ANTI-SEMITIC
STEREOTYPES

JOHNS HOPKINS JEWISH STUDIES

Sander Gilman and Steven T. Katz
Series Editors

ANTI-SEMITIC STEREOTYPES

A PARADIGM OF OTHERNESS IN

ENGLISH POPULAR CULTURE,

1660–1830

FRANK FELSENSTEIN

THE JOHNS HOPKINS UNIVERSITY PRESS

Baltimore and London

© 1995
The Johns Hopkins University Press
All rights reserved. Published 1995
Printed in the United States of America
on acid-free paper

04 03 02 01 00 99 98 97 96 95   5 4 3 2 1

The Johns Hopkins University Press
715 North Charles Street
Baltimore, Maryland 21218-4319
The Johns Hopkins Press Ltd., London

Library of Congress Cataloging-in-Publication Data
will be found at the end of this book.

A catalog record for this book is available
from the British Library.

ISBN 0-8018-4903-9

FOR CAROLE

WITHOUT WHOM

THIS BOOK

WOULD NOT

HAVE BEEN

CONTENTS

ILLUSTRATIONS

CHRONOLOGY

c. 1066   Settlement of Norman Jews in England

1144   Reputed martyrdom of William of Norwich (earliest blood libel)

1255   Death of Hugh of Lincoln (among the most prominent of many blood libels against the Jews)

1290   Banishment of the Jews from England under Edward I

c. 1589–90   First performance of Christopher Marlowe, *The Jew of Malta*

1594   Trial and execution of Roderigo Lopez

c. 1594–98   First performance of William Shakespeare, *The Merchant of Venice*

1655   Readmission of the Jews begins under Oliver Cromwell after petition by Menasseh Ben Israel

1680   Apostasy of Eve Cohan

1697   Number of Jews on London Exchange limited to twelve

1701   First performance of George Granville, *The Jew of Venice* (Thomas Doggett as Shylock)

1714   John Toland's *Reasons for Naturalizing the Jews* published

1732   Trial of William Osborne for publishing anti-Jewish libel William Hogarth's *A Harlot's Progress* published

1741   Charles Macklin's first performance of the part of Shylock in *The Merchant of Venice*

1753   Jewish Naturalization Act (26 Geo. II, c. 33) passed but repealed (27 Geo. II, c. 1) in the following parliamentary session

1757   William Hogarth's *Election* plates published

1765   Bishop Thomas Percy's *Reliques of Ancient English Poetry* published

1771   Chelsea murders

1787   Conversion of Lord George Gordon to Judaism

1794   First performance of Richard Cumberland, *The Jew*
         Richard Brothers begins his ministry to the Jews

1809   Founding of the London Society for the Promotion of
         Christianity among the Jews

1814   Edmund Kean's first performance as Shylock

1817   Publication of Maria Edgeworth, *Harrington*

1819   Publication of Sir Walter Scott, *Ivanhoe*

1829   Roman Catholic Relief Act (10 Geo. IV, c. 7)

1830   First Jewish Emancipation Bill defeated

1831   Restrictions on Jewish traders in the City of London removed

1833   First Jew called to the bar

1835   First Jewish sheriff of London and Westminster

1836   First Jewish Alderman of the City of London

1837   Moses Montefiore knighted

1837–39 Publication of Charles Dickens's *Adventures of Oliver Twist*

1841   First Jewish baronet created

1847   First Jew elected to Parliament

1855   First Jewish Lord Mayor of London

1858   Jewish Emancipation adopted

Fuller chronologies of Anglo-Jewish historical events are contained in Albert M. Hyamson, *A History of the Jews in England* (London, 1908), and H. S. Q. Henriques, *The Jews and the English Law* (Oxford, 1908). Old Style Julian Calendar dates (prior to the reform of 1752) have, where necessary, been silently emended in my text to accord with New Style dating.

PREFACE AND
ACKNOWLEDGMENTS

A S A YOUNG SCHOOLBOY, growing up in the nonorthodox environment of an outer London suburb during the early 1950s, I was seriously perplexed when a gentile classmate, with whom I had often
played, buttonholed me with the startling accusation that we Jews regularly engaged in acts of ritual sacrifice. I could only deny the charge by
lamely responding that I had never been witness to such an occurrence
nor indeed until that moment ever heard of its existence. My classmate
gave me a quizzical glance expressive of complete disbelief and informed
me that it *must* be true as his knowledge of it came with the authority
of his parents. A few days later, he again accosted me with a similar
allegation, declaring that his father had since related to him how it was
well known that the Jews commonly sacrificed young Christian children
in their temple, although he had conceded that in recent times they had
been constrained to the use of domestic animals. His mother, my fellow
pupil added, had as a consequence of this disclosure insisted that from
now on we boys no longer visit each other's houses nor even play together. Needless to say, after that he and I were hardly destined to continue as friends!

When I inquired of my own parents to confirm or refute the dreadful
aspersion that my erstwhile playmate had leveled against those of our
faith, they peremptorily dismissed it and assured me that I should not
believe such silly nonsense. Although I fully accepted their word that
what I had heard was but a flagrant concoction, I still remained perplexed
and slightly hurt. It was only when I was considerably older and maybe
a little wiser that I began to understand that the accusation made with
such callow impunity was neither more nor less than a still-intact ves-
tige of a much larger myth concerning the Jews that had persisted, perhaps increasingly on the fringes of Christian culture, for many hundreds
of years. The continuity of this myth from the late Middle Ages through
the "longer" eighteenth century, approximately 1660 to 1830, and the
growing challenge to its veracity, pointing by the end of the period to its
fragmentation more than its demise, furnishes the subject of this book.

The focus of my research is the existence of three remarkable collections of English books and pamphlets relating to the Jews. These are the Israel Solomons Collection in the Library of the Jewish Theological Seminary of America (New York), at which I was granted a research fellowship during the autumn of 1985, the Mocatta Collection (University College Library, University of London), and the Roth Collection (Brotherton Library, University of Leeds). In addition, extensive use has been made of graphic material in the British Library (Department of Prints and Drawings), the Library of Congress, and the privately owned collection of Mr. Alfred Rubens. The British Library, the Folger Library (Washington), the library of the Shakespeare Institute (Stratford and Birmingham), and the New York Public Library are among other collections that have provided essential—and often unique—material for study. Given their present rarity and diffusion, I have deliberately utilized extensive quotation from the works I have read to provide the staple for much of my discussion. In my employment of visual material, particularly satirical prints, I have in many cases endeavored to untie the narrative elements of the cartoon rather than discussing those more distinctly aesthetic qualities that might intrigue the professional art historian.

The pamphlets, prints, and so on, that I have examined are considerably more valuable as indicators of *English* attitudes toward the Jews than necessarily presenting an accurate or truthful depiction of the Jews themselves. Works of the kind can often tell us far more about the endemic beliefs and prejudices of those who are the *stereotypers* than they can reveal about the *stereotyped*. In a primitive sense, many of the stereotypical attitudes that were accepted as "facts" about the Jews during the eighteenth century prefigure similar forms of prejudice toward minority groups in the twentieth century. Although we would risk implicating ourselves in a reductive trap by assuming too readily that anti-Semitism diminished while approbation of the Jews was augmented during the period under study, it is apparent that their renewed presence in England called into question and sometimes attenuated many biases and assumptions once accepted more or less verbatim by the host population. In this sense, the study of the historical and literary representation of the Jew as "Other" provides an appropriate paradigm for our own age and for present-day research into patterns of ethnic discrimination.

The nine chapters of the book are conceived thematically, although their sequence here is to a large extent determined by chronology. For readers seeking preliminary signposting, the following is a very general synopsis:

In the opening chapter, "Stereotypes," I review several recent ideas on stereotyping, taken chiefly from theories current in social psychology, and endeavor to place these within the broader domain of cultural studies through referral to the innovative approaches posited by Edward Said, Sander L. Gilman, and others. The chapter is concerned to translate such ideas, particularly that of the Jew as Other, into a coherent methodology for the study of the stereotyping of Jews within the "longer" eighteenth century as a whole.

"Jews and Devils" (chapter 2) is a backward glance, examining the evolution of anti-Semitic stereotyping during the late Middle Ages and Renaissance period when (with the occasional exception of a few secret believers) no Jews lived in England. Despite—or perhaps partly because of—their absence, the rituals and practices of the Jews were frequently viewed in popular taxonomy as diabolically inspired. An earlier version of this chapter has appeared in *Literature and Theology* (March 1990) and I am grateful to the journal's editor, Dr. David Jasper, for permission to expand and reprint it here.

The focus of "Following Readmission" (chapter 3) is on the period from 1655 through the early eighteenth century, when the traditional diabolized stereotype was implicitly challenged by the renewed presence of actual Jews. The chapter examines also the demographics of the Jewish community, the imagined threat that it posed to the status quo in England, the verbal and proverbial employment of the word "Jew," and the perceived distinction between "rich" (Sephardi) and "poor" (Ashkenazi) Jews.

"Wandering Jew, Vagabond Jews" (chapter 4) juxtaposes the imaginary and the real. It examines the iconography of the Wandering Jew and shows how actual Jewish pedlars were interpreted as living proof of God's declared intention that those who were once his chosen people should be granted no respite until they came finally to recognize the "true" Messiah. The chapter also introduces a discussion of the literary representation of the Wandering Jew in the eighteenth century and of the dialectal peculiarities of the language of pedlars.

In "Conversion" (chapter 5), I look selectively at the very large body of pamphlet literature concerned with the endeavors of Christians to proselytize the Jews. The chapter pursues some of the arguments that were put forward by way of persuasion and at the treatment of converted Jews. It also examines the repeated fears of many Christians that the Jews were conniving to convert them. Parts of this chapter were originally presented as papers, "Conversion and Infanticide" and "Jews and Christian Jews" at annual meetings of the American Society for Eighteenth-Century Studies (ASECS) in Pittsburgh, Pa., April 1991, and in Charleston, S.C., March 1994.

"Ceremonies" (chapter 6) shows how anti-Semitic discourse in the eighteenth century proposed as witnessed fact a bizarre "alternative" liturgy and barbaric observance that it, quite unashamedly, ascribed to the Jews. In particular, it concentrates on the perverse representation of Jewish dietary laws (Jews as secret lovers of pork), circumcision, and the ritual murder myth.

" 'Ev'ry child hates Shylock' " (chapter 7) traces the history of the performance of *The Merchant of Venice* from the time of Shakespeare to the early nineteenth century. It appraises George Granville's adaptation of the play and the revival by Charles Macklin of Shakespeare's play with Shylock as the inveterate diabolized Jew. It shows how outside the drama Shylock became a kind of cipher revealing deeply embedded anti-Semitic sentiments, and the reaction to this from the late eighteenth century. A version of this chapter, "Money and Macklin's Shylock," was presented as a paper at the annual meeting of ASECS in Minneapolis in 1990.

In "The Jew Bill" (chapter 8), I examine the Act of 1753 and the plethora of tracts and satirical cartoons spawned by the ill-fated venture by the Pelham administration to naturalize certain Jews. The chapter reviews the reappearance in many of these pamphlets and prints of traditional anti-Semitic stereotypes and the longer term effect of the repeal of the act. As the bill was specifically intended to aid a small number of affluent Sephardim, this chapter also explores the representation of the Jew as plutocrat.

"Toward Emancipation" (chapter 9) investigates the extent to which the presence in England of actual Jews and awareness of them might have contributed to the presumed evolution of more liberalized attitudes in the early nineteenth century. Taking particular examples from Cobbett and Dickens, it also considers the persistence of forms of anti-Semitic stereotyping into the nineteenth century.

Finally, the Epilogue is an attempt to contextualize. It assesses whether (as has been claimed) attacks against the Jews should be understood by and large as the rhetoric of the age and little different from similar diatribes against other national and religious minorities all too common in English cultural discourse of the eighteenth century.

As well as the institutions already mentioned, my work has been valuably served by the following libraries: Birmingham City Reference

Library; Chetham's Library, Manchester; Avery and Butler Libraries, Columbia University, New York; Leeds City Reference Library; Leeds (Private) Subscription Library; Public Record Office, London; Senate House Library and the Institute of Historical Research, University of London; John Rylands Library, University of Manchester; New York Public Library; Bodleian Library, Oxford; Firestone Library, Princeton University; Jean and Alexander Heard Library, Vanderbilt University, Nashville. I am grateful to the staff at the University of Leeds Audio-Visual Service for their assistance with photography.

Among individuals whose insight and knowledge have helped to illuminate my own thinking I should like in particular to thank the following: Joel Baer; Douglas Bethlehem, Paul-Gabriel Boucé; Therese Boyd; Douglas Charing; Evelyn M. Cohen; Nina Collins; Margaret Doody; Bonnie Ferrero; Terry Friedman; Sander L. Gilman; Suzy Halimi; the late James H. Heineman; Nora Howland; Herb and Evelyn Jaffe; Douglas Jefferson; Sharon Liberman Mintz; David Lindley; Irma Lustig; the late Alexander Marx; Peter Meredith; Derek Nuttall; Irene Roth; Alfred Rubens; Tony St. Quintin; Judith Samuel; Agnes Sherman; Judith Stark; Loreto Todd; Jack Watt; Donez Xiques. I feel confident that none of those thanked here will feel even remotely slighted by my dedicating the book to my best advocate and most scrupulous critic, my wife Carole.

ANTI-SEMITIC
STEREOTYPES

INTRODUCTION

WHEN, IN 1941, Cecil Roth concluded his *History of the Jews in England* with a deferential tribute to what he called the "alembic of English tolerance," he was voicing a belief that had been diligently cultivated by several generations of Anglo-Jewish scholars. For Roth, the situation of the Jews in England could be summed up in terms of "a gradual acceptance based on common sense rather than doctrine, consolidating itself slowly, and never outstripping public opinion" (267). If there was an element of wishful thinking in Roth's assessment, it was in the belief that the advances in the status of the Jews from their readmission into the country in the seventeenth century to their emancipation in the nineteenth provided fit illustration of the broad common sense and instinctive tolerance of the English people at large. However well meant, his analysis smoothed over (and at times consciously chose to ignore) the extensive undergrowth of anti-Semitic allusion that permeates the rhetoric of eighteenth-century English popular culture. Until recently, few writers on the subject have shown any enthusiasm to disaffirm Roth's comfortable assumption that the acceptance of the Jews in England should be seen to exemplify *a fortiori* the triumph of native good sense over ancient prejudice.

Indeed, it was far easier for such writers to dismiss as inconsequential the stereotypical assertion so often enunciated and so deeply engrained in eighteenth-century popular wisdom that "the *Jewish* Nation . . . certainly are the most Perfidious and base People in the World" (*London Jests*, 1712, 15). Such a self-evident untruth could be excused as casual or meaningless and hardly the stuff of history. Yet, in the so-called age of Enlightenment, the nation that half a millennium before had been the first in medieval Europe to expel its Jews, a nation that (as far as records reveal) was also the first to promote the myth of the Wandering Jew and the obscenity of the blood libel, showed a purblind refusal to let go of its primitive superstitions with anything like the genial quiescence that many later scholars would have us suppose. If eighteenth-century England was a country that enjoyed a toleration almost unique for its era, it was also a country that harbored a host of popular fallacies concerning the Jews that would require more than the lights of reason and common sense to abjure. Should some readers come away at the end of this book with a sense that the case I put forward is overstated, they should recall that most previous writers on the subject have tended to minimize the aggressive strain of anti-Judaism that runs through eighteenth-century English popular culture.

Consequently, my aim is to probe the repertoire of anti-Semitic stereotypes and stereotyping in English pamphlets, popular literature, sermons, tracts, and prints of the "longer" eighteenth century (approximately 1660 to 1830). Ample work, though of greatly uneven quality, has been carried out in the past on the depiction of the Jews in the fiction and drama of Restoration and Georgian England, but little or no attempt has been made to situate this within the broader context of popular culture. The "longer" eighteenth century proves a compelling period to explore for it coincides almost precisely with, on one side, the readmission of the Jews into England after an absence of some three and one-half centuries, and, on the other, the beginning of the extended campaign in Parliament to grant them full-blown political equality and lawful citizenship. Inside this time span, their acceptance by the English was frequently compromised through the haphazard endurance of anti-Semitic myths and folktales, many of which can be traced back at least to medieval times and more often than not to exegesis of the text and meaning of the Bible.

Indeed, any reader familiar with the literature of the "longer" eighteenth century, in which they habitually appear as tenacious minor figures, may recall that allusion to contemporary Jews is as a rule less than flattering. One thinks of Daniel Defoe's blackguard Jew dealer in *Roxana* (1724) whose face contorts into that of the Devil at sight of the heroine's jewels and whose skullduggery is reflected in the stream of wicked epithets—such as "villain," "cursed," "rogue," "dog of a Jew," "traitor"—that are used to allude to this nameless fiend.[1] As my study will show, each of these tags has its own peculiar resonance in reflecting the larger negative image of what constitutes a Jew in the common perception. When deployed in eighteenth-century usage as a term of opprobrium or reprobation, the word immediately arouses the most deep-rooted apprehensions and prejudices. It is small wonder then to discover, by short example, that in Frances Burney's *Cecilia* (1782), the tender heart of the heroine "recoiled at the very mention of a *Jew, and taking up money upon interest*," or that in *The Adventures of a Guinea* (1760–65), Charles Johnstone asperses the "lower species of trade . . . engrossed by those people" in terms of "adulteration of wares, lying, perjury; in a word, every species of deceit that can impose upon ignorance and credulity."[2] Passing reference elsewhere to unscrupulous dealers by writers as diverse as Alexander Pope ("Jews, Jobbers, Bubblers, Subscribers, Projectors, ... &c."), Edmund Burke ("the whole gang of usurers; pedlars, and itinerant Jew-discounters at the corners of streets") and William Cobbett ("Jews, jobbers, dead-weight, ... place-men and sinecure people") rarely omit disparaging allusion to the Jews.[3] According to M. J. Landa, nine times out of ten the typical Jew of English drama appears as a scion of Shylock, "a money-lender ... , insisting upon his 'pound of flesh,' scheming and intriguing to get the Christian within his clutches."[4]

The Jew of the eighteenth-century imagination threatens to overturn and confound the fabric of the social order by the uneasiness that his being brings, although perhaps he unwittingly mirrors the cracks and tensions already inherent there. He is the perpetual outsider whose unsettling presence serves to define the bounds that separate the native Englishman from the alien Other. But his alterity is not confined to his imaginative representation. In law, the Jew and the infidel are deemed (according to the famous seventeenth-century jurist Lord Coke) "*perpetui inimici*, perpetual enemies ... , for between them, as with the devils, whose subjects they be, and the Christian there is a perpetual hostility, and can be no peace."[5] Theologically, too, it could be argued that the imprimatur of the Bible maintained an equivalent separation (2 Cor. 6:14–15), which finds popular expression (among other places) in the hymnologist Isaac Watts's well-known song for children in praise of the Gospel that begins:

Lord, I ascribe it to thy Grace,
And not to Chance, as others do,
That I was born of *Christian* Race,
And not a *Heathen*, or a *Jew*.[6]

The extraordinary survival of the Jews into the modern era, as well as their reputed forlorn condition, was frequently interpreted as witness of God's wish to hold them up as a paradigm or exemplum to the rest of humanity. The "very Preservation of that People," remarks John Breuhowse, "is certainly intended by Divine Providence for making the Judgments of God the more visible to Men."[7] In search of the intrinsic "Evidences of Christianity," Lord Chesterfield is reported to have observed that "there was *one*, which he thought to be invincible, not to be got over by the wit of man, viz. *the present state of the Jews*—a fact to be accounted for on no human principle."[8] Widespread curiosity throughout the whole period in the Jews and their fate is prompted almost exclusively by a desire to understand and interpret them not for their own sake but in terms of their meaning for Christianity. The impulse to try to speculate on contemporary Jews in their own right is negligible.[9]

Consequently, this book is not in any true or conventional sense a history of the Jews but of English cultural attitudes to them during the longer eighteenth century. Readers looking for a "straight" historical interpretation should turn to Todd Endelman's groundbreaking volume, *The Jews of Georgian England, 1714–1830: Tradition and Change in a Liberal Society* (Philadelphia, 1979), to which I stand indebted for many of its valuable insights. Endelman, however, is concerned primarily with what he terms the "acculturation" of Anglo-Jewry, whereas the purpose of the present book is to exhibit through a series of snapshots the shifts and mutations in English anti-Semitic attitudes from the readmission of the Jews in 1655 to the beginnings of their political emancipation. It is concerned to interpret an extensive English discourse about the Jews, which has as its problematic constant that it only incidentally touches the state of the "real" Jews themselves. The difficulty, however, of knowing how best to distinguish between reality and fiction or myth concerning the Jews poses a besetting obstacle, although it is not necessarily one that severely taxed English popular opinion during the eighteenth century, which only rarely acknowledged such a distinction. By way of illustration here, *The Times* of January 31, 1811, prints the ensuing report as a factual item of news:

> The following ludicrous circumstance occurred on Tuesday week at Bristol:-A couple of Jews being apprehended in the act of stealing several articles from the stables of the White Hart Inn, were hauled into the yard by two stout fellows, whither the whole fraternity of the currycomb were immediately summoned. The long beards of these disciples were then stuck together with pitch (their hands being previously tied behind them); and while thus face to face, a profusion of snuff, mixed with hellebore, was administered, which caused them to sneeze in such a manner, that by the frequent and violent bobbing of noses one against the other, a copious stream of blood issued from either nostril, while the enraged culprits were kicking and capering about in all directions.

The episode is cited by more than one social historian of the period as a bona fide example of the kind of retributive justice that might have been roughed out by the mob as punishment upon Jewish petty malefactors.[10] The farcicality of the incident appears to make it verge upon the anecdotal and I have not been able to determine beyond all dispute that it actually happened as described.[11] Yet, the best evidence to make us scrutinize its veracity more closely is the discovery that an almost identical account, set in London rather than Bristol, had appeared as a popular anecdote in jest-books published more than a decade earlier:

> Two Jews, old clothesmen, with venerable beards, were passing by a stable-door near Tottenham court-road, one Saturday, when a couple of jackets so fascinated them, that they could not resist the temptation to give them a place with their own wares. Whilst they were secreting the jackets, the two owners, who were drinking porter on the opposite side of the way, were observing the transaction. They rushed out, seized the Rabbies, locked them up in the stable, and went in quest of certain preparations, which promised better things than a jail, or lawyer's wig, or a fine. They then tied the Rabbies together, matted their beards, and smeared them with warm shoemakers wax. As soon as the wax was cooled, and the people around had enjoyed sufficiently the sight of the venerable patriarchs in this fraternal embrace, the postilions applied to each nose by intervals, a few pinches of snuff, which occasioned such a concussion of noses, and such sputtering, that, of five hundred spectators, there was not one who did not depart highly pleased with this spectacle of distributive justice.[12]

The more elaborate London version certainly differs from its Bristol counterpart in a number of details, although essentially they tell the same story. We should not exclude making the assumption that each is based, quite coincidentally, on a separate occurrence, although it seems unlikely that the "stout fellows" at Bristol would have come up with the equivalent punishment had they not been familiar with what would have circulated widely by word of mouth as well as in print as a popular tale or jest. If anything, the Bristol report reads as a watered-down version (with several local details added) of the earlier London account. Even were we able to uncover proof that the occurrence took place exactly as recounted in *The Times*, it would still raise the possibility of fact replicating fiction, of the punishment at Bristol being a kind of "real-life" carbon copy of a popular anecdote. As we shall see, the blurring of fact into fiction and vice-versa is a common qualification in the study of stereotypes.

Another important feature evident in either account (although more markedly in the London version on which we shall focus) is the sketching of difference between Englishman and Jew. The owners of the stolen jackets are depicted, like William Hogarth's honest English artisans in *Beer Street* (1751), imbibing porter, a brown ale "chiefly drunk by porters and the lower class of labourers" (*OED*) Their alertness in discovering the crime, their decision to punish the thieves summarily rather than relying upon the tedious processes of the law, and the prankish ingenuity of the chastisement itself attest to the capability and independence that the anecdote tacitly associates with the native Englishman. By contrast, the series of ironic euphemisms to describe the Jews and their actions ("the Rabbies," "the venerable patriarchs," "a couple of jackets so fascinated them, that they could not resist the temptation to give them a place with their own wares") reinforces the suspicion of their inveterate duplicity. That the crime was committed on the Jewish Sabbath may also be intended to reflect ironically on their deceitfulness. Their humiliation before a cheering crowd of 500 spectators is made complete by cruelly employing against each other two of the physiognomic characteristics most commonly associated in the popular perception with the Jews. By tying the Jews' beards together, and with the diligent addition of a few pinches of snuff, their noses can be bloodied to the delight of the mob. The anecdote implicitly sustains the sense of superiority of the English or indigenous group by its reiteration of the folkloric motif of "besting" or (as a late eighteenth-century writer sardonically expresses it) "out-jewing a Jew,"[13] a recurrent blueprint that can vary in scale from minor contretemps to the "pound of flesh" tale that imbues The Merchant of Venice.

The echo of Shylock should also alert us to the equally persistent motif by which the Jews are represented in anti-Semitic discourse as cutthroat butchers and demonic mutilators intent on wreaking havoc on innocent Christian lives. As we shall see, even the challenge of the rational Enlightenment failed to eradicate the grossest of imputations by which the Jews had been depicted in an unbroken tradition from medieval times as inveterate desecrators of the sanctity of the Cross. The currency of this crude mental image intrudes into eighteenth-century delineation of Jewish ceremony and into the rhetoric of conversionist texts. It colors the iconography of the Wandering Jew and the arguments put over with such pernicious conviction in 1753 against the naturalization of the Jews. Its cultural overtones are explicit in the belief periodically expressed throughout the century that rabbinical law made it a Jewish "duty" to murder Christians; its undertones are sometimes present, too, in anecdote and jest that warned of the Jews as cunning sharpers and cheats. Although it is doubtful that every aspect of the diabolized stereotype of the Jew that emanated from the Middle Ages continued to enjoy the same credence, it remained sufficiently intact to have widespread appeal in English popular culture throughout the eighteenth century.

Quantitatively, it is of course very difficult and perhaps in the long run impossible to measure with thermometrical precision the level or intensity of eighteenth-century anti-Semitism. In this study, I make use of such adjectives as "widespread," "traditional," "endemic," and "inveterate" to describe the persistence through the period of certain attitudes toward or rather biases against the Jews that can in most cases be traced back at least to the late Middle Ages. In employing them, I am fully conscious that such prescriptive terms can sound crudely all-embracing in their failure to take more fully into account both those who viewed the grosser prejudices of their own age with abhorrence or skepticism and also those who showed no interest in the problem. Similarly, the portmanteau term *popular culture* can exercise too great a hegemony if we rigidly confine its meaning by setting up uncrossable boundaries between what Peter Burke calls great ("learned culture") and little ("popular culture") traditions. As Burke acknowledges, any theory of cultural diversity must recognize a constant interaction or two-way traffic between these binaries.[14] His albeit brief remarks on the representation of the Jew as "the outsider who lived within the community, the traitor within the gates" place beliefs and traditions concerning the Jews as blasphemers, usurers, and eternal wanderers firmly within the compass of popular culture.[15] Yet, as we shall discover, many of the vilest aspersions persistently leveled against the Jews are intonated by the "learned" and the "great" no less than by the common man. Particularly in the furor instigated by the Jew Bill of 1753, it is apparent that anti-Judaic sentiments find lively expression as much in the august chamber of the House of Commons as on the streets in the *vox populi* of the mob. Our working definition of popular culture must take account of the diffusion and at least tacit acceptance of many of these beliefs through a broad spectrum of English society. Indeed, *public opinion*, although also a term fraught with difficulty, sometimes reflects more closely the elusive notion sought here of "what is generally believed" or "that which is prevalent among, or accepted by the people" than the more hierarchically loaded concept of "popular culture."[16] Pragmatically, though, the employment of popular culture within this book is self-defining by the use I have made of chapbooks, ephemeral pamphlets, tracts, jestbooks, prints, folklore, and proverbial expressions. These provide the staple for much of my discussion, although (without laboring the distinction between great and little traditions) I have not hesitated to turn to more "canonical" sources whenever I have felt them to be of value. Equally, the apparent geographical boundary in writing about *English* (and not British) popular culture is as much convenient as deliberate. I have not, however, excluded reference, when appropriate, to people and influences from other parts of the British Isles and beyond.

An even more slippery ideological hot potato is evident in the need to try to define the use I have made in this book of the term *anti-Semitism*. Many writers on the subject have expressed their unease in employing out of context what is essentially a nineteenth-century phrase first coined to describe "the avowed intention of racists to bar Jews from legitimate membership in the body politic in Germany or in other European states."[17] Its use, particularly in the twentieth century, has been colored by racial theories of the Aryan *Übermensch*, espoused with such brutal alacrity by Nazism as a pretext for the Holocaust, whereas prior to the second half of the nineteenth century hostility to and persecution of the Jews had their origin mainly in religious difference. Where once a Jew could at least escape Christian persecution by submitting to conversion, the creed of anti-Semitism under the Nazis offered only the horror of the "final solution." Despite the inappropriateness of the term *anti-Semitism* in the context of the eighteenth century and other earlier historical periods, no alternative word has really taken its place. Although in recent years some scholars have tried to differentiate between anti-Semitism (hostility to Jews) and anti-Judaism (hostility to the Jewish religion),[18] the distinction has shown little sign of catching on more widely. Consequently, for better or worse, I have continued to use both terms synonymously except when occasion has suggested discriminating between the two. The study of English anti-Semitism in the eighteenth century should make it apparent that its manifestation is far less coordinated than its twentieth-century equivalent. Its randomness is evinced in its employment by English authors whose religious allegiance ranges from Puritan to High Church Anglican and from Catholic to radical dissent. In politics, mainly because of the Jew Bill, it may be more common to find it used by the Tory opposition, but there is little shortage of examples of anti-Semitic diatribe in writers and parliamentarians of a Whiggish disposition.

Finally, what about the Jews themselves? It is a curious fact, too easily ignored, that throughout the period (with the rare exception of polemicists such as David Levi and Joshua van Oven) there was almost no direct involvement or contribution by those Jews settled in the country to a thriving English dialogue concerning their present and future condition. Nor did they of their own accord openly attempt (except perhaps privately) to refute the terrible charges made against them with such frequency and conviction in anti-Semitic discourse. Whether because of barriers of language and education or fears brought about by their precarious status as an unenfranchised minority or lack of effective communal organization, no distinct Jewish voice emerges to speak for them. But, then, the extravagance of some of the charges that were leveled against them and the rootedness of anti-Semitism in English popular culture would almost certainly have made any such attempt a futile exercise. The preoccupation of the eighteenth century with the Jews has its source more in the fertile domain of the imagination than in proven reality.

CHAPTER I

STEREOTYPES

The Writers of all Ages, from the Primitive *Justin Martyr* downwards, have born Witness of the cruel and implacable Malice the *Jews* have ever born against Christians; as by solemnly cursing them every day in their Synagogues, by raising Persecutions wherever they could in all Times against them, by stealing, and torturing, and oftentimes crucifying Christian Children; never professing to keep any Terms of Civility Truth, or Honesty with Christians; but always doing them all the Mischief in their Power, and murdering them by all the Tortures they could devise, by Thousands.[1]

—Nay! the very Existence of the *Jews* upon the Face of the Earth, now that they have neither King nor Priest, nor Prophet, is a Demonstration of a divine and watchful Providence, that has protected a Remnant of them to confirm a Proof of the coming of the Messias, and to be a fit Subject to be wrought upon by the powerful Motive of soft perswasion, that in time they may embrace the Christian Religion, and so in their Conviction fulfil the latter Prophecies of the Messiah.[2]

THESE TWO PASSAGES are culled from opposing pamphlets written within a short time of each other during the political controversy and upheaval excited by the Jewish Naturalization Bill of 1753. The first of the two amply exemplifies endemic anti-Semitic biases against the Jews that in England can be traced back at least to the Middle Ages. Such attitudes assume that the Jews have always behaved toward Christians with implacable hostility, that their religious ritual is devised specifically to undermine the moral foundation of the church and state of their host country, and that the habitual assassination of Christians is only the most extreme of their many heinous deeds. The attestation that "Writers of all Ages, from . . . *Justin Martyr* downwards" may be consulted by way of testimony inadvertently reveals the persistence of these outlandish claims as an aspect of Christian theology from the time of the Church Fathers.[3] That, by any rational consideration, the claims are absurd, having little or no basis in historical fact, does nothing to mitigate their potency as accepted myth. The passage proclaims an enduring enmity between Jew and Christian.

The second quotation typifies the far more conciliatory attitude favored by English philo-Semites, who considered that to embrace the Jews within the bosom of the nation was an indispensable first step toward encouraging the return of the Messiah and the fulfillment of the Christian apocalypse. The survival of the Jews from biblical times, according to this view, is a perfect manifestation of the verity of sacred revelation, of which their presence is a sign and a witness. But, despite the place allotted to the Jews as a living remnant of their forebears, "a Demonstration of a divine and watchful Providence," it is the duty of all good Christians to welcome them as brethren and to seek to enlighten them from their obdurate beliefs by gospel evidence. Through reconciliation, the Jews will recognize the error of their ways and their conversion into the true faith will be a semaphoric response that will enable the Almighty to distinguish the singular merit of the English Church. No less than the purveyor of traditional anti-Semitism, though perhaps with greater subtlety, the theological philo-Semite ultimately seeks to undermine the very existence of Jews as Jews.

The two views expressed in these excerpts, however contradictory, share a common mode of perception; each employs a particular cognitive process or habit of thinking to describe the Jews. Both rely on crudely oversimplified, yet readily understood, preconceptions of the distinctive attributes that characterize the Jews. For the one, the Jews are by their nature sadistic Christ-killers, blasphemers, and thieves, the irredeemable foes of the Church; for the other, they are the residue of God's chosen people, permitted to survive as a token of his enduring love for the true Christian, of whose redemption their presence is covenantal. Each defines the Jews not for their own sake but in terms of a distinctive Christian attitude. Each observes the Jews as outsiders, whose measure is only consequential in terms of the authority of the established faith. Each implies a bias or value judgment about the Jews which we may recognize as stereotypes that are based on traditional suppositions. The characteristics of these suppositions and the resultant written and visual stereotyping of Jews by Christians in eighteenth-century England will provide the focus to this study.

A *stereotype*, according to its standard definition, is a basic form of social insight, "a preconceived and oversimplified idea of the characteristics which typify a person, situation, etc.; an attitude based on such a preconception" (*OED*). By its nature, stereotyping may be seen as a necessary part of the categorizing process of the human mind, a simple but effective system of abstracting certain features, real or assumed, of a person or group and making those features represent the whole. Because of our cognitive incapacity to grasp the essence or whole of a perceived entity, we tend to categorize by accentuating certain salient qualities that in our minds come to embody that whole.[4] This crude process of evaluative categorization frequently emerges as no more than a form of inexact generalization that becomes by acceptance a fixed idea in our heads. Such acceptance may be unique to one person's thought processes but, more commonly, we tend to treat it as a stereotype if it is part of the accepted mental vocabulary of a larger group or society. In this context, we may wish to explore particular stereotypes as manifestations of the established prejudices and values that characterize a given society.

Since the word *stereotype* was first employed in its present usage by the American journalist Walter Lippman in an extraordinarily perspicacious book entitled *Public Opinion*, first published in 1922,[5] it has become a consequential and much-debated term in social psychology and sociology. Its use in literary and historical studies has until recently provoked little discussion.[6] In his employment of the term, Lippman was the first to recognize that the tendency to perceive through stereotypes, indicative though it can be of our own prejudices, is in itself an essential part of our mental makeup. Outside an ideal world it would be "unthinkable" to contemplate "a people without prejudices, a people with altogether neutral vision."[7] Lacking such neutrality, those stereotyped images of others that we carry around with us are frequently the defense mechanisms by which we try both to protect our own established beliefs and to come to terms with and to judge what we perceive as different or threatening. Stereotypes (as in the two examples with which we began) are far more revealing of those who invoke them than of those they attempt to describe. They are "loaded with preference, suffused with affection or dislike, attached to fears, lusts, strong wishes, pride, hope" (119). Such stereotypes emphasize supposedly typical characteristics of those they describe that would in many cases be hard to verify if subjected to rational scrutiny. Following Lippman, the study of stereotypes has become a measure by which social psychologists have tried to unravel the causes and the nature of different kinds of prejudice through the systematic analysis of collected data. In particular, studies in such areas as ethnic or gender prejudice have benefited from research into different aspects of stereotyping. For all its complicated ancestry, in social psychology the case of the Jews remains the classic paradigm of racial stereotyping.

Because, as we have seen, stereotypes so often reflect the received attitudes and beliefs of the men and women that employ them, they can be invested with a force or power far above their basic worth as crude assumptions. They can assume the status of myth by appearing to ar-

ticulate the indigenous values of the society that has created them. A
stereotype, says Lippman, "may be so consistently and authoritatively
transmitted in each generation from parent to child that it seems almost
like a biological fact" (93). Yet, paradoxically, for all its supposed authority a stereotype is almost invariably bipolar, having an affirmative
and negative aspect by which it may be put to service to justify either a
love-prejudice or a hate-prejudice.[8] As Sander Gilman, one of the few
literary critics who has seriously engaged in the study of stereotypes,
points out, "Every stereotype is Janus-faced. It has a positive and a negative element, neither of which bears any resemblance to the complexity
or diversity of the world as it is. . . . For every 'noble savage' seen through
colonial power a parallel 'ignoble savage' exists."[9]

Even as early as 1753, another pseudonymous pamphleteer, writing
about attitudes to the Jews at the time of the Naturalization Bill, shows
a rare percipience in observing the implausible fact of the coexistence
of such total contradictions:

> Certainly all that hath been said against the *Jews* must appear to be
> empty *tittle-tattle*, and trumpery Stuff.
>
> There is also all the Reason in the World to believe, they are not so
> despicable a People, as they have been represented to be by *some* Per-
> sons, to answer an End: Nor so much caressed and esteemed, as others
> have insinuated for the same Purpose. But whatever be the true state
> of the Case, 'tis certain, that their Opponents cannot be both Right.
> Those Suggestions seem to be Exaggerations and the *Offspring* of a
> warm Imagination; a Sort of *Chimeras*, or *Phantoms* conjured up to
> terrify or amuse: And being palpable Contradictions cannot be *both
> true*, and may possibly be *both false*.[10]

In the modern world, the contradictions are no less apparent. Konstantyn Jelenski describes well the predicament of the Jews as victims of
contrary stereotyping in his native Poland:

> Poles have never come out against Jews "because they are Jews" but
> because Jews are dirty, greedy, mendacious, because they wear ear-
> locks, speak jargon, do not want to assimilate, and *also* because they
> *do* assimilate, cease using their jargon, are nattily dressed, and want
> to be regarded as Poles. Because they lack culture and because they are
> overly cultured. Because they are superstitious, backward and ignorant,
> and because they are damnably capable, progressive, and ambitious.
> Because they have long, hooked noses, and because it is sometimes
> difficult to distinguish them from "pure Poles." Because they crucified
> Christ and practice ritual murder and pore over the Talmud, and be-
> cause they disdain their own religion and are atheists. Because they

look wretched and sickly, and because they are tough and have their own fighting units and are full of *khutspah*. Because they are bankers and capitalists and because they are Communists and agitators. But in *no* case because they are Jews.[11]

The bipolarity with which Jews are stereotyped is frequently implosive, their very contradictions making such stereotypes protean and unreliable. Despite that, the longevity of inveterate stereotypes of the Jews has the powerful consequence of making them seem irrefutably true and all the more potent in their imaginative force.

The authority accorded to the traditional stereotyping of the Jews is reinforced (as with no other common ethnic stereotype) by the imprimatur of the Bible, literally interpreted in Christian teaching as the word of God. Yet again in 1753, the bipolarity of the Jews as God's "peculiar chosen People" and simultaneously "a People of . . . most shocking Description and Character" is a recurrent motif in the flurry of pamphlets occasioned by the Naturalization Bill. An anti-Semitic writer, determined to thwart the supporters of the bill, can muster out of context a long inventory of God's own denunciations of the biblical Jews as a means to put their contemporary descendants on the whipping-block. God, he says, complains that the Jews were

> a most rebellious, disobedient, gainsaying, stiff-necked, impenitent, incorrigible, adulterous, whorish, impudent, froward, shameless, perverse, treacherous, revolting, back-sliding, idolatrous, wicked, sinful, stubborn, untoward, hard-hearted, hypocritical, foolish, sottish, brutish, stupid, ungrateful, Covenant-breaking Nation or People; a Seed of Evil Doers, a Generation of Vipers, doing Evil greedily with both Hands, according to all the Nations that were round about them; as bad, nay worse than *Sodom* and *Gomorrah*, casting all God's Laws and Ordinances behind them, trampling them under their Feet, rejecting, forsaking and despising God himself, provoking him continually to his Face, grieving him to the Heart, forgetting him Days without Number, always erring in their Hearts, and disobeying his Voice, &c. &c. And shall it be recorded that *Britannia*, the first among the Christian States, ever admitted such a Nation or People as this to become one People, and to enjoy the Privileges of a true born *Englishman?*[12]

By imputation, the vile characteristics attributed to the biblical Jews are perceived as shared by all Jews and, as a consequence, the veracity of the Bible is applied to give credence to an enduring stereotype, the persistence of which is seemingly supported by the word of God. The pamphleteer's diatribe against the Jews is a useful illustration of the mythical force of stereotypes and of their persuasive ability to supplant reality.

The attack is sustained by invoking familiar theological perceptions of the Jews that are nevertheless remote in time from contemporary actuality. Either through ignorance or deliberation, the writer avoids direct reference to the Jews of eighteenth-century England, focusing instead on their biblical forebears and employing them as epitomes of the outlandish behavior of the whole people. The passage concludes by rhetorically accentuating the sense of difference between the despicable conduct of an alien people and the moral primacy of "*Britannia*, the first among the Christian States." It implies an ideal counter-stereotype to the Jew in the "true born *Englishman*." It emphasizes the sense of the Otherness of the Jews.

This sense of difference between the host group and the outsider reveals that at the root of negative stereotyping is the need of the host group to defend its values and beliefs, which it presumes to be under threat from the intrusion of an alien culture that it does not fully understand. Lippman sees a system of stereotypes as "the fortress of our tradition." Behind its defenses, he states, "we can continue to feel ourselves safe in the position we occupy."[13] In social psychology, the pursuit of this idea has led to the promotion of a variety of psychodynamic and ego-defense theories by which it is suggested that projection of hostility upon innocent targets through stereotyping represents a form of displaced aggression.[14] Anti-Semitic prejudice arises, according to Gordon Allport, "because people are irritated by their own consciences. Jews are symbolically their superego," since historically they personify high ethical ideals that most people are unable to emulate. Only through the study of the history of the Jews, he argues, aided by close psychological insights into the nature of prejudice, may we begin to solve the exceedingly complex problem of anti-Semitism. For him, Freud's explanation that anti-Semitism is an extension of the repressed desire of most men to "kill the father" provides a useful clue to the choice of Jews as scapegoats, especially as from a Christian point of view the Jews may be perceived as killers of God, the eternal Father. Prejudice against the Jews may be seen as a release mechanism, conscious or otherwise, by which to express such dangerous desires.[15] The theory that stereotypes nurture their own contradictions becomes apparent in Allport's discussion with its emphasis on Jews as both morally superior and deicidal. In common with Lippman, he recognizes that, for all their self-contradiction, stereotypes are endemic within a particular culture, although the bias of his study tends rather more toward individual personality than broader anthropological considerations.[16]

Within the domain of literary and cultural studies, the concept of

Otherness as a key element in stereotyping has perhaps only comparatively recently achieved academic respectability, particularly through the exponential development in interest in black and feminist issues and in the "new" literatures of former colonies (e.g., Commonwealth and postcolonial studies). A few examples, which have been influential in shaping my own thinking, will illustrate the evolution of recent ideas about stereotyping. As early as 1954, in an all-too-underrated book, *Teague, Shenkin, and Sawney*, J. O. Bartley explored the incidence of Irish, Welsh, and Scottish characters in English plays from the Renaissance to 1800. Although Bartley eschews theoretical discussion and does not use the term *stereotype*, he examines in some detail what he describes as "stock characters" in the drama, looking at such aspects as speech, dress, manners, and the modes of identification of national types. Because "English generalizations about their particular nationality are false and libellous,"[17] such types are among the least respectable in the drama, often conventionalized into comic butts, rarely presented as serious or elevated characters. Bartley makes the important observation that "national" stock characters are more likely than others to "lend themselves to the crudest buffoonery" since "ignorance and prejudice are not, in this case, continuously countered by experience as they are with such generalizations as, for example, the heavy father, the strong minded aunt, the doctor or the fop" (4).

The lack of true knowledge or experience of Irishmen, Welshmen, and Scots means that they are more likely to function as figures on the English stage if presented through a series of accepted mannerisms that "enables the audience to apprehend quickly the outline of a character without elaborate description or explanation" (3). What Bartley describes is a process that is synonymous with stereotyping, which also relies heavily on the exaggeration of particular national or ethnic assumptions and is rarely the result of direct experience or knowledge of its subject. In the context of the drama, a later chapter will examine the fortunes through the eighteenth century of the most renowned stage Jew of all.

Most modern studies specifically concerned with the historical stereotyping of Jews have shown little regard for or awareness of theoretical problems. A notable exception is *From Shylock to Svengali: Jewish Stereotypes in English Fiction* (1960), in which Edgar Rosenberg concentrates on the literary stereotype of the Jew, particularly in nineteenth-century fiction. Rosenberg picks his words with considerable care in arriving at a definition of what he understands by stereotyping:

Shylock and Fagin are stereotypes—figures who conform to more or less identical patterns of behaviour, resemble each other physically, and subscribe to a relatively fixed moral code; who react in predictable ways to similar stimuli; and who may exist independently of historical changes and often in the very teeth of historical change.[18]

While accepting its inherent bipolarities, Rosenberg also emphasizes what he calls "the massive durability of a stereotype, which is almost by definition the least pliable of literary sorts, the one least sensitive to social vibrations" (14). For him, literary stereotypes are all but immutable because so deeply embedded in the popular consciousness. Rosenberg assumes that the patterns of behavior, moral code, and so on, of stereotyped Jew-figures are to be viewed as autonomous within literature rather than necessarily mirroring the biases and values inherent in the host group that created them. In fact, by studying individual works of fiction almost as independent entities, Rosenberg, through his own admission, "sidestepped or ignored altogether the question of personal bias toward the Jews in the authors whose work I discuss, and though I have naturally had to pay some attention to historical currents I have not stressed them" (13). The scale of this omission becomes apparent in his insistence that the literary conventions that govern stereotypes are fundamentally static and not sufficiently sensitive to be affected by changes in popular consciousness in different periods. The approach stresses the durability of specific character types in fiction but fails to recognize sufficiently that this endurance is dependent upon the far less predictable response of different audiences and readers in different periods. Shylock may appear immutable in his "persistent and international appeal" (15), but the response to and interpretation of his character will inevitably vary in each age. Rosenberg's more orthodox methodology with its persistent emphasis upon the stereotyped rather than the stereotyper commands little favor with later writers on the subject. If he contributes positively to the present discussion, it is in his recognition of the emotive power and consequent appeal of negative literary stereotypes. "A fiction," he says, "may be all the more convincing and durable for being a basic distortion, with deep seated attractions for the superstitious mass of men" (19).

More recently, in *The Conditioned Imagination from Shakespeare to Conrad: Studies in the Exo-cultural Stereotype* (1978), Michael Echeruo parallels Bartley in distinguishing between "cultural stereotypes," such as the braggart soldier whom the audience knows to be "a deliberate simplification or exaggeration," and what he calls "exo-cultural stereotypes," those of an ethnic background that is extrinsic to the audience or reader. In the case of the braggart soldier (Echeruo's equivalent of Bartley's heavy father or strong-minded aunt), "exploration of the character of the stereotype is also an exploration of the character of the audience," whereas with the exo-cultural stereotype no such identification takes place:

> This is because it is almost impossible for the audience and the artist to see the character as other than *an example* of some other group to which the character belongs. . . . The exo-cultural character functions within a frame of attitudes created by a tradition outside his person. . . .
> . . . What emerges from the application of the concept of the exo-cultural stereotype to the study of national literatures is an awareness of the extent to which the imagination of the artist (as well, of course, as that of the audience) can be conditioned by cultural prejudices and attitudes; or, more relevantly, how great works of art can be produced under the impetus of some of the basest of prejudices.[19]

Echeruo argues that the exo-cultural stereotype responds to and stimulates the culturally conditioned imagination. The stereotyped Jew-figure of *The Jew of Malta* or *The Merchant of Venice* is the "complex product of an imagination conditioned by the expectations of its audience" (34) and that conditioning springs from latent folk memory rather than from any kind of "local or topical momentum that gave immediacy to the plays" (26). Echeruo's short book is useful in its insistence that ethnic stereotypes may be understood as the product of particular cultures, and therefore may be explored as manifestations of cultural conditioning. Its acknowledgment of the semeiological significance of stereotyping little more than indicates a promising avenue of inquiry.

In a much more controversial book, Edward Said translates the preoccupation with discourse and myth of such thinkers as Michel Foucault and Roland Barthes into a wide-ranging and politically impassioned inquiry into the depiction of the Orient in Western culture. The perception of the Orient through the saturating hegemony of European culture, while a fertile stimulus to the literary imagination and ideologies of the West, is for Said a relationship of power and domination. "Orientalism," he believes, "is more particularly valuable as a sign of European-Atlantic power over the Orient than it is as a veridic discourse about the Orient."[20] The occidental view of the Orient is almost entirely a construct of historical standardization and cultural stereotyping, intensified through the hold since at least the late eighteenth century of the imaginative demonology of the "mysterious Orient" (26). Largely because of its roots in imperialist thinking, the Western perception of the Orient continues to maintain the cultural distinction between "us" (Europe) and "the Other" (the East) and ineluctably to reassert the inferiority of the Other. As a Palestinian, educated under and living in a Western culture, Said is particularly sensitive to the dehumanizing effects of occidental myths and ideologies concerning Arabs and Islam. The study of Orientalism makes sense only if we recognize it as a cultural discourse that reveals attitudes that have remained prevalent primarily in the West; yet, Said argues, because of the tyrannical hold of these attitudes and of the political hegemony of Western culture, their effects continue to have devastating consequences for the Muslim world. More than earlier writers, Said stresses that in both literary representation and so-called truthful texts (e.g., "histories, philological analyses, political treatises") what are often represented are far from correct or faithful depictions of the Orient as it *actually* is. "The exteriority of the representation," he writes, "is always governed by some version of the truism that if the Orient could represent itself, it would; since it cannot, the representation does the job, for the West, and *faute de mieux*, for the poor Orient" (21).

Despite holding severe reservations about the validity for our purposes of many of his conclusions,[21] I am influenced by Said's recognition that (a) ethnic stereotyping stresses the distinction between the dominant group and the Other; (b) stereotyping rarely distinguishes between and is endemic in the style, metaphorical strategies, and discourse of both imaginative and "truthful" texts; and (c) the prevalence in such discourse of mythical assumptions about a particular race often obscures, sometimes stands in for, and often takes the place of direct perception. Some of these ideas are already apparent in the works of Lippman and others, but Said is among the first to attempt to give them a broadly cross-cultural focus.

The newfound academic interest in stereotyping as a valid discourse in cultural studies is perhaps nowhere better reflected than in the work of Sander L. Gilman, professor at the University of Chicago. The pioneering aspect of his work is in his ability to widen the terminology of stereotyping and its scope as an important area of research from social psychology to literary and cultural studies. In a series of penetrating books, he has explored the function of stereotypes as markers or labels of sexuality, race, ethnic self-hatred, and madness. In their literary manifestation, as preserved in written and printed form, stereotypes lend themselves to examination as decipherable palimpsests of the mental representations of the world that are (or were) the accepted vocabulary of particular social groups.[22] Although often no more than myths that have become "powerful enough to substitute for realities," stereotypes deserve close study because of their encoding of categories of difference between the predominant or host group that employs them and the Other who is described by them.[23] So, for instance, writes Gilman, "The statement that someone 'looks Jewish' or 'looks crazy' reflects the visual stereotype which a culture creates for the 'other' out of an arbitrary complex of features."[24]

Yet, however arbitrary and protean this complex of features, all too easily it becomes the accepted means by which the host group perpetuates distinctions between itself and the Other that it is describing. Such stereotyping assigns qualities to the Other that "form patterns with little or no relationship to any external reality," although in the mind of the host group these qualities may be registered as inherent and immutable facts.[25] As a result, stereotypes are more reliable as indicators of the values and beliefs of the host group than necessarily of the Other that they claim to define. The presence of the Other accentuates the recognition of difference by the host group that feels its beliefs and values to be under threat through intrusion. In the process of stereotyping, an imaginary line of demarcation is perpetuated by the host group, creating a needed sense of difference from the Other that is essentially defensive. The paradoxical constant of this illusory line of demarcation is that, as a means of defense, it is "dynamic in its ability to alter itself."[26] The bipolarity of stereotypes is one exemplification of their protean nature.

Gilman argues that as a means of dealing with the instabilities of our perception of the world, stereotypes are an outward reflection of an internal cognitive process, and may therefore be interpreted as the closest approximation by which we may begin to understand the structure of that internal process.[27] By studying stereotypes almost as recurrent metaphors, we may untie a system of references that are part of a larger structural pattern. "Within the closed world they create," writes Gilman,

> stereotypes can be studied as an idealized definition of the different. The closed world of language, a system of references which creates the illusion of completeness and wholeness, carries and is carried by the need to stereotype. For stereotypes, like commonplaces, carry entire realms of association with them, associations that form a subtext within the world of fiction.[28]

Through the study of such stereotypes in their "idealized" or fixed form in printed texts, we may hope to approach an understanding of many of the myths, ideologies, and cultural beliefs of the society that employs them. Gilman develops a cogent theoretical framework by which we may recognize that the analysis of stereotypes provides an insight into the structural patterns that reflect the daily mental life of a particular culture. In the light of the developments in the theory of stereotyping from Walter Lippman through to the recent work of Sander Gilman, the aim of the present study is as an exposition of endemic English attitudes to the Jews, rather than in any true sense as a reliable account of Jewish realities. The Jew as Other provides the focus by which these attitudes may be gauged.

In historical terms, the period covered in this study is sometimes referred to as the "long" or "longer" eighteenth century, approximately from the Restoration of the monarchy in 1660 to the death of George IV in 1830.[29] What makes the period particularly interesting insofar as it concerns the Jews is that these dates coincide almost exactly with the readmission of the Jews after an enforced absence of over 350 years and in 1830, with Robert Grant's unsuccessful attempt to steer through the House of Commons the first Jewish Disabilities Bill, the beginning of the extended parliamentary campaign that in the following half century gave English Jews complete equality in law as full citizens of the kingdom. Between these dates, despite the one notable though disastrous attempt to naturalize the Jews in 1753, their position in English society was viewed as at least anomalous and sometimes pernicious by the majority of the indigenous populace. The paradigm of the Other as a threat to the status quo, jeopardizing the institutions of Church and State, is recurrent in anti-Semitic definition of the relationship of Jew and Christian. A writer at the time of the Naturalization Bill, by evocation of the biblical Fall, captures the prevalent mood of fear and hysteria that could be generated against too ready an acceptance of the Jews:

> If the Attempt now said to be on Foot, to incorporate them in Rights and Privileges with our natural-born *Englishmen*, should take place, I must look upon our own Destruction, as a People, to be the next Thing we have to expect; and that, after That, we shall never see happy Day more; but Their Sin and Guilt shall become ours; and their Judgment and Plague follow us, till God cast us out of this good Land which he hath given us; as He hath, so long since, cast Them out of Theirs.[30]

Even though reaction to the Jew Bill of 1753 should be viewed as representing the most vociferous expression of anti-Jewish feeling during the whole period, we would be mistaken to believe that such feeling went into abeyance at other times. Stereotypical attitudes, which may no more than subsist in the public consciousness of the host group, become catalyzed when the threat from the Other appears most immediate and dangerous. As will be discussed in a later chapter, the Jew Bill at one moment brought into focus so many inherent prejudices and assumptions that at other times by and large remained latent.

In terms of the study of stereotypes, the period from 1655 to 1830, from the readmission of the Jews to the beginnings of their political emancipation in England, has an almost unique validity and interest. Within this period the traditional stereotype that had come down from the Middle Ages of the mythical Jew, in league with the Devil as the inveterate enemy of Christianity and Christian values, is juxtaposed with and implicitly challenged by the presence once again in England of actual Jews. During the period, although largely unconscious of what was an almost imperceptible change, the English, while not yet fully accepting the Jews as equals, were to learn increasingly to regard them as fellow human beings in preference to reviling them in the traditional manner. Where at the beginning of the period, to the majority of Englishmen, the Jews were no more than bogeymen and aliens, by the end acceptance of their presence had advanced sufficiently for them to be able to enlist appreciable support in their protracted campaign for complete political emancipation. If the change in attitude may be attributed to any particular cause, it probably owes more to the wider social awareness and intermittent, direct contact that their presence in England allowed. If not in any formal sense, at least implicitly their presence may be shown to have had an educative effect in questioning the validity of many of the old negative assumptions.

In the present day, education has become a major area of critical debate in the study of ethnic stereotyping. By utilizing more or less accurate scientific data drawn from widely based survey work, social psychologists have endeavored to measure the effect of education as an important factor in alleviating negative racial attitudes. As early as 1922, Lippman had contended that the critical discernment that we acquire through education can give us the ability to begin to recognize the shortcomings and partialities of stereotypical attitudes. "It is only," he writes,

> when we are in the habit of recognizing our opinions as a partial experience seen through our stereotypes that we become truly tolerant of an opponent. Without that habit, we believe in the absolutism of our own vision, and consequently in the treacherous character of all opposition. For while men are willing to admit that there are two sides to a "question," they do not believe that there are two sides to what they regard as a "fact." And they never do believe it until after long critical education, they are fully conscious of how second-hand and subjective is their apprehension of their social data.[31]

Several studies in Britain and America since the 1930s have attempted to relate levels of formal education to reductions in ethnic stereotyping and prejudice. Education, it has been claimed, may be seen as the "key factor" in explaining anti-Semitism. The higher a person's level of education, the less likely that person is to express negative attitudes or feelings toward Jews.[32] Education is viewed elsewhere as one of a number of variables, including other factors such as class and intelligence, that help to determine ethnic prejudice.[33] Yet, curiously, a report of one American study also reveals a shifting nexus of negative associations in the perception of Jews by persons with higher levels of education. Instead of the more overt and largely uninformed anti-Semitism of those with no more than high school education, this study shows that persons with college and postgraduate degrees are more likely to base their contentions about the Jews on the supposition that Jews have too much power.[34] The study concurs with the view that anti-Semitic prejudice in America has been mitigated by higher levels of education, but it also demonstrates the ease with which stereotypes, given different circumstances, can transform themselves.[35]

The perception of Otherness as reflected in the putative stereotypical traits attributed to the Jews by anti-Semites may appear totally distinct in different ages. Apart from the recognition of a shared negativeness, comparison of such traits may seem of little value initially. Yet, in social psychology, the change in attribution and emphasis of such stereotypes over the more than half century in which survey work has been carried out has helped to suggest "the possibility that [during this time] stereotypes have genuinely assumed a more liberalized character."[36] The measurement of ethnic prejudice on a downward curve as a possible result of higher standards of education in American schools has been used to bolster the argument that "characteristics intrinsically associated with education, such as greater cognitive sophistication or different cultural values and tastes, . . . [are] the principal factors leading to a reduction in anti-Semitism."[37] In the earliest such survey, the frequently quoted checklist measurement of stereotypical traits published by Katz and Braly in 1933, a group of students at Princeton University selected out of a list of eighty-four bipolar attributes the following adjectives as characteristics that they associated with Jews: shrewd, mercenary, industrious, grasping, intelligent, ambitious, sly.[38] Later surveys of similar groups at Princeton carried out in the postwar years showed a distinct change from conspicuous racial prejudice to, on the whole, a supposedly more liberal outlook. Of the six traits first chosen, in later surveys only intelligence and ambition achieved higher scores, but significantly Jews were also rated by more recent students as aggressive and materialistic.[39]

Rather than necessarily showing a "fading effect," as claimed by Allport, by which ethnic clichés may be seen to be weakening,[40] the changes seem once again to support the contention that stereotypes mutate to reflect the cultural ethos of a particular age or group. Needless to say, the comparative simplicity of the Katz-Braly mode of measurement has been criticized for its insistence on checklist instructions that too readily encourage stereotypical responses and for its failure to elucidate what stereotypes really are.[41] Research by questionnaire of this kind has since undergone considerable refinement to try to minimize error factors and the almost inevitable artificiality of the process.

In attempting to analyze changes in the stereotyping of Jews in the longer eighteenth century, it is immediately evident that our methodology will be far less "scientific" than that adopted with varying degrees of rigor by researchers in the area of social psychology. Inevitably, the "data" that is available to us cannot be based on formal sampling by social survey but relies far more on the discursive observations of mainly minor authors who chose or found themselves impelled for whatever reason to write about the Jews in pamphlets, news sheets, and works of the imagination. Within such a protracted period, the views and attitudes about the Jews expressed by a wide variety of very different writers cannot necessarily be expected to be entirely homogeneous, although a notable feature of many remarks made about the Jews is that they are often reiterated. Because so many pamphlets about the Jews were published anonymously, it is usually difficult (with individual exceptions) to ascribe specific religious or political allegiances to their authors.[42] Indeed, for all their emotive impact, the employment in eighteenth-century England of anti-Semitic stereotypes is rarely confined to any one particular group or used (as most notoriously by twentieth-century fascism) as coordinated propaganda. The very haphazardness of anti-Semitism in eighteenth-century popular culture makes it arguably a more authentic discourse for the study of stereotyping because less likely than its modern counterpart to be disturbed and manipulated by external influences. If Gilman and others who have attempted to conceptualize the study of stereotypes are right, then the coding of Otherness in the case of the Jews should provide a relatively accurate reflection of many of the myths, cultural values, and prejudices of the host group at any given time. The differences between perceptions of the Jews in an earlier age and now reflect the shifts in the needs and values of the host groups and also the responses of the Other to those shifts. In each period, the vocabulary by which the Other is labeled and categorized may be interpreted as part of a pattern of association that reveals at a minimum some of the prevalent prejudices but, by extension, the deeper structure of embedded beliefs by which an age—or at least the host group in a particular age—defines itself.

Whether we choose to adopt Rosenberg's skeptical view that students of English anti-Semitism "are determined to come up with optimistic results" and therefore show "a tendency to slant the evidence,"[43] or whether we accept the record of social history that points unmistakably in the same direction, it is generally agreed that a more liberal attitude toward the Jews gradually emerged toward the latter years of the eighteenth century. "At this day," writes Joseph Priestley, addressing the titular correspondents of his *Letters to the Jews* (1787), "the cruel usage you have met with from christian nations is happily much abated. Christians in general, and especially the more civilized among them, are disposed to treat you with equity and humanity."[44] "Happily this moral degeneracy" between Christian and Jew, says another writer twenty years later, "has been wearing off in this country [England] for some years past, and the Jews, as well as others, have largely partaken of the general improvement in manners and appearance."[45] The readier acceptance of the social position of actual Jews toward the end of the eighteenth century presupposes an accompanying decline in the traditional theological anti-Semitism that had stereotyped them as fiendish mutilators of Christians and Christian values. Although unfortunately eschewing theoretical discussion, the most recent account of endemic anti-Semitism in the period *prior* to ours during which the Jews were expelled from England does at least provide at the end of the book a valuable index of traditional stereotypes found mainly in English sermons, drama, ballads, folklore, tracts, and conversionist literature written between 1290 and 1700. Jews are stereotyped as aliens, anti-Christs, bribers, "clippers and forgers," crucifiers, demons, desecrators of the ritual Host, enemies of Christians, hypocrites, murderers of innocent children, outcasts, poisoners, regicides, sorcerers, traitors, and usurers.[46] Without exception, these stereotypical traits are commonly repeated in the anti-Semitic literature of the eighteenth century, but their validity as established "facts" about the Jews is increasingly challenged.

Todd Endelman has argued convincingly that during the eighteenth century the "gradual decline in the appeal and the credibility of the older anti-Semitism was largely a function of the secularization of English life," although he cautions us not to mistake this as representing in any sense the complete disappearance of anti-Jewish feeling. Rather, he recognizes "that much anti-Semitism that had been expressed in an exclusively religious framework underwent transformation and reappeared in a variety of secular forms." Yet, the function of the Jews as a negative element in the "fantasy life" of Christians remained largely unchanged.[47] Whether represented in traditional theological terms or as flesh-and-blood Jews, the exigency of the host group to shape the anatomy of their Otherness persists unabated throughout the period. The study of anti-Semitism in English popular culture of the eighteenth century provides a fascinating insight into the almost intangible process by which a stereotype may mutate according to the psychological and social needs of the host group. By accepting, willingly or otherwise, the presence in their country of actual Jews, the English were obliged to modify many of the myths and superstitions with which they had previously beheld them. The changes in the perception of the Jews by the English during the eighteenth century offer valuable clues toward understanding the dynamics of prejudice for a later age in which the process of "education" of the host group has been much more closely documented.

CHAPTER 2

JEWS AND DEVILS

OUR ACCOUNT must begin with a backward glance. In pictorial representation, the earliest extant English caricature drawings of Jews stem from the thirteenth century. The best known, which may serve as our example, is the group caricature by an anonymous court scribe that appears at the head of a vellum Tallage Roll from the year 1233, now in the Public Record Office, London.[1] Whatever may have been in the mind of the sketcher, we cannot be certain of the precise intention of his drawing, perhaps little more than a doodle in an idle hour, for the contents of the roll do not allude to it. The figure, however, at the center of the sketch is identified as Isaac of Norwich, whose head surmounted by a crown has three faces, one full, the other two in profile, each of them

"Isaac of Norwich." Drawing, 1233. Exchequer of Receipt, Jews' Roll, no. 87. (Courtesy of the Public Record Office, London.)

protruding into a goatee beard. It has been suggested that a fourth face, behind the others, is to be understood, so that the crowned figure of Isaac is shown casting his eye over his possessions to the north, south, east, and west.[2]

In his day, Isaac of Norwich (d. 1235), the son of Jurnet, was probably the wealthiest Jew in England and the drawing seems to allude both to the sphere of his influence and to his double dealing. Some years earlier, Isaac is reported to have loaned huge sums of money to the abbot and monks of Westminster, despite the support they enjoyed of Pandulf, bishop elect of Norwich and former papal legate, a clergyman who had tried to have the Jews expelled from England.[3] Also in the mind of the anonymous caricaturist may have been the tallaging of the Jewish community during the reign of Henry III, by which Jews were forced to pay considerable levies to the Crown. We know that Isaac owned taxable assets and land at Norwich, but in 1231 the king, in an unusual step, granted him freedom from being tallaged for the rest of his life, although the records show that even after this he was sufficiently rich to remain among the most heavily taxed.[4]

Below the three faces of Isaac is a complex tableau that has been described by Cecil Roth as "the setting as it were of a contemporary miracle play," the drapery representing "the stage, and the architecture . . . that of the church where such plays were generally performed."[5] Of course, the texts of those miracle plays that have survived are of a later date than the thirteenth century, although the Jew characters portrayed in them were often intended to be vilified and hissed at by the audience. The caricature shows Isaac surrounded by a number of figures, some of whom are Jews, the others recognizably devils or pagan gods. To the left and right of him are the named figures of a Jew and Jewess, Mosse Mokke and Avegaye (i.e., Abigail). The fierce horned devil, called Colbif, that stands between them has his index finger upon the pronounced nose of each, as if he were both identifying their ethnic origin and claiming them as his own. We know of Mosse Mokke's criminal background from other sources, that he was involved in an assault in Norwich in 1230 and that he was subsequently hanged for coin-clipping in 1242,[6] so that there is every likelihood that the artist intended to stress Isaac of Norwich's underworld connections. The spiked hat that Mokke wears has been identified as the characteristic *pileum cornutum* worn by medieval Jews,[7] although the spike may also be seen to link him to the horned figures of the cosmic underworld. (Isaac is similarly linked by his goatee beard, often used to associate Jews and the Devil.)[8] Avegaye wears the costume of a well-born Englishwoman, a wimple and a coif, and since

her name appears immediately below the triple face of Isaac, it is possible that she is intended as his wife or mistress, dressed by him as a
lady of fashion.[9] Their intent, even libidinous, eying of each other and
the quizzical posture of the horned voyeur in the turret (identified as
Dagon) may suggest an illicit relationship between Avegaye and Mokke,
a union that has the sanction of the Devil. To the left of Mokke is another Jewish figure, who remains unidentified, holding up a pair of scales
filled with coins, symbolizing the usurious role with which Jews were
at once associated in the Middle Ages. Even if the exact significance of
the caricature as a whole remains obscure, the demonic figures to the
right make it clear that the Jews are to be viewed as agents of hell, to be
feared as well as vilified. With his crown, and standing as he does at the
center of the picture, Isaac may be seen to rule over this demonic world
and perhaps also, by inference, through the power of his connections, to
usurp the role of the true king, Henry III.[10] The Jew is portrayed as both
demon and traitor.

The caricature may be said to encapsulate in visual terms the prejudices and hostility of Christians in the England of the Middle Ages toward the Jews. The motifs that appear in the drawing recreate an image
of Jewry that is far from savory, in which Jews are presented at best as
coin-clippers and moneylenders, in league with the Devil. But behind
the portrayal is the larger, and far more sinister, stereotype of the medieval Jew as a bloody ritual murderer, the betrayer of Christ and a crucifier, one who is intent upon the very destruction of Christian society
and Christian values. That stereotype, reinforced as it was from the pulpit, in pageants and plays, engulfed and eventually submerged what Jews
were *actually* like in favor of a diabolical travesty. Part of the problem
for the present-day researcher concerned to trace the Jews of medieval
England is how to distinguish between reality and stereotype, for so
many early allusions to them are noteworthy only for the crudity of their
anti-Semitism. They are expressive of an attitude, the prevailing Christian attitude toward the Jews, rather than describing the actual Jews of
medieval England.

Those actual Jews—many of them settled in England from the time
of William the Conqueror—were shortly to become victims of the prejudice against them; in 1290, by royal decree of Edward I, the whole Jewish population, numbering about 16,000 people, was summarily expelled
from the country. For over 350 years after that, with the exception of a
few visitors and perhaps a handful of secret believers, there were no Jews
in England until, following the delegation of Menasseh Ben Israel (1604–
57), Oliver Cromwell finally acceded to their readmission in 1655. But

although the Jews themselves were expelled, the stereotype remained. There was no way of expelling that. On the contrary, in many ways it was often expedient to nurture the stereotype if only as a means to imbue belief by Christians in the righteousness of their faith. As Joshua Trachtenberg puts it,

> The mythical Jew, outlined by early Christian theology and ultimately puffed out to impossible proportions, supplanted the real Jew in the medieval mind, until that real Jew to all intents and purposes ceased to exist. The only Jew whom the medieval Christian recognized was a figment of the imagination.[11]

On the European continent, allusions to Jews in the late Middle Ages are with few exceptions stereotypical and hostile, showing a blind ignorance (or lack of comprehension) of the actualities of Jewish life and faith. In England, the hostility is no less apparent, although after 1290 there were no real Jews to compare with the stereotype. As a result, the stereotype remains practically the only yardstick by which English attitudes to the Jews may be gauged. And, for the English of the late Middle Ages, that stereotype, grotesque as it is, had become the "real" Jew, since for them no other existed.

If we examine the facets of the stereotype in England as it appears in literary and dramatic representation, it soon becomes evident that Jews could be accused of every conceivable crime and found guilty without regard. After all, unlike on the Continent, in the absence of Jews from England there could be no real harm in introducing them from the pulpit in demonic terms. There could be no question of revenge being meted out upon the Jews after the church service. Any ensuing violence could only be in the minds of the congregants.

At the root of the Christian stereotype of the Jew is the accusation that it was he who was responsible, as much as his forefathers, for the betrayal and crucifixion of Christ. The blame for the crucifixion is to be carried by every generation of Jews. Instead of being God's chosen people the Jews have become, through the death of Christ, eternally accursed. The prevalent attitude here may be illustrated by quoting from William Langland's *Piers Plowman* (c. 1362), a work that has sometimes been praised for entertaining a sympathetic view of the Jews.[12] In describing how they encouraged the stabbing of Christ's body upon the cross, Langland execrates the Jews as follows:

> For this foule vileynye vengeaunce to yow falle! . . .
> For be this derknesse ydo, Death worth yvenqisshed;
> And ye, lurdaynes, han lost—for lif shal have the maistrye.

And youre fraunchyse, that fre was, fallen is in thraldom,
And ye, cherles, and youre children, cheve shulle ye nevere,
Ne have lordshipe in londe, ne no lond tilye,
But al barayne be and usurie usen,
Which is lif that Oure Lord in alle lawes acurseth.[13]

The scourge that is upon the Jews following the Crucifixion is compounded by Judas's betrayal of Christ at the Last Supper. By extension, all Jews must be feared for their treachery. Medieval tales and ballads often depict Jews who in their cunning deliberately impose upon or trick their Christian neighbors. Similar tales are no less common in which the treacherous Jew is himself out-tricked. The most famous of these occurs in the *Cursor Mundi* of the fourteenth century, containing what appears to be the first rendering in English of the "pound of flesh" tale, which Shakespeare borrowed from a later version as one of the narrative sources of *The Merchant of Venice*. It is interesting that in the earliest examples of the "pound of flesh" tale (which is of continental origin) neither party in the bond is Jewish, although in England, once the connection with Judaism was made, there was no other way in which this popular story was told.[14]

In dramatic representation, the Judas-figure is made recognizable— and for the audience recognizably Jewish—by the red beard he wears, which can be traced back at least to the thirteenth century. According to Bernard Glassman, from the beginning the figure was associated with usury, for "[in] the summer festival of Corpus Christi, founded by Pope Urban IV in 1264, . . . Judas was portrayed by a person wearing a red beard who was bent beneath the weight of his money bags."[15] Hyam Maccoby points out that red hair was also an "identifying mark" of Herod in the Passion Plays of late medieval Germany and tantalizingly surmises that it "may be that redness, as the colour of blood was reserved for those taking the leading murderous parts—Judas for his acceptance of blood-money . . . and Herod because of his massacre of the Innocents."[16] Be that as it may, the red hair, deemed characteristic of Judas, was transferred in the English drama to any villainous Jew-figure. Most notably, Shylock from the time of Richard Burbage (who is thought to have first acted the part) to at least the middle years of the eighteenth century was invariably portrayed wearing a red beard.[17] That the significance of the color was well known in Elizabethan times is evident from a reference in Thomas Kyd's play, *The Spanish Tragedy*, "and let their beards be of Judas his own colour."[18] Even after the Restoration, following the period of closure of the theaters, the tradition remained alive, for Dryden alludes to it in *Amboyna* (1673), "There's treachery in that Judas-coloured beard."[19] Throughout, the Judas figure is associated with Jews as much as with treachery. "Judas," affirms the Protestant martyr John Bradford writing in the middle years of the sixteenth century, "bare a figure of the people of the Jews, which tribe only fell from Christ."[20] "Who sels Religion," echoes the seventeenth-century cleric and poet Henry Vaughan, "is a *Judas Jew*."[21] In popular culture, the equation through similarity of name of Jew and Judas marks out the Jew as one who both betrayed and killed Christ.

The deicidal image of the Jew in the England of the Middle Ages was reinforced by the further accusation that during Passover Jews were possessed by the fiendish desire to reenact the Crucifixion and satisfied this frenzy by desecrating the consecrated Host until it bled,[22] and sometimes by murdering young Christian children. Typologically, the action of Abraham, the patriarch of the Hebrews, with his knife offering the child Isaac as sacrifice, became in the medieval mind a telling antecedent to the fatal sacrifice of Christ by the Jews.[23] (Another explanation of this blood libel charge is that it derived from Crusading tales of the ruthlessness of the Saracens, who were said to use Christian blood in their demoniacal rituals. It was not difficult for the Crusaders to transfer the imputation to the Jews and use it as an excuse to wreak vengeance upon them.)[24] Ballads and tales abound describing the alleged fate of little Hugh of Lincoln who, it was claimed, had been put to death by ritual torture after having entered a Jew's house to play.[25] On that occasion, in 1255, despite a lack of evidence, the houses in the Jewish quarter of Lincoln were attacked and their occupants put to the sword or later hanged.

Even after the expulsion, the blood accusation remained the perfect means to incite mob hatred against absent Jews. As late as 1656, at about the time that Menasseh Ben Israel was suing Oliver Cromwell, a pamphleteer writing to prevent their readmission into England reminds his readers that the Jews "make it their annual practice to crucifie children" and that there is no safeguard against such people once again "imbruing their hands in the blood of yong and tender infants (crucifying them in scorn and derision of our profession)."[26] And, in the same year, the notorious Puritan pamphleteer, William Prynne, quite brazenly asserts that "the Jews almost every year crucify one child, to the injury and contumely of Jesus."[27] So deeply ingrained seems to have been the belief in the blood libel that in his petition to Cromwell to readmit the Jews, Menasseh himself found it necessary to include his own firm refutation and defense. The killing by Jews of the young children of Christians, he avers, "is but a meer slander, seeing it is known that at this day, out of Ierusalem, no sacrifice nor blood is in any use by them [the Jews], even that blood which is found in an Egg is forbidden them, how much more mans blood?"[28] Menasseh's plea, sufficient as it was to persuade Cromwell, appears to have had little effect in wiping away the blood libel from the collective consciousness of the Christian majority in England.

If the stereotype portrayed Jews in all their heinousness as ritual murderers and crucifiers, it was but a short step to link them with the Devil and Antichrist.[29] After all, it was possible to find gospel evidence of the satanic involvement of the Jews. "You are of your father the devil, and the lusts of your fathers ye will do," Jesus berates the Jews (John 8:44). As children of the Devil, the Jews seem to have been considered often as less than human, akin more to brute beast than humankind. Shakespeare's Shylock, for instance, is described as a "cut-throat dog" (I.iii. 106), "A creature that did bear the shape of man" (III.ii.274) and later as one whose "desires / Are wolvish, bloody, starv'd and ravenous" (IV.i. 137–38). Another contemporary author speaks in a typical vein when he lists in procession "Doggs, Turkes, Jewes, brute beasts, or filthy villaines."[30] Again, in *A Brief Compendium of the Vain Hopes of the Jews Messias*, published in London in 1652, within a few years of the readmission, Eleazar Bargishai, a known apostate, enunciates that Elias the prophet "shall become an Hunter, which shall gather through the voice of his Horn, all the Doggs (that is to say) the Jews of the whole world together."[31] A seventeenth-century proverb, concerned with the Jews' stiff-necked refusal of Christ, juxtaposes "five things" that "exceed in stubborness and pertinaciousnesse, the Dogge among Beasts, the Cock among birds, the Goat among Cattle, the Prickthorn among plants, and the Jew among men."[32] It is interesting that two of these "five things" have associations with the Devil, a further two with the betrayal and crucifixion of Christ, but, in the Christian mind, the fifth—the Jew—is associated with both.[33] If only by inference, the Jew-figure is debased to a level beneath even the bestial.

The typical occupation of such a figure, the lending of money at interest, is also to be seen as the work of the Devil and in contradiction to the Scriptures. In the Gospel according to Luke, Christians are enjoined to "Lend, hoping for nothing again" (6:35; "Mutuum date, nihil inde sperantes," Vulgate Version). In response to this, the medieval Church forbade, under pain of excommunication, the taking of interest by Christian usurers. Being outside the jurisdiction of canonical law and, in any case, prevented from pursuing those trades monopolized by the Christian craft guilds, Jews in many European countries turned to usury or money-lending as the one profession that gave them legitimized status, however dubious. In the popular imagination, Judaism and money-lending became synonymous: in England, on the medieval and the Elizabethan stage, a Jew-figure was nearly always a usurer. The scorn and jeering derision that his appearance produced may be linked to the earlier equation of Jews and Judas, for it was remembered that the latter had betrayed Jesus to the priests for thirty pieces of silver (Matt. 26:15). Like Judas, the Jewish moneylender was depicted on stage and elsewhere as completely unscrupulous and totally untrustworthy, a fiend-like agent who would sell his very soul for financial gain: "all they that live of usury," Bishop Latimer tells us, "they have their gains by the devil."[34] Francis Bacon, writing in mitigation of the practice in his essay "Of Usury" (1625), cites the many "witty invectives" that both castigate usury as the work of the Devil and enjoin "that usurers should have orange-tawny bonnets, because they do Judaize."[35] At the time of the readmission, Menasseh was once again impelled to argue against similar embedded prejudice by pointing out that "such dealing" in usury "is not the essentiall property of the Iewes," and that Jewish law insists that "it is a greater sinne to rob or defraud a stranger, than if I did it to one of my own profession: because a Iew is bound to shew his charity to all men." "If notwithstanding," adds Menasseh, "there be some that do contrary to this, they do it not as Iewes simply, but as wicked Iewes, as amongst all Nations there are found generally some Usurers."[36]

As well as finding himself obliged to defend his coreligionists against the charges of usury and blood libel, Menasseh refers to a third prejudice or false report in currency against the Jews, whereby it was feared that, should they be readmitted, they would set about inducing Christians to convert to Judaism. Again, Menasseh is adamant in contradicting this by categorically insisting that "the Iewes do not entice any man to professe their Law."[37] Nevertheless, the deeply rooted fear of the stereotyped Jew-figure, the threat that he posed to Christianity and his supposed cosmic connection with the Devil gave credibility to claims even more bizarre. One such story that circulated widely at that time was that, as the price of their readmission (for even that appears to have commanded a price), the Jews had offered to purchase St. Paul's Cathedral in order to make it into their synagogue and "the *Bodleian* Library at *Oxford*, to begin their Traffick with."[38] The eighteenth-century Oxford historian D'Blossiers Tovey recounts with wry cynicism the discomfort of the English clergymen shortly before the readmission in considering the possible fate that awaited them: "The *Fanatical Preachers* at that Time," writes Tovey,

> haveing so much Cunning as to perceive that if the Jewish Religion shou'd by a *Tolleration* at *first*, become *afterwards* the *Establish'd Re-*

ligion, they cou'd never expect to become *Rulers of Synagogues*, and be call'd *Rabbi*, without submitting to a *Circumcision*, which would be very painful to the Flesh of *Adult* Persons, and perhaps endanger their beloved lives.[39]

If the extreme unlikelihood of such insinuations makes them more comic than serious, the elements of fear and threat associated with them signify the extent to which the Jew-figure remained, in the popular imagination, an outcast or bogeyman even 350 years after the expulsion of 1290.

There are indeed lesser aspects of the stereotype that I have been unable touch on, as for instance, (a) the belief that, as punishment for their crime against Jesus, Jews emitted a peculiarly foul smell, akin to that of the Devil, which would instantly transform to a savor sweeter than ambrosia upon their willing conversion by baptism (Sir Thomas Browne furnishes his *Pseudodoxia Epidemica*, 1646, with a circumstantial chapter endeavoring most earnestly in their defense to disprove "received opinion" that the "Jews stinck naturally");[40] (b) the apparent addiction of Jews to swearing and foul language (perhaps derived from Matt. 26:74, describing the cursing and swearing of Peter in denying Christ), which seems to have been considered indicative of their cursed state;[41] (c) the imputation that menstruation by both men and women and hemorrhoidal bleeding was normal among Jews, and was to be considered "a very literal interpretation of the concept of guilt and corporate responsibility supposedly advanced in Matthew 27:25: 'His blood be on us, and on our children'";[42] (d) the charge that in their extreme lasciviousness Jews "seduced Christian girls, buggered Christian boys, and perpetrated profane orgies in parody of Christian ritual."[43]

All these aspects of the stereotype combined to portray a pariah, to be both hated and feared, who, with the mark of Cain upon him, was to be seen as the perpetual outsider, an analogue to the figure of the Wandering Jew. It has been claimed that the Wandering Jew, eternally seeking expiation for his supposed crime against Christ, derives from the late Middle Ages when mass expulsions of Jews took place throughout western Europe.[44] Again, however, it was not difficult to find scriptural support to justify the widespread belief that Jews were impelled to wander. "And among these Nations," says Moses to the Jews in Deuteronomy 28:65, "thou shalt find no Ease, neither shall the Sole of thy Foot have rest." At different times, in many places on the European continent, Jews were refused the right of settlement and became, in the German term, *Betteljuden*, the word *Bettel* having the double meaning of "mendicancy" and "trash." In England, William Prynne picks up both meanings when he says of the Jews that they are "disposed like so many Vagabonds over the face of the whole Earth, as the off-scowring of the world."[45] As a punishment for his deicidal deeds and for his refusal to acknowledge Christ through accepting conversion, the Jew will never be permitted to rest but must wander the world to be execrated as a living symbol of his crime against mankind.

The anti-Semitic stereotype outlined here is not always made up of every one of the features I have described. Frequently, however, semeiological allusion to a single feature will be sufficient to invoke the larger stereotype without the necessity of cataloguing all its connections. The associations that the Jew-figure evokes make him instantly recognizable and immediately abhorrent. It is difficult—indeed, perhaps impossible—to trace specific sources for each aspect of the stereotype. What is apparent, though, is that two things in particular seem to have given sustenance to the apparent "truth" of the stereotype, even at such moments when by any rational consideration the existence of such a diabolical figure could only be considered as preposterous.

The first of these is the perversely literalistic interpretation of the Holy Scriptures, whereby clergymen and controversialists could make charges against the Jews and offer irrefutable typological evidence for their arguments by claiming the support of the word of God. As we have seen, scriptural "proof" could be uncovered for many facets of the stereotype, and biblical text was not infrequently used to determine Christian attitudes toward contemporary Jews. So, an anonymous pamphleteer writing about fifteen years before the readmission into England of the Jews speaks of them as the descendants "of the most viperous generation . . . that ever were as Christ chargeth them" (Matt. 12:34, 23:33).[46] And the episcopal author of the sermon, *The Devilish Conspiracy, Hellish Treason, Heathenish Condemnation, and Damnable Murder, Committed, and Executed by the Iewes, against the Anointed of the Lord, Christ the King* (1648), switches from past to present tense, thereby implicating all Jews through apt biblical quotation:

> to be rightly informed what the reall true causes were, which moved these accursed Jewes to so horrid an act as to kil *Ch[rist]:* the King: And the generall leading cause is one word, that they are *Hypocrites, a Generation of Vipers, Sonnes of Belial, Children* (indeed) *of the Devill:* for so *Ch[rist]:* told them.[47]

It is important to realize, in reviewing the stereotype as we have, that it is essentially a Christian invention or myth, and that as such it actually tells us far more about Christianity and Christian attitudes in late medieval and Renaissance England than it can reveal about real Jews. Equally, we should not forget that a very different though also literalistic interpretation of biblical text by Christian scholars could lead—as it did in seventeenth-century England—to the strong philo-Semitic movement that greatly aided the readmission of the Jews. By a curious paradox, explicable in terms of our theory of bipolarity, the diabolical stereotype and the view of the Jews as God's chosen people were to exist side by side in the England of the later Renaissance.[48] Indeed, it has been claimed that they remain that way even to the present day.[49]

A second and related source for the endurance of the stereotype is the nearly complete ignorance or misunderstanding of Jewish ritual by which, for instance, the almost simultaneously celebrated festivals of Passover and Easter could be viewed as mutually antagonistic. That the Jews practiced religious ceremonies that were not those of Christianity already served to mark them out as different, and from there it was but a short step to cast Jewish ritual in a diabolized mold. Such a practice as circumcision, physically a source of fear, could be employed as a further means to distinguish between Christian purity and Jewish immorality. From biblical text, both of the Old and New Testaments, it was predicated that the act of circumcision should be viewed as one of spiritual cleansing. In Genesis (17:6–14) it is described as "a token of the covenant" between God and the seed of Abraham, although Saint Paul argues in his epistle to his proselytes in Rome that the physical cutting of the prepuce may be deemed purposeless if it is not coupled with a similar spiritual purification. Writes Paul:

> Circumcision verily profiteth, if thou keep the law: but if thou be a breaker of the law, thy circumcision is made uncircumcision.
> Therefore if the uncircumcision keep the righteousness of the law, shall not his uncircumcision be counted for circumcision? (Rom. 2:25–26)

Paul's argument here, by which he intends to offer salvation through Christ to a wider circle of new believers, easily becomes the means by which later commentators could berate the Jews. So, for example, the martyrologist John Foxe, in a sermon preached upon the conversion of a Jew in 1578, execrating the Jews for their "heynous abominations, insatiable butcheries, treasons, frensies, and madnes," accuses them of vaunting "your selues lustily in speach of the circumcision of your foreskinnes, and your uncircumcised hearts ouerflowe with spyderlike poyson."[50] By extension, the act of circumcision becomes in another writer of the mid-seventeenth century the focal point of the Passover ritual whereby

> When they were in *England* ... the Jews used every year to steal a
> young Boy (the child of a Christian) and to circumcise him, and then
> in their Synagogue sate in a solemn Assembly, chusing one of them-
> selves to be *Pilat*, who out of their Devillish malice to Christ and
> Christians condemned the child, and crucified him to death; and
> this was discovered at *Norwich*, where they circumcised a Christian
> child ... , and condemned him to be crucified.[51]

The supposed use of circumcision as part of a larger diabolical ritual,
still being practiced, is impressed by populist Christian thinking about
the Jews, despite the attempts of a few more enlightened writers to dispel
the myth.[52]

The initiating or consecrating role of circumcision in Judaism has its
counterpart in Christianity in the act of baptism by holy water. The similarity of purpose of the two rites may be behind a further charge against
the Jews that they deliberately set about to poison well water as a means
of wreaking damage and desecration upon Christendom. During the
Black Death (c. 1348/49), the cause of which was attributed to well poisoning by the Jews, dreadful pogroms were a common occurrence across
Europe,[53] and the charge of poisoning by Jews became a recurrent one,
despite the fact that outbreaks of plague made no distinction in also selecting the alleged perpetrators as victims. The boast by Barabas, the
eponymous villain of Marlowe's play, *The Jew of Malta* (c. 1591), that
"sometimes I go about and poison wells" is indicative that the charge
was known and repeated even in England.[54]

By extension, Jews were thought to use poison as a means to further
their treachery against the state. The imputation was even given some
credence when the Portuguese Roderigo Lopez, a converted Jew and phy-
sician to Queen Elizabeth, was found guilty in 1594 of attempting to
poison her, although the more common assumption was that he was the
paid agent of the Catholic Church and of the king of Spain. Lopez's
treachery, according to an early seventeenth-century broadsheet, was
"Hatcht by the Pope, the Devil, and a Jew."[55] "This practice of poyson-
ing," says George Carleton writing of Lopez, was "reckoned among the
sinnes of the *Anti-christian* Synagogue, and taught for Doctrine by the
Romish Rabbies."[56] The prosecuting counsel at his trial described the
"vile Jew" Lopez in terms that leave him indistinguishable from the Jew
stereotype, "a perjured and murdering traitor and Jewish doctor, worse
than Judas himself."[57]

The rituals of Judaism were viewed by many as having the express
aim of subverting the English Church. At best, such ritual is seen as an
admonition to Christians, a reminder that "the egregious Sin, of an in-

grateful, disobedient, and obstinate mind, with which the nation of the Jewes hath been in all ages branded . . . is worth our remembrance, and serious meditation."[58] More commonly, as the Elizabethan divine Bishop Thomas Cartwright has it, their "Ceremoniall Law" is to be seen as "a Law of Enmity," a perpetual hindrance to "the Gentiles from joyning themselves unto the Jews."[59] Both the interpretation of biblical text and the persistence of popular belief on the nature of their rituals cast the Jews as enemies of Christ, outsiders, and devils. As we have seen, the stereotype flourished in the virtual absence of Jews from England. It was the unavoidable and unsought inheritance of those Jews who came to England following the readmission of 1655.

CHAPTER 3

FOLLOWING READMISSION

EVOLVING STEREOTYPES

W HAT KIND OF mental and visual image of the Jews was to evolve in English eyes during the first century pursuant upon their readmission into the country? How, if at all, might it have differed from the traditional perception that we explored in the previous chapter? Was there any discernible mollification of the old hateful stereotype?

Given the strange history and tenacity of anti-Semitism during the long absence of the Jews from England, it would have been even stranger if their subsequent return, welcome as it was by some, had passed without criticism or adverse attention. In fact, the spate of pamphlets published around the time of Menasseh Ben Israel's petition before Cromwell testifies that their readmission was regarded as nothing short of controversial.[1] Certainly, for some it was a nigh godsent opportunity to stir the hornets' nest of medieval assumptions anent the Jews.

The author of *Anglo-Judaeus, or the History of the Jews Whilst Here in England* (1656), who may be identified through his initials on the title page as one William Hughes of Gray's Inn, is fairly typical of a motley legion of negative pamphleteers who responded to Menasseh's plea. In common with others, he sustains in loathsome detail a repertoire of anti-Semitic allusion that stems from the traditional diabolization of the Jews. He reminds his readers that at the time of their expulsion in 1290, the Jews had been in England for some 220 years, a period "longer by five or six then [*sic*] their Ancestors were in *Egypt*" and, he claims, throughout their stay "we may easily see the *English* Nation was in bondage."[2] The character of this oppression by the Jews, he explains, is to be understood in terms of their extortionate behavior and their cruel— although seemingly visceral—need to "make it their annual practice to crucifie children, conspire against City and people, [and] still clip and spoil the coyn, as very earnest to undo themselves."[3] Not only was their earlier banishment from England justified by the heinousness of their crimes, but it has also left such "antipathy in English hearts against these men . . . , that though it be now more than 365 years since their expulsion, yet not at all doth it seem to moderate, or be abated; an ill sign of their future agreement, if ever permitted to meet again" (47).

In fulminating against the Jews, Hughes's motive is not strictly to reiterate the nature of their alleged behavior in medieval times but to forewarn contemporary Englishmen what may be expected from an unreserved compliance with Menasseh's recent pleas in favor of readmis-·sion. For, Hughes contends, the early history of the Jews in England and their consequent punishment by expulsion have had no effect in abating their known deicidal instincts. To him, the Jews of the mid-seventeenth century are potentially no different from their medieval forefathers:

> And can we conclude they have left their old qualities? their hatred against Christ, and them that worship him, their Gripings, Usuries, and cruel Oppressions? May we not judge them to be the same as before? and if their actions be not so enormous as formerly, is it not for want of opportunity, more by restraint, then [sic] any change of nature? (48)

The anti-Judaic rancor that Hughes generates, which he presumes is instinctively shared by all Englishmen, has no grounding in contact with actual Jews, of whom he seems almost certainly to have no direct knowledge. (Curiously, he maintains that if they were already settled in England "and the [English] Nation had sufficient experience of their faithfulness and good behaviour," there would be none "so cruel, as to desire their expulsion.") Rather, his opprobrium is directed and achieves effect by reactivating the familiar diabolized stereotype, which, in 1656, is still the only way by which most Englishmen could claim to be able to recognize a Jew. The reactivation is not simply of a pasteboard figure that is intended to have no life beyond the printed page. For, claims Hughes, Gentile and Jew in England have a "more than ordinary repugnancy to each other," that will inevitably unfold again in Jewish perfidy and cutthroat dealing (48). The impact of the stereotype is as a focus for populist fears and prejudices, even if it can bear little or no relation to those Jews, insignificant and small in number, who would shortly settle in England.

To the English at large in the mid-seventeenth century then, it would have been difficult to represent the Jews of their own day in any other recognizable form, so absolute was their lack of familiarity with and knowledge of them. In puffing at the embers of anti-Semitism by reactivating in all its crudity a mythical chimera, polemicists such as William Hughes and William Prynne show an almost total ignorance of contemporary Jews, and of their customs, ceremonies, and beliefs. During the first half of the century, far too few Jews had subsisted in England to have made a recognizable group, and given the secrecy of their religious observance, such recognition would have been the last thing they might have sought. Even occasional tracts, much more common in a later period, describing the public conversion of a Jew, were unlikely to give more than a garbled account of Judaic practice or creed.[4] Despite a wealth of exegetical scholarship into their biblical forebears and fervid debate about the fulfillment of the chiliastic prophecy of their ingathering to the promised land, there was little opportunity in England to learn with any accuracy about contemporary Jews, and, more to the point, little real popular interest in doing so.

On the whole, in reactivating the diabolized stereotype, English writers in the first fifty years or so of the seventeenth century eschew or, rather, prove themselves unable to delineate or describe the Jews in human, physiognomic terms. To say of them, as for instance did William Prynne, that "unconverted Jews are both Unbelievers, Infidels, Darknesse, Belialists, and the very Synagogue of Satan,"[5] would have served simply to invoke and reactivate in the popular imagination the horned figures of medieval times. The Jews who are thought to have been in England during the early seventeenth century were too few to have elicited detailed comment or criticism, and it is doubtful that their presence would have been sufficient to affect or influence popular attitudes. Only those Englishmen able to travel abroad, for example to Amsterdam or Venice, where there were established and sizable communities, were likely to be able to record at first hand authentic Jews that they had seen, and their accounts are for the most part sparing of palpable forays at diabolization.[6]

One of the most important of early seventeenth-century descriptions, that of Thomas Coryat, who traveled mostly on foot across Europe during the year 1608, is valuable for the contrast it establishes between anticipation and actuality in its description of the Jews. "I obserued," says Coryat, on his visit to Venice,

> some fewe of those Iewes, especially some of the Leuantines to bee such goodly and proper men, that then I said to my selfe our English prouerbe: To looke like a Iewe (whereby is meant sometimes a weather beaten warp-faced fellow, sometimes a phreneticke and lunaticke person, sometimes one discontented) is not true. For indeed I noted some of them to be most elegant and sweet featured persons, which gaue me occasion the more to lament their religion.[7]

Far from reinforcing particular physiognomic associations, the proverb reveals itself as utterly inapplicable in the presence of the unexpectedly agreeable Venetian Jews described by Coryat.

The absence of Jews from England is also implicit within a fictional character book, *The Wandering-Jew, Telling Fortunes to English-men* (1640), in which the fortune-teller, "an antient Gentleman, in an odde Jewish habit," transpires to be an Englishman, one Egremont, who has disguised himself as a Venetian Jew. In the narrative, we learn that Egremont, who had "been a Traveller many yeares, and felt the heate of the Sunne in change of Countries," became acquainted when at Venice with a certain Jew, "whom meeting upon the Rialta, diverse Venetians noting his face and mine, said we were so like, we might very easily be taken for brothers." After some enticement, Egremont agrees to pass himself off as the Jew's brother by donning "a rich Jewish habit."[8] On his return to London, where his reputation soon spreads, an assortment of characters, including a drunkard, an extortioner, a roaring boy, and a "fond fantastick" lover, seek him out to have their fortunes told, all bar one of them failing to recognize him as a fellow Englishman. In addition to his dress—"a Jewish gowne girt to him, and a Jewish round cap on his head" (12–13)—the other principal endeavor within the tract to make him appear before the world as a descendant of Abraham is the assumption for Egremont of the supposedly Hebraic appellation, Gad Ben-arod, Ben Balaam, Ben Ahimoth, Ben-Baal, Ben-Gog, Ben-Magog. The more common association of several of these names with the Antichrist suggests that the unknown author of the pamphlet has not wholly released his otherwise innocuous Jew-figure from his diabolized background. Indeed, fortune-telling had long been considered a peculiar forte of the Jews, often connected with their putative involvement in the black arts of sorcery and witchcraft.[9] If the pamphlet is remarkable, it is in the assumption that an English traveler could so easily take on the role of a Jew, although this is obviously a convenient fiction by which to introduce his wonderful prophecies.

It is interesting, too, as Alfred Rubens points out, that the woodcut showing Egremont telling fortunes is the earliest English graphic depiction of a Wandering Jew, although documentary representation of the theme can be traced back to Roger of Wendover in the thirteenth century.[10] The long cloak or outer garment of the fortune-teller is the typical apparel worn in seventeenth-century Europe solely by Jews, and it is made even more distinctive by the badge (commonly in the form of a yellow circle) that they were obliged to wear from the thirteenth century as a mark of their separation in many European city states.[11] In contemporary Venice, the Jews were forced to don red hats or bonnets to distin-

The Wandering-Jew Telling Fortunes to English-men. Woodcut title page, 1640. (Courtesy of the British Library.)

guish them from the rest of the populace, and (as many English travelers discovered) similar regulations pertained in almost every European country with the exception of the Netherlands.[12] The inclusion by the anonymous xylographer of all these details in the print provides some confirmation that the traditional dress of continental European Jewry, the "Jewish gaberdine" to which Shakespeare alludes in *The Merchant of Venice* (I.iii.107), will not have been totally unheard-of to English artists and writers.[13] Despite the apparent innocuousness of the presentation and the epithets "honest" and "noble"[14] to describe the Jew, there are sufficient indicators both in the woodcut and in the pamphlet to reinforce our sense of his exo-cultural Otherness. The reference in *The Wandering-Jew* by one of Egremont's clients that "store of Jewes we have in England; a few in Court, many i'th Citty, more in the Countrey" (17) remains unexplained and (surely) historically incorrect. It anticipates in a curious way later debates concerning the populousness of the Jews.

Following their readmission, the advent and the development of the Jewish community from the middle years of the seventeenth century to 1830 may be spelled out demographically. It has been estimated that at the time of the resettlement there were perhaps twenty-seven Jewish families already living in England, most of whom had been secret observers until Cromwell's toleration.[15] Although such figures, in the absence of formal statistics, remain far from definitive, it is believed that by 1677 the Jewish population of London already numbered at least 500 souls.[16] More than half a century later, D'Blossiers Tovey reckoned the number of Jews in England at 6,000, at a time when the total population of the country was some 7 to 8 million.[17] An unidentified writer in 1753 acknowledges that he veers toward overestimation when he computes "that the number of JEWS in England doth not amount to ten thousand."[18] Other figures for the same period variously guessed the Jewish population of the country at between 7,000 and 8,000.[19] By the 1790s, Patrick Colquhoun could consider "that there are about twenty thousand Jews in the city of London, besides, perhaps about five or six thousand more in the great provincial and sea-port towns."[20] However, this figure has been challenged as veering toward the high side and that actually the total number of Jews in England only reached 25,000 by or after 1830.[21] In the 1831 census, the population of England and Wales fell just short of 14 million. By any calculation, even taking the most generous figures, the Jewish population of England between 1656 and 1830 remained throughout the period no more than a tiny fraction of the whole.

Yet, in popular belief, following their readmission and particularly at a time of rampant agitation as that which greeted the Naturalization Bill of 1753, it was fairly regularly proposed that the Jews existed in such large numbers as to be on the point of overwhelming both Church and State. The proposition is all the more bizarre if it is remembered that even in the late eighteenth century, apart from the occasional itinerant pedlar, the majority of Britons had rarely, if ever, encountered a flesh-and-blood Jew. As early as 1661, shortly after their readmission, the controversialist Thomas Violet denigrates the toleration given by Cromwell, that had caused

> a great number of Iewes to come and live here in *London*, and to this day they do keep publick Worship in the City of *London*, to the great dishonour of Christianity, and publick scandal of the true Protestant Religion, and to the great damage of the Kingdome, especially our Merchants, whose Trade they engross, and eat the childrens bread.[22]

For Violet, writing within a year of the Restoration of the monarchy, responsibility for their readmission must be blamed on the confused times of Cromwell's interregnum, and his petition to Charles II is intended to persuade the new king to repeat the work of his royal ancestor, Edward I, and once again expel the Jews. In fact, Violet refines upon the notion of expulsion by suggesting that those Jews who had settled in England should be sold to their brethren abroad, who "over all the World will ransom these Iewes Bodies at a great rate, and they have mighty Estates at this day among us" (7). Some of the supposed ill-gotten gains of the Jews, he suggests, may at least be retrieved in this way.

Fortunately for the Jews, Violet's appeal fell on deaf ears. But his petition sets a note that is echoed in a variety of similar strains by later writers. Even if it was grudgingly accepted that the Jewish population of England remained relatively small, pamphleteers could remonstrate that those dispersed in different parts abroad, once given permission to settle, were "more than sufficient to occupy all the Lands, Houses, &c. in this Kingdom."[23] The naturalization of the Jews, according to a writer in 1753, will bring a hundred thousand of them teeming into the country, many of them acquiring estates and displacing the native population.[24] The threat to the very props of the English political hierarchy is compounded for John Tutchin in the early eighteenth century, who asks his readers to recollect that at the time of Edward I when "the *Jews* were so very Numerous, and Insolent withall . . . they not only Stole Christian Children and Crucify'd them in Mockery of our Saviour, but they became a *Pestilent Grievance* to the *Commonwealth*, and seem'd Powerful enough to Subvert a *Government*." In spite of his acknowledgment that "we have not the same occasion (at least visibly) to punish the *Jews*, as had our Ancestors," there are strong indicators in Tutchin's argument to encourage the supposition that were the Jews allowed to become once more so populous, it would be difficult to prevent them from returning to their vicious practices.[25]

The effect upon the Church of a large-scale influx of Jews, asserts the author of a satirical pamphlet of 1748, will be that fifty new Christian places of worship now proposed by act of Parliament will be immediately converted into so many synagogues, and "a greater Number of Jews will flock hither than those Churches of Synagogues will be able to contain."[26] Another pamphleteer writing in 1753 cynically calculates that following the proposed naturalization, because the synagogues shall be so "numerous in our Land ... instead of *Great-Britain*, our famous renowned Island may acquire the Name of *Little-Jewry*."[27] The consequence of naturalizing the Jews, he surmises, will be "our own Destruction, as a People," for God will "cast us out of this good Land which He hath given us; as He Hath, so long since, cast Them out of Theirs" (29). Far from any desire to integrate or assimilate the Jews into the fabric of English society, these writers all perceive such prospective immigrants as agents who, in pursuance of their own selfish ends, will undermine and ultimately destroy the institutions of Church and State. Throughout this period, such writers help to sustain a popular myth that the Jews both in England and on the Continent were far more abundant than could ever have been the case, and as a body actively conspiring to take over and "swamp" the state. Inescapably, the Jew as Other is still perceived as a radical threat to the status quo and values of the host group. Despite the very small total of Jews actually there, the story told by an essayist on a visit to England from Scotland in 1753 is indicative of the prevalence of the myth. He recounts a conversation he had with "an old gentlewoman," who told him she "believed the *Jews* were like locusts to cover the whole face of the land; and that they would eat up all the fruits of the earth, and establish Judaism in place of our religion."[28]

If the supposed number of Jews in England always grossly exceeded the actual number, it is perhaps hardly surprising that there are comparatively few accurate first-hand descriptions of English Jews until well into the eighteenth century. The image of the Jew in popular literature does not appear to have undergone any significant transformation for at least the first half century following readmission, although the stage Jew, an immediately recognizable figure in Elizabethan and Jacobean drama, all but disappeared from the Restoration theater.[29] In physiognomic terms, representation of the Jews in these early years hardly seems to have progressed beyond the horned figure of the Middle Ages. In character with the diabolized stereotype derived from that era, even later in the eighteenth century the Jews could still oftentimes be fouled with the accusation that they were bloodthirsty crucifiers and blasphemers of the cross. At a time of widespread agitation against them, as in 1753 when the naturalization of the Jews became a national issue, there was hardly an aspect of the medieval stereotype that was not reactivated in some extreme form. Jews were accused of being less than human, akin to dogs, "Children of the Devil," "Infidels and *Antichrists*," "the nastiest People by Nature under Heaven," "Vagrants, Infidels, Blasphemers, and Crucifiers," "the Scum and Outcast of the Earth," and so on.[30]

Throughout the period, in addition to the common use of the epithet "Jew" as the noun to describe a person of the Hebrew religion or race, a descendant of Abraham, the label retained a secondary meaning, probably deriving from medieval times, as a term of opprobrium or reprobation.[31] That the nasty use of the appellation was already deep-rooted in the English language and in popular culture by the time of the readmission in 1656 is evident from its employment by William Hughes, who remarks:

> The very name of a Jew [serves] . . . as a perfect measure, either to notifie the height of impiety in the agent, or to sound the depth and bottom of an abject worthless and forlorn condition in any patient. . . . Lower we cannot prize any one of the most abject condition, then [sic] by comparing him to a *Jew*. For so in common speech men use to exaggerate enormous wrongs. *This had been enough for a Jew to suffer*, or, *I would not have done so to a Jew.*[32]

In the eighteenth century, the opprobrious usage of the epithet is sustained, among others, by Jonas Hanway who observes that "as the word *Christian* is frequently made use of among the *vulgar*, to express the *idea* of *man*; so when a *Jew* is spoken of, among those who are not conversant with people of this faith, they *hardly* associate the *idea* of *man*."[33] When Henry Simons, a Polish Jew and the victim of a vicious assault and robbery in 1751, appeared in court, he was constantly referred to not by his own name but impersonally as "the Jew." In one of a series of trials implicating Simons, a constable involved in the case is reported to have had it on hearsay that "these wicked Jews carry about with them snickersnee knives and very mischievous weapons," suggesting the homicidal connotations associated with the name of "Jew."[34] Even fifty years later, at the start of the nineteenth century, a Jewish writer could complain to his correspondent that "the word Jew is still deemed as an opprobrious epithet, and is almost sufficient to damn any cause in a Civil or Criminal

Court; it is a term invidiously made to imply usury or knavery, and is often too successfully employed in that sense."[35] "*Jew*," echoes the journalist and politician William Cobbett, writing in the early 1830s, "has always been synonymous with *sharper, cheat, rogue*. This has been the case with no *other race* of mankind."[36]

In proverbial usage, too, embedded prejudice against the Jews is no less apparent. "Better we cannot express the most cut-throat dealing," claims Bishop Simon Patrick in 1700, "than this, you use me like a Jew."[37] Similarly, the usurious role in which the Jews are so often depicted is behind the phrase "to play the Jew." In *The Wandering-Jew, Telling Fortunes to English-men*, a voluntary bankrupt who comes to Egremont to have his fortune told confesses: "I have playd the Jew with my Christian-brother-Citizens; have got into my hands the goods of many, to enrich one" (58). The combined phrase, "Jews, Turks, Infidels and Heretics," first found in 1548 in *The Book of Common Prayer*, recurs as a general term of abuse in various forms throughout the eighteenth century.[38] The novelist Maria Edgeworth resurrects a familiar preconception when she alludes to "the old proverb of '*as rich as a Jew.*'"[39] Even a defender of the Jews, writing in 1753, opens his case far from auspiciously by evoking a traditional association: "If I may be allowed to use a very homely, yet sensible Proverb . . . as the *Devil is not so black nor so ugly as he is painted*, so the *Jews*, who have been drawn in such odious Colours, we may charitably suppose, have something to say in their Justification."[40] Whatever the Jews may have had to say could do little to eradicate such deep-rooted sociolinguistic patterns of prejudice from everyday usage.

The strength of popular prejudice in keeping alive the diabolized stereotype is perhaps best illustrated by the experience of the Deist John Toland, one of a few moderate defenders of the Jews in the early decades of the eighteenth century. He recounts:

> I know a person, no fool in other instances, who labor'd to perswade me, contrary to the evidence of his own and my eyes (to mine I am sure) that every *Jew* in the world had one eye remarkably less than the other, which silly notion he took from the Mob. Others will gravely tell you, that they may be distinguish'd by a peculiar sort of smell, that they have a mark of blood upon one shoulder, and that they cannot spit to any distance, with a world of such extravagant fancies, exciting at once laughter, scorn, and pity.[41]

It is one of the more intriguing minor paradoxes of an age that regularly vaunted its supposed rationality, its empiricism and common sense, that for so long it also gave succor and credence to so many inveterate superstitions concerning the Jews. Arguably, the most serious challenge to the persistence of the old diabolized stereotype and the absurd beliefs associated with it is the fact that actual Jews were once again settling in England. Their presence did not necessarily act as a counter to traditional stereotyping—if anything, it initially acted as a catalyst to such responses—but it also encouraged others to confront these strange new neighbors and to describe them at first hand.

The majority of the earliest Jewish settlers in England after the readmission belonged to the Sephardic community that had been driven out of Spain and Portugal two centuries before to find refuge mainly in the Low Countries. Consequently, those few accounts that we have of visits to the synagogue distinguish these Sephardic Jews in physiognomic terms by the darkness of their eyes and swarthy complexion and occasionally also by their handsome appearance. Rarely is there any endeavor to diabolize, even though the descriptions are not usually flattering. "The Jews," says the Reverend Robert Kirk of Aberfoyle, who visited the Creechurch Lane synagogue (the earliest in London after the readmission) in 1690, "were all very black men, and indistinct in their reasonings as gipsies."[42] "They are all generally black," writes the schoolmaster John Greehalgh to his friend the Reverend Thomas Crompton in 1662, "so as they may be distinguished from Spaniards or native Greeks, for the Jews hair hath a deeper tincture of a more perfect raven black, they have a quick piercing eye, and look as if of strong intellectuals; several of them are comely, gallant, proper gentlemen."[43] But, more often than not, Christian visitors to the synagogue were far more concerned to describe what they saw as the outlandish rituals of the Jews than to essay physiognomic delineation. For Samuel Pepys, who attended the Creechurch Lane synagogue on October 14, 1663, the interest of the visit was in seeing "the men and boys in their Vayles," the men carrying "their Laws, that they take out of the press . . . round about the room while such a service is singing." He records dismissively in his *Diary* that "to see the disorder, laughing, sporting, and no attention, but confusion in all their service, more like Brutes then people knowing the true God, would make a man forswear ever seeing them more."[44] Another visitor in 1686 describes the "strange worship" of the Jews, "so modish and foppish; and the people not much serious in it as it is."[45]

These early accounts of encounters with Jews at worship, none published until a much later date, set the tone of the new era following the readmission. The reaction of English visitors to the synagogue intermixes curiosity to witness (if not always to understand) Jewish ritual and a near congenital aversion toward the race itself. Paradoxically, the presence of actual Jews both served to perpetuate and at the same time to modify the old stereotype of the Jew as devil figure. If the Jews of Restoration and Georgian England were tolerated, which for the most part they certainly were, they were by no means accepted with any great willingness and enthusiasm as fellow citizens, merchants, or tradesmen. Whatever role they were to carve out for themselves or have thrust upon them in English life, the renewed presence of the Jews was considered by most natives as a manifest intrusion. Much of the antipathy that the English felt toward the Jews from the time of the readmission had its origin in popular prejudice that had flourished in the collective imagination over many centuries and had become embodied in the traditional stereotyped figure. Even with the active presence of actual Jews in England, that figure refused to go away. In fact, because of their developing influence from the time of the readmission in the commercial life of the city, it was (as we shall see in later chapters) not at all difficult to cast the Jews in their traditional role as usurers and counterfeiters, and so to invoke afresh, by a little exaggeration, an important aspect of the stereotype.

The earliest Jewish settlers in England in the second half of the seventeenth century came from the wealthy Sephardic community on whose behalf Menasseh Ben Israel had petitioned. Almost all the known descriptions of English Jews during the seventeenth century appear to refer to the Sephardim, although by the end of the century there had followed a sizable influx of Ashkenazic Jews from Germany and Poland. It has been estimated that before 1720 the number of Ashkenazim in England had outnumbered the Sephardim, and that by 1750 they accounted for perhaps three-quarters of the Jewish population.[46] The majority of the Ashkenazic Jews who came to England were poor, eking a living by peddling or petty trading rather than the more lucrative mercantile and brokering activities with which the Sephardim were associated. Although there certainly were wealthy Ashkenazim and also impoverished Sephardim, it became quite common in the eighteenth century to distinguish the Jews in England as either "rich" (i.e., belonging to the Portuguese community) or "poor" (i.e., German-Polish). However, the fact that they had been the first to settle and that they were indeed not infrequently well-to-do gave the Sephardic community an initial preeminence in any account of the two groups. "Those of *Spain* and *Portugal*," says one writer, "value themselves highly upon their Extraction, and conceive a very contemptible Idea of their Brethren in *Germany*, *Italy*, and *Holland*, with whom they are always at Variance, as well as upon civil as religious Pretences." Ultimately though, he adds caustically, their differences blur into a shared "Love of Gain," which "has obtained such an absolute Empire in their Souls, that there is not the least Remains, the least Umbrage of Candor or Virtue in either."[47] There is "*almost as great an Animosity*" between Sephardim and Ashkenazim, according to another writer, "*as betwixt* Calvinists *and* Lutherans."[48] But this animosity does not appear to have been sufficient to prevent a skittish pamphleteer at the time of the 1753 Jew bill from suggesting that, at "the trifling Expence of an *Hundred Pounds* per Man," the rich Jews "will be at the Expence of naturalizing the poorer Sort," so that they too will be "enabled to purchase a landed Estate" as soon as their fortunes permit.[49]

Whatever distinctions may have been noted between Jews of varying historical backgrounds are made inconsequential by reference to the familiar conspiracy theory of a Jewish plot to take over the state. In any final analysis, as "Britannicus," a correspondent in the *London Evening-Post* avers, there is little to choose between the two groups: "How then have the Rich ones got all their Wealth? By State Jobbs, Lotteries, and other iniquitous Arts of Exchange-Alley. How do the Poor Jews get their Bread? . . . By peddling about and cheating the Publick with bad and counterfeit Commodities?"[50] The awareness among anti-Semitic writers of the period of the distinction between Sephardim and Ashkenazim is at best superficial, but it is a distinction that is deployed to show that the Jews, irrespective of their background, whether rich or poor, are everywhere the same in their love of gain and grasping nature.

In visual terms, the distinction between Sephardim and Ashkenazim or, at least, between "rich" and "poor" Jews, becomes immediately most conspicuous and is reflected for the first time in Georgian England in caricatures and satirical prints. From shortly after the readmission, those well-to-do Jews of the Sephardic community aspired to present themselves with all the external trappings that they associated with the English gentry. Even though at home and in their place of worship, they may have adhered to their religious practices, in public they appeared in the fashionable dress of the day, the men normally clean-shaven, the women indistinguishable in their dress from their Christian neighbors. Endelman sees this desire to conform in clothing and appearance as evidence of what he calls "the acculturation of the Anglo-Jewish Middle Class" (120–22), the desire to acquire the manners and attitudes of native Englishmen, while at the same time preserving their own religious beliefs and traditions. It should be remembered, too, that the need to conform, at least in their appearance to the outside world, was almost an inbred characteristic of the Sephardim, who from the time of their official expulsion from Spain and Portugal had survived as crypto-Jews in many countries.

On the other hand, the Ashkenazim from Poland and Germany were for the most part far more traditional in their dress and outward appearance, many of the men wearing the distinctive long cloaks of eastern European Jewry and considering shaving a severe transgression of their faith.[51] In addition, those Ashkenazim who traveled through England as itinerants, peddling wares brought over from the Continent, spoke very little English, conversing in a mixture of Yiddish, German, and broken English. In one of the accounts of the robbery of the Polish Jew Henry Simons, the victim is reported to have "call'd out, *my Gilt!* [gelt, i.e., money] *my Gilt, my Gilt! my Ducats in Pocket . . . ne, ne, not dat Pocket toder* [the other] *Pocket.*"[52] From the middle of the eighteenth century, the dialectal oddities of these Ashkenazic Jews were often the focus of linguistic ridicule and, indeed, to this day the accent remains a recognized form of mimicry in recounting jokes about the Jews. Because the Ashkenazi pedlar was a sufficiently well-known street figure in Georgian England, his image became one of the more common ways by which Jews were popularly depicted and recognized. According to the humor of Thomas Bridges, so familiar were such figures by the early 1770s that a gabbing widow he portrays in his episodic novel, *The Adventures of a Bank-Note*, is less than willing to believe that Abraham, Isaac, and Jacob were Jews, for nowhere in the Bible does it say that they "ever sold a black-lead pencil, or a roll of hard pomatum, or a pair of sleeve buttons in their lives."[53]

It is to the most celebrated English artist of his day that we are indebted for the earliest widely known graphic representation of the Jew, for the two types of Jew, "rich" and "poor," are depicted in two separate engravings by William Hogarth. In the second plate of *A Harlot's Progress* (1732), Hogarth's prostitute, the fittingly named Moll Hackabout, has become the paid courtesan of an unnamed Sephardic Jew.[54] The print shows the Jew's discovery of her unfaithfulness, the Christian lover she has taken tiptoeing out of a door to the side. The richness of her accommodation reflects the affluence of the Jew and his ambition (perceived, for instance, in his elegant apparel and the taking of tea) to adopt the mannerisms of an upper-class Englishman. However, his sharp features, thick black brows, dark eyes and complexion make him appear distinctly un-English and, as in other prints, Hogarth reserves the mute figure of an animal to furnish moral commentary on the scene. The Jew's shocked expression at Moll's infidelity is literally aped by the startled monkey, its visage contorted in the same direction as his. The monkey

William Hogarth, *A Harlot's Progress.* Engraving, 1732. Plate 2. (Courtesy of the British Museum, Department of Prints and Drawings.)

mirrors both the Jew's expression and the flight of the lover, in its scurried escape reflecting the impropriety of the situation.

The plate's significance is not simply in its graphic depiction of the bamboozling of a fashionable Jew, but in the extraordinary cultural influence that it was to have. Within a year of its publication, the moral fable of Hogarth's series had been dramatized by Theophilus Cibber as a pantomime entertainment, *The Harlot's Progress; or, the Ridotto al 'Fresco,* introducing to the theater "the first real stage Jew of the century,"[55] a significantly different figure to Shylock or Barabas. In Cibber's pantomime, he appears with the name Beau Mordecai, which was to become one of the more common appellations for a stage Jew in the eighteenth century. Further echoes of Hogarth are to be found in the anonymous ballad opera, *The Jew Decoyed; or, The Progress of a Harlot*

(1735), in Henry Fielding's farce, *Miss Lucy in Town* (1742) and, less directly, in Charles Macklin's *Love à la Mode* (1759).[56] Hogarth's plate served as a graphic prototype both in the reactivation of the Jew-figure in the popular imagination as a lascivious reprobate, willing to lay out significant sums to entice young gentile women into prostitution, and also as one who is sometimes himself the unsuspecting victim of his kept mistress's duplicity or sexual infidelity. For example, as a counterpart to Hogarth's Moll Hackabout, the almost equally aptly named Miss Forward in Eliza Hayward's bestseller, *The History of Miss Betsy Thoughtless* (1751), when abandoned by her former lover, shows no scruples in accepting "the offer made her by a rich Jew merchant of five guineas a week to be his mistress." Yet, scarcely less inured in vice than Moll before her, "Miss Forward could not content herself with the embraces nor allowances of her keeper, but received both the presents and caresses of as many as she had charms to attract."[57] Elsewhere, the echoes of Hogarth are perhaps not always as clear-cut but, as we shall discover, the already long established stereotypical motif of out-tricking or cheating on a Jew recurs in a variety of forms throughout the eighteenth century.

Twenty-five years after *A Harlot's Progress*, in the second of his four *Election* plates, *Canvassing for Votes* (1757), Hogarth depicts as a minor figure a Jewish pedlar, a box of wares strapped 'round his shoulders, vending gewgaws to a political candidate, who in turn offers them as favors to the ladies in the balcony above. Among the items the Jew is selling is a crucifix hanging from the side of the box, a sly allusion perhaps to the selling of Christ. As the sequence of plates refers to the Election of 1754, in which the Jewish Naturalization Bill of the year before was still a hot issue, the presence of the pedlar, indirectly influencing the ballot, is particularly ironic. Although Hogarth does not dress him in the full-length coat or cloak of continental Jewry, his black beard, pronounced nose, and dark complexion leave us in no doubt of his ethnic origin. According to Ronald Paulson, the inclusion of the pedlar in the plate picks up and gives visual currency to a report in common circulation at the time of the Naturalization Bill of an unsuccessful attempt by one of the tribe to defraud some unsuspecting females. The story, as reported in a contemporary newspaper, runs as follows:

Huntington, Aug. 3 [1753]. On Wednesday a Jew Hawker in this Town persuaded some young ladies to look at his Toys, &c. among which was a Diamond Ring, but the Ladies not chusing to buy any Thing, he pretended to look over his Goods, and said, he missed his Diamond Ring; the Ladies declared they knew nothing of it, but he insisted they

William Hogarth, *Election.* Engraving, 1757. Plate 2: (a) *Canvassing for Votes;* (b) detail of same. (Courtesy of the Brotherton Library, University of Leeds.)

did, and that they should pay for it; during the dispute a young Gentleman, a Relation of the Ladies, came in, and being told of the Affair, had the Jew immediately before a Magistrate, where his Box was searched, and the Ring he had charged the Ladies with found conceal'd in a private Part of the Box: The Fellow being had back to the Ladies, and having nothing to say in his Defence, the Mob seiz'd him, took him to a Horsepond, and duck'd him in a very severe Manner.[58]

Hogarth's pedlar is the first of a long line of such figures, usually cari-

catured and often engaged in similar forms of trickery, who are represented in prints from this time through to at least the mid-nineteenth
century.[59] If anything, the poor Jew, the pedlar, was to become during
this period the most common way in which Jews were to be depicted
and recognized at large. His mythical reembodiment in the figure of the
Wandering Jew will be looked at in the following chapter.

CHAPTER 4

WANDERING JEW, VAGABOND JEWS

O F ALL CHRISTIAN LEGENDS concerning the Jews, that of the Wandering Jew is perhaps the most persistent and one of the most extraordinary. The legend's endurance through many centuries of Christian folklore, even to the present day, may be seen as a popular reflection of a theological impulse in Christianity to come to terms or at least to define the relationship with its own paternity. The adaptability of the myth of the Wandering Jew over the ages is witness to an ongoing preoccupation in Christian apologetics to comprehend and to justify the often uneasy kinship between the two religions. As with other legends relating to the Jews, the story has roots that derive piecemeal from various readings of the Scriptures. Those roots may be unearthed out of the Bible even though no figure specifically identifiable as the Wandering Jew is to be found in either the Old or the New Testament.

In the Gospel according to Matthew, Jesus prophesies, "Verily I say unto you. There be some standing here, which shall not taste of death, till they see the Son of man coming in his kingdom" (16:28). Christ's import here seems to be to assure his immediate auditors that many of them will live to witness the advent of the kingdom of God. But over time the prophecy came to be read as also suggesting that one or several of these disciples was destined to remain on earth far beyond the era of the Bible, right through to the period of his return and redemption of humankind.[1]

The blow struck against Jesus by one of the officers of the Jews in the court of the high priest, as described in the Gospel according to John (18:22–23), is also seminal to the conception of the myth of the Wandering Jew. By way of expiation for this crime against the Lord, Christian legend had it that the offending Jew, sometimes depicted in later versions as Pontius Pilate's porter and sometimes as a shoemaker of Jerusalem, was impelled to a life of eternal wandering for which no amount of contrition would be sufficient. Forgiveness, such a central tenet of Christian teaching, seems to have had no effect here in reducing the punishment or assuaging the guilt of the sinner. Penitence in this case is for all time or at least until the promised second coming of Christ.

From Genesis, the story of Cain, "cursed from the earth" (4:11) for the murder of Abel, his brother, helped promote the belief that not only he, but also the people of the Old Testament, should in later ages be "a fugitive and a vagabond in the earth" (4:14). Significantly, the slain figure of Abel had been "a keeper of sheep" (4:2), offering unto God the firstling of the flock, in symbolic terms prefiguring the sacrificial role of Christ in the New Testament. Christian typologists descried no obstacle in forging parallels between Abel's treatment at the hand of Cain and the treatment of Christ by the Jews. Cain's subsequent punishment of eternal wandering could be transposed and deemed to be the fate of the Jews in general. During the Middle Ages, this accumulation of episodic biblical details had solidified into an accepted myth that was given further credence by the actual expulsion of the Jews out of many European countries, including England, from the thirteenth century on.

In the most comprehensive modern survey of the legend, George K. Anderson assembled well over 100 distinct folktales of the Wandering Jew from central and western Europe, illustrative of the remarkable prevalence of the myth between the seventeenth and the nineteenth centuries. Comparing them with their continental counterparts, Anderson complains that the British versions of the tale are mainly but "poor specimens" of an otherwise rich and varied folk tradition. What seems clear is that the recorded versions of the legend of the Wandering Jew that survive in British folklore and literature do not appear to be significantly different from (and are probably indebted to) similar tales found in France, Germany, Switzerland, and the Low Countries. By way of speculation, Anderson suggests that the "stunted growth of the Legend in Britain" may be accounted for in terms of "the temperament of the British countryman of the seventeenth and eighteenth centuries, who would of all Britons be most likely to accept the Legend" as it stands without the capacity of developing it further on his own. The lack of vitality of the legend in its various manifestations in Britain contrasts sharply, according to Anderson, with an otherwise remarkable wealth of indigenous folk traditions and legends, from which he surmises that the British have a preference for "local native legend" over a migratory one imported from abroad.[2]

If Anderson is right that the legend of the Wandering Jew hardly took root in the popular culture of seventeenth- and eighteenth-century Britain, that should not lead us to assume that the story remained little

known. A ballad entitled "The Wandering Jew Or the Shoemaker of Jerusalem," included by Bishop Thomas Percy in his *Reliques of Ancient
English Poetry* (1765),[3] can be traced back through several printed editions at least to the early seventeenth century,[4] and, in the eighteenth
century, a prose chapbook with the same title was many times reprinted.
From an undated copy of this chapbook in the Solomons Collection of
the Jewish Theological Seminary, New York, the following is extracted
to give an outline of what Anderson calls "the traditional picture of the
Wandering Jew"[5]:

> This Jew was Born at Jerusalem, and was by Trade a Shoe-Maker; when
> Our Saviour was going to the Place of Crucifixion, being Weary and
> Faint, he would have sat down to Rest at the Shoe-Maker's Stall; but
> the Shoe-Maker came to the Door, and spitting in our Lord's Face, buf-
> fetted him from the Door, saying, That was no Place of Abode for
> him.—On which Christ said, For this Thing thou shalt never Rest, but
> Wander till I come again upon the Earth: From this he is called, The
> Wandering Jew of Jerusalem.—Now, according to this saying of our
> Saviour, who was Crucified, this Man had no Power to retu[r]n Home,
> but went about wandering from Place to Place ever since even unto
> this Day.
> After travelling through Asia and A[f]rica, he roamed to America,
> and is now upon his Journey to visit every Town in Europe. . . .
> If he hears any one Curse or Swear, or take the Name of God in vain,
> he tells them they crucify their God again.—If any one offers him
> Money, though it were the richest Lord or Lady in all the Land, he will
> take no more than one Groat, and that, he says he takes for Christ's
> Sake, and gives it to the next poor Person he meets.—He is always
> Crying and Praying, and wishing to see Death; but that Ease from his
> labouring Pilgrimage, he says can never happen until Christ comes
> again upon the Earth. . . .
> And he prophesies, that before the End of the World the Jews shall
> be gathered together from all Parts of the World, and return to Jeru-
> salem, and live there, and it shall flourish as much as ever, and that
> they, and all others, shall become Christians, and that Wars shall cease,
> and the whole World live in Unity one with another.[6]

In the context of our study of stereotypes, the traditional figure of the
Wandering Jew as outlined here presents a useful paradigm, for the myth
both asserts the values and beliefs of the Christian host group and at the
same time preserves and perpetuates the alien or exo-cultural Otherness
of the Jew. By constantly acknowledging the magnitude of his crime, the
Jew affirms fundamental Christian verities, while also connoting the unhappy fate of those who fail or refuse to recognize what he now views

as the true faith. In his desire to embrace Christianity and in his prophecy that all others will finally be converted, he manifests a zeal to proselytize that is an essential canon of Christian rather than Jewish teaching. Equally, his fear of blaspheming the name of the Lord and his refusal to accept money except to relieve the indigence of others suggest qualities that were popularly thought to be distinctly Christian and as distinctly un-Jewish. Yet in his purgatorial state of wandering his inescapable Otherness as a Jew is perpetually reaffirmed. The legend underlines the sense of difference between host group and Other, while simultaneously defending the vested beliefs of the host group. The Wandering Jew as Other, it is now generally recognized, is primarily a projection of Christian beliefs and values.[7]

Despite acknowledging the striking plasticity of the tale and the frequency with which "other legends . . . mix with it until it becomes distorted almost beyond recognition," Anderson seems to assume that, behind all the transformations and transpositions that he so diligently records, the "true" legend of the Wandering Jew somehow subsists in an uncontaminated state. He cites examples of the tale that sustain but "frail bonds with the *true* Legend" and "instances in which the Legend in its *pure* form collides with a local legend in such a way as to produce considerable deviation from the norm." Evidently, as a compiler of the legend in its innumerable manifestations, Anderson felt it necessary to adhere to what he calls the *"true* core of the Legend" as distinct from that which he considered to be later encrustations that are "merely peripheral" to it.[8] If only by implication, Anderson gives to the "true" legend a rigidity that he may not have fully intended.

At worst, the difference in emphasis of my argument may amount to little more than semantic quibbling that emerges from the uneasy burden that I believe Anderson places upon the word "true." But my simultaneous intention is to question some of the consequences of his frequent insistence on reverting to the supposed "true core" of the legend. For I shall maintain that the enduring strength of the legend, its ability to propagate itself through time in so many motley forms, makes its periphery no less valuable than its core as an exponential source of study. Anderson records and shows interest in the many configurations of the legend but the strategic emphasis of his inquiry is throughout more centripetal than centrifugal. Such an approach, however valuable as a practical yardstick for documenting the central core of the legend, does not necessarily fully succeed in communicating its ongoing locomotion as discourse, its disposition to transmute and recast itself at its periphery. In particular, Anderson's account of its supposed "stunted growth" in England pays little or no attention to those very margins of the legend at which, as we shall see, it can be argued that it is actually at its most vital.

Essentially, the story of the Wandering Jew should be considered as a legend that thrives on its ability to adapt in different circumstances to the exigencies of those who employ it. Edgar Rosenberg is surely exactly right when he contends that the legend may be most profitably approached as a reliable and "readable" barometer "to the kind of civilization, ideology, and literary convention in which it flourishes." The Wandering Jew, he maintains, "can mean all things to all men and all ages," for each generation recreates the figure in its own image. If we endeavor to follow it through all its changes "there is always the chance that at the end of the line the Wandering Jew no longer bears the remotest resemblance to the ancestral portrait." In the end, its fissile nature makes it particularly difficult to legitimate the core of the legend.[9] Its character may best be understood in terms of its chameleon-like ability to take on a form that reflects a given age.

For the English of the eighteenth century, the character of *their* depiction of the Wandering Jew owed as much to the novelty of the readmission of actual Jews into the country as to the ancient roots of the legend itself. Although, as we have seen, the first settlers were mainly fairly affluent Sephardi merchants and stock-jobbers, before long these were overtaken in number by a continuing influx of Ashkenazic Jews from Poland and Germany whose poverty often forced them into a livelihood of peddling and huckstering.[10] Because the occupation of these poorer Jews, the hawking of portable items and gewgaws or the door-to-door trade in old clothes, was necessarily itinerant, it was not long before popular association linked them with the legendary figure of the Wandering Jew. "There is," says the author of a pamphlet warning of the desire of the Jews to settle at the time of the Naturalization Bill,

> a certain Person commonly and emphatically stiled *the wandering Jew*, who, though already upwards of 1700 Years old, is however sure of living several hundred Years longer. . . . Now if this strange old Vagrant should chance to be tired of his present pedling way of Life . . . what alas! may be apprehended from a Man in his extraordinary Circumstances?[11]

A satirical print, *Moses Gorden or the Wandering Jew*, published in Birmingham some years later in 1788, integrates pedlar and Wandering Jew by depicting the lank-haired and bearded figure of Lord George Gordon, a famous convert to Judaism, dressed in traditional Ashkenazi fashion

Moses Gorden or the Wandering Jew. Engraving. Birmingham, 1788.
(Courtesy of Mr. Alfred Rubens, London.)

as a street-dealer with a bag of old clothes under his arm and some rabbit-skins in the other hand.[12] By the middle years of the eighteenth century, the sight of such ragamuffin pedlars plying their wares up and down the country was so common that it had become in anti-Semitic discourse a primary means by which to identify and describe the Jews in general. There are, hyperbolizes one writer, "a thousand Beggars to one wealthy Jew."[13] The Jews, writes another, are but "a Nation of Huckstering Pedlers and voracious Usurers." They "have been, and are to be Vagabonds in all the World, and an Abominating to all People, being never hitherto incorporated in Privileges with any."[14] "The JEWS," declares an anonymous late eighteenth-century pamphleteer, "are held in utter and universal abomination, and are scattered up and down the earth like wandering vagabonds, for having disbelieved his [Christ's] Holy Word, for having crucified him, and denied his being the TRUE son of the LIVING GOD."[15] Like the Wandering Jew of legend, they are to be seen as perpetual aliens whose raison d'être may only be signalized through their difference from the host group and their apparent incapacity to assimilate.

Broadly speaking, the fate of the Wandering Jew images the fate of the Jews in general, but the image is a refracted one in which many of their supposed imperfections have been mollified or translated into positive qualities. The impulsion of the Wandering Jew is in his desire to seek pardon for his crime against Christ. In this perpetual search, he attests to all he meets the verity of the Crucifixion and, in so doing, helps to authenticate for the skeptical among them the historical truth of Christ's sacrifice. On the other hand, the fate of the real Jews, as reflected in popular discourse in eighteenth-century England, ratifies their dispersion as the consequence of their crime against Christ, which has made them eternal outcasts throughout the world. Typically, they are to be regarded as "vagabond Jews" (Acts 19:13), who, in their scattered state and in their obdurate refusal or inability to understand the gravity of their wrongdoing, are visible confirmation of God's resolve that their punishment must continue.[16] Witness the messianist Henry Francis Offley, writing in 1795, who tells us that

> the Son of God, who came into the world to purchase salvation to sinners [was] at length ignominiously crucified by the hands of unbelieving Jews. But mark the result! The Almighty hurled down vengeance instantaneously on their heads, death and ruin to themselves and destruction to their country; hated by God, and despised by man, they were driven from society, and became vagabonds on the face of the earth.[17]

In common with many other writers, Offley shows a blissful lack of compassion and want of awareness of the un-Christian nature of the sentiments he expresses. His argument presupposes the willing acceptance of divine odium as fair game if directed against the Jews and of an attendant aping of God's wrath by true believers. Such an account of the history of the Jews accentuates the idea that God deliberately wishes to brutalize them for failing to believe. The eternal lot of the Jews as wanderers is manifest again, according to Offley, in their present condition as pedlars and dealers in old clothes:

> Certainly the Jews almost ever since the destruction of their kingdom by Titus Vespasian, have been without a fix'd abode, and have been scattered all over the earth, neglecting the Lord their God—and I believe there is not a kingdom in the known world but there are Jews to be found in it; *"yet among those Nations shall they find no ease"* and truly may it be said that their *"feet find no rest,"* for every where these unfortunate people are derided, insulted and abused. Even to England, if we confine ourselves alone, a Country professing the greatest humanity to stranger and foreigners—we see them wandering about the streets, particularly in the metropolis of London, in the most menial occupation, that of carrying a bag at their back, and crying old cloaths from door to door, the objects of universal ridicule and contempt . . . —nay, so much are they held in derision in this Christian Country, that even children despise them and *laugh them to scorn.* (8–9)

The Jews described here share with the traditional figure of the Wandering Jew the inability to settle as a punishment for their treatment of Christ. Their outlandish garb and lowly status are to be seen as markers of their perpetual alienation, the fulfillment of biblical prophecy that in the countries to which they have been dispersed they may find no rest or ease (see Deut. 28:65). By some, it was further believed that the abhorrence with which they were held obliged the Jews to "disperse themselves throughout all *Europe,* and traffic in the Manner they do." For if they attempted to settle "in a much larger Number in any one Country, and attempted to set up any Manufacture, or to exercise any Trade, practised by the Natives of the Country, they would rise, as one Man, against them."[18] Consciousness of Christian antipathy toward them is to be seen as a self-perpetuating motive for the peculiar disposition of the Jews.

In fact, anti-Semitic discourse frequently reiterates a common belief that the punishment supposedly meted out by God against the Jews made it requisite that Christians continue to treat them with befitting contempt. At the very least, due caution should be exercised by the Christian community in all dealings with those whom God has "sentenc'd and decreed . . . to be *Captives* among all Nations, and *Vagabonds* like *Cain.*"[19] "As Nature will not allow Sheep to associate with Wolves," insists the author of a frequently reissued tract, "no more will the Law of the Gospel allow Christians to associate or intermix with Jews; Christians are promised the State of Grace, and the Jews, without their Conversion and Repentance, totally excluded."[20] If anything, avers John Tutchin, after "1700 Years . . . in a *Fugitive* and *Vagabond State* . . . the Subjects of *Divine Wrath,*" the Jews have become increasingly "hardned in *Impenitence.*" However duty-bound Christians may be "to pity their *Ignorance* and *Obstinacy,* and to Pray for their Conversion," they should also beware "not to Encourage their *Impieties,* so as to obstruct the Currency of the *Christian Religion.*"[21] Such utterances reinforce the notion that the separation of the Jews is ordained from above as a manifestation of heavenly displeasure and as a perpetual reminder of the truth of the Christian faith. It is for "murdering and blaspheming Christ," urges William Romaine, that "God drave them out of the Holy Land, and made them Vagrants all over the Earth."[22]

A more subtle, though less prevalent, articulation of the reasons for the nomadic state of the Jews and their inability to settle hinges upon the assumption that their ingathering from exile would naturally precede the coming of the Messiah. To obviate widespread fears whipped up at the time of the Naturalization Bill that the Jews planned to settle en masse in England, Edward Weston avers that the Jews live in enduring anticipation of an apocalyptic summons from the Holy Land. Their uprooted state throughout the world may be explained by their desire to be ready at an instant to return to their own country to welcome the Messiah. Even their avocation as itinerant tradesmen and stock-jobbers may be understood in these terms:

> The constant Practice of that Nation has been to convert every thing into portable Wealth. Cash, Stocks, Remittances, Jewels, &c. are what, I believe, they have been chiefly known to deal in; and the Reason of it is very evident, that as they live in a constant Expectation of the Completion of the Prophecies, and of a sudden Summons from the Messiah to return and take Possession of the holy Land.[23]

More commonly, the dispersion of the Jews is used as evidence of divine censure, by which there is little or no hope that such a return will be allowed to come about. So in writing to the Jews Joseph Priestley takes their present abject state as testimony of their rejection. "Many christians," he says, "who have the same respect for the books of the Old Testament with yourselves, judging from present appearances, consider

you as abandoned of God, and do not believe that you *will ever* be restored to your country again." Rather, the Jews should recognize their
dispersion as an explicit challenge to the very validity of their faith, an
opportunity for them to question the causes of their present tormented
state. Only in the unlikely event of their messianic return to the Holy
Land would they succeed in convincing others of the veracity of their
creed:

> It will be your *restoration* to your own country, and not your present
> *banishment* from it, that will be the means of convincing all the world
> of the truth of your prophecies, and consequently of the truth of your
> religion, and of confirming them in the faith and pure worship of the
> God of your fathers to the end of time.[24]

For most, the state of the Jews driven from their own land and dispersed
is confirmation of their abandonment since the advent of the Christian
era. "The *Cities* of the Land of *Israel*," one writer tells us, "do still *lie
waste* and *uninhabited*; neither are the *People* yet *planted in their Land*,
nor are, in any Respect, likely so to be at present. They being, on the
contrary, *desolate Vagabonds* all over the Earth to this Day."[25] The "Almighty Creator and Preserver of all Things," declares another, "utterly
extirpated and ejected the *Jews* from *their own promised Land*, . . . and
scattered and dispersed them into other Nations like Chaff before the
Wind, where they should be *totally* deprived of all divine Ordinances,
and be despised and contemned by all People."[26]

If writers and controversialists saw little likelihood of the prophetic
mass return of the Jews to the Holy Land, it was but a simple volte-face
to argue that England could become the new focal place of their ingathering. Indeed, during the seventeenth century, philo-Semites had based
many of their arguments in favor of the readmission of the Jews on the
supposition that their presence in England and eventual conversion to
the true faith would inexorably lead to the Millennium. The involvement of the English, it was assumed, would enhance the redemption not
only of the Jews but of the whole nation.[27] In his life of Menasseh Ben
Israel published early in the eighteenth century, Thomas Pocock captures the essence of these beliefs in writing about the Jews:

> After all these Iliads of Afflictions, they remain at this Day scatter'd
> over the Face of the whole Earth; and because they continue peaceable,
> by the Connivance of our Laws they are not disturb'd. And good rea-
> son; for if (as most learned Men agree) they will all be converted to the
> Christian Religion, no place can be more proper to promote this Con-
> version, than a Christian Country.[28]

Under the guise of amity, such arguments became the standard by which proselytizing Christians were able to justify their support for the presence of the Jews in England. Gathering the Jews together and easing their sufferings were, it was thought, but the first steps toward their redemption.

However, in the expulsionist rhetoric of anti-Semitic discourse, such notions are once again turned on their head. To bring together a people that ostensibly God has scattered is not a fulfillment but a dangerous repudiation of his commandments. "And shall any Christian Kingdom or State," shrills a professed opponent, "presume to collect whom God has dispersed?"[29] At the time of the Jew Bill of 1753, a frequently repeated charge was that, wishing to reunite, the Jews had chosen England as the site of their ingathering. The bill, it was argued, by granting them the same rights as indigenously born subjects, merely encouraged the Jews in their belief that Providence had appointed England as an asylum from their wanderings. In particular, it was felt, those Jews most likely to migrate to England were not the rich Sephardi merchants whose trade connections might be of benefit to the nation but destitute Ashkenazi pedlars who would become an immediate burden upon the state. "It is not at all impossible," writes a contemporary pamphleteer, "that numbers of them may flock over; not because they are *wealthy*, but because they have *no property*; yet hope to find the *promised land*, with an opportunity of acquiring riches, without labour."[30] Just as philo-Semitic and chiliastic writers had invoked the name of God to bolster their case for the readmission and the naturalization of his chosen people, so these propagandists employ a similar strategy to keep them out and perpetuate their dispersal. If they are allowed to "become native free-born *Englishmen*," claims one such author, "they then cease to be Vagrants, and find such a Rest, as will frustrate, so far as Man is able, the Truth of God's infallible Prophecies."[31] "I say, upon no other Terms" but their prior conversion to Christianity, argues another, "can they be permitted to have Rest or Peace, which GOD has appointed otherwise, without sinning against Heaven; for the Almighty Will must be a Law to all Men."[32] The bipolarity inherent in the process of stereotyping is no less evident even in the contracting of the divine fiat for altogether contrary motives in defining the relationship between Christian and Jew.

Despite the radically different ways by which the "vagabond" state of the Jews was interpreted, it was generally agreed by nearly all Christian writers that their present miserable condition should be understood as an indubitable sign of divine displeasure toward them. Given such an attitude, it might be asked why, instead of eradicating them, God had allowed the Jews a kind of purgatorial reprieve on earth. By way of answer, almost all these writers concur in suggesting that the scattered survival of the Jews should be interpreted as a Christian miracle, a fulfillment for later ages of biblical prophecy. The *"dispersion of the Jews,"* it is warranted, "is a standing monument of the truth of the *christian* faith."[33] Their existence to the present day is affirmation of the revealed word of God and of his desire that a remnant of the biblical Jews should be allowed to endure as testimony to the world of the mysterious truth of gospel prophecy (see Matt. 16:28). "They are," maintains the antiquary Jacob Bryant, "a lasting monument of prophetic veracity; and wherever their fortune has driven them, they have been *an astonishment, a proverb, and a by-word among nations."*[34] Even the anonymous author of *An Historical and Law-Treatise against Jews and Judaism* (1732), a virulently anti-Semitic tract advocating the enforced separation of Jew from Christian, has to confess before gloatingly cataloguing the long history of their persecution that "it is wonderful to see a Jew living upon the Face of the Earth, considering how they have been banish'd, frequently slaughter'd, massacred, hang'd and burnt all the World over."[35]

The survival of the Jews as unsettled wanderers across the earth is witness of God's determination to apprise those of the true faith of his larger design. Even the commonality of England may find corroboration of this in their encounters with itinerant Jewish pedlars. The point is well made by Lewis Stephens, the archdeacon of Chester, in a sermon delivered to an Exeter parish in 1735 for the benefit of a recently converted Jew:

> But God himself has not intended the utter Excision of the *Jews;* for altho' they are *dispersed,* yet by a singular Circumstance of Punishment, as *miraculous* as their Dispersion, they remain *unincorporated* with any Nations of the Earth, with whom they dwell: This is a visible Argument of the Truth of the Prophecies of the Gospel: This is a standing Miracle, which subsists even at this Day in all Nations and all Cities, and is seen and perceived by every Christian. And let no Nation ever seek to root them out or destroy them.[36]

What better argument in favor of the veracity of the Christian faith than to witness in everyday life the impoverished and piteous remnant of the Jews, the scattered descendants of those who in biblical times had been God's chosen people? To convert such people can be seen as an act of piety, an opportunity to save a few poor souls among them from the futility of their everlasting wandering. Beyond that, one may only contemplate their debased condition. Whether considering them as objects of pity or as seasoned enemies, eighteenth-century English commentators on the Jews largely concur in viewing their survival as having a validity that can be measured only by reference to the Christian cosmos. The lowly place accorded by God to "vagabond Jews" in the postbiblical world clearly demonstrates that his providence has passed them over. The closed-minded treatment of these Jews in English popular culture mirrors the assumption that they are to be deemed a fallen people. Only too well, their predicament is writ small in the figure of the pedlar. How he was received and depicted must now occupy our attention.

In his print, Too Many for a Jew (1785), Thomas Rowlandson depicts a vivid moment in the rural course of an itinerant Jewish pedlar.[37] On the village green, beneath a sturdy English oak tree, we see just such a figure, his customary box of wares strapped over his shoulder, held open and supported between his arms, displaying a variety of linens, smalls, and knicknacks. The writer and poet Robert Southey lists among the typical contents of just such a Jew's box, "haberdashery . . . , cuckoo clocks, sealing wax, quills, weather glasses, green spectacles, clumsy figures in plaister of Paris . . . , or miserable prints of the king and queen." "You meet," adds Southey, these "Jew pedlars every where" and they will do "any thing for money."[38] Rowlandson's Jew pedlar is evidently a habitual figure in the neighborhood since his arrival is greeted by the importunate attention of a group of local children, with whom he appears to be on familiar terms. Although not shabby, his apparel is plain and utilitarian, fit for one whose livelihood is ambulatory. He wears a good strong coat and thick breeches to cover him against the elements. From his right hand hangs a small change bag, in traditional iconography an emblem of the monetary design of the Jews. On his head, he wears an unfashionable type of wide-brimmed slouch hat. His long hair and particularly his beard are specific features that distinguish him as a Jew. As we look, we see that the pedlar appears to be staring skyward. His gaze is riveted not in heavenly contemplation but on two small objects in the air, which we perceive to be a couple of coins that have been thrown up by the fair-haired youth standing in front of him. At the very moment that he is being distracted, a small boy, quick as a flash, reaches under the Jew's arm and filches from his box. By humorously illustrating in Too Many for a Jew how a group of children consort to out-trick him, Rowlandson imputes that trickery should also be seen as a characteristic of the behavior of Jewish pedlars and, by extension perhaps, endemic to all Jews.

In many ways, the reputation of Jewish pedlars for trickery and petty

Thomas Rowlandson, *Too Many for a Jew.* Engraving, 1785. (Courtesy of Mr. Alfred Rubens, London.)

cheating was far from ill-founded. Particularly in the cities, where the main traffic of these street pedlars was in the buying and selling of old clothes, there was ample reason to distrust them, since it was well known that their trade often extended to stolen goods and counterfeit money. The dealing in old clothes, according to police magistrate Patrick Colquhoun, writing in the last decade of the eighteenth century, barely concealed a much wider network of misdemeanor in which these street hawkers were involved:

Their chief business really is to prowl about the houses and stables of
men of rank and fortune, for the purpose of holding out temptations
to the servants to pilfer and steal small articles, not likely to be missed,
which these Jews purchase at about one third of the real value.—It is
supposed that upwards of two thousand of these depraved people are
employed in diurnal journeys of this kind, by which, through the me-
dium of bad money, and other fraudulent dealings, many of them acquire property, and then become Receivers of stolen Goods.[39]

Unfortunately, there is plenty of evidence throughout the eighteenth
century to support Colquhoun's inculpation of such Jews in the underworld economy of London, but it remains unproven that their involvement, except perhaps in the lucrative business of receiving stolen goods,
was any greater than that of non-Jews of a similar urban background.[40]
Yet, published and hearsay stories of Jewish criminal duplicity merely
helped to confirm or revive existing prejudices and presuppositions. The
latent anti-Semitism of the age required very little prompting to transform itself into popular hostility, if not usually to open violence.

Solitary itinerant pedlars were, however, considerably more at risk
from violence and physical assault than those Jews who did not need to
rely on wayfaring for their livelihood. There are many instances of their
brutal treatment at the hands of English Gentiles. For instance, in January 1760, the *London Chronicle* carries the following report under
"Country News":

> *Plymouth, Jan.* 11. We hear from Plymstock, that some days since a
> murder was committed upon the body of a Jew, who went by the name
> of Little Isaac: his body was found hid in a wood. His goods being of-
> fered to be sold, the goods and people were stopt, and a militia man
> taken into custody on suspicion; who confessed where he hid the Jew's
> box; and himself, and some other militiamen, went and found it, but
> the goods were all gone. He denied the murder.[41]

A few days later, the story is taken up and unfolded in the same newspaper:

> *Sherborne, Jan.* 21. Edward Jackson, a militia-man, has confessed that
> he met with the Jew, who was lately found murdered near Plymstock.
> After drinking a pint of beer together, which the Jew paid for, they both
> went together, and after walking about two miles towards Plymstock,
> the Deceased stopt to rest himself, and putting a long stick he had in
> his hand behind his back to rest his box upon, Jackson took the stick
> from behind him, and knocked him down, and when he was on the
> ground gave him two more blows, which finished him. Then taking
> his watch out of his pocket, and some goods out of the box, he hid the
> box in the wood. When he offered some of the things to sale, being

asked how he came by them, He said he found them in a box, and would shew it to Mr. Sherenbeare; which he accordingly did, taking him into the wood where he had left it, and presently after said his conscience troubled him, and he confessed the murder.[42]

Other such unconscious reenactments of the tale of Cain and Abel, with the Jew as victim, are recorded periodically throughout the eighteenth century.[43] Even by the standards of a violent age, attacks on itinerant Jews, although not usually descending to murder, were of a particular viciousness, suggesting that Jew-baiting was as integral a motive as robbery. "When a Jew was seen in the streets," recalls Francis Place, describing their situation in the early 1770s,

> it was often the signal of assault. I have seen many Jews hooted and hunted, kicked, cuffed, pulled by the beard, and spat upon, and so barbarously assaulted in the streets without any protection from the passers-by or the police, as seems impossible to have existed at any time. Dogs could not then be used in the streets in the manner in which Jews were treated.[44]

Nevertheless, apart from being most sorely threatened by such terrifying incidents and by a simmering cauldron of malicious abuse and libel that bubbled up from time to time, the Jews of eighteenth-century England were never en masse made the victims of orchestrated violence. In his *Letters from England* (1807), written from the point of view of a fictitious Spanish traveler, Robert Southey attributes anti-Jewish actions in the countries of Catholic Europe to the perpetual reminders in pictures and crucifixes of the sufferings of Christ at their hands. By contrast, he argues, without such constant exposure, the English have become "indifferent to the crimes of the Jews" and England "the heaven of the Jews," for in no other country do they enjoy a comparable unbounded liberty. Yet, he acknowledges that "even the most trifling ceremony" may serve to reactivate latent feelings. "At one of the public schools here," he writes,

> the boys on Easter Sunday rush out of the chapel after prayers, singing
> He is risen, he is risen,
> All the Jews must go to prison.
> This custom is certainly very old, though I cannot learn that it was ever usual to imprison this wretched people upon this festival. Some of these boys cut the straps of a Jew's box one day, and all his gingerbread nuts fell into the street. Complaint was made to the master; and when he questioned the culprits what they could say in their defence, one of them stepped forward and said, "Why, sir, did not they crucify our Lord!"[45]

In common with the legendary figure of the Wandering Jew, Christian populist culture presupposes that all Jews, even the poor itinerant pedlar, must share the blame for Christ's suffering. That succeeding generations of Jews should in turn be compelled to suffer as a result of the putative crimes of their biblical forebears may seem primitive justice and a particularly cruel irony in its equation of their fate with the eternal lot of the Wandering Jew. But, where the affliction of the Wandering Jew is internalized and manifested in his tearful contrition and in his perpetual search for redemption, the real Jew—the Ashkenazi pedlar—is afflicted by forces outside himself in the widespread antagonism of the majority gentile community. He is a figure far less capable of arousing Christian sympathy than his mythical counterpart for, despite his empirical presence for all to see, almost no attempt is made to understand him in terms that recognize him in his own right. Instead, his strange garb and physiognomy, his broken English and itinerant trade, and those further stereotypical evocations associated with his race mark him out as an outsider who is to be suspected (and even accursed) in all his dealings. In populist discourse, by a tradition that may be traced to the usury practiced by his ancestors in the Middle Ages and earlier to the money-changers cast out by Jesus from the Temple (Mark 11:15, John 2:15), the Jew pedlar's love of pecuniary gain and of bartering becomes the primary expedient by which he is identified and, seemingly, the motivating force of his character.

Recurrent allusions, perhaps echoing the biblical alignment of the endurance of his faith with his cunning ("If I forget thee, O Jerusalem, let my right hand forget her cunning" [Ps. 137:5]), tell of the base sharpness and notorious impudence of the Jew in what he is deemed best at, the fine art of bargaining. "What have we to learn of the *Jews*," inquires one particularly hostile pamphleteer, "except to cozen, trick and cheat[?]"[46] It would demand the miraculous power of "that which could raise men from the dead," opines William Cobbett in a crushing derogation, to induce the Jews "to cease to live by cheating, traffic, and usury."[47] By extension, trade becomes a recognized means by which to describe the Jews in general. "The *Jews*," we are told, "are the subtlest and most artful People in the World, and are so dexterous in bargaining, that it is impossible for Christians to expect any Advantage in their Dealings with them."[48] From their earliest youth, claims the novelist Charles Johnstone, the Jews are initiated into "the mysteries of that lower species of trade called peddling," reducing to a fine science every species of deceit so as "to wear off every hesitation of conscience, and make the practice natural and expert."[49] The effect of naturalizing such a people, avers a lukewarm proponent of the Jew Bill of 1753, will be to "make this Island the Mart and Emporium of the whole World."[50]

In the treatment of their shrewd dealing and of their love of gain, persiflage and whimsical anecdote are staples of the rhetoric of popular discourse concerning the Jews. For example, in his novel, *Tom Jones* (1748), when a £100 note falls unexpectedly from a pocketbook offered to the hero, Henry Fielding quips in passing that "a *Jew* would have jumped to purchase it at five shillings less than 100 *l.*"[51] From time to time across his writings, Fielding shows an unsympathetic attitude to the Jews, but it is a sign of how proverbially ingrained this is that such a remark should appear in a novel that is absent of Jewish characters or themes. A humorous story probably of English or Dutch origin but reprinted by Benjamin Franklin's *Pennsylvania Gazette* tells of a "Jew pedlar" who, having cuckolded a farmer by offering his wife a piece of calico, then attempts to regain from the husband the material he had earlier exchanged for her charms.[52] Such tales, in which business and sexual transactions are intermixed, are not uncommon in anecdotage concerning the Jews, as we shall see in a later chapter.[53] A satirical print, undated but probably from the 1830s, shows a young Jewess pleading with the cashier at a theatrical box office. "You must return me Sixpence, Sir!" she urges, "—My little brother Moses has tumbled out of the Shilling Gallery; he has broke his Neck and only seen half the play!" A similar story, concerning a "Jew boy" who fell to his death in the pit while attending a performance of the actress Sarah Siddons and whose mother, despite very charitable treatment by the theater managers, asked for the money back for his ticket, had appeared in a popular jest-book a few years before. In the same book, another jest tells of a capitally condemned Jew who was reprieved on his way to the gallows, but insisted on attending the hanging of two fellow prisoners in order to be able to bargain with the hangman for their clothes.[54] Another print, dated May 1830, by the caricaturist William Heath, depicts a devout Jew with a deed of bond showing from his pocket, reciting the eleventh commandment, seemingly intended for those of his faith: "Get all you can—keep what you get—give away NOTHING." In all these instances, Jews (and not just those of the peddling class) are represented as grasping traffickers whose sole motivation is money.

If the representation of the "bad" Jew frequently shows him as all too willing to outsmart his gentile neighbors, it is no less common to illustrate his being bested by "good" Christians or (nearly the same thing) by native sons of England, as in *Too Many for a Jew.* Cutting the hawker's straps, forcing him to eat what his religion forbids, or ultimately con-

"You must return me Sixpence, Sir!" Lithograph, c. 1830s. (Courtesy of the Library of the Jewish Theological Seminary of America.)

"Get all you can—keep what you get—give away nothing." William
Heath, 11th Commandment. Engraving, 1830. (Courtesy of the Library of
the Jewish Theological Seminary of America.)

vincing him by whatever means of the falseness of his creed and of the need to embrace the true faith are all in their varying degrees manifestations of the same thing, the blind need of the host group to justify and defend its own values against the perceived threat from the stereotyped Other. The imaginary exact line of demarcation between the host group and the Other and the presumed perpetual distinction between Christian and Jew are made "real" by reference to external features that are deemed peculiar to the Jew pedlar, particularly his apparel, the language he speaks, and, above all, his physiognomy. Some of these features may also have influenced contemporary depiction of the Wandering Jew, although in the symbiotic relationship of the legendary figure with the actual itinerant pedlar, the real Jew seems destined almost always to be portrayed in a darker light than his mythical counterpart.

By way of trade, itinerant Jews would often congregate in the metropolis where they could earn their livelihood by hawking, among other things, such imported commodities as spices, sponges, oranges and lemons, and even accordions. But if there was one trade that was most readily associated with the street Jews of London and some other cities it was the buying and selling of old clothes, often considered by commentators as a peculiarly Jewish form of mendicancy. "Most of the *Germen Jews* . . . now in England," remarks one writer, "have emigrated from Germany, Holland, Denmark, and Poland; for the sole purpose of obtaining a subsistence by *Begging*." "When . . . they get to London," he adds, "they embrace the most pitiful and mean employments to procure them food . . . as buying and selling Old Clothes, Buckles, Buttons, Sealing wax, Wafers, Oranges, Lemons, Pencils, or such like."[55] In graphic depiction, the Jewish old-clothes dealer is usually portrayed carrying under one arm a bag or sack in which to put his stock of second-hand clothes and often, on his head, he is shown balancing a pile of old hats. The bag and the hats are as much symbols of the old-clothes dealer as the traveling box is associated with his brother, the itinerant pedlar. Typically, the dealer's clothing is ragged and patched. The lowly social status of such an occupation and the importunity of some of these traders were sometimes put forward as further evidence of the debased condition of the Jews since biblical times. "The two images farthest removed from each other which I can comprehend under one term," perceives the poet Samuel Taylor Coleridge, "are, I think, Isaiah,—'Hear, O heavens, and give ear, O earth!'—and Levi of Holywell Street—'Old clothes!'—both of them

Jews, you'll observe."[56] Where the Wandering Jew with his long gown and flowing beard is portrayed, for all his suffering, as one who retains characteristics that are (at least vestigially) quasi-biblical and prophetic, the real Jew in his physical and spiritual impoverishment manifests for the Christian world the present fallen position of those who were once God's chosen people. They have been plunged from their elect status of old to become, according to Lord Byron, "a name for every race / To spit upon—the chosen of disgrace."[57]

In many accounts of the Wandering Jew, a great deal is made of his remarkable facility with languages. Wherever he travels, he is able to converse with ease in any tongue, learned or vernacular, a talent that may be understood as miraculous confirmation of the magnitude of his message. By contrast, the itinerant Jew pedlar or dealer in old clothes, whose own closed language is Yiddish, is usually represented as incapable of much more than the most halting English. The language spoken by such people, observes one writer, is

> but a kind of *Gibberish*, or fulsome compound of Hebrew, German and Dutch, which none but the *German Jews* are capable of understanding; so that neither a real Hollander or German, can understand a German Jew; or a German Jew, a Dutchman or German; except they have by frequent intercourse & connection, as is commonly the case, laboured out a construction of each other; which might be done by People the most opposite in their language of any in the world.[58]

By the middle years of the eighteenth century, the broken English of Ashkenazi Jews had become a recognized way of identifying them as also a common means of linguistic ridicule, in particular through their appearance as characters on the stage and in graphic satire.[59] The guttural dialect of these Jews is usually represented by the substitution of hard and soft consonants (e.g., "d" for "th"), by toning down or flattening sibilants (e.g., "sh" for "s"), and by the introduction of Germanic-sounding words. A late eighteenth-century caricature of *A Jew Pedlar*, with his box of knickknacks and cheap jewelry, shows him holding up and pointing to a gilt-framed portrait as he exclaims: "Dere ish de Pictures of de King and de Queen—ash fine ash de life itself—who buys? who buys? no more den twopence for de two—and de gold be worth all de monish without de pictures!"[60] Another, *Mo Isaacs*, also titled *The Jew in Grain*, dated 1824, depicts a typical pedlar selling a watch to an unsuspecting customer whose pocket is being picked by an accomplice. The text to the print, to be spoken and sung, is entirely in dialect and includes the following:

To cry old cloash I go my rounds,
I cheat um all so clean;
The coat what cost a tousand pounds
I buy um for fifteen.

I sell a vatch for moshe good deal,
With fine gay seal and chain,
I get a tief de vatch to steal
And puy um pack again.[61]

In both these examples, the humorous disposition of the caricaturist attenuates any real nastiness, but in each case the dialectal peculiarities spell out clearly the wider Otherness of the Jew. By convention, it is at least tacitly recognized that the semiotic employment of such a dialect in the drama and elsewhere is specifically intended to represent not just a foreign Jew struggling with an unfamiliar language but one who is so totally dominated by a love of gain that he will sell (as Mo Isaacs gleefully informs us) "life, and body, and soul, and every ting in the world, and trick the very Tevil himself, for the monish." While having some crude basis in their actual impoverished condition, the stereotypical representation of Jews in this way indiscreetly substitutes for any conceivable desire to understand them. All too rarely, but mainly toward the end of our period, a few writers reveal an awareness of this. In her novel *Harrington* (1817), Maria Edgeworth expresses through her eponymous hero an awakened realization of the deleterious consequences of thoughtlessly linking these putative traits as so many have done before:

> Wherever the Jews are introduced, I find that they are invariably represented as beings of a mean, avaricious, unprincipled, treacherous character. Even the peculiarities of their persons, the errors of their foreign dialect and pronunciation, were mimicked and caricatured, as if to render them objects of perpetual derision and detestation.[62]

In a similar vein, Coleridge percipiently inquires whether the real cause of the mercenary behavior of the Jews is more readily attributable to the way in which they have been treated than to any endemic failings of their own:

> If they have been hard and griping in their dealings, may it not have been occasioned by the treatment they have received? To treat men as if they were incapable of virtue is to make them so. If it be said that the Almighty has decreed them to be wanderers and outcasts, we reply that that Divine Being has no where told us to persecute them.[63]

The much more common reaction, however, is to see no redeeming virtue in the Jews. Their importunity in the streets and markets of London

A Jew Pedlar. Engraving, c. 1790–1800. (Courtesy of the Library of the Jewish Theological Seminary of America.)

Mo Isaacs (or) *The Jew in Grain.* Engraving, 1824. (Courtesy of the Library of the Jewish Theological Seminary of America.)

is often commented upon and considered indicative of their present corruption. According to John Badcock, writing in 1828,

> The Jews of *Russell-court* and of *Holywell-street,* Strand, are not only enabled by their situation to *interrupt* a greater number of persons, but, in addition to all other annoyances, hurl abuse, scurrility, and threats at those who refuse to become purchasers of their base apparel and ricketty furniture.[64]

An unpleasant slang term to describe a Jew, a *smouch* or *smouse*, in common English usage from the early eighteenth century until after 1830, owes its origin to what the *Oxford English Dictionary* euphemistically describes as "the persuasive eloquence of Jewish pedlars," the word deriving from the German dialect word *schmus*, meaning "patter" or "talk."[65] In England, dialectal ridicule of the linguistic impediments of Jewish pedlars almost invariably channels their patter into an all-absorbing capacity to seek out and snatch a bargain. Whatever difficulties such Jews might have had with English does not seem to have blunted their presumed cardinal motivation.

Perhaps because their Yiddish dialect made their English appear on the verge of gibberish but more potently because of a reputed addiction stemming from biblical times, Jewish pedlars (in common with their race at large) are usually represented in popular culture as given to cursing and foul language.[66] So ingrained was this conception even before the readmission of the Jews that Thomas Collier, one of the more eloquent apologists on their behalf in 1656, deemed it necessary to offer by way of admonition that "a severe penalty might be inflicted upon them, if they curse or speak reproachfully of Christ, of which they should be made well acquainted before they come."[67] The allegation to which Collier refers boils down simply to the belief that, as a people supposedly cursed by God, the Jews themselves were preternaturally disposed to cursing. "Those who know any thing of the disposition of the *Jews*," asserts a pamphleteer writing at the time of the Jew Bill, "must know also, that they are great scoffers at *Christianity*."[68]

For denying Christ as the true Messiah, litanizes another contemporary inkslinger, the Jews "have been regarded and treated hitherto as Vagrants, Infidels, Blasphemers, and Crucifiers." "Their Books," he argues vaunting evidence that is nonexistent, "are full of the bitterest Curses and Blasphemies against Jesus Christ, and they say such shocking Things of him, as we dare not repeat."[69] A bilingual conversionist tract in Spanish and English, published early in the eighteenth century, is marginally more specific, although on testimony that has no basis in actuality, when it claims that

> The *Jews* labour as much against God by their Blasphemies, Impieties and Immoralities, as all the World besides labour the contrary. The Hatred of the *Jews* against *Jesus Christ* is so great, that in their ordinary Conversation they frequently call him the Son of an Adulteress, and likewise *Elganafa* the hanged.[70]

Although the imputation of blasphemy is leveled against the Jews with persistent regularity, it is as insistently contradicted by their refracted better self, the Wandering Jew, who constantly admonishes those that curse or take Christ's name in vain by reminding them that in so doing they crucify their God again.

The belief, derived from the Gospels but found in many accounts of the Wandering Jew, that in rebutting Christ before Calvary he had spat in his face, may be behind a further conviction that the Jews had since lost the capacity to expectorate, as a perpetual reminder to them of their cursed state. Writing toward the middle of the nineteenth century, Henry Mayhew, the celebrated chronicler of the London poor, recounts the following anecdote as evidence of the persistence of the superstition:

—A gentleman of my acquaintance was one evening, about twilight, walking down Brydges-street, Covent-garden, when an elderly Jew was preceding him, apparently on his return from a day's work, as an old clothesman. His bag accidentally touched the bonnet of a dashing woman of the town, who was passing, and she turned round abused the Jew, and spat at him, saying with an oath: "You old rags humbug! *You* can't do that!"—an allusion to a vulgar notion that Jews have been unable to do more than *slobber*, since spitting on the Saviour.[71]

It is instructive to recall that in the scriptural account, Christ is spat upon not by the Jews but by the Roman soldiers of the governor before being led away to be crucified (Matt. 27:30, Mark 15:19). Once again, through transference, the sins of others are visited as punishment upon the Jews.

In physiognomic representation, it is generally accepted that the late eighteenth-century English literary *locus classicus* and source for many subsequent depictions of the Wandering Jew is the tale of "Raymond and Agnes, or the Bleeding Nun," a kind of subplot within Matthew Gregory Lewis's notorious and much-reprinted Gothic novel, *The Monk* (1795). The intrusion of the Wandering Jew into this fantasy of horror has been much discussed and need not detain us here.[72] What should concern us, however, are specific features of his appearance as they are delineated by Lewis in the novel. In particular, the narrative (introduced through Don Raymond) gives prominence to the Jew's visage:

He was a Man of majestic presence: His countenance was strongly marked, and his eyes were large, black, and sparkling: Yet there was something in his look, which the moment that I saw him, inspired me with a secret awe, not to say horror. He was drest plainly, his hair was unpowdered, and a band of black velvet which encircled his fore-head, spread over his features an additional gloom. His countenance wore the marks of profound melancholy; his step was slow, and his manner grave, stately and solemn.[73]

Later, in a dramatic gesture that for Don Raymond is almost too unbearably shocking in its intensity, the Jew draws "the sable band from his fore-head" to reveal "a burning Cross impressed upon his brow" (172). The awesome sight of this cross is sufficient to exorcize the demoniac specter of the Bleeding Nun, who had haunted poor Raymond's every sleeping hour. After the exorcism, not only she but also the Jew are seen no more. His disappearance is almost as elemental to the aura of mystery that surrounds him as is his highly visible stigma. By introducing such a fateful mark on his brow, it has been claimed that Lewis broadened the popular appeal of the legend, subsequent picturizations of the Wandering Jew frequently portraying him with a flaming red cross on his forehead.[74] In addition, most critics agree that the piercing and hypnotic glance of the Jew is also Lewis's own particular contribution, significantly influencing the handling of the legend by many later writers.[75] While retaining all the burden of guilt that traditionally is forever his lot, Lewis's Wandering Jew becomes the supernatural agent by which an evil spirit is laid to rest. However, as Rosenberg points out, "the object is not to remind the reader of some awful power conferred by Christ on a great sinner; it is to create a spectacular effect."[76] Lewis's desire for melodrama smothers any incipient moral or theological overtones. But, for all that, the positive action of the Jew in aiding Don Raymond may be viewed as indicative of an emerging interpretation by writers of the Romantic age for whom he has become a figure who is often more noble than reprobate.

If the mark of the burning cross upon the Wandering Jew's brow and the mesmerizing glance of his black eyes are in fact Lewis's own enhancement of the legend, scholarly investigation has endeavored with rather limited effect to pinpoint analogies that may help to explain his innovation. At best, it is generally agreed that there are obvious affinities between the mark of Cain (Gen. 4:15) and that of the Wandering Jew. Anderson even cites Pierre Bayle's *Dictionnaire Historique et Critique* (1697), which had insisted that the mark of Cain was in the form of a cross.[77] Such piecemeal accretions to the legend as those found in *The Monk* are far from easily traceable to particular sources, and it seems much more likely that Lewis was responding to or rather echoing endemic beliefs about the Jews that were already deeply rooted in popular culture. Some of these beliefs may reflect past contact with actual Jews but more often than not they belong within the realm of vulgar error that stems from the medieval diabolization of the Jews. As early as the twelfth century, according to one account, a Jewish delegation bearing gifts and pledges of allegiance was excluded from the coronation of King

Richard the Lionheart in 1189 because it was considered sacrilegious to permit them to gaze upon the crown. The imputation of this report is founded in the belief that the Jews were possessed of the evil eye, which they were fully capable of using for nefarious purposes.[78] The material (and presumably ungodly) aspirations of the Jews are reflected in the English proverbial expression "to be worth a Jew's eye," that is, to be of sufficient value to captivate the eye of a Jew, which can be traced back at least to the late sixteenth century.[79] Writing in the early seventeenth century, Robert Burton may be alluding to a related tradition when, citing Buxtorf as his authority, he refers to the "goggle-eyes" of the Jews.[80] However, before their readmission into England, there is a paucity of evidence to suggest that physiognomy was used as a means of Jewish identification except in terms of their chimerical or diabolized image.[81]

In an earlier chapter, we saw how seventeenth-century Christian visitors to the newly reestablished London synagogue remarked upon the Sephardi Jews' quick, piercing eyes and swarthy complexion.[82] By the eighteenth century, such observations have been hybridized in popular belief with the traditional evil stereotype to engender a Jew who is made recognizably distinct from the rest of humanity by the addition of a peculiar physiognomic mark or stigma. For William Hurd, author of a frequently reissued account of global customs and religious rites, first published in the 1780s, the nature of the mark remains unspecified, although there can be no question as to how it originated: "God was to set a mark upon them, by which they were to be distinguished from all other persons in the universe, and what man can look upon a Jew without knowing he is such? The person who beholds a Jew, and denies Divine Revelation, must be an infidel indeed."[83]

A pamphleteer of 1753 refers more specifically to the generally held belief that the Jews are born with "an *unfortunate Cast*" in the eye, which is to be interpreted as "a Mark of Reprobation."[84] In the same year, another anonymous writer gives us a much fuller account, that most thoroughly illustrates the "new" physiognomy:

> It is Matter of Fact, that the *Jews* do live in continual Uneasiness, tormented and haunted, like Murderers, with a Legion of Horrors: Their Crimes deserve these several Lashes of Conscience, and how severe they are you may read in their very Faces. You know a *Jew* at first Sight. And what then are his distinguishing Features? Examine what it is peculiar that strikes you. It is not his dirty Skin, for there are other People as nasty; neither is it the Make of his Body, for the *Dutch* are every whit as odd, aukward Figures as the *Jews*. But look at his Eyes. Dont you see a malignant Blackness underneath them, which gives

them such a Cast, as bespeaks Guilt and Murder? You can never mistake a *Jew* by this Mark, it throws such a dead, livid Aspect over all his Features, that he carries Evidence enough in his Face to convict him of being a Crucifier.[85]

If the distinguishing mark is not yet a burning cross etched upon his brow, at least here the "malignant Blackness" beneath the Jew's eyes and his tormented conscience, the "Legion of Horrors" forever reminding him that it is he who is held responsible for the Crucifixion, are endowments that have a shared lineage with Lewis's Wandering Jew. There seems little doubt that the innovations to the countenance of the Wandering Jew in *The Monk* owe their existence as much to popular tradition concerning the singularity of Jewish physiognomy as to its author's fertile imagination. In turn, the mesmerizing capacity of Lewis's Jew provides us with a collateral ancestry for the "glittering eye" of Coleridge's ancient mariner (1798) and for that aspect of the literary and artistic depiction of the Wandering Jew in the age that followed.[86]

Although writers in the nineteenth century often took pride in their more liberal attitude and only infrequently attempted direct reactivation of the old medieval stereotype, the tradition that even in a crowd one could always tell a Jew continued to flourish. There is, declares the journalist James Grant, writing in 1839, "something so very peculiar in all their physiognomies, that any one acquainted with the conformation of a Jewish face would be able, in almost every instance, to single out a Jew by his face alone, from among a thousand other persons."[87]

Typically, Jewish physiognomy is increasingly cast in terms of what were perceived as distinct ethnic characteristics, supposedly deriving from their oriental ancestry but probably loosely based on observation of Jews of Sephardi descent. For John Fisher Murray, Irish poet and humorist, writing for *Blackwood's Magazine* in the early 1840s, in the Jew's "oval phiz, high, pale forehead, [and] dark, protuberant flashing eye," may be read "a volume of the romance of history more eloquent than Josephus ever writ." Within the Jewish Quarter of London, "every brow [seems] pencilled in an arch of exact ellipse; every nose modelled after the proboscis of a Toucan; locks as bushy and black as those of Absalom abound, and beards of the patriarchal ages."[88] The rampant orientalism of such an account is far from unique. "In various circumstances, at home and abroad," remarks William Rae Wilson in the early 1820s,

all Jews may be said to appear the same. Look at their face, the dark forehead, flashing eye, raven locks, bushy beard and eyebrow. A strong eastern character is in fact stamped on every countenance. Whether they are among their own people, or surrounded by those of other lands, Jews appear as the most extraordinary beings on the face of the earth.[89]

Although the fairer skinned Ashkenazi Jew, in his street trade as itinerant pedlar, had for at least a century been the far more common sight, it is the darker complexion of the Sephardi or "Portuguese" Jew that in so many accounts is made to exemplify the race. Both Jew and Wandering Jew from the second quarter of the nineteenth century are unable to escape this new tendency to "orientalize."[90] The tenuous bond that for more than a century had linked the mythical figure with his humble counterpart, the Ashkenazi pedlar, is severed.

In tracing this strange symbiosis of the legendary and the real during the eighteenth century, we have seen that the Wandering Jew is invariably depicted in a manner more favorable than that accorded to actual Jews. His portrayal by a number of writers of the Romantic period consciously idealizes him, representing him more as victim than sacrificer.[91] There is insufficient evidence to allow us to assert with complete conviction that such writers also wished to contribute to the promotion of more liberal attitudes toward actual Jews. Yet, Wordsworth's encounter at Grasmere with an old man, taken by his brother John for a Jew because of his dark eyes, long nose, and bundle of clothes, led to his imaginative reinvigoration as the noble (albeit non-Jewish) figure of the leech gatherer of "Resolution and Independence."[92] In the same year, Wordsworth also wrote a short "Song for the Wandering Jew." Coleridge's acknowledgment in his *Table Talk* of having "had a good deal to do with Jews in the course of my life" accompanies an anecdotal account of several humorous contretemps with itinerant pedlars.[93] From his early Note Books, we know that Coleridge contemplated "a romance" on the Wandering Jew before settling on the Ancient Mariner, a parallel figure whose nightmarish search for atonement infuses the ballad.[94] In his essay on the "Treatment of the Jews" in *The Courier* (June 18, 1816), Coleridge remarks that "if the age we live in, be in deeds, and not only in words, the enlightened age it is said to be, it will be shewn in a juster treatment of the Jews."[95] Given such an attitude, is it possible that Coleridge deliberately suppressed his original plan of writing a poem describing the expiation of the mythical Jew? Shelley's several forays on the theme, in which the protagonist is depicted as victim rather than villain, accord well with his acknowledged liberal views.[96] It is unlikely that the identification of these writers with the plight of the Wandering Jew could have been totally divorced from an awareness of contemporary Jews and of their commonest manifestation in the figure of the itinerant pedlar.

Uniquely, within our period, wanderer and vagabond, the legendary and the real Jew, shared the same ambulatory path. With the advent of the railways and the economic advancement of street Jews from hawkers to shopkeepers, the itinerant life of peddling was no longer viable or attractive. The gradual disappearance of the peripatetic Jewish pedlar from the rural life and byways of England toward the middle of the nineteenth century was to leave the Wandering Jew once more to pursue his eternal journey alone.

CHAPTER 5

CONVERSION

THE OFTEN UNEASY INTERACTION of Christianity with Judaism traceable even to the infancy of the common era may at least be said to articulate facets of a shared inheritance. Defying the unecumenical sentiments of those who would prefer that it were otherwise, the roots of Judaism and Christianity continue to be fed by a common soil. However, a prominent doctrinal distinction that remains to this day fundamental to the ultimate separation of the two religions rests in their respective attitudes to conversion. In traditional Judaism proselytism is discouraged, whereas almost all Christian denominations actively encourage conversion to their faith. Where Christianity is intent on spreading its "good news" to all corners of the world, a missionary zeal to advance the conversion of the Gentiles is nowhere apparent in Judaism. A highly important, though to date inadequately studied, literature of the longer eighteenth century documents Christian endeavors throughout the period to persuade the Jews of England of their obduracy in failing to recognize the truth of the younger faith. Such literature takes, among its many forms, occasional pamphlets describing the conversion of a particular Jew, learned tractates unfolding the arguments in favor of Christ as Messiah against received Judaic opinion, and sermons and epistles written specifically to enlighten the Hebrew nation by pointing out the error of its ways.[1] Many of the conversionist arguments put forward during the eighteenth century are largely indistinguishable from those advanced at other times. Only in their application to given circumstances may we perhaps isolate distinctive characteristics. The present chapter will not attempt to do more than scratch the surface of a vast printed source material that still awaits far closer investigation. In addition, use will be made of other works concerning the Jews, particularly anti-Semitic tracts, in which the subject of conversion is broached.

In one immediate sense, conversionist literature can be distinguished from most other Christian discourses concerning the Jews, since it is almost unique in being addressed directly to or indirectly at the Jews themselves. Its avowed aim being to persuade, it often tacitly assumes a dual readership of believing Christians requiring affirmation of their faith and nonbelieving Jews who remain to be convinced. It implies a dialogue between Christians and Jews even if on this issue no such thing exists or is in reality primarily one-sided. For most practicing Jews, such literature has little more than nuisance value and would be better directed if it was allowed to circulate no further than among those missionaries or evangelists who composed it. It seems to reflect the constant need in Christianity for self-definition, the very nature of which inevitably invites comparison with Judaism, usually to the detriment of practitioners of the older religion.

For Christian conversionists, on the other hand, Jews are considered stiff-necked in their inability or refusal to recognize in Jesus the true Messiah. Even if there is little tangible return in the number of individual Jews persuaded to convert, at least such evangelists are fulfilling their biblical duty (as set out most particularly in Paul's Epistle to the Romans, chaps. 9–11) by aspiring to alert God's people of their cardinal error.[2] In this sense, the conversion by baptism of a Jew, which would be confirmed by his or her unqualified acknowledgment of Christ as Messiah, may be considered almost as a greater triumph and of more temporal significance than, say, the conversion of a pagan. The importance accorded by evangelical thinkers in Georgian England to work of this kind is reflected in the founding at the turn of the nineteenth century of the London Society for Promoting Christianity among the Jews, an institution that has continued to strive toward the final attainment of its proclaimed mission even to the present day.

From the time of the Jews' readmission in the mid-seventeenth century, one of the most persuasive philo-Semitic arguments in favor of a Jewish presence in England has turned on the assumption that this will accelerate their eventual conversion to Christianity. Far from making it part of a hidden agenda, English philo-Semites have rarely been anything other than frank in conjoining their desire to welcome the Jews with a parallel goal of wishing to offer them new hope through Christianity. For them, the process by which a Jew will come to recognize and acknowledge the messianic role of Christ may be greatly assisted by suitable counsel and gentle persuasion rather than by compulsion or trickery. During the eighteenth century, the idea that Jews might be compelled into Christian belief is frequently associated in English minds with the inquisitorial methods of the Roman Catholic Church on the Continent, while the notion that they might be duped into converting belongs more accurately to folk mythology than to actual practice.[3] In most cases, the fear that a conversion to Christianity could be anything but a sincere act of faith functions as an effective barrier to any serious attempt to trick a Jew into such a step. The majority of Jewish proselytes to Christianity during the period turned to their new faith more by their own volition than necessarily by external persuasion. Their individual reasons for taking this fundamental step varied radically, from the visible demonstration of a deep-seated spiritual belief to a desire merely for wider or freer acceptance within English society.

The status of conversion as a central tenet of the Christian faith is among the more habitually reiterated assertions in eighteenth-century philo-Semitic discourse. "One of the great Glories of the Christian Faith, is the endeavouring to convert others to their Belief," writes a mid-eighteenth-century pamphleteer, in typical vein of those declaring their sympathy for the Jews. "No just Means," he adds, "are left untried to forward this pious Work."[4] The Jews, it is felt by these avowed philo-Semites, are in need of gentle reassurance rather than latter-day persecution to soothe them into a readier acceptance of Christian fellowship. The point is well put by another contemporary writer:

> We must particularly wish and labour to effect the Conversion to our Faith of All, who are unhappily prejudiced against it; and most especially of the *Jews*. . . . This can only be done by kind and gentle, by friendly and brotherly Treatment; not by calling-down Fire from Heaven, or rather calling-up Fire from Hell, upon them: we must reverence and adore the Depths of divine Wisdom, in the Dispensations of Providence to Us and to Them.[5]

Coupled with the recognition that the Jews are more liable to respond positively to those who, instead of condemning them as less than human and kin to the Devil, seek to behave toward them in a more tolerant manner, is a sense of shame at their treatment in former ages. Richard Kidder, bishop of Bath and Wells, writing in the final years of the seventeenth century, expresses just such a view:

> Very often, *Force* hath been used instead of *Reasoning*; and instead of allowing them [the Jews] to be Men of Wit and Sense, (as in truth they are) and treating them humanely, we have used them barbarously; and with great Inhumanity *persecuted them* whom we ought to have *convinced.*[6]

In similar vein, Lewis Stephens, archdeacon of Chester, in a sermon of 1735 to celebrate the rescue from imprisonment of a recently baptized Jew, spells out what he sees as the particular virtue of conversion within the liberal observance of the Anglican Church:

Of all the different Sects of Christians none are more indulgent to them [the Jews] than the present *Protestants:* For our Laws do not require any Mark of Distinction in their Habit as at Venice; nor impose any particular Tax upon their Heads, as in the former Reigns here in *England;* nor establish any *Bloody Inquisition* for *imprisoning,* and *racking,* and *burning their Bodies,* as is frequent in Popish Countries; but receive them first *freely* and *kindly* into our Country, in hopes of receiving them into *Our Church.*[7]

Eighteenth-century English philo-Semitic writers are often at pains to play down the differences and in turn to give due emphasis to the similarities that exist between Judaism and Christianity. By appealing to the intelligence and reasonableness of those (supposedly more enlightened) Jews that they are addressing, such writers aspire to engage them in a dialogue that will eventually prompt them into a fuller consciousness of their fundamental misunderstanding of Christ. So, writing directly to them, the Unitarian minister and scientist Joseph Priestley meticulously searches for common ground between the Jews and himself with which to earn their trust. Ties of kinship by which both he and they ("the *elder branch* of the family") worship and serve the same God are shrewdly employed by Priestley as a means of soliciting the attention of their reason:

Since, therefore, well-informed christians believe in the same one, living, and true God, with yourselves, it may be hoped that our mutual prejudices will in time abate, and that you will be prevailed upon to attend with calmness to the reasons that may be laid before you, why you should believe in the divine mission of Christ, as well as in that of Moses, and consider his religion as designed to be a blessing to the gentile world as well as to you.[8]

Among the more compelling reasons put before the Jews is the argument that, according to Christian exegesis of the Old Testament, their conversion had been foretold to them (e.g., Ezek. 11:17–20) and should therefore be understood as an inevitable first step prior to the longed-for advent of the Messiah. "There wants, methinks," writes the poet Abraham Cowley in 1656, "but the *Conversion* of . . . the *Jews,* for the accomplishing of the *Kingdom of Christ.*"[9] How that conversion could be brought about was the subject of hot dispute among seventeenth- and eighteenth-century Christian theologians, whose typological stratagems to unravel some of the more obscure pronouncements of the biblical prophets become as elaborate as trying to piece together a complex jigsaw. A received opinion among advocates of the Jews at the time of their readmission is that their conversion would be expedited by their being made welcome in England, a natural staging post before their expected eventual return to the Holy Land. In a truly Protestant country, the Jews would more easily come to recognize their blindness and prepare themselves for their spiritual ingathering. "This Nation of ENGLAND," runs a petition published a few years before their readmission, "shall be the first and readiest to transport IZRAELLS Sons & Daughters in their Ships to the Land promised to their fore-Fathers, ABRAHAM, ISAAC, and JACOB, for an everlasting Inheritance."[10] By coming to the help of the Jews in this and other ways, it was believed, the English would in turn receive God's blessing at the time of the approaching Millennium. If falling short of outright altruism and frequently naively impractical, millenarian assumptions about the Jews created a climate that helped to catalyze the debate leading to their readmission.[11]

Although it is often far from clear whether the restitution of the Jews to the Holy Land should precede or follow their conversion, eighteenth-century English philo-Semitic writers are no less attracted than their forebears to the idea of such a return. After all, a major prophecy spelled out in the Book of Isaiah that "the Lord shall set his hand again the second time to recover the remnant of his people" was hardly less specific in stating that the Gentiles, too, should partake in the new messianic age that was promised.[12] Philo-Semitic discourse is full of references to the restoration of the Jews to their ancient home in Israel. The English nation, asserts one such millenarian,

> cannot but look with Pleasure and Delight at any Step; which may seem to tend, how remotely soever, to their Restitution to their own Land; whether before or after their Conversion to Christianity: and we must ardently wish to be Instruments of so glorious an event, in the hands of the Almighty.[13]

A tenet of faith supporting the common belief by most Jews and Christians in the biblical prophecy of the return of the chosen people to the Holy Land presumes that (when he wishes so to do) God will reveal himself through miracle and other mysterious ways. The survival of the Jews as a separate people from biblical times through centuries of persecution perfectly exemplifies the workings of such Providence. Paradoxically, an argument sometimes put forward by eighteenth-century Christian messianists utilizes this shared faith in Revelation as endorsement of the suitability of the Jews for conversion. "It is alledged," writes Philo-Patriae, a pseudonymous pamphleteer at the time of the Jew Bill, that the Jews are

> stubborn Unbelievers, and no Way proper Objects on which we should turn our Thoughts to endeavour their Conversion. I must differ in that

Sentiment, as I fear those hardest to be drawn over, are such who give no Credit to any Revelation at all: Now, the *Jews* do all believe in Revelation, therefore, are much nearer Christianity than such Unbelievers; 'twill be hard to have any Doubt of the *Jews* Belief in Revelation, as no Man that did not believe it, would adhere to a Sect reviled by so great a Part of Mankind. . . . Credit being given to Revelation must greatly tend towards Christianity.[14]

The *idée fixe* of messianist thought toward the Jews is that, despised though they may be, and whether they wish it or not, they are verily but ripe plums for conversion to Christianity. Almost no legitimate strategy or argument is too mean if it will help to bring about an end that can only be to the greater glory of the Christian faith. If eighteenth-century English philo-Semitism is in many ways less blinkered than traditional anti-Semitism, its rhetoric is hardly less insistent in its acceleration of certain stereotypical attitudes that are made to imbue Christian behavior toward the Jews. In viewing the survival of a remnant of the Jews (Isa. 10:23, Rom. 9:27) as a visible token of a larger millenarian plan, Christians would be culpable of denying the Scriptures and showing infidelity to the Lord if they did not strive to effectuate their perpetual salvation through conversion.

Perhaps the most extravagant of a tally of English millenarians during the eighteenth century was the pseudo-prophet Richard Brothers (1757–1824), who predicted the impending apocalypse by linking the European turmoil brought on by the French Revolution with the restoration, under his deliverance, of the Jews to their patrimony and the recovery of the English as true descendants of the ten lost tribes of Israel. Brothers proclaimed himself to his people, "the Hebrews in all nations," as "the Shiloh mentioned in the scripture . . . , the descendant of David that is to be your king to conquer all your enemies and give peace to the world."[15] His mission, according to one of his followers, was to redeem God's ancient people from "the awful darkness" that has veiled their minds for so long, to call upon them "to believe in the true MESSIAH, and to order them to depart from all countries, where they are now scattered, to rebuild Jerusalem."[16] The extreme literalism of his interpretation of biblical text frequently crossed the margins of absurdity. As a former naval lieutenant turned prophet, his reading of Isaiah 11:12, "he shall set up an ensign for the nations, . . . and gather together the dispersed of Judah from the four corners of the earth," prompted him to ordain a national flag

to be the ensign of all Hebrew ships, agreeable to the instruction of God to me . . . as follows:—the field green with the form of the sun in gold near the middle, inclining to the upper corner next the staff, having twelve rays of light pointing from the body: in the centre of which is to be inscribed in blue letters of an inch in length the following words—"The kingdom is the Lord's."[17]

Believing himself to be the "Nephew of the Almighty," Brothers publicly called upon the English to lay down their arms before the French, the agents of God's wrath against hereditary monarchy, and for King George III to resign his throne to him. When in 1795, the year after he began his ministry, he was arrested at the behest of the Privy Council on a charge of encouraging treasonable practices, he was presumed to be insane and ordered to be locked away in an asylum, where he languished until 1806. "I wish to heaven," he wrote from his incarceration, "you had complimented me, as the announced King of the Jews, with a residence in Kensington palace, instead of one as a falsely supposed lunatic in Islington mad-house" (170).

A satirical print, The PROPHET of the HEBREWS—the PRINCE of PEACE—conducting the JEWS to the PROMIS'D-LAND, published by James Gillray in March 1795, the month that he was arrested, shows a maniacal Richard Brothers, the Mosaic rays of enthusiasm shining from his forehead, leading onwards a bemused flock of Jews and Gentiles. From the sack upon his back, marked "BUNDLE of the ELECT," peeks the recognizable visage of the politician, Charles James Fox, often depicted in caricature as a swarthy Jew, and here trussed up with those other leaders of the political opposition in England who, before the execution of Louis XVI, had expressed open sympathy for the French Revolution. The vanquished seven-headed beast of monarchy (Rev. 13:1, 17:3), its crowned heads fallen, is being trampled underfoot by the advancing rabble in anticipation of the new egalitarian age. To the lower right of Gillray's hieroglyphic tableau, we can see St. Paul's Cathedral and the city of London brilliantly aflame at their augured moment of eternal destruction as Brothers points his followers toward an apocalyptic future state that is symbolized by a bloody sun in frenzied sweat under the cap of liberty, and the gate of the new Jerusalem in the form of a burning gallows. That the messianist is made to carry a flaming sword alongside the Book of Revelation, yet is ludicrously dressed as a French sansculotte with a fool's chapeau on his head, signifies the extreme confusion of his mission. The dizzy owl above his head, gripping an olive branch in its beak, delivers an ironic token of an illusory universal peace. At the upper left of the engraving, a joyous circle of fallen angels and devils dance 'round a crescent moon, hovering over the simple crowd of converts headed by a rabbi and a Jew pedlar with an open

James Gillray, *The Prophet of the Hebrews.* Engraving, 1795. (Courtesy of
Mr. Alfred Rubens, London.)

box of knickknacks. Gillray imagines the conversion of the Jews as the
trigger that unleashes an apocalyptic nightmare, in which the anarchic
forces of the infernal world are ultimately triumphant. The print is a
stunningly clever parody of the philo-Semitic dream of converting the
Jews as a prelude to the Christian apocalypse. The shortcomings and the
folly of philo-Semitic evangelism have rarely been so urgently exposed.[18]

In reality, Brothers's ministry attracted very few Jews, its appeal drawing far more widely from the gentile populace, possibly due to external
exploitation for revolutionary ends. Its witheringly sarcastic refutation
by the Jewish polemicist David Levi is indicative of the contempt with

which Brothers was received by those that he claimed to reign. "I cannot conceive," writes Levi,

> how he can be accounted a Jew, (and which he certainly must, before he can lay claim to be their prince) while he is deficient in the most essential qualification of a Jew: namely God's covenant in his flesh: circumcision is an indispensable rite, and no one can be incorporated into their society till he has undergone the operation. How the prophet came to overlook this, which is so essential to his mission, I know not: but it is plain to me that, he has not learned his business, and that he is but a bungler at best: otherwise, he would have taken care, to have had the operation performed in a very secret manner, and then have given us a pompous account of its having been performed in a miraculous manner by the angel Michael, or Gabriel. . . . This would have been doing business like an adept: but alas! he has now marred all, as the Jews, who are strict observers of the rite, will sooner remain in bondage, than consent to be led home by an uncircumcised Philistine. So much for the Prophet.[19]

In response to those of his disciples who claimed that the skepticism of the Jews toward Brothers was comparable to their biblical disbelief of Moses, David Levi peremptorily dismisses his pseudo-messianic writings as unworthy of serious attention, made up of "mean, low expressions, destitute of all harmony of arrangement, and as much inferior to the grand, majestic, and sublime language of the Prophets, and truly inspired men among the ancient Jews, as is that of the most trifling poetaster of our days, to Homer's."[20] In Brothers, the Jews had certainly not found the prophet to lead them to the Holy Land. In general, messianic evangelism from its roots in the seventeenth and eighteenth centuries has always had a far greater and more immediate appeal to Christians than to Jews.

If eighteenth-century philo-Semitic messianists and writers created for themselves an image of the Jews as a people awaiting spiritual awakening through kindly sustenance leading ultimately to conversion and the kingdom of God, anti-Semitic diatribe during the same period activates a counter-image that stresses their total obduracy in refusing to countenance Christ as their true redeemer and, by extension, their inveterate enmity to the Christian faith. At least on the first of these two charges, such discourse is closer to the mark than the somewhat unctuous image of philo-Semitic aspiration. The construction of a twofold (or even a multiple) argument in which at least one of the elements has a quota of truth is not unusual in anti-Semitic exposition. For instance,

William Romaine, perhaps the most notorious mid-century disseminator of anti-Judaic dogma, claims with some veracity that through firsthand experience of living "much among them," he can "solemnly declare, that [he] never met with one *Jew*, who had any inclination to be converted." With rather less veracity and with no solemn declaration to uphold the libel, he can shortly after aver that the Jews are "all Infidels," who, in "their public and private Devotions . . . pray constantly for the sudden and univeral Extirpation of Christ's Kingdom, and of all his Christian Members." "Is not this," he adds, "as far as Hatred can go, without cutting our Throats?"[21] By merging the theological or doctrinal fact that they are not particularly receptive to conversionist rhetoric with the mythical belief that their ritual is intentionally subversive to Christianity, Romaine can invoke and give credence to the specter of the Jews rehearsing through prayer for their age-old avocation of ritual murder.

Similarly, in a curious variant to the traditional blood libel myth, the friction and bitter sense of loss felt by Jewish parents should an offspring become an apostate to Christianity is frequently represented in conversionist tracts by the imputation that they would rather put to death their own child than acquiesce to his or her conversion. So, Richard Kidder describes in vicious detail their obstinate behavior in refusing the profession of Christianity by one of their number:

> The *Jews* do not onely call by the opprobrious name of *Apostates*, but are wont to follow with the most direful and dreadful Execrations imaginable those who forsake *Judaism* and embrace *Christianity*. They teach that such an Apostate as this, *Shall have no part in the world to come;* That, *his sin shall never be forgiven, to eternal Ages.* They *spit at him,* They call *his Children Bastards, and his Wife polluted and defiled;* They refuse *to eat and drink with him;* They *Anathematize,* They *Curse him, three times a day, Morning and Evening,* And in this Curse, they pray that *he may be cut off from hope;* They *esteem him as an Epicurean and an Heretick;* They *contemn him and his Family, And decline all Affinities with them, be they never so wealthy;* They *insidiously lay wait for him;* Him *that kills him,* they *indemnifie,* and affirm, *that he needs not Repentance, but is to be esteemed as if he had brought about an Oblation.*[22]

Only at the tail end of an extensive account seemingly based on his own observation does Kidder, who in the same work denounces the inhumane treatment of the Jews during earlier times, acknowledge that it is all copied from the work of an apostate Jew, who had lived nearly 300 years before!

Another version of the same imputation appears in a short pamphlet, describing the persecution by the Jews of Elizabeth Verboon, the name taken after marriage and conversion by Eve Cohan, baptized at St. Martin's-in-the-Fields in London by Gilbert Burnet, Lord Bishop of St. Asaph, on October 10, 1680. According to the pamphlet, as Eve Cohan, the daughter of wealthy Jewish parents in Holland, she had been courted and won by Michael Verboon, a family servant, described as a Protestant, "descended of honest Parents, though but of a mean condition."[23] Her father being no longer alive, she had been threatened by her mother with poisoning (yet another crime traditionally associated with the Jews) if she changed her religion, and her brother and Jewish suitor had engaged in various abusive forms of vengeful mischief against her. In a report that is blatantly weighted against them, their villainous endeavors to prevent her from converting include having her imprisoned, manhandling her husband, and causing her to miscarry a "Conception [that] had been some days dead, and wasted within her" (21). But, ironically, the strongest presumption of the larger cosmic guilt of her aggrieved family, as exposed in the pamphlet, rests in their Jewishness: "those, whose Ancestors in Unbelief, had with so bloody a Malice crucified our Blessed Saviour, would have spared no invention of Mischief, to execute their Revenge on one, that was now resolved to believe in Him" (12). The author writes in a tone of admonition, warning his countrymen to be on their guard against this style of Jewish perfidy, which if no longer directed at those born of the Christian faith is still targeted against its neophytes:

> This Recital was thought necessary, to let the Nation see what a sort of People these Jews are, whom we harbour so kindly among us; who, as they yet lie under the guilt of that Innocent Blood, which their Fathers wished might rest on them and their Children: so continue not only in their obstinate Infidelity, but do still thirst after the Blood of such of their Nation as believe in Him whom their Fathers Crucified. (25)

In a supposedly more tolerant age, the traditional blood libel of the Middle Ages has been made once again credible by discreet redefinition. Instead of emphasizing the widespread belief that Jews indulge in the ritual murder of innocent Christian children, the transposed version of the myth, as we find it in conversionist discourse of the longer eighteenth century, has them seeking to kill apostates to Christianity, most particularly their own children.

When, more than forty years later, one Moses Marcus, the firstborn son of a Hamburg Jew who had made a fortune in the India trade, converted to the Protestant faith, he too was ostracized by his family. So determined, according to Marcus, was his father, now settled in London, to prevent him from conversion that he threatened that

> if I should turn Christian he would not allow me one single Farthing; but would rather spend a hundred thousand Pounds in Law against me, and would also seek Means that I should be destroy'd. And once he did almost effect it, by striking a Case-Knife at me; but I avoided the Blow, and it pleased the Almighty, that I came to no Mischief.[24]

In an eloquently written confession of faith, Marcus describes the predictable reaction to his conversion of his

> once most endearing and indulgent Parents, who spared for nothing of their precious Treasures, wherewith they abound, to make me Great and Happy in this World; but have now conceived a mortal Hatred to me, upon the Account of this religious Difference; and deny me Bread to eat, and Raiment to put on. By whom being rejected, I quickly found my self like a shipwrack'd Man, plunging in an Ocean of Hardships, under which in all human Appearance, I had utterly sunk, had not one of my Susceptors in Baptism, with the greatest Tenderness, took me under his Roof, where he still continues to entertain me, and supports me with the Necessaries of Life.
>
> When my Parents had reduced me to these melancholy Circumstances and imagined that the Bitterness of my Sufferings had shook my Resolutions, and brought me to repent of what I had done, they then courted me with the most advantageous Offers of a plentiful Share of their Substance, and a very agreeable Marriage, provided I would return to them and Judaism again. (viii–xi)

Despite his earnest protestations in favor of his new faith, Marcus appears to have succumbed to the bait, or at least attempted a reconciliation with his parents, since it is reported elsewhere that he soon after returned to Jewish worship, voluntarily residing for almost a year and a half in Holland, and publicly abjuring his Christianity before a synagogue congregation there. Nevertheless, this may not have been an entirely frank renunciation, for in 1726 he was still prepared to swear before an English court that he remained a Christian.[25]

From the standpoint of stereotyping, a significant feature of the published accounts of both the Verboon and Marcus conversions is the prominence given to the response of the parents, casting them in the primordially malevolent role that, by reflex or otherwise, is so often assigned to the Jews. If the immediate purpose of these tracts is to record the spiritual circumstances that led a person to Christian faith and joy, a secondary function only of little less consequence is to portray in a negative cast those who remain unenlightened. By imputing that the

Jews, in their unregenerate state, will resort even to infanticide rather than let their children convert, such accounts exacerbate traditional divisions. In each case, the threat of poisoning or of being stabbed with a case-knife (whether or not these actions really took place) is a convenient metonym by which to allege the compulsive reenaction by the Jews of a far greater iniquity. The cosmic menace of the unholy Jew as a crucifier and ritual murderer exacerbates the putative misdeed of a concerned parent into a potent and ungodly crime against humanity. His imagined omnipresence as the perpetual enemy of Christ attests to the Jew's incessant villainy. In demonstration of his Otherness, he is seen to block the way for the fledgling Christian. At her moment of greatest joy, when she was to be initiated into the Christian faith, Bishop Burnet tells us that Elizabeth Verboon caught sight of "a Jew in the Church, looking and laughing at her in the very time" that she was being baptized. Although we are assured that his unwelcome intrusion "did not a whit disorder her," the killjoy aspect of the Jew but underlines the larger external threat that he is presumed to pose.[26] His voyeuristic presence in church at her baptism connotes an inescapable evil.

That the allegation of ritual killing remained deeply ingrained in popular culture concerning the Jews is evident from a court case of 1732. In that year, one William Osborne, a printer with an address in the Minories, London, published a paper attesting in ugly detail how certain Portuguese Jews living near Broad Street had committed a heinous murder on a Jewish woman and her young child, the root cause of their alleged crime being that the infant was begotten by a Christian. The paper likewise claimed that their wicked action was common behavior among the Jews in these circumstances. After several vicious mob assaults in the vicinity of Broad Street and threats of death upon innocent Jews, a case was brought before the King's Bench against Osborne for publishing what transpired to be no more than a fictitious libel. Although the court ruled that the persons libeled were unknown and that no definite person had been defamed, it ordered that the paper be withdrawn and found Osborne punishable for having published a work that struck at "the whole community of the Jews . . . [by] necessarily tending to raise tumults and disorders among the people and inflame them with an universal spirit of barbarity against a whole body of men, as if guilty of crimes scarce practicable and totally incredible."[27] A further intention of the ruling may have been to make it that much more difficult in future to publish defamatory libels against the body of the Jews, although it has to be admitted that libels of this sort could easily be encoded in such a way as to make the precedent of the Osborne case ineffectual. For example, although the reference is far from specific, no one could mistake the slurring allusion in a pamphlet of 1753 to "a Crew of *Homicide unconverted Jews*" as anything other than a consciously nasty echo of the ritual murder libel.[28] Nor, it must be assumed, could a court ruling have much effect in eradicating the widespread belief in the validity of the libel shared by many English Christians, who would decipher the reference with little or no perplexity. Its association with conversionist discourse is one of the more unexpected ventilations of the blood libel encountered in the eighteenth century.

That unconverted Jews were supposedly by their nature given to vile behavior toward Christians was often seen as the unhappy consequence of their spiritual darkness. "They are a People," runs an early eighteenth-century conversionist tract, "who have stop'd their Ears that they might not hear the Truth, and have shut their Eyes lest they should see the light of the Gospel of *Jesus Christ*."[29] Their pernicious hatred, it was argued, could be traced back to biblical times, when their usage of apostates proved to be equally cruel and unenlightened. In particular, their treatment of St. Paul, spiritually the declared prototype for future converts, provided an apt exemplum of the continued fortitude necessary among Jewish proselytes to Christianity. "From the Time that St. *Paul* became a Christian Convert," asserts Archdeacon Stephens, "his Life was one continued Scene of Persecutions. . . . And the same Malice, the same Hatred, the same Bitterness of Spirit towards Christian Converts has continually reigned in the Hearts of the rigid *Jews* thro' all succeeding Generations."[30]

Despite the negative image that is so strenuously propounded in the rhetoric of conversion, most writers show little surface ambivalence in their expressions of desire to bring the Jews into the Protestant fold. As their eventual conversion (according to Christian exegesis) has been so clearly prophesied, at a minimum one must play along with their recalcitrance and, however impatiently, abide the time. "Like the lamb, lion and wolf which eat from one fodder," vouches a seventeenth-century proverb, "the Jew and the infidel will someday embrace Christ's Gospel."[31] Yet the perennial inability of the Jews to put aside their stiff-necked refusal of Christ as Messiah considerably raises the odds of their accepting the olive branch of conversion. As a rhetorical strategy, anti-Semitic writers are often only too ready to cast themselves in a more favorable light by offering what they instinctively realize will be (except rarely) tenaciously refused or ignored. In the ill-tempered and impassioned conflict of 1753 over whether to grant a right of naturalization, those most opposed to the Jews rarely deny them the prospect of conversion to the Christian faith as the one avenue that may consequently lead to English citizenship. The order of events, as Jonas Hanway knowingly informs us, remains clear-cut, with conversion a strict priority before any other considerations may begin. If, he says, a Jew "becomes a *christian*, it may give him a title to naturalization," but it will "certainly be no reason to a JEW to profess *christianity* merely because he is naturalized." "Would to God," adds Hanway, "they already possessed *that title*, that we might receive them into our bosoms!"[32]

It is not our duty, asserts another contemporary controversialist echoing St. Paul to the Corinthians, to be "*unequally yoked with Unbelievers*, . . . *making an* unnatural *Concord of Christ* with Belial," yet if the Jews "will once *lay aside their Unbelief*, and *receive Jesus* as the *Messiah*, it will be then Time enough to think of granting them their present Requests."[33] "The *Jews* in their *Judaism*," reports Archaicus, a pseudonymous pamphleteer, "are *Robbers*, Mat. iii. 37. *Traitors* and *Murderers*, Acts vii. 53. whom the *Divine Vengeance* pursues. . . . Neither is there any *Asylum* at all open to them, but *this one of Christianity*; to which they were invited in the Days of the *Apostles*, and are yet invited."[34] Notionally, the assumption of these and of other less polemically motivated writers and proselytizers throughout the period seems to be that in their moment of conversion the Jews will shed their diabolized selves and emerge spiritually cleansed from the waters of baptism. Their consecration into their new faith will somehow exorcize them of their inherited evil, since by it they will have at last willingly acknowledged the primacy of Christ as Messiah. "Such," maintains Archdeacon Stephens, "is a *Jewish Convert* when the Christian Religion is engrafted upon him; the Fierceness and Cruelty of the *Jew* is softened and converted into the better Fruit of Meekness and Gentleness."[35] "When converted," writes James Grant over a century later, "they almost, in every instance, become zealous and effective advocates of the cross and cause of Christ."[36] The cosmic threat of the Jew as Other, if we may believe these views, is at once miraculously attenuated through the transforming grace of conversion.

In actuality, good Christians though they may have become, their conversion from Judaism was more often than not a negative factor in determining their acceptance either by the host group that had so assiduously encouraged them into radically altering their spiritual and everyday lives, or by their former coreligionists who (as we have seen in the cases of Elizabeth Verboon and Moses Marcus) would painfully goad them to renounce their recent vows. In the popular image, the convert from Judaism is represented as one who, far from losing or relinquishing his Jewishness, has been translated into a living stereotype of marginality, one who because he cannot fully shed his Otherness may never fully be accounted a "real" Christian.[37] In almost all cases, his own spiritual acclimatization and his acculturation into the ways of English life are more immediate than his acceptance into a society for whom he remains either indelibly a Jew or, at best, a *Christian* Jew. His own perception of himself as a Christian is not necessarily fully shared by those whose religion he has just joined. The procrustean bed of the new convert is only partly of his own making. Perhaps no shrewder verbalization of his marginality may be found than that offered by the dramatist Richard Brinsley Sheridan in his ballad opera, *The Duenna* (1775), whose proselyte Jew, Isaac Mendoza, "a christian these six weeks," is declared by his unwilling inamorata as standing "like a dead wall between church and synagogue, or like the blank leaves between the Old and New Testament."[38]

The efforts from the time of their readmission to win over the Jews inevitably attracted converts whose motives were less than sincere. Bishop Kidder, for instance, rebukes the wretched misbehavior of those whose conversion to Christianity may have been prompted by ulterior causes. "Stories to this purpose," he declares, "are too well known. The fear of torments, the hope of Preferment and Gains, have prevailed with too many to profess the *Christian* Religion, who are still *Jews* in their hearts." He cites by way of example from his own experience:

> It is not many years since that I was informed, that there was a certain learned *Jew* who was desirous to become a *Christian:* but then he that informed me, added, That at present this *Jew* wanted some Pounds to redeem him out of Prison. I replyed that he should be redeemed thence, and the Money be deposited which he desired. I sent a very learned Man to the Prison to give me an account of the Man: He found him, and inquir'd of him upon what *Motives* he was inclined to turn *Christian*, he having declared his desire to change his Religion; but soon found that it was a Matter that he had never considered, and was not able to make any kind of Reply unto: It was all Artifice, to get money and relief.[39]

The intention of the anecdote is, of course, to delineate the equivocal conduct of a Jew attempting to seek release from prison by fraudulently posing as one who desires to turn Christian, and by extension to impute that this is by no means atypical behavior among his fellows. "I will not be so uncharitable," comments Kidder, "as to think they are all Hypocrites and bad Men; God forbid I should entertain such a thought: but I have too much cause to fear that too many of them are" (92). If not condemning them outright, the story clearly inculpates the Jews as insincere and untrustworthy partners in the business of conversion. Their moral code is shown here to be simply one of expediency. However, by its omissions, the story also admirably illustrates how, in their conversionist zeal and in the service of their own ends, Christian proselytizers often themselves employ moral criteria that may be deemed equally suspect. It is significant that at no time does Kidder question or seem to recognize the dubious morality inherent in his own action, of being prepared to pay for the Jew's freedom from jail (whatever his debts or wrongs) on the assumption that this may gain a convert. What kind of conversionist bribery is this? Does a Christian have a divine sanction to use whatever means to win the soul of a Jew? For all its homiletic intentions, the anecdote even fails to divulge whether, after the discovery of the Jew's perjury, the bishop could still agree to his release as a simple and unindebted act of mercy. The fate of the Jew has become unimportant once his false marginality has been exposed and his "true" self revealed.

Correspondingly, Christian attitudes toward those wealthy Jews, primarily of Sephardic descent, who chose to convert merely as a means of gaining social acceptance or preferment are also defined in terms of their marginality. The best-known Jewish financier in the middle years of the eighteenth century, Samson Gideon (1699–1762), not only took for himself a Christian wife but insured that all his children were baptized. However, in part because he himself never formally abandoned his Judaism but as much because of widespread hostility toward him, he had the greatest difficulty in finding an aristocratic wife for his half-Jewish son, despite the financial advantages to be gained by such a connection.[40] Horace Walpole's amusing sketch of the son's Christian education is indicative both of endemic attitudes and of the perplexity of a nine-year-old in coping with his mixed breeding:

> I must . . . tell you a story of Gideon. He breeds his children Christians: he had a mind to know what proficience his son had made in his new religion; "so," says he, "I began and asked him, who made him? He said, "God." I then asked him, who redeemed him? He replied very readily, "Christ." Well, then I was at the end of my interrogatories, and did not know what other question to put to him—I said, "Who— who—" I did not know what to say—at last I said, "Who gave you that hat?" "The Holy Ghost," said the boy."—Did you ever hear a better catechism?[41]

Some three-quarters of a century later, Isaac D'Israeli (the father of Benjamin) reminds us that even adult male converts to Christianity, who had been circumcised at birth in token of the covenant between God and his chosen people, are similarly perplexed in being forever reminded of their true ancestry. "The Jewish apostate," he writes, "is haunted, or betrayed by the indelible testimony, while the loyal Israelite who bears the sign proudly calls himself 'A son of the covenant.' "[42] Significantly, although he too never formally renounced the faith of his forefathers, Isaac D'Israeli had all four of his children baptized in 1817, the year after his own father had died. Given the religious barrier that prevented their political and social enfranchisement, it is perhaps understandable why many gentrified Jews and their families yielded to the trend of the ritual of baptism, even though for some it was hardly more than a matter of form. Caustic recognition of the apparent unassimilability of many of these anglicized Jews and the seeming lack of true conviction in their new faith invigorates Charles Lamb's complaint against such converts in one of his *Essays of Elia*, first published in the early 1820s:

> I boldly confess that I do not relish the approximation of Jew and Christian, which has become so fashionable. The reciprocal endearments have, to me, something hypocritical and unnatural in them. I do not like to see the Church and Synagogue kissing and congreeing in awkward postures of an affected civility. If *they* are converted, why do they not come over to us altogether? Why keep up a form of separation, when the life of it is fled? If they can sit with us at table, why do they keck at our cookery? I do not understand these half convertites. Jews christianizing—Christians judaizing—puzzle me. I like fish or flesh. A moderate Jew is a more confounding piece of anomaly than a wet Quaker. The spirit of the synagogue is essentially *separative*.[43]

For all his endeavors through the entry card of conversion to emulate the life and manners of the English gentleman, these examples help to illustrate that, in the popular perception, far from being able to escape his ethnic origins, the eighteenth-century upper-class Jew merely entrapped himself in his own marginality. If a distinction is sometimes made between a *Christian* Jew and a *real* Jew, the telling common factor is that they are both considered *Jews*. Neither, it is fair to say, has to suffer the indignity of complete ostracism by the host group, yet neither will be fully accepted as a social equal. At least for the real Jew the relationship between himself and the host group remains on both sides easier to define.

The spiritual and social dilemmas that oftentimes led the well-to-do Jew on the path to conversion are a far cry from the material poverty and hardship suffered mainly by his Ashkenazi brethren, who after 1750 made up at least three-quarters of the Jewish population of England. Their common avocation as pedlars and dealers in old clothes has already been discussed: their impoverished condition was often interpreted as visible evidence of God's neglect or punishment of those who, until their rebuttal and denial of Christ, had been his chosen people. The need to try to save these scattered vagabonds may not have been an immediate priority for those who explained their miserable plight as divine revelation of the near irredeemable spiritual darkness that had supposedly enshrouded them since biblical times. In its perverse way, the recognition that even these fallen souls might be made aware, through the hope that comes with conversion, of the sheer futility of enduring further suffering is symptomatic of the more liberalized disposition toward the Jews that gradually emerges during the latter years of the eighteenth century. To show love toward these debased creatures, the living descendants of those who had so grievously bloodied their hands and hearts, and to lead them out of their blindness, is veritably the apotheosis of Christian love, since it offers enduring forgiveness for an eternal sin. Few if any Christian messianists of the period seem troubled by the implicit paradox of such a position, whereby the Jews are at one and the same time both blessed and reviled. That the path of conversion was attractive only to a handful and that the rump of Jews remained unregenerate make it possible for such ambivalent attitudes to be held simultaneously. The contradictions are nevertheless inherent in the very rhetoric of conversion, as we shall now see by examining the work of J.S.C.F. Frey (1771–1850), the leading luminary of the early years of the London Society for Promoting Christianity among the Jews, founded in 1809 in response to the growing consensus of the necessity of such an apostolic mission.

As a German-born convert from orthodox Judaism, who claimed to have been trained in his former religion as a *chazan* (synagogue reader) and a *schochet* (ritual slaughterer of kosher meat), Joseph Frey considered himself particularly qualified to lead a movement with an impetus directed initially toward the Christian salvation of impoverished Ashkenazi Jews. Like St. Paul, to whom he often without modesty compares himself, he maintains that the experience of his own conversion has left him far more capable of sympathizing with the Jews and their predicament than other, Christian-born, philo-Semites. "He who has just been rescued from a dangerous fit of sickness," observes Frey, "feels more for a sick person than he who never knew what sickness means."[44] Throughout his writings, the Jews are usually referred to in endearing and familial style, for example, "my dear brethren of the house of Israel" or "my own brethren and kinsmen according to the flesh" (50, 52). Yet, for all the sweet talk, his actual depiction of them is in particularly negative terms. He stresses among other things their stubborn ignorance, their blaspheming of Christ, and the moral depravity of their private lives.[45] On evidence that remains unsubstantiated except in terms of his constant claim to "know" their ways and of remote biblical precedent, he is able, within a sentence of praising their close kinship, to invoke the conversionist myth of the Jews, making it a recurrent practice to murder those of their faith who become apostates to Christianity:

> In all my travels among different nations, I have never found a people more attached to each other, and ready to assist to the utmost of their power in every affliction, than I have witnessed among the Jews; and especially the ardent love and affection which subsists between parents and children. Yet I do not doubt the truth of the assertion, that even some parents have put to death some of their children because they would not renounce the name of Jesus with blasphemy.[46]

Frey explains this putative form of Jewish infanticide by reference to the patriarchal figure of Abraham, who, despite his tender love for Isaac, loved God still more and was accordingly prepared to kill his son as an act of obedience. "Even so," continues Frey,

> every Jew is commanded that if any of theirs should worship another God he is to be put to death, and believing Jesus to have been but a *mere man*, they look upon every Jew who professes Christianity, and consequently worshipping Christ as he does the Father, to be an idolater, and that therefore it becomes their duty as much as it was that of Abraham to put him to death. It should, therefore, not be considered strange or surprising to find that multitudes of the Jews, whose confidence in the present Judaism is shaken, and who feel a strong desire of inquiring into the evidences of Christianity, yet stifle their convictions for fear of the awful consequences. (5–6)

By simple psychology and convoluted logic, Frey attributes to the Jews en masse a secret desire to convert which only the threats of their rabbis and their own obduracy prevent from happening. He describes them as "everwhere hungering after the pure Word of God" (201), but unable to find fulfillment in the Old Testament alone. He imputes their abhorrence of Christ and hatred of Christian values to their education which deliberately cuts them off from the Gospels, and contends that only through conversion may they find the ultimate antidote to their present misery in the true happiness that belongs uniquely to the Christian faith.

Frey's arguments in favor of the conversion of the Jews, although more obsessive and repetitious in their mode of presentation, may be said to differ little from those of other Christian messianists of his age. They are distinguished only by the way in which they employ what is known as Jewish self-hatred, the pathological rejection of his Otherness in favor of the values of the host group, as a justification of the author's own spiritual conversion and subsequent career.[47] Frey's antipathy toward the Jews, combined with his acknowledgment of them as his brethren, presents a classic paradigm of self-hatred as a reflection of his own marginality. By endeavoring to be more Christian than even the Christians, he proclaims his stereotypical Otherness, albeit as a lapsed Jew. In his memoirs, he records how, after writing to his "dear parents" following his conversion to explain to them his unshakeable belief in "the Lord Jesus Christ as the true Messiah, the Son of God. . . . , they performed the same ceremonies as if they had been informed of my death, and never corresponded with me after that, and of course I was disinherited. But blessed be the Lord I have never wanted bread nor friends."[48]

If his conversion to Christianity caused his family to perform such obsequies, these appear as a very muted version of the fable of Jewish infanticide he invoked in the same memoir, yet his "death" as a Jew seems to have intensified his need to seek umbrage in his marginality as a *Christian* Jew, which, in early nineteenth-century England, he found he could often exploit to his own advantage. In his narrative, describing his first arrival from Germany as a convert from Judaism who could barely speak the language, he portrays the emotional effect upon an Anglican congregation at Fareham of his preaching to them from the New Testament in broken English ("Never in my life have I witnessed a scene like that morning; tears, like streams of water, flowed from every eye, and the people blessed and praised God for what they saw with their eyes, heard with their ears, and felt in their hearts"); and, later, he records the frequency with which Christians would accompany him on his missionary work simply for the vicarious pleasure of being able to witness a Jew inculcating his brethren with the Gospels (57–58, 65).

But by capitalizing on his marginal status as a Christian Jew, Frey seems to have more than once caught himself in a tenuous bind, whereby he was perceived to have behaved in a manner totally unbecoming for a Christian minister but stereotypically associated in the popular imagination with the Jews. In 1816, it was widely circulated that he had absconded with £3,000 that really belonged not to him but to the London Society for Promoting Christianity among the Jews. Similar charges were recurrent throughout his later life, despite Frey's strenuous and increasingly neurotic denials of the truth of these allegations (108,

160). In the same year, he was accused of breaking his marriage vows by involving himself in a tawdry affair with an ex-prostitute, the wife of one of his own converts, a liaison that he refrains from mentioning in his several memoirs. Whether or not he was guilty of such an immorality, the elders of the London Society chose to dispense with his services in that year, and Frey set sail to America, where he settled and was responsible for founding a close carbon copy of the London Society in the American Society for Meliorating the Condition of the Jews.[49]

The desperate methods Frey sometimes employed to attract converts among the Jewish poor during his seven years in the service of the London Society were also the subject of much debate and criticism. According to a pamphlet published shortly after his unseemly departure from England, Frey would charge his followers to ply the young Jewish street vendors of London by again and again purchasing their wares for many times their true value. When, as a consequence,

> the *snare-laid* youth *humbly* solicits to know to whom he is indebted for such mighty goodness. The answer is—*My dear child, this is nothing at all; I mean to make your fortune, if you take the FRIENDLY advice I shall give you,*—accompanying the last words with a guinea or two. Before the youth has time to recover himself from his surprise, he is informed that such a *lovely* fine lad would look handsome in a new suit of clothes, and that *if he will come next Sunday and hear Mr. Frey preach, he shall have as fine a suit as can be made.*[50]

It has been estimated, through studying the receipts of the London Society, which received widespread financial support for its mission, that the approximately 100 converts it claimed between 1809 and 1816 cost them on average a handsome £500 each person.[51] Even then, as a contemporary versifier humorously avers, many so-called converts of the London Society eventually reverted to their old faith or expediently took advantage of both:

> 'Tis true 'tis strange, and strange 'tis true,
> Cash *buys* but cannot *keep* a Jew.
> The meanest, trembling, bribed to lie,
> Back to the "God of Israel" fly. . . .

> So Cohen can both faiths unite,
> Still Jew, and yet a Christian quite;
> Receives the rites and pay of both,
> And serves two masters nothing loth.[52]

For all its millenarian ambitions and afflatus, the scale of success of the London Society in its venture to save the Jews was ultimately very limited. Although it created quite some disquiet and fear among those it sought to convert, its far greater effect was in galvanizing prevalent Christian attitudes toward the Jews by giving them for the first time an institutional focus. Many of those attitudes concerning conversion that we have seen elsewhere are subsumed in the early nineteenth century under the banner of the London Society.

Just as solicitation by missionaries caused more jitters than converts to Christianity among the Jews, so their renewed presence in England from the mid-seventeenth century became the seedbed for widespread and irrational fears of their counter-intent to apostatize the nation. That such hysterical deductions should emerge is one of the more surprising side effects of conversionist rhetoric, especially so when we recall that (except occasionally among its own) Judaism has never encouraged proselytism to the faith. In a curious way, the reiterated anti-Semitic charge that the Jews would stop at nothing to convert or "Judaize" the English may be interpreted as a distorted mirror-image of the message of Christian hope offered by evangelists to the survivors of God's biblical chosen people. That message, already frequent, becomes obsessive when viewed in reverse, portraying the Jews as willing to resort to vile practices and even to debauchery in their lust to seduce innocent Christian souls.

Despite the strict assurance made to Oliver Cromwell by Menasseh Ben Israel at the time of their readmission that the Jews had absolutely no desire to seek converts among the English,[53] it soon became part of the established furniture of anti-Semitic discourse to charge that they were already about their business of corrupting good Christians. As early as 1661, the controversialist Thomas Violet, whom we have elsewhere encountered as a bitter enemy of the Jews, alleges that

> since this Toleration many people have bin seduced, and the Iewes Exercise of their Religion, being every day solemnly kept in *London,* between seven and eight of the clock in the morning, and about three in the afternoon, multitudes of men and women seeking after novelties, and seduced by the devil, have been wavering in their Religion, and at length turned absolute Iewes, keeping Saturday for Sunday, and in many other Iewish Ceremonies are their Proselites.[54]

For all the considerable interest in their return, there is without doubt a great deal of exaggeration to this particular deposition against the Jews. An apparently less biased Christian witness, the schoolmaster John Greenhalgh, counted but one proselyte among a congregation of at least 100 Jews when he visited the synagogue at Creechurch Lane, Aldgate, in the following year.[55] Yet, according to some, proselytism had been rife among the Jews in all ages, to the extent that it was no longer possible to distinguish amid them those who were truly descended from their biblical forbears. The Reverend Charles Leslie, for instance, prefaces his popular and frequently reprinted conversionist treatise on the Jews by questioning the purity of the tribe:

> They have Intermarry'd with their Proselites of all Nations, and some-times with Others. Insomuch that they cannot be sure of one Jew now in the World, who is of the Pure and Unmix'd Blood of the Jews. Nay more, whether most of them, be not sprung from Proselytes of the Heathens, Mahometans, and Apostat-Christians.[56]

The issue of racial purity, such a telling factor against the Jews in the propaganda of a more recent period, rarely enters popular discussion in the eighteenth century. The more common reaction to their alleged conversionist tendencies is to wield the threat of punishment against those of the Christian faith putatively intending to become Jews. At its most hysterical, this manifests itself in calls that such proselytes to Judaism should be scourged from the state before they can contaminate others. "Why truly," avers an anonymous writer,

> if one, descending from English Parents should turn Jew, I verily think, for the Safety of our Religion, Honour of our Country, Good of the Publick and himself, he should be banished; lest he should infect others, breed his Children (for he either has, or may have some) in the same Principles, and so make them and their Descendents little Anti-christ's, and by this Means increase his own Damnation.[57]

Ironically, the punishment suggested here, by which an apostate to Judaism would be so totally ostracized as to be theologically given up for dead, differs little from that supposedly meted out by Jewish parents upon their Christian convert children. The imputation of infection by converts to Judaism links up very closely with similar fears of conspiracy by the Jews to take over both church and state.[58]

Indeed, although flying against all the historical evidence, so persistent was the wild rumor of the Jews seeking to convert the English that on a number of occasions during the eighteenth century, their defenders labored (almost certainly in vain) to try to quash its spread. For instance, a philo-Semitic author at the time of the Naturalization Bill of 1753 argues that as the Jews know full well that English Protestants already have their own established notions of salvation, it would be an illogical and futile endeavor to bind them by conversion to rituals that were never intended for them. In any case, he adds plainly, "the Jews can have no

View to give the Church the least Trouble," for the conservative truth remains that "they don't attempt making Proselytes."[59] A few years later, Edward Goldney Sr. recalls a conversation he once had with the late Aaron Hart (1670–1756), rabbi of the Great Synagogue in London from 1722 to his death, who maintained, on the anticonversionist rationale that each should be left to adhere to the faith of his birth, that "we English Jews, are not fond of gaining proselytes." "As for his part," records Goldney of this venerated spiritual leader, "his father, grandfather and great-grandfather were Jews; and . . . if it had been his fortune to have been born and bred a Mahometan, or in the principles of any other religion, he should have continued as such."[60]

The trickle of actual converts to Judaism in eighteenth-century England mainly comprised Christians, and usually women, who had intermarried. Even then, their passage to their new faith was far from easy, both because of the difficulty in traditional Judaism of recognizing marriage as a "reason" for conversion and also because (following the assurance of Menasseh Ben Israel) many English Jews, particularly those of Sephardi origin, seem to have understood it as a matter of honor if not of law that their resettlement forbade them from encouraging proselytism.[61] However, these self-imposed barriers rarely impinged upon popular belief. Much more common was the presumption, alluded to by Sarah Fielding in The Adventures of David Simple (1744), that, if a Christian woman would not accede to conversion to his faith, a Jew would rather take her as mistress or "obtain her on any other Terms than Matrimony." The unnamed "rich Jew" in Fielding's novel negotiates with the father of the young lady, the focus of his "great Passion," in the "hopes, that for a Sum of Money, he himself would sell her." Knowing "it to be impossible" to impose on a Jew and staggered by the immense sum offered, the father agrees to terms by which his daughter will convert as a condition of the marriage settlement. Her own compliance to change her religion being speedily assured by the "rich Presents the Jew made her, and his Promises of keeping her great," their marriage is shortly after "celebrated with great Pomp and Splendor." The passage to Judaism, though sweetened by bribes, exemplifies the patriarchal belief (expressed by the Jew) that "Women's Souls were of no great consequence, nor did it signify much what they profess." Belying (or rather ignoring) rabbinical injunction concerning intermarriage, the process of conversion here could hardly have been made easier.[62]

In reality and testimony of how fact can be sometimes far more complex than fiction, the most famous, perhaps the only famous, conversion to Judaism in the eighteenth century was that of George Gordon (1751–

93), a peer born in London of an ancient Scottish family. As an erstwhile ardent champion of Protestantism, Lord George had achieved considerable notoriety and, for a time, popular acclaim as a demagogue, for inciting the violent "No Popery" (or as they are more commonly known, "Gordon") riots of 1780, still recalled today as the historical setting of Dickens's novel, *Barnaby Rudge* (1841). When in 1787, having swum in and out of the public eye during most of the decade, he was prosecuted for having published a libel against Queen Marie Antoinette of France, Gordon disappeared before sentence could be passed. On his return to public attention only a few months later, a total transformation had taken place, for Lord George Gordon, the former leader of the Protestant Association, presented himself to the world with straggling reddish brown hair and an unkempt beard as a recent convert to Judaism. In embracing his new faith, he seems to have lost nothing of his former religious zeal, for as a Jew he was, if anything, even more conspicuous in his observance and practice. Stories abound, some of them discernibly magnified, reporting his entrance into Judaism by painful circumcision during the period of his absence, his subsequent arrest in the house of a poor Birmingham Jew where he had come to study the Talmud, his adamant refusal to allow entrance into his cell at Newgate (in which, following sentencing, he was incarcerated) to any male Jew who had his chin shaved clean, his insistence on being served only kosher victuals by his jailers, and his keeping in permanent attendance two Jewish handmaidens to answer his every private whim.[63] In innumerable pamphlets, ballads, and caricatures, Gordon is depicted in all his outlandish eccentricity as a spoof of the popular perception of what constitutes a Jew. In the print *Moses Chusing His Cook* (1788) by the Hanoverian artist Johann Heinrich Ramberg, we see a bearded Lord George in Newgate gaol surrounded by a *minyan* (a quorum of ten males for prayer) of devout Ashkenazi Jews, some obsequiously offering their noble proselyte a rarefied selection of the finest kosher delicacies, while others indignantly chase away the prison cook who has brought in a platter containing a suckling pig. Gordon and the English cook are the only figures not caricatured, thus exaggerating the incongruity and sense of Otherness of the grotesque crowd of Jews unctuously trying to please their latest convert.[64] Similar prints portray Gordon dressed as an Ashkenazi pedlar, underlining the metamorphosis from noble lord to disreputable Jew.[65] "And wonder not," goes the verse caption of one such caricature, "he stole to misbelievers, / Since they of stolen things are oft receivers."[66]

On the theme of a Christian turned Jew, ballads of the period also disparagingly play upon the negative outcome of Gordon's conversion,

Johann Heinrich Ramberg, *Moses Chusing His Cook.* Engraving, 1788.
(Courtesy of the British Museum, Department of Prints and Drawings.)

from which, according to one versifier, he may only be brought to his
senses by the old anti-Hebraic nostrum of anointing him with swine's
grease:

> To a Jew he turn'd, with beard long as a goat,
> The Mosaical law he has now got by rote.

What a glorious defender of Protestant laws!
With pork or fat bacon I'd well rub his jaws.[67]

Despite the tirades of ridicule, Lord George adhered to his new faith with all the resolution of an inspired enthusiast until his premature death from a fever in 1793. He was never released from Newgate. Public reaction to his conversion and subsequent imprisonment, transforming him from a maverick aristocrat into a figure of derision, provides a litmus of prevalent stereotypical attitudes toward those few (but rumored to be many) who became Jewish proselytes in eighteenth-century England. These attitudes infuse Edmund Burke's scornful dismissal of his sometime friend in his *Reflections on the Revolution in France* (1790). The richly allusive passage defending Queen Marie Antoinette of France against her libelers and the mob only fully makes sense if we recognize how insidiously it echoes popular sentiment regarding Gordon's conversion to Judaism:

> We have Lord George Gordon fast in Newgate; and neither his being a public proselyte to Judaism, nor his having, in his zeal against Catholick priests and all sort of ecclesiastics, raised a mob (excuse the term, it is still in use here) . . . have preserved to him a liberty, of which he did not render himself worthy by a virtuous use of it. We have rebuilt Newgate, and tenanted the mansion. We have prisons almost as strong as the Bastile, for those who dare to libel the queens of France. In this spiritual retreat, let the noble libeller remain. Let him there meditate on his Thalmud, until he learns a conduct more becoming his birth and parts, and not so disgraceful to the ancient religion to which he has become a proselyte; or until some persons from your side of the water, to please your new Hebrew brethren, shall ransom him. He may then be enabled to purchase, with the old hoards of the synagogue, and a very small poundage, on the long compound interest of the thirty pieces of silver . . . the lands which are lately discovered to have been usurped by the Gallican Church. Send us your popish Archbishop of Paris, and we will send you our protestant Rabbin.[68]

By addressing his remarks to a young French admirer who had sought his views on the Revolution, Burke stresses the aberrant nature of Gordon's neglect of his hereditary responsibilities in favor of the values of the mob and implies that such behavior will never be deemed acceptable in England. In France, on the other hand, where the *Assemblée Nationale* had recently voted for the naturalization of the Jews and also the confiscation of church lands, it is hardly surprising that the confused rabble are calling for the execution of their bishops. By adopting or converting to the values of the Jews, the French have contrived their own downfall as a civilized nation, whereas in England the most notorious proselyte to Judaism has been locked up and the status quo protected. As an oratorical tour de force, the passage brilliantly defends native English values against a combination of French mayhem and Jewish dealing. It exploits exactly the perceived sense of difference between the host group and Other by portraying Lord George as a proselyte not simply to Judaism but, by corollary, to the cumulative forces of anarchy, of which he as a seasoned rabble-rouser is truly no novice. As we have noticed, the imputation that conversion to Judaism may be a threat to the very fabric of church and state is not new, but its rhetorical employment to telling effect in this famous passage reveals how deeply such a belief is embedded in eighteenth-century popular culture.[69]

On a more intimate level, it was also commonly believed that the Jews found means to undermine the fabric of English society by taking innocent Christian women as their mistresses and thus seducing them to their faith. The charge of Jewish lasciviousness may be traced back to ancient times,[70] although its combination with the calumny that they actively employ their sexual prowess for the purpose of "Judaizing" is a later refinement. Because in its combined form the charge is so impossibly farfetched, it is almost always presented in a manner that is nonspecific, more a general libel against the Jews than necessarily a particular accusation against an individual. So John Tutchin early in the eighteenth century merely offers by way of unpleasant speculation that it "may not be amiss to enquire, what *Jews* there are in *England,* who Cohabit with *Christian Women,* and how many *Christians* have been perverted to *Judaism* for some Years last past."[71] And, an anonymous pamphleteer of the late 1730s indiscriminately charges that the Jews may without warning use their wealth and riches to further their nefarious seductions. They are, he writes,

> possess'd of Jewels and other Curiosities, with which Women may be easily tempted, and which, indeed, are dangerous Instruments in the Hands of Men less skill'd in the Arts of Corruption and Debauchery than the *Jews,* who of all People in the World, understand them best.[72]

Their licentious hankering after diamonds and damsels infuses Alexander Pope's well-known couplet in praise of Belinda's complexion in *The Rape of the Lock* (1714):

> On her white Breast a sparkling *Cross* she wore,
> Which *Jews* might kiss, and Infidels adore.[73]

The double entendre leaves it open to prurient question whether Pope's amorous Jews aspire to the cross or to Belinda's breast.[74] Conversion (or a blasphemous mimicry of it) and sexuality are ingeniously confused.

The effect of naturalizing the Jews, it is argued by extension, will be to corrupt and defile not just womankind but the populace at large. "The probability of their being converted to the *Christian* faith," avers a writer of 1753, "seems to bear no proportion to that of their debauching the minds of *Christians* by their immoralities, for which they are so remarkably distinguished."[75] If trying to pin these "immoralities" to the behavior of contemporary Jews proves largely unfeasible, tales told about their depravity are not infrequently invigorated by chapter and verse reference to episodes from the Bible, which could be read as an ongoing record of "their roguish fornicating tricks."[76] For example, the revenge meted by the sons of Jacob on the family of Shechem the Hivite, who had defiled their sister (Genesis 34), forms the basis for a bizarre parable in the *London Evening-Post*, also of 1753, in which the Jews are depicted as lascivious betrayers, who, not satisfied with having deflowered the maidens of England, proceed to circumcise their menfolk and "whilst their Private Parts were sore, . . . took up their Swords, and slew every Male of the Britons."[77] Similar attitudes are as commonly encountered in visual representation. In the mezzotint, *One of the Tribe of Levi Going to Brakefast with a Young Christian* (1778), a rich Jew, like the biblical Solomon, is seen in his drawing room admiring an opulently bedecked courtesan that his procuress has just presented to him. On the walls behind where he sits hang pictures of biblical (or possibly classical) scenes, showing the ravishment of young women. The lavishness of the décor belies the sordid nature of the liaison.[78] In another print, *The Jew Rabbi Turn'd to a Christian* (1772), a rabbi in oriental dress is making up to a richly attired Christian woman, who holds a cordial glass in one hand and a moneybag in the other. The implication is that her seduction is expedited by inebriation but has been bought for cash. The lovers' eyes are locked in each other's gaze so that neither is made aware of the emblematic presence of the horned devil voyeuristically staring down at them from a mounting on the wall. The "conversion" of this particular Christian, we are made to believe, has been fully sanctioned by the underworld. The visual iconography of her seduction betokens a greater moral threat of the Jew in his traditional role as a desecrator of fundamental Christian values.[79]

Those few writers who endeavor to vindicate the Jews from the variety of pernicious falsehoods concocted against them in conversionist discourse have most difficulty in dispelling the charge of Jewish immorality. Some, like the Reverend Josiah Tucker, a staunch supporter of

One of the Tribe of Levi Going to Brakefast with a Young Christian.
Mezzotint, 1778. (Courtesy of the Library of the Jewish Theological
Seminary of America.)

The Jew Rabbi Turn'd to a Christian. Mezzotint, 1772. (Courtesy of Mr. Alfred Rubens, London.)

the principles of the Naturalization Bill, simply counter by reminding us that sexual depravity is far from being the province of the Jews alone. It is apprehended, he writes, that

> if foreign *Jews* were permitted to settle in *England* . . . they would corrupt us.—Corrupt us, Sir! In what Instances? And what vicious Principles or immoral Practices can they introduce from abroad, for which *England* is not infamous already? For indeed, there is no Country under the Sun, where Vices of all Kinds reign so triumphantly, or where the Christian religion is so outrageously attacked. Therefore, bad as *unconverted Jews* are, surely they are not worse than *apostate* [lapsed] *Christians;* and these are all of our own Growth, true *English-born* Subjects.[80]

Others accept their immorality almost as a kind of sine qua non in describing the Jews, but account for it in terms of their religion and background, as explained in a rather stumbling defense by an anonymous advocate of the Jew Bill:

> Some of their Vices are the natural Consequences of their Habits and Manners; their Religion, by the Detestation it inculcates of the Crime of Sodomy, and its Indulgence of Polygamy, in great part accounts for their amorous Disposition, to which, if we join their being generally descended from Inhabitants of warmer Climates, this will fully account for their Propensity to that Vice; they are nevertheless, very seldom guilty of Adultery.[81]

In defending the Jews, such writers seem unable to refute the charge of immorality except in qualified terms, suggesting that the belief was too deep-rooted to be simply contradicted. Although it encroaches into conversionist discourse in an almost ubiquitous assumption among the propagators of anti-Semitic diatribe that, given the opportunity, Jews would willingly seduce others to their faith, it belongs as much to wider beliefs that their ceremony and ritual involve practices that were equally heinous. To these we shall turn our attention in a separate chapter.

CHAPTER 6

CEREMONIES

A PROSE EPISTLE tucked among others in a mid-eighteenth-century poetical miscellany and purportedly written by Onesimus, a Christian, to Eleasar, a Jewish rabbi, furnishes an apposite prologue to the present chapter. In directly addressing his rabbinical correspondent, the fictitious Christian rues the present state of the Jews in England, who despite their acceptance into "a Land where strong, meridian Light beams around thee" remain "still wandering in the Desart of *Supersti-tion*, darkened in thy *Heart*, as all thy *Fathers* were." The Jews, he claims, while continuing to be solidly impervious to the redemptive virtues of Christian grace and compassion, are perpetually laboring to lead others into the selfsame "Snares of palpable *Error*" that have cast them in a never-ending state of spiritual darkness. Indeed, Eleasar the rabbi is portrayed within the letter as zealous in his endeavors to persuade Onesimus to have himself circumcised as a pledge of Christian submission to the "rigorous *Law*" of Judaism. Gesturing to absurdity, Eleasar is represented as armed with his "Instruments of *Circumcision*" and energized by the brutal conviction that the Almighty will be "propitiated by *Foreskins*, . . . *Sacrifices* with which he [God] is *pleased*." Jewish ritual in the postbiblical world is depicted as subversive and persecutory, its adherents seen as blindly obdurate in their anachronistic refusal or inability to appreciate that "true" salvation may be accorded even to them if they were but to convert to Christianity: "That Yoke of *Rites* and *Ceremonies* which was once imposed on thy *People* for wise Purposes, and which they now submit to without Reason, thou not only bearest with a *Camel-like Patience*, but thou kickest at every one who would ease thee of thy *Load*."[1]

In contriving a view of the Jews as compulsive circumcisers, obstinate as those beasts of burden deemed by pentateuchal writ as unclean to their faith (Lev. 11:4), Onesimus's letter, consciously or otherwise, reflects the inherent nature of anti-Semitic discourse that thrives upon exacerbating the sense of dissimilarity and the appearance of hostility between Christian and Jew. Where (as we saw in the previous chapter) philo-Semitic conversionist texts are commonly disposed to stressing similitude between the two faiths and their respective adherents, the more virulent rhetoric employed by opponents of the Jews is emphatic in its amplification of difference.

It will be recalled that, even during the more than 350 years when they were forbidden settlement, the abusive conjunction of Jews with unclean animals and with creatures less than human is an established feature of English anti-Semitic allusion. During the period following their readmission, no less than in the previous age, the expression of difference may still find focus by degrading the Jews to the level of the bestial. The Bible and sacred texts, to the evident relish of anti-Judaic writers, provide a veritable menagerie by which to engender invidious comparison. A citation in a verse from Paul to the Philippians to an animal considered unclean—"Beware of dogs, beware of evil workers, beware of concision" (3:2)—can lead to the grotesque exegesis that this should be understood for later ages as an appropriate "Apostolic Warning to Christians, to avoid the Jews, under Terms of extreme Malediction and Reproach, viz. 'Beware of *Dogs* . . . an impure Animal, representing the *unclean Reprobates* that are cast out of the Church.'"[2] Elsewhere, in similar vein, the Jews are compared to ravenous wolves preying upon innocent Christian sheep.[3] Drawing upon the reptilian world, they are sometimes equated with snakes and serpents. A polemicist of 1753, by way of dismissing the allegations in their favor that "the *modern Jews* have lost much of *the old Jewish Venom*" parabolizes that

> it may be advisable to remember that a *Serpent* when *benumm'd* and *render'd Unactive* with the *Cold*, is still what he was, a *Serpent*; and if you bring him into *your House*, and *cherish* him a little with the kindly *Warmth* of your *Fire*, he will soon recover his *Serpentine Qualities*, to fill all the Place with his Hissings, and, perhaps, drive you out of your own Habitation.[4]

As "the most *Implacable Enemies* of the *Christians*," they are portrayed by a writer early in the century as infidels, who, congenitally attracted to their own, "Love a *Turk*, a *Heathen*, a *Barbarian*, nay, a *Toad* better than they do a *Christian*."[5] By analogy with insects, they are represented as an infestation of locusts overwhelming and engrossing both church and state. "And as Locusts are to Corn," avers one writer in quasi-biblical vein, "so are the Jews to Christians; the former consumes the Grain, and the latter undermine the Commonwealth."[6] "I verily believe," echoes a pamphleteer writing from London during the political controversy of 1753, "that if the Naturalization Bill should occasion a second Swarm of this Kind of Locusts to come and settle in the Town, we should have a Kind of Plague or Sickness as often as they have at *Constantinople.*"[7]

Although the function of these analogies is to reduce the Jews to the level of predatory or unclean beasts and to view them as irredeemable in their hostility to Christianity, it would be difficult to argue that such comparison, with its insistent biblical overtones, goes much beyond being a form of rhetorical gambit by which to exacerbate existing differences. If far less frequently, philo-Semitic writers will also employ a similar language to describe not the supposed nefariousness but the chronic suffering of the Jews down the ages. The Deist John Toland, for example, in recording the cruelties and barbarities of Christians against Jews in former times, remarks: "Very often they [the Jews] were massacred by thousands, without the least cause pretended: all sense of humanity being cast off to such a degree, as if the *Jews* had been but silly sheep, and their enemies ravenous Wolves."[8]

It is interesting that Toland can employ an identical quasi-biblical metaphor for completely opposite purposes to those of the avowed enemies of the Jews. Such references are far from static indices by which to denigrate one particular group. A parallel study (that has just been published) of anti-Catholic allusions in English Protestant texts of the same period unfolds impressively the use of similar metaphors, containing resonances of the text of the Bible, as a means of belittling the Church of Rome.[9] The flexibility with which such images are employed makes them fairly haphazard units by which to denote ethnic or religious difference. Out of context, it would be close to impossible for most readers to associate these references to camels, dogs, wolves, serpents, locusts, and so on, specifically with the Jews rather than with any other group under rhetorical assault.

Only in the abusive conjunction of Jews with a certain common domestic or, more properly, farmyard animal, forbidden to them by biblical code and expressly proscribed by their dietary laws, is it possible to argue that an association is forged in the popular imagination that, however perversely, links God's chosen people with unclean beasts. The injunction prohibiting the Jews from partaking of the meat of this particular animal appears most prominently in Leviticus 11:7–8, describing to them what beasts they may or may not consume:

And the swine, though he divide the hoof, and be clovenfooted, yet he cheweth not the cud; he *is* unclean to you.

Of their flesh you shall not eat, and their carcase shall ye not touch: they *are* unclean to you.

For all the fundamental ignorance in eighteenth-century popular culture concerning their everyday ceremonies and rituals, at least two main facts, each deriving from the Bible, remained well known about the religion of the Jews, namely that they were forbidden the eating of swine's flesh and that several days after birth their male children were subjected to circumcision. As we shall see, awareness of these facts became conjoined in anti-Semitic discourse with a third belief or common superstition, deriving in this case from the Middle Ages, that they actively sought and employed Christian blood for the fulfillment of their sacrificial rites. Despite the existence of works of scholarship that strove with varying degrees of accuracy to detail the actualities of their religious practice,[10] these three notions formed the piecemeal linkage for the refinement of a number of outlandish beliefs about the Jews and their ceremonies. The bizarre "alternative" ritual and barbaric observance ascribed to them will form the subject of the present chapter.

Echoes of the known abhorrence of the flesh of the swine among Jews verge upon the proverbial in English usage. "Do not conceive that antipathy between us," pronounces a character in Ben Jonson's play, *Every Man in His Humour* (1616), "as was between Jews, and hogs-flesh."[11] In corresponding thespian vein almost a quarter of a century earlier, Christopher Marlowe has his Jew, Barabas, dismiss those of the faith he abominates as "swine-eating Christians."[12] A proverb recorded by Thomas Fuller in 1732 but probably in parlance at least a century and a half before posits by way of cautionary advice, "Invite not a Jew to pig or pork."[13] Alexander Cruden, the eighteenth-century minister who compiled the famous Concordance to the Authorized Version, reflects the correct or legitimate Christian understanding of a familiar Jewish prohibition when he describes the swine as "an animal well known, the use of which was forbid to the Hebrews. . . . It is said, they had the flesh of this animal in such detestation, that they would not so much as pronounce its name, but instead of it said, *That beast, That thing.*"[14]

Consciousness of this particular dietary prohibition rather than any other provides a habitual butt for jocular allusion to the Jews. In Shakespeare's *The Merchant of Venice,* so tellingly rediscovered on stage during the eighteenth century as we shall see in the next chapter, we find the newlywed Jessica, Shylock's errant daughter, banteringly reproaching her Christian husband that "in converting Jews to Christians, you

raise the price of pork."[15] By quick sample of some of the more conspicuous (out of a host of often tediously strained or plain silly) references
of a similar kind in eighteenth-century writing, the following may be
cited. A fictitious epistle in *The Spectator* describing degrees of incongruity between dress and behavior among several fashionable personages
attending a masquerade includes one in the habit of "a Jew [who] eat me
up half a Ham of Bacon."[16] A passing comment in an actual epistle of
Thomas Gray, the poet, to his longtime correspondent, Horace Walpole,
reverberates with dismissive irony: "As to the Jews (though they do not
eat pork) I like them because they are better Christians than Voltaire."[17]
In revealing to his readers his opinion concerning the pathetic fate of Cor-
poral Trim's brother, Tom, who, before the auto-da-fé at Lisbon had married a "Jew's widow," Sterne's Tristram Shandy offers by way of meager
solace: "Had it pleased God after their marriage, that they had but put pork
into their sausages, the honest soul [Tom] had never been taken out of his
warm bed, and dragg'd to the inquisition."[18] The Jews, it is maintained by
Charles Johnstone in his novel, *Chrysal* (1760–65), will always make the
best butchers for bacon and sausages since, unlike their Christian counterparts, "they never cut out the nice bits to eat themselves."[19] An incidental anecdote recorded by James Boswell, concerning Dr. William
Barrowby, tells how the latter in his great fondness for swine's flesh jested
that he wished he were a Jew. On being asked why, when the Jews were
themselves forbidden to eat of his favorite meat, his reply was that he
"should then have the gust of eating it, with the pleasure of sinning."[20] In
all these examples, recognition of their abhorrence of pork has created a
deliberately incongruous metonym by which their difference as Jews is
made unsubtly conspicuous, albeit for an intended comic or sardonic effect.

By extension, perhaps as a grotesque reflection of the eccentric belief
shared by many Christians that despite their obduracy the Jews actually
nurtured a deep desire to convert, it was not uncommon to depict them
as secret lovers of pork, openly despising that for which they supposedly
had the greatest craving. At its most extreme, the presumed Jewish hungering after the flesh of the swine or (as it has become known) the *Judensau* had long been a common motif in the iconography of German
anti-Semitism. Isaiah Shachar, who made a particular study of the
theme, shows that what was originally a Christian allegory of vice became over the centuries a potent stereotype of anti-Semitic abuse. He
describes the visual representation, mainly in German prints and ecclesiastical statuary, of this disgusting motif:

> The stereotypic character ... of the *Judensau* was chiefly due to its
> aggressive obscenity. It is noticeable that, in spite of local and period

variations, all examples of the motif share clear common features of rudimentary obscenity. The sucking [by the Jews] of the sow's teats is shown in all but two, which show the sow embraced and kissed. Additional occupation with the animal's hind quarters, and the eating and drinking of its excrement, are shown in most.[21]

So prevalent was the acceptance of this abominable stereotype that in many German states it was well into the late eighteenth century, according to reports published in England a few years after, before attempts were made to abolish a despicable highway toll levied indiscriminately on the passage of pigs and itinerant Jews.[22]

Even though it is unusual to find the stereotyping of Jews as idolaters of pork emulating the unpalatable extremes so deep-rooted in traditional German delineations of the motif, it would be a mistake to suppose that Hanoverian England was in any special sense immune to the obscenities associated with the *Judensau*. English representation of the Jews' supposed private appetite for the pig and its flesh is sufficiently prevalent, particularly in graphic caricature, to leave little doubt as to its acceptance as a facet of popular lore concerning their habitual behavior and religious custom. Thomas Rowlandson's print, *Humours of Houndsditch, or M*rs *Shevi in a Longing Condition* (1813) depicts an Ashkenazi dealer in old clothes who has set out to gratify his wife's carnal impulses by purloining for her a sow and its litter of seven piglets. We see him, one arm affectionately around her plump shoulder, holding before her a fine young suckling pig that she kisses with an almost uninhibited eroticism. As she leans across the doorway, with her wanton breast, pouting lips, and closed eyes, Mrs. Shevi all too obviously incarnates in her "longing condition" those bestial instincts associated in popular belief with the Jews. Her promiscuous indulgence with the piglet denotes a brutishness that is less than human except shared by others of her faith, as may be seen by the complicity of her husband and the bejeweled woman companion standing behind her admiring the porker and perhaps awaiting her own turn. The leaning figure in the adjacent window or doorway may be, as Dorothy George proposes, "an elderly Jew . . . registering outraged horror," although iconographically his forelock and goatee beard indicate that Rowlandson wishes us to recognize in him the voyeuristic face of the Devil grimly sanctioning the lascivious behavior before him.[23] The supposed irrepressible hankering among Jews after the flesh of the pig rarely renders itself in England in a manner more explicitly immoral.

In another print of the same period, *Suitors to the Pig Faced Lady* (1815), George Cruikshank portrays a Jewish old-clothes dealer among an unsuitable crowd of would-be bridegrooms to a fabulously wealthy Christian heiress, unhappily blessed with a hideously porcine visage.

Thomas Rowlandson, *Humours of Houndsditch.* Engraving, 1813.
(Courtesy of Mr. Alfred Rubens, London.)

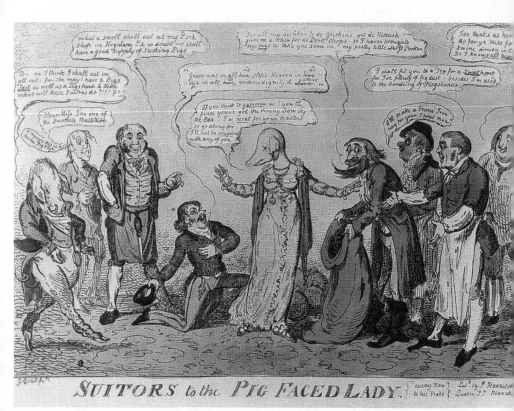

George Cruikshank, *Suitors to the Pig Faced Lady*. (a) Engraving. 1815;
(b) detail of same. (Courtesy of Mr. Alfred Rubens, London.)

Here, the Jew standing to her immediate right with his familiar sack held
open to receive her, his beard erect to define his state of arousal, exclaims, "For all my dislikes to de Griskins—yet de Monish gives me a
relish for de Pork Chops—so I have broughts mys *bags* to take you home
in . . . my pretty little Miss Porker." She responds, "If you think to *gammon* me? you'll find you've got the Wrong Sow by the Ear." The caricature bespeaks a more common attitude toward the Jews in its light-
hearted reflection of the longstanding belief that they remain persistently impervious to any distinction between venal and sensual desires,
as well as importunately desirous of precipitating any liaison, however
incongruous, with a Christian maiden.[24]

As a folk motif, tales recounting the unsuccessful wooing of a legendary pig-faced heiress may be traced back at least to the mid-
seventeenth century, and the association with the Jews seems to have

been established early on. According to one version of this inveterate tale, the divine punishment that is meted upon a certain luckless English Christian, who embraced Judaism supposedly at about the time of the readmission controversy, was that his first child born following conversion, a daughter, was pig-faced. Unable to express his paternal love by kissing or touching her through fear as an observant proselyte to Judaism of coming in contact with an unclean beast, and after suffering in trepidation for many years, he eventually consults a Dutch monk, who advises that the only antidote to his plight is for both father and daughter to undergo conversion to Christianity. Miraculously, if at the same time predictably, the instant the girl is baptized her porcine visage vanishes to be replaced by a numinous human one.[25] The inevitable conclusion to the tale adds further weight to our earlier contention that the secret love of the pig attributed to the Jews may be read as replicating a perverse Christian belief in their ferociously stifled but supposedly irrepressible desire to convert to the true faith.

Arising out of this widely held conviction that despite their stated abhorrence the Jews were actually covert lovers of pork, it was sometimes assumed in popular lore that forced feeding could be used as a crudely effective means of expediting their conversion to Christianity. The biblical example of Eleazar the scribe, who had suffered a horrid death rather than be constrained to eat swine's flesh (see 2 Macc. 6:18–31), may not have been too well remembered in eighteenth-century England but similar stories echo an implicit belief that impelling a Jew to partake in what his religion forbade him was tantamount to converting him. The verse text to Thomas Bonner's print, *The Conversion of Nathan* (1764), iterates just such a theme:

A wandering Levite who visited Fairs
A dealer in Penknives and such Sort of Wares
At a little Hedge Ale House fell deep in dispute
With a Butcher of Swine a Man of Repute
After Canvassing o'er the Mosaical Laws
Old Customs and soforth they came to the Cause
Why Hoggs Flesh to Jews was so horrid a treat
When Christians esteem'd it most Excellent Meat
But Nathan whose System put a side all his Art
On Bacon and Pork was now somewhat too tart
Swore Christians were fools & D—m the whole Nation
Which (soon fill'd) the Butcher with terrible Passion
He brandish'd his Cudgell—the Jew on his Knees
Frighted out of his Sences would his wrath fain appease
But on this Condition the Butcher relents

To instant turn Christian, poor Nathan Consents
But what could be done n'er a Priest to be got
When the Butcher conceiv'd a most excellent thought
A Yard of Pork Sausage to carry the farce on
Shou'd make him a Christian as well as a Parson
That this was not legal the Jew would have pleaded
But he saw the strong Cudgell—so Silent proceeded
All the folks were call'd in to behold the droll sight
Sure there ne'er was a Scene of such mirth & delight
The sanctified Morsel at length having eaten
He became a Stanch Christian & so sav'd his Bacon.[26]

In the crowded but uncomplicated illustration to which the text is an accompaniment, a fraternity of good folks in their cups rowdily celebrate Nathan's enforced conversion. With the "butcher of swine" standing menacingly over him, the terrified Jew is down on one knee, his traveling box of penknives and cheap spectacles laid to the side, while a young boy points at him in derision and feeds him the last of a long string of pork sausages.[27] It is not known whether the print is based, however loosely, upon an actual incident although, sadly, the base treatment of Jews in this or similar ways was far from uncommon. Traveling toward Bath in 1793, Thomas Telford, the architect, records paying for bread and cheese for a ragged German Jew to avert the brawny landlord of an alehouse, who "all at once with his formidable Knife—sliced off above a pound of raw Bacon from a ham which hung over our head, and swore that . . . he [the Jew] should swallow that Bacon raw as it was."[28] Almost a quarter of a century earlier, the *Annual Register* catalogues the conviction of Abel Prosser at Monmouth Assizes "for barbarous treatment to a poor Jew"; he had roasted his victim (most likely an itinerant pedlar) by tying his hands behind his back, sitting him before a large fire, and stuffing hot bacon down his throat.[29] In yet another recorded case, heard before the Lambeth Street magistrate toward the end of our period in 1824, Joseph Jones, a donkey driver, was accused of an attempted assault upon Leah Meldola, the daughter of the Haham (chief rabbi) of the Sephardi community, having allegedly tried to force her into a nearby house to eat pork. The case, brought by the young lady's father against Jones and the woman who owned the house, was summarily dismissed by the presiding magistrate, the Reverend Mathias, as "frivolous," and the plaintiffs themselves were castigated for belonging as Jews to "a quarelling people" and reprimanded for having wasted the court's time.[30] It must be assumed that similar incidents were not unusual, although, given the demeaning nature of such a case and the difficulty of

Thomas Bonner, *The Conversion of Nathan.* Engraving, 1764. (Courtesy of the Library of the Jewish Theological Seminary of America.)

obtaining a successful prosecution, but rarely tested in the courts and by consequence only exceptionally preserved for our much later attention.

Nevertheless, to threaten to grease a Jew's beard or chin with pork fat was to become by the end of the eighteenth century a near proverbial means of taunting or humiliating him. "With pork or fat bacon I'd well rub his jaws" runs a line from a ballad of 1788 ridiculing the conversion to Judaism of Lord George Gordon.[31] A few years earlier, the *Gentleman's Magazine* summarizes the outcome of a case brought before the Quarter Sessions at Westminster, in which a Jew was awarded damages of £10 after a woman who kept a public house was found guilty of assaulting him and greasing his chin with pork.[32] Sir Walter Scott perhaps alludes, albeit distantly, to the same practice in *Ivanhoe* (1819), set in the reign of Richard I, when Wamba the jester opposes to the beard of Isaac the Jew "a shield of brawn . . . the abomination of his tribe," causing him to miss his footing and roll down the steps, "an excellent jest to the spectators."[33] Similarly, in an unpublished dramatic interlude, *Mordecai's Beard*, performed at Drury Lane on April 20, 1790, the anonymous author has an uncouth Irishman grease a Jew pedlar's beard with a flitch of bacon. In retaliation for this misdemeanor and in the hope of making some money out of it, the Jew has recourse to a Justice, who fines the Irishman half a crown and reprimands him for failing "to respect the benign laws of this country, which protect equally men of all religions, and opinions." However, Mordecai, no less a scoundrel than his antagonist, almost risks losing his lawsuit, for on the way to court he naturally cannot resist licking his beard nearly clean of its all-too-delicious evidence.[34] The anointment of the Jew's beard with swine's grease, while having the primary purpose to humiliate or degrade him, may also be perceived in at least the final of these examples as a facetiously unholy replication of the sacred act of Christian baptism. "If I can't convert your whole body," exclaims the Irishman to the Jew in *Mordecai's Beard*, "I will at least christen your beard, my jewel."

At a no less primitive level, popular awareness of their prohibition upon pork leads to the conviction that the Jews gluttonously devour in private what their religious edicts have expressly forbidden them. By way of grotesque illustration here, Thomas Bridges, the author of the fictitious *Adventures of a Bank-Note* (1770–71), has his eponymous narrator carried home to the dinner table of

> the ugliest dog of a Jew that the sun ever shone upon. . . . I expected . . . that I should see him sit down to a head of garlick, with a piece of bread and salt, and, perhaps a sallad; . . . but how was I surprised to see a fine leg of pork and a pease pudding come smoaking upon table; the Hebrew, without a single ejaculation, or so much as lifting up his eyes, fell at the pork with such eagerness, that I expected he would not so much as leave the shank unswallowed.[35]

Elsewhere in the same work, he depicts another Jew who celebrates having comprehensively cheated a shopkeeper by polishing off "a pork-griskin that he had bespoke when he first made the bargain . . . , for he always indulged with pork when he had a lucky hit" (2:98). Bridges sarcastically endorses the double standard by which the Jews' trespass is against the precepts of their own faith yet open to public condemnation by the wider gentile world. "Let them turn Christians," he counsels, "there's no objection to their being rogues if they do; and then, when pork is not forbid, they won't eat a tenth part they do at present; by which means the Christian poor . . . may come in for a rasher or a steak, because the price must fall" (4:132).

Although primarily an emblem of the Jew's Otherness, his unseemly association in popular mythology with that which his religious practice finds most foul and abominable becomes also a significant feature by which his contrary neighbor, the Christian, who enjoys living under no such prohibition, may consciously distinguish himself. At Eastertime, the antiquary John Aubrey informs us, " 'twas always the Fashion for a man to have a Gammon of Bacon, to shew himself to be no Jew."[36] By hyperbole but probably with this tradition in mind, a fictitious correspondent writing in a periodical essay during the year following the Naturalization Bill, when inflammatory sentiment against the Jews remained particularly rampant, describes a sumptuously laden election dinner in an English country town at which

> a great variety of pig-meat was provided. The table was covered from one end to the other with hams, legs of pork, spare-ribs, griskins, haslets, feet and ears, brawn, and the like. In the middle there smoked a large barbecued hog, which was soon devoured to the bone, so desirous was every one to prove his Christianity by the quantity he could swallow of that anti-Judaic food. After dinner there was brought in, by way of dessert, a dish of hog's puddings; but as I have a dislike to that kind of diet (though not from any scruple of conscience), I was regarded as little better than a Jew for declining to eat of them.[37]

Another essay in the same periodical, sarcastically reinforcing the abhorrence of pork by the Jews as a mark of their distinction, occasions a proposal to have engraved a print of Christ conjuring the Devil into the herd of Gadarene swine (Mark 5:1–20, Luke 8:26–39), "being very proper to be had in all Jewish families, as a necessary preservative against pork and Christianity."[38]

A further distortion of the identical biblical narrative becomes for the poet William Blake the telling factor by which Christ has distinguished the Jew by endowing him with a porcine physiognomy or, more accurately, the pig with a Jewish visage:

He turn'd the devils into Swine
That he might tempt the Jews to dine;
Since which, a Pig has got a look
That for a Jew may be mistook.[39]

The perverse mixture of the Gospel and the folkloric illustrated here typifies the fluidity with which such elements become synthesized within anti-Semitic discourse into a potent reiteration of difference. As creatures deemed by an ultimate irony to be more porcine than human, the alleged semblance of the Jews to pigs becomes sometimes the pretext that explains their well-known abhorrence of swine's flesh. The "JEWS are not permitted to eat pork," jibes the Tory satirist William King because that would constitute "a kind of fratricide."[40] Only by immediately and sincerely embracing Christianity or ultimately through the second coming of the Messiah, which it was widely believed would be preceded by their conversion, could the Jews be freed from a prohibition that separates them from the rest of humanity. "The very Rabbies," avers a late seventeenth-century apostate from Judaism, "themselves generally agree the distinction of Meats should cease in the times of Messiah, and Swines Flesh should be as pure as the rest."[41]

Until the millennial fulfillment of these expectations, even the secularized, well-to-do apostate who has openly turned his back on the observance of his former religion may be jolted into recalling his continuing marginality by iconographic allusion to an unsought linkage with the pig. In Gillray's print of *"Mr. Franco"* (1800), a stout young man, said to be a personage well known on the turf, is shown in full profile, dressed in high fashion as a gentleman of leisure. However, his unavoidable Otherness as a Jew by birth is marked by his exaggerated nose and more particularly by the pigs, like him turned tail on themselves, scampering off at either side. The pigs' tails, forked as the horns of the Devil, have become Gillray's way of indicating that Mr. Franco remains more a converted or Christian *Jew* than true Englishman. To adopt the diet and manners of the native English gentleman is ultimately no escape from an all-too-familiar slur.[42]

If the consciously scurrilous association with the pig remained (and probably still remains) indelible in popular discourse concerning the Jews, a parallel link, equally denotative of difference in many Western cultures, arises from the biblical ordinance that on the eighth day after birth every man child among them should undergo ritual circumcision of the flesh of his foreskin. Far from being a prohibition, as that forbidding the Jews to partake of the pig, an "unclean" beast, the converse

James Gillray, *"Mr. Franco."* Engraving, 1800. (Courtesy of Mr. Alfred Rubens, London.)

function of circumcision is purificatory and as a token of the covenant established from the time of Abraham between God and his chosen people (Gen. 17:10–14, Lev. 12:1–4). As is well known, circumcision is in common practice not only in the Jewish but also (among others) in the Muslim faith, although for the latter it is traditionally viewed as a rite of initiation usually to be performed at a later age. It is both the oldest and the most widely practiced surgical operation in the world.

Because of its recurrence from ancient times as a totemic rite performed by many different civilizations of the Near East, circumcision was less evidently portrayed negatively there as an emblem of the Otherness of the Jews than it was later to become in occidental Christian cultures. The exegetical belief that its covenantal function had been divinely abrogated to be supplanted by a supposedly more humane consecration by baptism belongs entirely to Christian thinking. According to one standard eighteenth-century commentary, that of the Reverend Matthew Henry, the cutting of the foreskin as practiced by the Jews is to be interpreted as a "bloody ordinance" that pertained when "all things by the law were purged with blood. . . . But, the blood of Christ being shed, all bloody ordinances are now abolished; [and] circumcision therefore gives way to baptism."[43] That Christ himself (as if alone among the Jews) had submitted to this *"painful* operation" when "they *circumcised* him" is seen by the same intrepid commentator as indicative of what the Savior was prepared to undergo "that he might own himself a surety for our sins, and an undertaker for our safety; that he might justify the infant seed of the church to God, by that ordinance which is the instituted seal of the covenant, as circumcision was . . . and baptism is."[44]

How far such commentary elaborates on primitive biblical text may be judged by reference to the single account of the circumcision in the Gospel according to Luke (2:21), which simply states: "And when eight days were accomplished for the circumcising of the child, his name was called JESUS." In Henry's commentary, the supposed pain Christ felt at his circumcision and the loss of blood typologically anticipate his later agony upon the cross. Implicitly, at least, the commentator lays blame by contrast between what he sees as the initiating sacraments of Christianity and of Judaism.[45] As a "bloody ordinance," circumcision becomes emblematic of Christ's greater suffering at the hands of the Jews. The commentary reinforces, however innocuously, the occidental fear of circumcision as a ritual that has been invalidated or made taboo by the introduction of a "new" sacrament by baptism.[46]

The eighteenth century provides plenty of evidence that fear of circumcision could easily be harnessed into the wider fabric of anti-Semitic discourse. The theory that circumcision is the symbolic substitute for castration, associated most closely in the twentieth century with Freudian thinking, lends itself as a useful postulate (if not perhaps completely convincing in all its detail) by which to explain the recurrence of the theme.[47] Certainly, anecdotal allusion to the act of circumcision then as now almost always represents it as a simulation of deeper pathological fears, a fantasized threat to the props of masculinity or of the status quo.[48] By way of illustration, let us cull an anecdote concerning a man condemned to death for coin-clipping from *Joe Miller's Jests*, of its day the most widely known and frequently reprinted English jest-book:

> Mr. Smith, the ordinary of Newgate, in the reign of King William, one of the most famous scruple-drawers of his time, had an impenitent clipper once to deal with. "Why," says the fellow, "what harm have I done? A parcel of overgrown shillings fell into my hands, and I only par'd off their superfluities. They would have bought but twelve pennyworth of beef and turnips at first, and they will buy twelve pennyworth of beef and turnips still." "Ay, but hark you my friend!" cries the ordinary, "what is to clip a thing but pare it round? And what is paring round called in scripture, but circumcision? And who, under the evangelical dispensation, dares practise circumcision, but one that has actually renounced the Christian-Religion, and is a Jew, a most obstinate and perverse Jew in his heart?" Upon this the poor clipper threw himself at his feet, owned the heinousness of his sin, confessed that sabbath-breaking had brought him to it, and wept like a church-spout.[49]

Plainly, the anecdote or jest is only incidentally concerned with the Jews. It assumes (as, of course, we are unable today) that its audience knows that coin-clipping in the age of King William III was a capital offense and that the "impenitent clipper" will shortly be hanged.[50] The response by Mr. Smith, the "ordinary," whose unenviable task it was to prepare a condemned prisoner for death, to the clipper's initial failure to acknowledge his crime links the paring of the coinage of the realm with the severing of the prepuce, both activities traditionally associated with the Jews.[51] Having established the connection, he insures the hitherto unpliant prisoner's immediate breakdown or collapse, all the more understandable given his grievous circumstances but exacerbated by the clever casuistry of the scruple-drawer's argument. The scruple that brings about the clipper's sudden confession is effective because of its amplification of existing, although partly subconscious, fears of circumcision and of the Jew as Other. By throwing himself at his confessor's feet and weeping like a church-spout, the condemned man emasculates the grounds of his earlier defense but, in his penitence, gains our absolute sympathy. He is, as it were, translated back from "obstinate and perverse Jew" to contrite "Christian." The subtlety of the anecdote depends upon its supposition of irreconcilable ritual and attitudinal differences between the behavior of a Christian and that of a Jew, although paradoxically (at least as we have it) it contains no hint of Christian pardon for the sinner. The "jest" is simply in the revelation of the means by which he is made to own up.

In the anecdote just discussed, the impenitent clipper is charged by the scruple-drawer with having renounced his Christianity and regressed into a "Jew in his heart." Not uncommonly, a similar parody of conversion is tendered in anti-Semitic representation by emphasizing the diligence of the Jews in their endeavors to circumcise into their own faith. In George Farquhar's play, *The Twin-Rivals* (1702), for instance, we learn how a rich Jew, Mr. Moabite, appears with his kept mistress at the house of Mother Midnight, a bawd and midwife, who tells her own story:

> One Evening as I was very grave in my House. . . . What hears me I—but pat, pat, pat very softly at the Door. Come in, cries I, and presently enters Mr. *Moabite*, follow'd by . . . a fine young Virgin just upon the point of being deliver'd.—We were all in a great hurly burly for a while, to be sure; but our Production was a fine Boy.—I had fifty Guineas for my Trouble; the Lady was wrapt up very warm, plac'd in her Chair, and reconveigh'd to the Place she came from . . . but the Child was left with me—the Father wou'd have made a *Jew* on't presently, but I swore, if he committed such a Barbarity on the Infant, that I wou'd discover all—so I had him brought up a good *Christian*, and bound prentice to an Attorney.[52]

The "Barbarity" to which Mother Midnight alludes is, of course, circumcision, implicitly seen as an operation that a Jew, unless hindered, will endeavor to execute with an almost missionary zeal. An important aspect of popular mythology concerning circumcision depends upon the anxiety that, given but half an opportunity and with unseemly dispatch, the Jews (traditionally imagined brandishing sharp knives) will perpetrate their antique ritual upon those menfolk they indiscriminately single out for conversion. The possible threat of circumcision by the Jews persists, it appears, from the cradle to the grave. The infant that Mr. Moabite in Farquhar's play tries to circumcise is not eight days old but newborn, and, perhaps because orthodox Jews insist on its necessity for those who convert out of choice, there seems to have been a residual belief that even among their own the operation was sometimes withheld to a later age. A memoir by César de Saussure, a Swiss visitor to London in 1729, describing an actual circumcision that he witnessed at the Ashkenazi synagogue helps confirm the persistence of such fears beyond the merely fictive:

> On that same day a child was circumcised. Some of the Rabbis stood up on a sort of wooden stand, together with the father and the infant's sponsor, whilst sentences were read out of the Bible in Hebrew. The sponsor then sat down in a chair in the centre of the stand, the priests chanting alone. I was by chance seated next to a young Englishwoman, who had evidently also come out of curiosity. Seeing no infant (for it had not yet been brought in), she imagined that the sponsor, the young, good-looking man who was seated on the chair, was the intended victim. I could not resist confirming her in this view, and she then made as if she would retire, and even rose to leave the synagogue, but I cannot tell whether her curiosity got the better of her modesty. Anyhow, she pretended that the crowd around her prevented her from leaving, but by this time the infant had been brought in, and she understood her mistake.[53]

Seeming modesty apart, the young Englishwoman's discomfort and need to leave the synagogue are aggravated by de Saussure's transference to her of his own subjective fear of circumcision, evinced in the cruel pleasure with which he encourages the impression that a relatively simple initiation rite is to be perpetrated not on a child but upon a fully grown man. On its own, the testimony as we have it here is probably too slight to be wholly convincing but an incipient equation of adult circumcision with fear of castration is at least implied. The motif is a common one elsewhere, underscoring the supposed barbarity of the ceremonial practices of the Jews. "In the Fury of their Devotion they set about circumcizing him," runs a bogus memoir describing the narrow escape of a wretched Gentile, but "no sooner had they forced open the Armour, and applied the holy Instruments to his Flesh, than he bounded out of their Hands, and roar'd about like an angry Lion."[54] The uneasy humor with which this and similar contretemps are reported simulates deeper endemic anxieties concerning the invasive rituals of the Jews.

At the time of the bill of 1753, such recurrent fears are at their most explicit. Anti-Judaic writers revel in exaggerating the effect of naturalization, one result of which will be that the Jews will take over the kingdom and immediately insist on mass circumcision of all gentile males. In the countryside, they will set about circumcising their tenants, and in the city, as well as "clipping our coin" as of old, they will now (if we wish to credit the claim made in some wretched verses) "add sin to sin" by "clipping our skin."[55] The penalty of acceding to Jewish naturalization, according to another versifier, must be submission to the same dreaded operation:

> That I hate ev'ry Jew,
> Believe I speak true,
> Nor shall they be naturalized;
> For them if I vote,
> Or e'er turn my Coat,
> I myself will be first circumcised.[56]

Similarly, a pamphleteer jocularly resigning himself to the inevitability of his fate, solicits for "a Priestess to Circumcise me, because they have the lighter Hand"[57] and a lukewarm proponent of the bill, sarcastically inverting widespread fears that the Jews will undermine the state, argues that, on the contrary, "if what is said of its Physical Use be true," circumcision will soon be brought into fashion as therapy against the spread of "a Distemper [syphilis] to which . . . our Youth are so very subject, to the great Endangerment of their own Lives, and the Health and Prosperity of their Neighbours and Families."[58] The currency of the absurd belief that the Jews would introduce mandatory initiation into the Abrahamic covenant is also reflected in political prints, at least half a dozen of which allude to the alleged practice.[59] In one of these, *A Stir in the City, or some Folks at Guild-Hall* (1754), issued after the repeal of the Naturalization Bill but when hopes were entertained by its supporters that it might once again become law, an orator is shown standing on a tub, recommending to the mob a corps of butchers as surgeons fit to perform the rite.[60] In another, *A Scene of Scenes for the Year 1853* (i.e., 1753; see chap. 8), the seated figure of Sir William Calvert, a strong advocate in favor of the naturalization of the Jews, is being circumcised on the steps of St. Paul's Cathedral, while several bishops and judges impatiently await their own turn. The print gives an idea of what would happen in the future once the Naturalization Bill had become law.[61]

Such anxieties, however, are by no means unique to the period of the Jew Bill. A good thirty-six years earlier, Alexander Pope exploits similar apprehensions in a malicious prose squib describing an imagined circumcision by the "*barbarous and cruel* Jews" upon the bookseller Edmund Curll (1675–1747). Pope had objected to Curll's false attribution to him of several poems published by the bookseller in 1716 and the pamphlet describing the latter's circumcision is the last of three lampoons against him that the poet tossed off to fuel the quarrel.[62] According to the narrative, prompted by "the filthy Prospect of Lucre," Curll had resolved to quit bookselling for 'Change Alley, where he fell into com-

pany with the Jews "at their Club at the Sign of the *Cross* in *Cornhill*,
. . . [who] began to tamper with him upon the most important Points of
the *Christian Faith*." From zealously defending the creed, Curll is lured
toward conversion by vain promises that he will become as rich as a Jew,
and that "if he would poison his Wife and give up his *Grisking* [pork],
. . . he should marry the rich *Ben Meymon*'s only Daughter." These and
similar temptations prove too attractive and a few days later, without
informing his wife, he returns to the tavern to complete the initiation:

> At his Entrance into the Room he perceived a meagre Man, with a
> sallow Countenance, a black forky Beard, and long Vestment. In his
> Right Hand he held a large Pair of Sheers, and in his Left a red hot
> Searing-Iron. At Sight of this, Mr. *Curll*'s Heart trembled within him,
> and feign would he retire; but was prevented by six Jews, who laid
> Hands upon him, and unbuttoning his Breeches threw him upon the
> Table, a pale pitiful Spectacle.

Inevitably, at the critical moment of the operation, Curll in his fright
jerks upward and loses "five times as much as ever Jew did before." Levitical law decrees that he is too much circumcised ("worse than not
being circumcis'd at all") and so may not be declared a Jew, and he is
consequently cast forth from the synagogue, having voided all contracts.
To add insult to injury, at their club the Jews proudly expose to the world
at large the physical memorial to his wife's loss and her husband's indignity. The sad moral of the squib is reserved to a short admonitory
prayer at its close that "all good and well-disposed Christians be warn'd
by this unhappy Wretch's woful Example to abominate the heinous Sin
of *Avarice*, which sooner or later will draw them into the cruel Clutches
of *Satan, Papists, Jews,* and *Stock-jobbers.*"[63]

As a piece intended to lampoon Edmund Curll, the squib emerges as,
if anything, more emphatic in its scurrilous vilification of the Jews. The
moral at its end makes only passing mention of Curll but aggressively
implicates the Jews as inexorable enemies of true Christians in league
with the Devil and the Catholic Church.[64] Their practice of circumcision, deemed in the pamphlet as primary among "the *outward* and *visible* Signs of *Judaism*," is fundamental in marking their continual
distinction from the rest of the populace in England.[65] Their conspira-
torial dealings in entrapping and manhandling Curll for the purpose of
circumcision betoken their larger crime against Christianity, of which
the pamphlet provides perceptible echoes. A later reference to the supposed incident in a lampooning pamphlet published at the time of the
Naturalization Bill certainly suggests that the Jews' treatment of Curll
was viewed as indicative of their wider hidden agenda. "The Attempt

which some of these Miscreants made not many Years ago on a late eminent Bookseller," writes the anonymous author, "is a plain Proof that they have not forgot their old Practices of circumcising, crucifying, &c."[66] Ultimately, Pope's pamphlet achieves its effect by reigniting the traditional charge against the Jews that casts them as a cosmic menace against Christian kind.

In similar vein, even possibly distantly indebted to Pope, is a satirical pamphlet entitled *The Reply of the Jews to the Letters Addressed to them by Doctor Joseph Priestley* (Oxford, 1787), indicting the missionary exertions of the famous Unitarian minister, who had advocated that instead of mutual prejudice there should be a new dialogue between the two faiths to awaken the Jews to the divinity of Christ. The work is proffered as coming from the pen of "Solomon de A.R.," representing the Jews, but has long been ascribed to George Horne (1730–92), later bishop of Norwich, a fierce critic of Priestley's ministry. Under the guise of his nom-de-plume, Horne reminds Priestley of the approbation he had shown toward the practice of the Ebionites, an obscure Judeo-Christian sect of the second to the fourth century, who observed all the Jewish rites but acknowledged the messianic character of Jesus. If, he argues, the principles of the Ebionites should be retained as a model for present-day Jews, then they should also be adopted by the very man who has set himself up as their intercessor. If, he adds tenuously, Priestley expects to offer a true defense of his theology, then he must lay aside such idle subterfuges as his time of life and the "fancy that the operator's hand may slip," and "with the boldness and confidence of a man" submit to circumcision as the most indispensable of Jewish rites.[67] As an unsavory refinement, Horne describes in wicked detail the byzantine apparatus, supposedly employed by the Jews, for the "safe" initiation of older proselytes to their faith:

A table is prepared, something in the form of a hog's back, six feet in length, *i.e.* in the chord. Upon this the subject is laid, and incurvated to the utmost of his bent; and in this position he hath in some measure the appearance of a piece of wood that is incurvated for the purpose of becoming the felly of a cart wheel. Across his neck, his hands and arms, and legs and thighs, are thrown proper ligatures, which fasten him so completely to the table, that he can neither shrink downwards nor jerk upwards. But this is not all. After he is thus fastened to the table, side boards are applied close to his body, and screwed up as tight as possible, which take from him entirely all power of wriggling or motion of any kind, except in thought; and in this posture, the operator being secured against all hazards of interruption in his operation, it is performed with the utmost safety and expedition. (30–31)

Although purely a flight of fancy seemingly with little indebtedness to any identifiable source, the description is crudely effective in spreading the imputation that the torture of its neophytes (ironically here as a form of safeguard from the greater risk of castration) is a common trait of Jewish ceremony. By barbarizing their ritual, Horne can both traduce the Jews and ridicule what he sees as misplaced Christian compassion on Priestley's part. As with the account of Curll, the Jews end up disavowing Priestley, here not because of a botched initiation, but through realization that he will never "prove faithful to the Law of Moses" and "would be trimming and new modelling the Pentateuch" with the same abandon that he had hitherto "served the Gospel of the Christians."[68]

As we can see, two reiterative charges against the Jews become verbalized in popular response to their rite of initiation, namely that they engage in barbarous practices and that they remain unequivocally different from the rest of mankind, their covenantal seal appearing as a tribal mark of that abiding difference. Fear of circumcision as a taboo still perpetrated by the Jews is, however, occasionally rationalized into a broader assault on the rite as a seeming breach of man's natural state. A salvo in an anonymously published late eighteenth-century anti-Judaic pamphlet repudiates circumcision as

> a barbarous violation of the principles of Humanity, and an insult to the God of Nature. For what can be more unhuman, than to punish an Infant by a cruel operation on a part of its body, done by a bungling Butcher of a Priest! or what can be more insulting to the all wise Creator, than for a stupid Fool of a Fellow, to presume to correct His workmanship, by finding one superfluous part, and taking that away to reduce the subject to perfection?[69]

But more logically conceived attacks of this sort are fairly rare. The commoner representation of the rite from at least the sixteenth century onward is to embody it in metonymic terms whereby the Jews are referred to—and not always in a consciously derogatory context—as "the Circumcis'd," "the unforeskinn'd race," "the circumcised Sons of *Eve*," "fore-skinne clippers," "They of the circumcision," and "Circumshission-Men."[70] The metonym is used both descriptively and as an elementary means to distinguish the Jews from the rest of mankind. An anecdote, recorded by Horace Walpole, concerning Robert Nugent, an Irishman who successfully stood for Bristol in the rambunctious elections of 1754, is usefully illustrative:

> The great cry against Nugent at Bristol was for having voted [the year before] for the Jew Bill: one old woman said, "What, must we be rep-

resented by a Jew and an Irishman?" He replied, with great quickness, "My good dame, if you will step aside with me into a corner, I will show you that I am *not* a Jew, and that *I am* an Irishman."[71]

What began for the Jews as the seal of an enduring covenant between God and the sons of Abraham has become in gentile eyes the intractable mark of an almost anthropological difference. In the popular imagination, circumcision connotes the perpetual stigma of the Jewish people in their self-inflicted Otherness.

The mainstay of an "alternative" ritual as constituted in anti-Semitic discourse fastens upon the popular belief that the nefarious use of Christian blood is essential to the most intimate ceremonies of the Jews. Ignoring the clearest pentateuchal evidence to the contrary (e.g., Gen. 9:4; Lev. 3:17, 7:26–27, 19:26), such discourse cultivates the erroneous notion that the Jews utilize human blood in their sacrificial rites, by their implacable hostility to Christ particularly delighting in blood culled from his disciples. Many explanations, sometimes deriving from biblical exegesis, have been put forward to account for the origins of this terrible superstition. For example, the advocate of Jewish readmission into England, Rabbi Menasseh Ben Israel, who, it will be recalled, had strongly defended his coreligionists against charges that they sacrificed children and drank human blood, proposed that the source of these calumnies may have been from a misreading of Ezekiel 36:13, "Thou land [of Israel] devourest up men."[72] More convincingly, others have supposed that the collective guilt of the Jews is enshrined in their answer to Pilate, "His blood be on us, and on our children" (Matt. 27:25). It is also quite feasible to suggest that the seed of the blood accusation may be traced to parallels between Jewish and Christian ceremonial practice. The totemic function of the Christian Eucharist by which (at least symbolically) the blood and flesh of the Savior become incorporated has links both with pagan fertility cults involving sacrifice and also with the Jewish Passover and Sabbath rituals, at which blessings are recited over cups of red wine that are then imbibed. These two distinct anthropological roots to the eucharistic sacrament become strangely entwined in the popular fallacy that at their feasts the Jews consumed not wine but human blood.[73] Similarly, the associated charge of desecration or poisoning by the Jews of the sacramental wafer may derive from its physical likeness to matzo, the flat unleavened bread eaten to commemorate the Passover and mythically said to be baked with innocent Christian blood.[74] As is well known, the ubiquity of these groundless charges has been a prominent motive behind the persecution and indiscriminate slaughter of Jews on the European continent at different times from the thirteenth through the twentieth centuries.

Among a tally of related blood libel myths concerning the Jews, the most persistent, and also the most appalling, remains the imputation that as a crucial part of their Passover ceremonial they actively encouraged and sought the kidnapping and ritual slaughter of young Christian infants. The recurrence even into the twentieth century of this disreputable myth as a pan-European phenomenon may too easily cause us to forget that the first documented persecution of Jews as a consequence of the accusation was not on the Continent but in Middle Age England, where the stories of William of Norwich and Hugh of Lincoln, supposed boy-martyrs respectively in 1144 and 1255, quickly gained canonical status. One of the earliest English chronicles containing gruesome details of the alleged avocation of the Jews in ritual murder is that of the thirteenth-century Benedictine monk, Matthew Paris (d. 1259), whose *Historia Major* is replete with examples intended to reveal the heinousness of their practices. Once chronicled, these stories were repeated for the most part uncritically by later historians and, as a consequence, accepted into popular culture as verifiable fact. After the mass expulsion of the Jews from England in 1290, similar tales enjoyed a wider circulation in oral narratives, finding common expression in such ballads as "Hugh of Lincoln and the Jew's Daughter" and "The Jew's Daughter: A Scottish Ballad,"[75] and also, of course, in Chaucer's *Prioress's Tale.*

The infiltration of such charges into later mythology about the Jews is evident from Menasseh's explicit rebuttal at the time of the readmission, although their recurrence into the eighteenth century often includes acknowledgment of medieval sources as empirical "proof" of their veracity, suggesting that the tempering effect upon popular belief of the Amsterdam rabbi's eloquent defense was negligible. A pamphlet of 1656, *The Case of the Jewes Stated,* typifies well the persistence of the ritual murder motif as a subject still to be considered by anti-Judaic writers as irrevocable dogma. "When they were in *England*," writes the anonymous author, citing Matthew Paris as his authority,

> the Jews used every year to steal a young Boy (the child of a Christian) and to circumcise him, and then in their Synagogue sate in a solemn Assembly, chusing one of themselves to be *Pilat*, who out of their Devillish malice to Christ and Christians condemned the child, and crucified him to death; and this was discovered at *Norwich*, where they circumcised a Christian child . . . , and condemned him to be cru-

cified[;] it was discovered, for which four Jews being convicted were drawn at horses tails, and hanged on a Gibbit, and 18 Jews were drawn and hanged for thus crucifying of one *Hugh Lincoln*.[76]

The murder of the child is portrayed as a visceral and consciously staged reenactment of the crucifixion of Christ, the Jews performing their allotted part as the perpetual enemies of all true Christians. Jewish ceremony is perceived here as an expression of their collective guilt as Christ-killers, the annual Passover ritual functioning as a kind of sinister continuum into modern times of the slaughter of the innocents (Matt. 2:16). The punishment meted out against the Jews, however harsh, is presumed fit for those who show themselves to be no less inclined to deicidal deeds than their biblical forefathers.

Significantly, the circumcision of the stolen child is represented as being as much a focal point of their supposed ritual as his subsequent crucifixion. The blood accusation against the Jews may only be properly understood if we recognize that its basis lies in the crudest awareness of their *actual* religious practice coupled with a need to perpetuate for later generations the blame for the death of Christ. Its survival as a bizarre stigma into the eighteenth century and beyond has only the most slender connection with true Judaism insofar as it reflects a tenebrous awareness that ritual circumcision and an interdiction to eat pork are both integral to Jewish religious life. The imputation that their child sacrifices were preceded by the ritual cutting of the victim's foreskin may be behind a related and equally outlandish belief, first encountered in fifteenth-century Germany, that the Jews required Christian blood as an unguent to heal the wounds inflicted on their own infants by circumcision.[77] Although this absurd notion does not appear to have taken root in English popular culture, considerable credence seems to have been given, as we saw earlier, to the belief that the Jews were consummately plotting to inflict their painful rite on those outside their faith. The perception that they supposedly engaged in torture both in their rites of initiation and of sacrifice is sufficient pretext to link the two ceremonies in anti-Judaic discourse.

A more surprising juxtaposition is that sometimes forged between the blood accusation against the Jews and their renowned abhorrence (but supposed secret partiality) for the flesh of the pig. Because it was well known that in adhering to their dietary laws "the more rigid *Jews* always choose to kill and dress their own meat,"[78] it required but a short leap in the popular imagination to combine this with their reputation as Christ-killers and cast them as a people by barbaric instinct given to venal butchery. The alleged covert consumption of roast pork by the Jews and their presumed ritual need for Christian blood become strangely interlinked. So the author of a satirical pamphlet of 1753, consciously echoing Swift's outrageous sham remedy for Irish indigence in *A Modest Proposal*—the breeding of the infants of the poor for food—ironically estimates that "the Flavour of a roasting Pig, from which the *Jews* are debarred, may be happily imitated by the proper Management of a young sucking Child."[79] The serving of a roasted piglet at a clandestine Jewish feast, a resilient motif in English graphic caricature, distantly parodies their supposed blood sacrifice of Christian babes.[80] The persistence of the association is vividly reconstructed by Maria Edgeworth in her novel, *Harrington* (1817), in which a nursemaid frightens the infant hero with gruesome anti-Judaic yarns, the most nightmarish of which concerns a Jew at Paris "who professed to sell pork pies; but it was found out at last that the pies were not pork—they were made of the flesh of little children."[81] A taunting jingle popular among schoolchildren,

> Get a bit of pork
> Stick it on a fork
> And give it to a Jew boy, a Jew

is conjoined with another in the recollection of the author, James Leigh Hunt, a pupil at Christ Hospital, the London charity school, during the 1790s. "At Easter," proceeds Hunt,

> a strip of bordered paper was stuck on the breast of every boy, containing the words "He is risen." It did not give us the slightest thought of what it recorded. It only reminded us of an old rhyme, which some of the boys used to go about the school repeating:-
>
> "He is risen, he is risen,
> All the Jews must go to prison."
>
> A beautiful Christian deduction; Thus has charity itself been converted into a spirit of antagonism; and thus it is that the antagonism, in the progress of knowledge, becomes first a pastime and then a jest.[82]

Hunt's virtuous embarrassment here is in his discernment not merely of the ignoble treatment of the Jews but of the hypocrisy by which anti-Judaic prejudices are so readily ingrained in the Christian consciousness from an early age. In the lore of schoolchildren, the punishment of the Jews for their supposed deicidal deed is openly to bait them with that which they consider most unclean. To taunt them thus, it seems, is to remind them of the unceasing error of their ways.

For the contemporaries of Matthew Paris in the late Middle Ages,

there had been no easier way of instilling a sense of the perennial significance of Easter as a festival solemnizing the passion and resurrection
of the Christian God than to lay continuing blame for the crucifixion on
their contrary neighbors, the Jews. The alleged kidnapping and immo-
lation of Christian children by the Jews during Easter as represented in
the traditional blood libel may be said to symbolize their supposed appetite to reiterate their cosmic misdeed against humanity. Their recalcitrance in refusing to acknowledge the deity of Christ was ample
evidence of their incessant infamy. By the eighteenth century, the sustenance of the libel at least in England belongs more to folk memory than
to provocation from the pulpit. If anything, the signals of its endurance
are contradictory, ranging from dogmatic assertion that the Jews still
even now engaged in their vicious practices to enlightened dismissal of
what was interpreted as a self-serving and terrible myth fabricated by
the monks in an age of Gothic darkness. It is revealing to examine these
polarities, although we must caution ourselves from believing that they
ever really provoked serious dialogue or debate in place of hectoring
claim and sporadic counter-claim. If there was less real credence in the
blood libel as fact by the end of our period, the shift was by gradual ero-
sion rather than by sudden change.

Those anti-Judaic writers in the longer eighteenth century who invoke the specter of ritual murder do so by cunning combination of direct
reference and innuendo. The direct reference is to the alleged behavior
of the Jews in former times and the innuendo in arousing the suspicion
that their present descendants will act no differently. The *"former Jews*
Crucified and the *present* justify their so doing, by defending the Religion of their Ancestors," spells out a typical mid-eighteenth-century
commentator.[83] "In the spite of their hearts and pravity of their dispositions," avers the fictional Mr. Jolter in Smollett's *Peregrine Pickle*
(1751), the present Jews remain "the genuine offspring of those who crucified the Saviour of the world."[84] These "wretches not only do not believe," resonates William Cobbett more than three-quarters of a century
later, "but boast of being the descendants, and of retaining all the principles, of those who murdered him, in whom we profess belief."[85] Their
very name as Jews, Cobbett insists elsewhere, "indicates that they
would, if they could, crucify him again!"[86] Almost every popularly
known facet of their ceremony becomes concocted within anti-Judaic
discourse as an abominable travesty of Christian values consciously pre-
meditated by rabbinical edict in specific opposition both to the person
of Jesus and to his Church. Within "a *Jewish Chappel*," insists John
Tutchin evincing a widely held belief, one may witness "the Saviour of

Mankind publickly Blasphemed every Week."[87] The Jews, urges William Romaine in a brazen stroke of historical revisionism, are "the only People upon the Earth, whose Principles lead them to abhor and persecute Christians." "As Subjects to the Devil," he adds, "they are in perpetual Hostility with Christ, so that there can be no Peace between them and Christians."[88]

The supposed robotic antagonism of the Jews toward the person of Christ continues to express itself in their visceral handling of his newly baptized disciples. Their aggressive behavior remains nowhere more vilely conspicuous than in their alleged ceremonial slaughter of innocent Christian infants. The accusation is nearly always represented during the eighteenth century in general rather than specific terms. "The Christian Religion is an Object of Scorn and Contempt to the *Jews*," begins a characteristic deposition, "and 'tis well known that their zeal has often push'd them so far, as to murder Christian Children, upon Crosses, in derision to the Christian Sacrifice."[89] The "high Contempt and Despite," charges another,

> they have frequently discovered against the Person and Passion of *Christ*, . . . they have maliciously acted over and over again, in Representation, not only by piercing his Image with Swords and Spears; by abusing the Sacramental Bread; and by crucifying a *Ram* at *Easter*; but by crucifying several *Christian* Children on *Good-Friday*; as could be instanced by seven or eight Facts in *England*, of which they were detected.[90]

The graduation of the list of their putative crimes gives final prominence to what is often viewed as the most clandestine of Jewish ritual practices, widely accepted as fact although authenticated only by the hearsay of folk memory.

One of the few eighteenth-century expositions describing in detail the atrocious rite at the core of the blood accusation occurs in Charles Johnstone's popular episodic novel, *Chrysal or the Adventures of a Guinea*.[91] The narrative, fictionally set in the vicinity of Hesse in the northern part of Germany during the late 1750s, begins by revealing that among the Jews "the most secret and mysterious ceremony of their religion" is the observance of a most solemn festival:

> This was the sacrifice of the Passover, which, by a secret tradition, never committed to writing for fear of being betrayed, was changed from the typical offering of a lamb to the real immolation of human blood, for which purpose the most beautiful children were purchased at any expense, and under any pretext, from the ignorance of necessitous parents, or the perfidious avarice of servants, if they could not

be obtained by stealth, and brought from all parts of Europe for these ceremonies, it being a long received opinion that the original sacrifice of a lamb was designed only for that one occasion, to conciliate the favour of Heaven to the escape of their forefathers out of Egypt; but that to render it propitious to their restoration to their country, and to the consummation of their promised happiness and glory, the type must be changed for the thing typified, and human blood, in the purest state of infant innocence, be offered instead of the ineffectual blood of a brute. (224)

The tangled biblical prophecy that the Gentiles will have a vital role in bringing about the restoration of the Jews to their promised land (Isa. 11:10–12, Rom. 15:12), a prominent factor in English millenarian assumptions, takes an unexpected and gory twist in Johnstone's bizarre exegesis. The atavistic recourse to human sacrifice as a means to appease their deity casts the Jews as primordial savages whose undeniable brutishness is at last exposed in their most intimate ceremony. Instead of the totemic sacrifice of the lamb (in reality long discarded by the Jews, although still symbolized at table by a single shank-bone upon the Passover plate), their religion bids them lustrate themselves with Christian blood. Because of their superstitious hatred and desire of revenge against Christians, they have no trace of natural affection for those infants they choose for slaughter, but coldly appoint a number of conditions in selecting their prey:

The rules laid down in the institution of the Passover were literally observed in respect to the victim, who was to be without blemish, a male of the first year, that is, the first-born of his mother, and to be kept fourteen days before he was sacrificed, during which time they fed him with the richest food, to raise him to the highest perfection of his nature.

The place chosen for the celebration of this ceremony was a summer-house in a garden, belonging to one of the rulers of their synagogue, where they all met at the appointed time. As soon as they were placed in order, one of the elders stood up, and in a long speech, declared the occasion of their meeting, and read the original institution of the Passover, and then recited the tradition, which changed the sacrifice to be offered, ... concluding with an oath of secrecy, which all present joined in, and confirmed with the most dreadful imprecations, and which was to be sealed by the participation of this horrid mystery. (224–25)

The description draws eclectically from folk mythology without (as far as I have been able to ascertain) showing indebtedness to any one particular source. Johnstone ensnares the worst popular prejudices concerning the Jews and presents them as witnessed fact. The climax of the narrative reveals their deep heinousness even as they are in the nick of time prevented from consummating their terrifying ritual:

> All things being prepared, the victims were brought to the altar, naked and bound, the instruments for slaying, and the fires for roasting them (for, horror to human thought! they were to have feasted on their flesh) in readiness, and the butchers, . . . just going to begin their work, when the doors of the house were burst open, with an outcry that heightened the terrors of the guilty wretches, and a band of soldiers rushed in and seized them, as they stood stupefied with fright. (226)

In the dénouement of the scene, one of the children rescued from the sacrificial pyre reveals himself pathetically to be the son of the army officer in command, with the inevitable outcome that the enraged soldiers at once turn upon and massacre almost all the Jews. Those few who survive are put on trial and, shortly after, publicly burned alive on the very spot where they had planned to perpetrate their crime, the torching of the site eliminating all physical evidence of their dastardly agenda. In debasing the ceremony of the Jews to the level of cannibalism, the narrative utilizes the camouflage of secrecy as perhaps the only way of making its repugnant charges against them appear in any sense credible. But to cast contemporary Jews as child-eating savages is merely straining to the last ounce the sensationalist element in the blood libel myth and enfeebling its already tenuous bond with its roots in a bygone medieval theology. It is little wonder that scrutiny of the myth in the eighteenth century is accompanied by a progressive skepticism.

The renewed presence from the mid-seventeenth century of a Jewish community in England acted as the primary challenge to fears that they would revert once again to their alleged vicious practices. Despite sporadic but largely uncoordinated attempts at different times to whip up hysteria against them, their peaceful and nonaggressive behavior provided perhaps the strongest counterargument to belief in the blood libel. Indeed, as early as 1656, Joseph Copley is among the first to pour scorn on the imputation that the Jews had ever engaged in ritual infanticide. In Protestant England, where fear of a renewal of Catholicism posed a much more serious threat than the supposed medieval crimes of the Jews, Copley can refute the blood accusation by squarely dismissing it as a monastic fabrication. Who, he asks, were the true

> actors of the crimes? none but the Monks and Friers, men, who besides their practice of Necromancy and other unlawful Arts, did frequently murder children in their Monasteries, [but] to keep their unclean conversation from the knowledge of the world, they moved by envy at the

prosperity of the Jews, crucified Children, and poisoned Wells, that laying the blame upon the Jews, they might provoke the hatred of the common people towards them.[92]

It is on these lines that counterarguments to the charge of ritual murder are sustained in eighteenth-century discourse concerning the Jews. When Bishop Percy published "The Jew's Daughter, a Scottish Ballad" in his *Reliques of Ancient English Poetry* (1765), he prefaced it with an extended rebuttal of "the supposed practice of the Jews in crucifying or otherwise murthering Christian children, out of hatred to the religion of their parents." He upholds that the false allegation merely provided "excuse for the cruelties exercised upon that wretched people," yet, he adds, the practice "probably never happened in a single instance." "*For,*" writes Percy,

> if we consider, on the one hand, the ignorance and superstition of the times when such stories took their rise, the virulent prejudices of the monks who record them, and the eagerness with which they would be catched up by the barbarous populace as a pretence for plunder; on the other hand, the great danger incurred by the perpetrators [the Jews], and the inadequate motives they could have to excite them to a crime of so much horror, we may reasonably conclude the whole charge to be groundless and malicious.[93]

The view promulgated so influentially here by Bishop Percy deserves our attention both because it helps to reflect the more liberal attitude toward the Jews that gradually gained ascendance during the century and also because of its implicit supposition of difference between medieval barbarousness—"the virulent prejudices of the monks"—and Percy's own age, in which the "ignorance and prejudice" of earlier times have been supplanted by a more enlightened intellectual skepticism. Although it remains far from unusual to encounter allusions in the pamphlet literature and fiction of eighteenth-century England to the ritual murder myth and its recurrent association with the Jews, it is as common to find it dismissed as the fabrication of a former age. If the blood libel is still leveled at contemporary Jews, its purpose seems to be more to exacerbate the sense of their continuing Otherness than to nail them with charges too farfetched ever to be substantiated. Common sense casts equal doubt on the validity even of the myth in its traditional form. It has been "undeniably prov'd," avers John Toland writing earlier in the century, that "this murder of Children [by the Jews] . . . be a gross fable, invented out of perfect malice and calumny" by fanatical priests riding upon the back of the monstrous superstition of the mob.[94] It is, argues William Hazlitt over 100 years later, "the test of reason and refinement to be able to subsist without [such] bugbears. While it was supposed that 'the Jews eat little children,' it was proper to take precautions against them. But why keep up ill names and the ill odour of a prejudice when the prejudice has ceased to exist?"

Hazlitt's defense of the Jews usefully distinguishes between the enduring presence of "vulgar prejudices," preserved at all levels of English society but (he insists) "longest in the highest places," and the more liberal bias favored by what he calls "the reflecting part of the community." Writing at the very end of our period and toward the beginning of the parliamentary campaign that was to lead to the Jews' eventual political emancipation during the Victorian era, Hazlitt laments that, despite the advance of reason and philosophy, the former attitude toward the Jews, however attenuated, still persists in popular culture.[95] For an era that, at least publicly, often emphasizes its conviction in judicious inquiry over hearsay speculation, echoes of the blood accusation are, paradoxically, never too far away in speculation concerning the Jews. The rational Enlightenment of the eighteenth century may have cast doubt upon and dispelled belief in the blood libel, yet it was quite unequipped to purge it completely from folk memory. The mutability of the libel makes it extremely durable. It emerges by discreet redefinition in conversion literature in which the neophyte from Judaism is pursued and persecuted, yet invariably succeeds in narrowly escaping from the clutches of a vengeful father and his hired assassins. Among its other manifestations, it appears in the undiminished narrative popularity of the related imputation that the Jews actively seek out the Christian Host in order to desecrate it as a compulsive reenactment of the crucifixion.[96] Sometimes, it will surface unexpectedly (as it does at a slightly later date) in a humorous punning allusion to a scion of the leading Anglo-Jewish family of merchant bankers as Baron Roast-child (i.e., Rothschild).[97] Hazlitt's "reflecting part of the community" may have expedited the fragmentation of the old myth of the rabid Jew compulsively consuming the blood of Christian children as an essential function of his religious ceremony, but it failed to dislodge the more general association that cast him as a reiterative killer willing to run amok among the congregation of Christ.

Yet one further powerful manifestation of the stereotype of the murderous Jew, that remains all-too-prevalent in the popular culture of Georgian England, finds expression through William Cobbett, who depicts him as a villainous plunderer who willingly squeezes from the poor Christian "the last drop of his blood; . . . [and] stands with his bond in one hand and the sharp knife in the other, the water from his mouth moistening his beard, ready to make the incision and take the pound of flesh."[98] The Jew here may have momentarily demurred from perfecting the business at the heart of the blood libel, the sacrifice of innocent Christian children as the centerpiece of an elaborate "alternative" ceremony, but in his portrayal as a latter-day Shylock he has lost little of the taste of the assassin. The strange conversion of Shylock from stage figure to cipher will bear much closer examination in the subsequent chapter.

CHAPTER 7

"EV'RY CHILD HATES SHYLOCK"

Writing to his friend George Selwyn in October 1757, Horace Walpole conjures a crafted metaphor to describe the reputed miserliness and political animus of Philip Yorke, first Earl of Hardwicke, who after an almost unprecedented nineteen years in office had the previous year resigned as Lord Chancellor of England. "I believe," says Walpole, "the late Chancellor Shylock, that Jew who loves human blood better than anything but money, is whetting a cleaver—that he has borrowed; for even for murder I believe he would grudge a penny to have his own new-set."[1]

The force of sentiment by which Walpole expresses his antipathy to Hardwicke simultaneously articulates a deeply embedded prejudice against the Jews that we may read as a kind of cipher.[2] For Walpole constructs his attack by linking Hardwicke's putative avarice to that associated, at least in the common perception, with the Jews. In addition, Walpole's metaphor stirs the embers of ancient hostility by invoking the medieval stereotype of the deicidal Jew intent on iterating his deed of ritual sacrifice, the shedding of innocent Christian blood. More particularly it alludes, of course, to Shakespeare's stage character of Shylock in *The Merchant of Venice,* whose inhuman insistence upon the payment of a pound of Antonio's flesh as forfeiture for the loss of his bond becomes all the more chilling and uncomfortable when we discover in his actions so many reverberations that link him with the stereotypical murdering Jew of the medieval imagination. Walpole's choice of metaphor is colored by two further factors. The first is that "Chancellor Shylock," Lord Hardwicke, best remembered perhaps as the sponsor of the celebrated Marriage Act of 1753 that made it statutory to publish in the parish church the banns of Christian marriage, and himself the father of a future bishop of the Church of England, may well have balked at being called a Jew. The second factor is that, in employing the metaphor in a letter to a friend, it is most unlikely that Horace Walpole would have considered even for a moment that in another age his remarks could be construed as racially offensive. Rather, he is using an accepted idiom that in the language and rhetoric of the day divulges a shared attitude toward the Jews of many eighteenth-century Englishmen, gentrified or otherwise. The coding of Jews as compulsive misers and ritual murderers can only make sense by appealing to a set of references readily understood by both writer and reader. Even after almost two and a half centuries, it remains not too difficult today to recognize these references and decipher the attitudes represented by them. What is far less familiar and also more intriguing is how these attitudes came to be perpetuated. The case of Shylock will provide valuable clues to their endurance.

From the heyday of the Elizabethan stage to the Jews' readmission into England in the mid-seventeenth century, it has been estimated that perhaps fifteen plays were produced in which at least one of the characters is Jewish.[3] For present purposes, only two, which also happen to be the most famous, need take our attention, namely Marlowe's *The Jew of Malta* and Shakespeare's *The Merchant of Venice*. It is well known that there exist many parallels between the two plays, suggesting a strong likelihood that in his characterization of Shylock, Shakespeare was himself influenced by Marlowe's portrayal of Barabas.[4] But whereas even recent criticism has been unable to release Marlowe's Jew entirely from Charles Lamb's complaint that he is "a mere monster . . . [who] kills in sport, poisons whole nunneries, invents infernal machines,"[5] Shakespeare's Shylock, it is generally agreed in twentieth-century interpretations of the play, can command considerable sympathy from the audience. "One has only to compare Shylock with the melodramatic travesty of Barabas in *The Jew of Malta*," writes Derek Traversi, "to see how the Shakespearian capacity to provoke contrasted reactions to his figures humanizes the Jew, provides him with motivations for the behaviour expected of him in the light of established conventions."[6]

Yet, this more sympathetic and dramatically complex interpretation, however sustainable in criticism and actual performance, may be traced back probably little further than production of the play in the second half of the nineteenth century, most notably to that of Henry Irving, first staged at the Lyceum Theatre, London, on November 1, 1879. Irving as Shylock, we learn through contemporary reviews, manifested "a dignity that seem[ed] the true expression of his belief in his nation and himself." His portrayal, we are told, was of "a picturesque figure with an air of a man feeling the bitterness of oppression, and conscious of his own superiority in all but circumstance to the oppressor." "In point of all intelligence and culture he is far above the Christians with whom he comes in contact, and the fact that as a Jew he is deemed far below them in the social scale is gall and wormwood to his proud and sensitive spirit."[7] As Toby Lelyveld concludes in his valuable historical survey, *Shylock on the Stage,* through Henry Irving, "for the first time in the long and varied history of the character, the sympathy of the general audience has been enlisted and secured."[8] If but a distant model for more recent portrayals, Irving's mid-Victorian depiction has made it wellnigh impossible for later actors and directors to ignore the compelling paradox of Shylock as both villain *and* one more sinned against than sinning. Interpretations of the play before Irving were rarely, if ever, concerned to emphasize such moral ambivalences. In particular, as we shall see, the contemporaries of Horace Walpole would not have been aware of any other Shylock than the bloodthirsty Jew of popular association with the "pound of flesh" story.

We know almost nothing about the stage presentation of *The Merchant of Venice* in Shakespeare's time. One argument that has been put forward quite frequently, although on evidence that still remains flimsy, is that the play was written in response to popular clamor against the Jews occasioned by the trial in 1594 of the Portuguese doctor Roderigo Lopez found guilty of attempting to poison his royal patient, Queen Elizabeth I. Sir Sidney Lee, who was among the first to advance this theory, contended that "it cannot surprise us that caterers for public amusements gave expression to the popular sentiments respecting" Dr. Lopez. In terms of his physical representation in the theater, Lee believed that "the kind of beard that has been for centuries a stage-tradition with Shylock" seems to have imitated that worn by Lopez, who "doubtless had [been] previously introduced" to Richard Burbage, supposedly the first player to act the part of Shylock.[9] Reviewing these ideas, John Russell Brown, the Arden editor of the play, considers the connection "insecure," although he does acknowledge that Gratiano's equation of Shylock's "currish spirit" with that of "a wolf . . . hang'd for human slaughter" (IV.i.133–34) may contain a translated pun on the name Lopez,[10] a curiously covert allusion to a figure of such public notoriety. Even if it proves impossible on existing evidence firmly to link Lopez and Shylock, at least it can be said that the trial and execution of Lopez were sufficient *causes célèbres* in the mid-1590s to give added topicality to any play containing a treacherous Jew-figure. *The Merchant of Venice* has been variously dated as having been written between 1594 and 1598, at its latest date within about four years of Lopez's execution.

A further clue to the popular reception of the play is provided by the quarto title page of 1600, which reads: "The most excellent / Historie

of the *Merchant / of Venice. /* VVith the extreame crueltie of *Shylocke*
the Iewe / towards the sayd Merchant, in cutting a iust pound / of his
flesh: . . . / *As it hath beene diuers times acted by the Lord / Chamberlaine his Seruants.*" Shylock's "extreame crueltie" is given dramatic
focus within the play in his obdurate insistence upon the exaction of his
bond, a pound of the Christian Antonio's flesh. As one who would marry
his daughter to a scion of "the stock of Barrabas" (IV.i.292) rather than
to a Christian, he is linked both with the biblical murderer whose life
was spared by the Jews for that of Jesus (Matt. 27:15–26), and, most immediately for an Elizabethan stage audience, with the similarly named
protagonist of Marlowe's *The Jew of Malta*, a villain who revels in the
ruthless manner with which he can

> kill sick people groaning under walls;
> . . . go about and poison wells;
> And now and then, . . . cherish Christian thieves (II.iii.177–79).

As with *The Merchant of Venice*, almost nothing is known about how
The Jew of Malta was performed. What we do know is that the play,
which is usually dated c. 1589–90, making it at least four years earlier
than *The Merchant of Venice*, was much in demand during the final decade of the sixteenth century and the first decade of the seventeenth
century. Between February 1592 and June 1596, the actor-manager Philip
Henslowe records that it was put on at least thirty-six times by different
companies, mainly at the Rose Theatre in Southwark. In the weeks surrounding the execution of Dr. Lopez in June 1594, Henslowe has six performances of the play noted in his diary. A significant number of literary
echoes in the works of other writers during the same two decades is
further attestation of the dramatic impact of Marlowe's play. The quarto
title page of 1633, the only surviving early edition, refers to the play as
a "*Famous* TRAGEDY," and adds a puff that it was played before King
Charles I and Queen Henrietta "IN HIS MAJESTIES / Theatre at *White-Hall*," one of the last recorded performances in Stuart England. After the
closure of the theaters in 1642, the play vanished completely from the
repertoire until its revival at Drury Lane in April 1818, with Edmund
Kean playing the part of Barabas, perhaps riding on the back of his previous triumph in the part of Shylock. There is no record of its having
been performed during the eighteenth century.

Within the insistently ironic patterning of *The Jew of Malta* Marlowe
missed few opportunities to stress the antagonism between Gentile and
Jew, with the intention (it has been argued) not merely of dramatizing
for its own sake Barabas's extreme cruelty and by association that of all

Jews, but also to expose the unabashed self-righteousness of the Christians who refuse or are unable to recognize their own complacency and their own rapaciousness.[11] In Marlowe's black humor, Barabas's cruelty is even shown to act as a necessary prop to the Church, enriching "the priests with burials" (II.iii.185) of Christians who have perished by his stratagems. The prevalent Christian attitude toward Jews within the play is best enunciated not by one of their own faith but by Ithamore, Barabas's treacherous Turkish slave. "To undo a Jew," he avers, "is charity, and not sin" (IV.iv.80). Coming from a heathen turned against his master by his uncontrolled lust for a Christian courtesan, the statement is a shockingly ironic parody of the "charity" practiced by the Christian clergy in their repeated attempts to save Barabas and his daughter through conversion. Barabas's own attitude by which he asserts that "it's no sin to deceive a Christian" (II.iii.311) is equally antagonistic and perhaps more forceful, because undiluted by any similar hypocritical desire to proselytize the Christians. In portraying Barabas as a relentless miser (one who "smiles to see how full his bags are crammed": I.i.31) and murderer (a counterpart to his biblical namesake), Marlowe is both eliciting the stereotypical response in his audience to a conventional Jew-figure who glories in his inordinate brutality, and implying that such cold-blooded and ruthless behavior is hardly different in the rest of humanity. However we wish to interpret *The Jew of Malta*, we cannot avoid recognizing that its dramatic effectiveness relies far more than Shakespeare's play upon its display of "extreame crueltie," particularly that of Barabas.

Of early literary echoes of *The Jew of Malta*, only one need detain us briefly. In William Rowley's satirical squib, *A Search for Money* (1609), a usurer figure is described as having a visage "like the artificiall Jewe of Maltaes nose" and stage tradition has it that it was usual, even well into the eighteenth century, that a Jew-figure would be seen wearing such an appendage. Ithamore's genuflective remark, "O brave, master, I worship your nose" (II.iii.175) seems to allude to this, and there is evidence that Barabas's false nose was early on transferred to Shylock. As it was not uncommon during the sixteenth century for the Devil to be depicted wearing a long misshapen nose, the physical appearance of a Barabas or a Shylock on stage must have instantly reinforced the traditional popular association of devils and Jews.[12] In an age when actual Jews were virtually unknown in England, Barabas and Shylock replicate and revivify the stereotypical Jew of the medieval imagination.

The few details that survive are insufficient to reconstruct anything more than the barest outline of the mode of performance of Shakespeare's *The Merchant of Venice* during the seventeenth century. Like *The Jew of Malta*, the play does not appear to have been revived beyond the closure of the theaters, and in fact there is no specific record of its performance after 1605, when it had been put on before James I by the King's Men as a Shrove-tide entertainment. The closest recollection of the play extant from the middle years of the century—and the nearest to a record that the play might have been performed again before 1642— occurs in a ballad entitled "The Forfeiture," published as late as 1664 and attributed to Thomas Jordan, a one-time actor. Jordan retells in a mangled fashion the Venetian story of the "vilde" Jew and the pound of flesh. There is a strong likelihood that the verses were actually written in the previous decade at the time of the readmission since their author ends his ballad by wishing that "such Jews may never come / To England, nor to London." His delineation of the Jew, although aiming to activate a prejudiced response, verges, perchance unintentionally, on the comic:

His beard was red; his face was made
   Not much unlike a witches.
His habit was a Jewish gown,
   That would defend all weather;
His chin turn'd up, his nose hung down,
   And both ends met together.[13]

The references to the Jew's beard and to his peculiar nose allude more directly to the traditional stage appearance of Shylock than to Shakespeare's text of the play, despite its availability in print during most of the seventeenth century.[14] If the vicious Jew stereotype of the Middle Ages once subsisted as little more than an abstraction, at least on stage it had gained dramatic embodiment through the appropriation of the character of Shylock. In the absence of any further performance of Shakespeare's play before 1741, that embodiment was to remain dormant for most of the first century following the readmission of the Jews.

Thomas Jordan's comic depiction of a usurious Venetian Jew in "The Forfeiture" unwittingly anticipates the fortunes of Shylock in the early years of the eighteenth century. In an era that looked back to Renaissance drama as the product of a barbarous age, it was not uncommon to endeavor to "improve" upon Shakespeare and his contemporaries by attempting to rewrite their plays according to the rules of neoclassical criticism and (not always the same thing) to the refinements in taste of the age. Nahum Tate's rewriting of *King Lear* (1681) with a happy ending is only the most famous of many such adaptations. In 1701, George Granville (later Lord Lansdowne and one of the first patrons of Alexander Pope) endeavored to rewrite the play, endowing it with the curiously misleading title *The Jew of Venice*. Granville gives prominence not to the role of Shylock but to that of Bassanio, first played in this adaptation by Thomas Betterton (1635–1710), the leader of the company "at the THEATRE in Little-Lincolns-Inn-Fields,"[15] and, though no longer young, still considered the foremost actor of the day. Bassanio's noble love for Portia becomes the focus for what is essentially a romantic comedy. In the prologue, written by Granville's kinsman Bevill Higgons, the ghost of Shakespeare, his tongue refined from blank verse to heroic couplets, is ludicrously ingratiating in his praise of the improvements to the play:

These Scenes in their rough Native Dress were mine;
But now improv'd with nobler Luster shine;
The first rude Sketches *Shakespear*'s Pencil drew,
But all the shining Master-stroaks are new.
This Play, ye Criticks, shall your Fury stand,
Adorn'd and rescu'd by a faultless Hand.[16]

It is outside the scope of the present discussion to offer anything other than a brief critique of this appalling adaptation, "rescu'd" from Shakespeare. Among its more preposterous departures is the handling of the negotiation of the bond between Shylock and Antonio, in which Granville's Jew fumbles pathetically in his indecision as to which feature of his enemy's anatomy to claim:

Let me see, What think you of your Nose,
Or of an Eye—or of—a Pound of Flesh
To be cut off, and taken from what Part
Of your Body—I shall think fit to name.
Thou art too portly, Christian!
Too much pamper'd—What say you then
To such a merry Bond?[17]

Elsewhere, Granville uses the part of Gratiano, played by and perhaps written for another well-known actor, Barton Booth (1679?–1733), as a humorous foil to Bassanio in the romantic scenes and, less than fortunately, as a commentator upon the course of the action. In the second act, Gratiano's description of Shylock's daughter, Jessica, upon learning of Lorenzo's scheme to run away with her, "Young, handsom, willing, with Gold and Jewels to Boot! / Plague on't, when shall I have such luck?" (act II, p. 10), merely degrades his friend's motive to the opportunism of a fortune-hunter, familiar enough a stock figure in Restoration comedy. In a later scene, Jessica becomes, in Gratiano's words, a "pretty Infidel," an erratic label for a Jewess turned Christian; and, after learning that it is she who has rescued Antonio, he dismisses Portia's role, for all the quality of *her* mercy, as that of a "little Smerking Lawyer" (act III, p. 25; act V, p. 45).

In the trial scene, Granville seeks out every opportunity to enlarge upon the heroism of Bassanio, who melodramatically interposes by standing between Antonio and Shylock, offering the latter "Interest upon Interest in Flesh." "Take every peice of mine," he pleads in his finest histrionic vein, "And tear it off with Pincers." By contrast, at the turning point of the scene, when Portia confronts the Jew with her judgment that he must not shed a single drop of Christian blood, Shylock "starts surpriz'd" and replies with an inarticulate "Humph," the same semi-expletive he had used earlier when he learned from Bassanio of Antonio's need to borrow money from him: "Three Thousand Duccats—humph—I think I may venture to take his Bond" (act IV, p. 36; act I, p. 6).

Faced with such a ridiculous travesty, it is perhaps too easy for us to dismiss *The Jew of Venice* as a theatrical aberration that falls below even the standard of other late seventeenth- and early eighteenth-century adaptations of Shakespeare. However, in his "Advertisement to the Reader," Granville compares his effort with that of "those Great Men who have employ'd their Endeavours the same Way" and asserts that his intention has been to bring out the "many Manly and Moral Graces in the Characters and Sentiments" of the play, "the Foundation of . . . [Shakespeare's] Comedy being liable to some Objections." The reader, he adds, may be prepared to "excuse the Story, for the Sake of the Ornamental Parts." In giving prominence to Bassanio, it would appear, Granville is not only extending a role for Betterton, but is also attempting to make the play generically clear-cut as a kind of romantic comedy and to rid it of its more awkward moral ambiguities. In part, he has done this by making expendable such characters as Launcelot Gobbo, Gobbo the father, Tubal, Solanio, and the princes of Morocco and Arragon, none of whom has had the dubious good fortune to survive his mangling. More pertinently, he appears to have tried to translate Shylock from a murderous Jew-figure into an object of comic ridicule, a ludicrously caricatured representative of his race, who is depicted raising his glass to "Money . . . my Mistress" and, in intentional anticipation of Bassanio's dramatic gesture in the trial scene, proffering a toast to "Interest upon Interest" (act II, p. 12). Bevill Higgons's prologue (spoken again here by the ghost of Shakespeare) hints at a contemporary applicability to Shylock's role that is not at once evinced from a reading of the text of the play:

> Less Heinous Faults, our Justice does pursue;
> To day we punish a Stock-jobbing Jew.
> A piece of Justice, terrible and strange;
> Which, if pursu'd, would make a thin Exchange.

The depiction of Shylock in *The Jew of Venice*, if only by a strained insinuation, was intended by Granville as a topical thrust against those first- and second-generation immigrant Jews on the London Stock-Exchange, whose unpopular presence as members had been limited by a statute of 1697 to a maximum of twelve.[18] A dictionary of 1700 defines *stock-jobbing* as "a sharp, cunning, cheating Trade of Buying and selling Shares of Stock in East-India, Guinea and other Companies; also in the Bank, Exchequer, &c." (*OED*). Such activities would have been associated by a Tory aristocrat like Granville with the mercantile aspirations of the Whigs, who controlled the financial institutions of the city and enjoyed the strong support of the Jews.[19] The implied connection of the stage figure with those actual Jews settled in London since the readmission goes some way to secularize Granville's Shylock. As the type of a stock-jobber, he is more a petty dealer who has overreached himself, a comic villain to be scorned and ridiculed by the audience, than a fiendish agent nurturing murderous instincts akin to those of the medieval theological stereotype of the Jew. Unlike Shakespeare's Jew, he is not forced to undergo the ultimate humiliation of conversion to Christianity, suggesting that this aspect was of little interest to Granville.

The role of Shylock in *The Jew of Venice* was first performed by and became associated with Thomas Doggett (d. 1721), an actor who was famous for playing "low" comic parts. It is without doubt to his performance that Nicholas Rowe alludes in 1709, when he remarks that he had seen *The Merchant of Venice* "Receiv'd and Acted as a Comedy, and the Part of the *Jew* perform'd by an excellent Comedian." Yet, adds Rowe, distinguishing between Granville's play and the original, "I cannot but think it was desig'd Tragically by the Author [Shakespeare]."[20] Of Doggett's stage appearance, Anthony Aston tells us that "he was the best face painter and gesticular" of his day, and his friend Colley Cibber records that in presenting "lower life" characters at which he was most successful, he "could be extremely ridiculous, without stepping into the least impropriety to make him so."[21] Another contemporary, John Downes, in 1708, recommends Doggett's performance in *The Jew of Ven-*

ice and other plays, when he claims that he "is the only Comick Original now Extant." "On the Stage," says Downes, "Mr. *Dogget* . . . [is] very Aspectabund, wearing a Farce in his Face; his Thoughts deliberately framing his Utterance Congruous to his Looks."²² All the evidence that we have suggests that he played the role of the "stock-jobbing Jew" Shylock in order to be droll, a deliberately "low" comic counter to Betterton's noble portrayal of Bassanio.²³ The "celebrated Dogget," we are told, "performed the *Jew* almost in the style of broad farce."²⁴

From 1701, Granville's version of the play held the stage, through a succession of actors after Betterton and Doggett, for forty years, and during that time went through six printed editions.²⁵ Its performance as romantic comedy with Shylock as a comic butt became the accepted interpretation of the age. Writing in 1710, Charles Gildon expresses the prevalent attitude of those familiar with Shakespeare's original play when he complains of its lack of "Probability and Verisimilitude" and its errors "too visible to need Discovery," which he blames on its author's "Ignorance . . . of the *Greek Drama*." However, adds Gildon, "This play has receiv'd considerable Advantages from the Pen of the honorable *George Granville*, Esq."²⁶ Those "Advantages" meant that Shakespeare's play was largely unknown during this time, ceding favor to Granville's perversely admired adaptation. Paradoxically, the same period saw a wider acceptance of Shakespeare's canonical status, a reputation that was greatly enhanced by the diligent endeavors of Nicholas Rowe (1709), Alexander Pope (1723), and Lewis Theobald (1733), each of whom edited separate multivolume editions of his complete works. The availability of edited versions of the plays also prompted fresh critical readings and, in many cases, new interpretations on the stage. In the case of *The Merchant of Venice*, as Nicholas Rowe was among the first to recognize, the discrepancy between theatrical performance, by which Granville's comic adaptation held the stage, and critical assessment of the play could hardly have been greater. "There appears in it," says Rowe, "such a deadly Spirit of Revenge, such a savage Fierceness and Fellness, and such a bloody designation of Cruelty and Mischief, as cannot agree with the Stile or Characters of Comedy."²⁷ On stage, that darker side to the play remained in limbo until 1741.

The theatrical rehabilitation of Shakespeare's play must be credited to the dramatic genius and perhaps also to the longevity of one man, Charles Macklin (1690/99?–1797), a petulant Irish actor whose stage vocation had been primarily as a comedian.²⁸ Macklin's career in the theater can be traced back at least to the early 1720s. By the time that he first performed the role of Shylock, his reputation was well established as a theatrical jack-of-all-trades and as one who favored a more natural style of acting rather than the traditional declamatory mode that had for long been in favor. Although the titular "merchant" is Antonio, Macklin recognized that in Shylock, despite the fact that he appears in only five of its twenty scenes, Shakespeare had created a dramatic role that can dominate the action as no other character in the play.[29] However, the legacy of Tom Doggett meant that in the popular perception and as far as most actors were concerned, the only way to play Shylock was as a clown or buffoon with an immense nose, and in any case in Granville's adaptation it was not Shylock but Bassanio who had been given dramatic prominence.

When Macklin revealed to members of the company at Drury Lane his design to revive Shakespeare's *The Merchant of Venice* and to play the part of Shylock *seriously*, he was merely laughed at. Their skepticism increased his determination but also persuaded him to keep secret from them exactly how he intended to interpret the part. During rehearsals, according to an early biographer, "whilst he enjoined the rest of the performers to do their best, he himself played both under his voice and general powers, carefully reserving his fire till the night of representation."[30] So vocal were the complaints of his fellow players about the feebleness of his portrayal of Shylock in rehearsal that, but for his categorical insistence, the play would have been abandoned even before it was presented to the public. Only shortly before the curtain went up on the first night, Macklin tells us, did he finally reveal himself to the other actors, "dressed for the part, with my red hat on my head, my piqued beard, loose black gown, &c. and with a confidence which I never before assumed" (92).

Meanwhile, by way of preparation outside the theater, it was later reported, Macklin went out of his way to try to learn the mannerisms and peculiarities of real Jews: "He made daily visits to the centre of business, the 'Change and the adjacent coffee-houses; that by a frequent intercourse and conversation with 'the unforeskinn'd race,' he might habituate himself to their air and deportment."[31] At home, he pored over his copy of the Old Testament and of Josephus's *History of the Jews*. In his commonplace book, he jotted down headings of various attributes of the people of the Bible that he thought might inform his dramatic performance:

> Jewes Their history, an instance of human incertainty—from the Creation to the Flood—in Egypt leaving it—robbing their masters, mu-

tinying—Jericho—wilderness—murder of the Innocents—captivity—
lion's den—Shadrack, Meshak, Abednigo, Babel. go through the history of it—act the great characters.[32]

Throughout his preparations, while dispensing with the traditional stage
nose, Macklin made strenuous efforts to "authenticate" the appearance
of his Shylock, even, as he informed Alexander Pope a few days after the
first performance, using his reading to determine specific details of the
actual dress he would wear:

> Pope particularly asked him, why he wore a *red hat?* and he answered,
> because he had read that Jews in Italy, particularly in Venice, wore hats
> of that colour. "And pray, Mr. Macklin," said Pope, "do players in
> general take such pains?"—"I do not know, Sir, that they do [replied
> Macklin]; but as I had staked my reputation on the character, I was
> determined to spare no trouble in getting at the best information."[33]

By such a strange amalgam of actual and supposed Jewish traits—biblical
and historical, mythical and contemporary—his interpretation of Shylock was conceived.

The first performance of *The Merchant of Venice* (the first recorded
since the time of Shakespeare) with Charles Macklin playing the part of
Shylock took place at Drury Lane on February 14, 1741, and, given the
extraordinary acclamation with which it was received, subsequently became the role most readily associated with the actor in a stage career
that continued for nearly another half-century. Overnight, as many years
later the novelist Maria Edgeworth expressed it with percipient irony,
Macklin had become "the most celebrated Jew that ever appeared in
England."[34] Something of the extraordinary effect of the performance can
be reconstructed from its witnesses over the years. A German visitor,
the writer Georg Christoph Lichtenberg, who saw the play in December
1775, describes well the phenomenal popularity of Macklin's Shylock
as well as the dramatic impact of his first entrance upon the stage at the
commencement of the third scene:

> When he appeared he was received with great applause, thrice given,
> each time lasting a quarter of a minute. It is not to be denied that the
> sight of this Jew suffices to awaken at once, in the best-regulated mind,
> all the prejudices of childhood against this people. . . . Picture to your-
> self a somewhat strong man, with a sallow, harsh face and a nose which
> is by no means lacking in any one of the three dimensions, a long dou-
> ble chin or dewlap; and in making his mouth, Nature's knife seems to
> have slipped and gone all the way to his ears, at least on one side, so
> it seemed to me. His cloak is black and long, his pantaloons also are
> long and broad, and his hat three-cornered and red, probably in accor-

dance with the style of the Italian Jews. The first words which he utters are spoken slowly and deliberately: *"Three thousand ducats."* The *th* and the *s* twice occurring and the last *s* after the *t* have a lickerish sound from Macklin's lips, as if he were tasting the ducats and all that they can buy; this speech creates for the man, upon his first appearance, a prepossession which is sustained throughout. Three such words, thus spoken and at the very first, reveal a whole character.[35]

In the same scene, according to an account that describes Macklin's first performance in 1741,

> Upon the entrance of *Anthonio*, the Jew makes the audience acquainted with his motives of antipathy against the Merchant. *Mr. Macklin* had no sooner delivered this speech, than the audience suddenly burst out into a thunder of applause, and in proportion as he afterwards proceeded to exhibit and mark the malevolence, the villainy, and the diabolical atrocity of the character, so in proportion did the admiring and delighted audience testify their approbation of the Actor's astonishing merit, by still louder and louder plaudits and acclamations.[36]

Of the opening scenes, which he considered "rather tame and level," Macklin himself tells us that he did "not expect much applause," but he adds that to his encouragement,

> I found myself well listened to—I could hear distinctly, in the pit, the words, "Very well—very well, indeed!—This man seems to know what he is about," &c. These encomiums warmed me but did not overset me—I knew where I should have the pull, which was in the third act, and reserved myself accordingly. At this period I threw out all my fire; and, as the contrasted passions of joy for the Merchant's losses, and grief for the elopement of Jessica, open a fine field for an actor's powers, I had the good fortune to please beyond my warmest expectations—The whole house was in an uproar of applause—and I was obliged to pause between the speeches, to give it vent, so as to be heard.[37]

In Lichtenberg's description, we can still gain an impression of the absolute sway that Macklin as Shylock had attained over his audience by the middle of the play:

> In the Scene [III.i] in which he first misses his daughter he appears hatless, with hair all flying, some of it standing up straight, a hand's breadth high, just as if it had been lifted up by a breeze from the gallows. Both hands are doubled up, and his gestures are quick and convulsive. To see a man thus moved, who had been hitherto a calm villain, is fearful.[38]

But the consummate savagery of his performance came through most powerfully of all in the trial scene (act IV, scene 1). In Johann Heinrich Ramberg's engraving of "Mr. MACKLIN in SHYLOCK," drawn for Bell's edition of Shakespeare of 1785, the Hanoverian artist shows the actor, a pair of scales in his left hand and a long sharp knife in his right, preparing to claim his pound of flesh ("Most learned Judge!—a Sentence, come, prepare" [IV.i.300]) in the manner of a ritual murderer.[39] In performance, at this point Macklin would stoop down and whet his knife on the stage floor, this mute action causing on one occasion a young man in the pit to faint dead away.[40] "When he whetted his knife," John Doran informs us, "a shudder went round the house and the profound silence following told me that he held his audience by the heart-strings."[41] Of this final scene in which he appears, Macklin writes, "The *trial scene* wound up the fulness of my reputation: here I was well listened to; and here I made such a silent yet forcible impression on my audience, that I retired from this great attempt most perfectly satisfied."[42]

Macklin's Shylock became the measure by which other actors playing the part were to be judged. As late as 1825, James Boaden, who knew Macklin personally, could claim that the dramatic effect of his Shylock "has remained to the present hour unrivalled."[43] That effect is corroborated from many quarters. Alexander Pope, who saw the play on its third night in 1741, was so moved that he is supposed to have enthusiastically pronounced a wretched doggerel couplet that has become forever linked with Macklin's interpretation of Shylock:

This is the Jew,
That SHAKESPEARE drew.[44]

If not merely apocryphal, the encomium is all the more consequential coming as it probably does not only from the greatest poet of his age but also from one who had undergone the rigors of editing Shakespeare. After George II had seen the play, he was so affected that he was unable to sleep that night, and shortly after, when Sir Robert Walpole solicited his advice as to how to subdue a recalcitrant House of Commons, the king is reported to have replied, "What do you think of sending them to the theatre to see that Irishman play Shylock?" For "Anthony Pasquin," a pseudonymous poet of the late eighteenth century, Macklin's "blood thirsty SHYLOCK" was so infernal that "could Shakespeare behold him, e'en Shakespeare would tremble."[45]

The consensus of all these opinions is that Macklin had transformed *The Merchant of Venice* into Shylock's play (as it has remained ever since through very different interpretations) by portraying him with

Johann Heinrich Ramberg, *Mr. Macklin in Shylock*. Engraving, 1785. (Courtesy of the Brotherton Library, University of Leeds.)

such remarkable and seemingly uninhibited energy as a malignant Jewish moneylender turned fiendish assassin. The demonic aspect of Macklin's Shylock is frequently remarked upon. Mrs. Inchbald's editorial comments, prefatory to a text of the play included in her multivolume compilation, *The British Theatre* (1808), reflect an enduring attitude: "Macklin was the soul, which, infused into Shylock, first animated this favourite drama—no fiend-like malice, no outrageous cruelty, no diabolical joy in human misery, seemed too excessive for the nature of mankind, when he depicted those extraordinary crimes." Macklin as Shylock, says the anonymous author of *A Guide to the Stage* (1750), had "the looks of a Judas, and the howl of a Hyena."[46] By tradition, William Hazlitt tells us, Shylock came to be depicted on stage as

> a decrepid old man, bent with age and ugly with mental deformity, grinning with deadly malice, with the venom of his heart congealed in the expression of his countenance, sullen, morose, gloomy, inflexible, brooding over one idea, that of his hatred, and fixed on one unalterable purpose, that of his revenge.[47]

Despite high expectations at the time, in a comparable Shakespearean "demonic" role for which he prepared himself with similar intensity and deliberation to that of Shylock, Macklin was anything but a success. This was his unfortunate attempt to play the title role in *Macbeth* at Covent Garden in October 1773. In large measure, its failure can be put down to the enmity of a faction of rival actors, who took prominent positions in the gallery and hissed at Macklin's every entrance, resulting in the patentee, George Colman, ordering the play to be taken off after only four performances. On November 18, in a vain attempt to appease the audience on what should have been the fifth night of *Macbeth*, Colman ordered his troupe to put on *The Merchant of Venice* in its stead. But the mob that had been brought in for the occasion by his enemies, ignoring the change of role from Macbeth to Shylock, booed and pelted Macklin off the stage, before smashing up a large part of the theater.[48] A satirical engraving of the time, *Roscius in Triumph, or the downfall of Shylock alias Mackbeth*, shows Garrick (who was thought by many to be behind the disturbances) triumphantly astride the figures of Comedy and Tragedy, while Macklin dressed as Shylock in a furred gown is being pulled down to the underworld by two fierce demons.[49] The print furnishes graphic reiteration of the popular assumption of Macklin's devilish connections. Such assumptions were also commonplace in the iconographical representation of Jews.

In the popular perception, too, Macklin was thought to share in his

Roscius in Triumph, or the downfall of Shylock alias Mackbeth.
Engraving, 1773. (Courtesy of the Folger Shakespeare Library,
Washington, D.C.)

own life many of the diabolic traits that he had elicited from the character he portrayed in his greatest dramatic triumph. The compiler of his memoirs, William Cooke, warns us that,

> although Macklin got and merited the greatest applause in Shylock, this very applause in his public, often drew from the merit of his private character; as many people, who knew nothing of him but as he appeared on the stage, and there saw the passions of *revenge* and *malice* so forcibly and naturally displayed . . . that they judged he must be something like the monster in private life which he was upon the stage.[50]

There were grounds, however, that helped to give some validity to the association. Macklin's reputation for irascibility was well founded. In 1735, several years before his performance as Shylock, he had quarreled behind the stage with a fellow actor, Thomas Hallam, over the possession of a greasy black stock wig that he claimed he had played in the night before and wished to wear again. Suddenly losing his temper, Macklin lunged at Hallam with a long stick. The latter, turning unhappily at that very moment, was caught in his left eye by the stick, which Macklin, his passion unabated, wrenched back and threw into the fire. At once, Hallam clapped his hand to his eye, groaning that the stick had gone into his head and that his eye had been pulled out. "No," said Macklin, tearing Hallam's fingers aside and probing inside the socket with his own, "I feel the ball roll under my hand." A bizarre anecdote records that Hallam then turned to a young actor (who happened to be dressed for a role requiring women's garments) and said, "Whip up your clothes, you little b——h, and urine in my eye," but as he could not Macklin himself immediately supplied the relief of this sovereign panacea.[51] Yet, despite the further efforts of a surgeon, Hallam died the following day, and after fleeing the scene, Macklin was obliged to give himself up to stand to the charge of willful murder. At his trial later that year, he was found guilty on the lesser indictment of manslaughter and sentenced to branding, a token punishment that was probably carried out with a cold iron.[52] In the cryptic text to a print of 1750, *An Infallible Recipe to Make a Wicked Manager of a Theatre*, published at Chester by a disgruntled actor who had worked under him, the ingredients of Macklin's wickedness include "the Eye of a Miser," "a Murderers Heart," "the Kiss of a Judas," and "the Bowels of Herod." Neither Shylock nor Macklin is alluded to directly in the text, although these references seem to be intended to link them. Above the text is a posthumous portrait of Hallam, holding the disputed wig in his left hand and pointing to the recipe with the index finger of his right hand. To Hallam's left, we can just see the sleeved hand of Macklin thrusting a stick or rapier straight into his vic-tim's eye.[53] Oddly and (I think) quite coincidentally, an analogue to the well-known "pound of flesh" story, which Shakespeare may have drawn from as one of the narrative sources of the play, had had "an extorting Usurer" stipulating as the price of his bond the forfeiture of an eye.[54]

Macklin's apparent indestructibility also may have contributed to his demonic reputation. The endurance of his Shylock certainly insured his fame. Depending on which birthdate we choose for him, when he first played the part of Shylock, he was already well into his forties, and he continued reviving the part until he was at least into his ninetieth year.[55] During its first season, *The Merchant of Venice*, with Macklin playing Shylock, was put on twenty times in three months, and it was regularly restored to the stage in London and on tour (particularly in his native Ireland) for nearly fifty years.[56] As one of the great Shakespearean roles, inextricably linked as it was to the performance of the famous old actor who had rediscovered it, theater managers knew that its showing was almost guaranteed to fill every seat in the playhouse. An account of a performance at Covent Garden in October 1788 imparts a sense of the veneration with which the elderly Macklin as Shylock was held in the long evening of his dramatic career:

> A crowded audience was collected . . . by what may be truly termed a phenomenon, a man in the ninetieth year of his age, sustaining a char-acter that requires the strongest exertions of faculties in their meridian blaze, and not merely sustaining them, but embodying them with such a force that would make the most inanimate spectator "live o'er the scene." A few trivial lapses of memory excepted, his performance of the character betrayed no symptoms of declension to the observation even of the oldest. On his entrance all hands and voices united in expressing the warm pleasure which the sight of him, who had entertained their fa-thers, and still retained the powers vigorous as the stoutest of their sons.[57]

Unluckily, when, on May 7, 1789, after several lackluster performances in different roles, he last attempted the part of Shylock, his memory, which had been failing for some time, finally betrayed him. After deliv-ering two or three speeches "in a manner that evidently proved that he did not understand what he was repeating," he ceded the stage to another actor, informing the audience (so Cooke tells us)

> "That he now found he was unable to proceed in the part, and hoped they would accept Mr. [Thomas] Ryder as his substitute, who was al-ready prepared to finish it." The audience accepted his apology with a mixed applause of indulgence and commiseration—and he retired from the Stage for ever.[58]

An Infallible Recipe to Make a Wicked Manager of a Theatre. Engraving, Chester[?], 1750. (Courtesy of the Harvard Theater Collection.)

In *Shylock on the Stage*, Toby Lelyveld speculates why it was that Macklin's Shylock remained such a success for so long:

> Although Macklin's genius brought about the innovation of a serious reading of Shylock's lines, a number of contemporary critics believed that he did not seem to have delved deeply enough into the character of the Jew and that he never succeeded in making the character come to life. His lasting popularity in the role, therefore, remains something of a puzzle.[59]

It is, of course, very difficult, probably impossible, to attribute such success to a single cause. Although he was throughout his career a very versatile actor who played many different parts, no other role came anywhere close to attaining the reputation (and it should be said, the notoriety) of his Shylock.[60] Undoubtedly, the impact of the part, its ability to awe and to hold an audience, must have relied heavily on his capacity to dramatize malevolence in all its "forcible and terrifying ferocity"[61] in the figure of a Jew. (Significantly, that capacity failed him when he attempted to portray a similar butchery in the Scot, Macbeth.) Macklin's villainous Shylock in no small measure owed its long-lasting appeal to his ability to ventilate in his audience those ingrained prejudices and irrational fears that are so deeply embedded in the traditional stereotyping of the Jews. The devastating effect of his performance was nurtured in the recognition most succinctly expressed a few years earlier by Pope that "ev'ry child hates Shylock."[62] Despite all the assiduous efforts Macklin took in preparing the part and the claims that his Shylock helped to introduce on to the English stage a more natural style of acting, the character that he brought to life was essentially a reactivation of the mythical Jew bogeyman of the medieval imagination. Perhaps more than anyone else, Macklin succeeded in transplanting that pariah figure out of the history books and into the everyday world of the eighteenth century. The cipher that emerged refused to be confined to the playhouse.

In *The Merchant of Venice*, Shylock is far more often referred to as "the Jew" than by his own name. As a term of opprobrium, the *Oxford English Dictionary* classifies the word *Jew* as one that is specially "applied to a grasping or extortionate money-lender or usurer." Correspondingly, it defines *Shylock* as a word that may be used allusively to describe "an extortionate usurer."[63] It is almost entirely due to the performance of Charles Macklin that from the middle years of the eighteenth century "Jew" and "Shylock" became synonymous in this usage. Henley's remarks in the 1805 Dublin edition of *The Merchant of Venice* are a good indication of the firmness with which the two epithets had become linked. "Perhaps," he says, "there is no character through all Shakespeare, drawn with more spirit and just discrimination, than Shylock's. His language, allusions and ideas are everywhere so appropriate to a Jew, that Shylock might be exhibited as an exemplar of that peculiar people."[64]

As an abusive name for a Jew, "Shylock" turns up with some frequency. It is one of a string of names flung at the essayist Richard Cumberland's fictitious Jewish correspondent, Abraham Abrahams, who describes the indignity suffered by being the object of "the vulgar fun of *smoking a Jew*" from the theater:

> As I should really take great pleasure in a good play, if I might be permitted to sit it out in peace, I have tried every part of the house, but the front boxes, where I observe such a line of bullies in the back, that even if I were a Christian I would not venture amongst them; but I no sooner put my head into an obscure corner of the gallery, than some fellow or other roars out to his comrades—*Smoke the Jew!—Smoke the cunning little Isaac!—Throw him over*, says another, *hand over the smouch!—Out with Shylock*, cries a third, *out with the pound of man's flesh*— . . . and so on through the whole gallery, till I am forced to retire out of the theatre, amongst hootings and hissings, with a shower of rotten apples and chewed oranges vollied at my head, when all the offence I have given is an humble offer to be a peaceable spectator, jointly with them, of the same common amusement.[65]

We have already seen that mob agitation in the theaters of Georgian England was far from unusual. Although fictional, Abraham Abrahams's account is almost certainly inspired by the common sport of Jew-baiting readily enjoyed by the rabble in the middle years of the eighteenth century and rarely confined to the theater.[66] Commenting on Abrahams's letter to him, Cumberland considers it inconceivable that such opprobrious entertainment could be condoned if it were but recognized by the English that "a Jew is their fellow-creature, and really has fellow-feelings with their own." The false association of all Jews with the dehumanized "monster" and "blood-thirsty villain" of Shakespeare's play helped to make them an easy target for the vile humor of the common people. The complaint by Cumberland's correspondent that "the odious character of Shylock has brought little less persecution upon us poor scattered sons of Abraham, than the Inquisition itself" conveys, for all its hyperbole, the devastating effect upon actual Jews of the Shylock figure.[67] Through Macklin's Shylock, stereotype and reality had become dangerously interchangeable in the popular perception of what constitutes a Jew. Cumberland's liberal plea, recognizing the need for more toleration toward the Jews, is a good indication of the potency and the persistence of stereotypical attitudes against which he waged a long campaign.[68]

At a time of popular clamor, as occasioned by the notorious Jew Bill of 1753, it is perhaps not surprising to discover that prejudice against the Jews was invigorated by reference to Shakespeare's play. The diarist Richard Cross, attending a performance of the opera at Drury Lane at the height of the unrest against the Jews, records the reaction of the audience: "Ye Naturalizing Bill having made some Noise against the Jews, some people call'd out for ye Merchant of Venice, & a Letter was thrown upon ye Stage desiring that play instead of the Opera, but we took no notice of it, some little hissing but it dy'd away."[69] By contrast, a malicious rumor put out at the time suggested that several eminent Jews were assiduously working together to have Macklin excluded altogether from Drury Lane to prevent him from appearing again in the character of Shylock.[70]

Elsewhere we find Shylock employed as a cipher to add weight to the traditional tally of accusations against the Jews, by which they are to be perpetually distinguished from the Christians. For instance, the author of one of the many pamphlets written against the naturalization of the Jews, condenses the dialogue of Shylock's scenes in *The Merchant of Venice* to furnish dramatic evidence of "the Mercy of the *Christian* . . . and . . . the inveterate Hatred of a *Jew.*" Rather than resorting to argument, he simply quotes the play as ample testimony of how "the *Jew* Glories in Revenge," before descending into jingoistic abuse (Christian forgiveness laid aside!) to clinch a muddled argument:

> And now, *Englishmen* and Countrymen, judge ye, What Advantage can it be to you to have these *Jews* natualiz'd! What can you get by *them?* They are all griping Usurers. And what can they get out of you, but your very Blood and Vitals? It can never be your temporal Interest to see such Persons made *Englishmen,* and I am certain it can never be the Interest of your Religion; because they are its professd Enemies. They are a Nation of Infidels. They blaspheme and curse your savior with the most dreadful Imprecations; and their TALMUD, which they revere as much as the Law of Moses, allows them to hold no Faith with us; to break their Oaths with us, to cheat us, and even to murder us, is doing God Service. Such are the vile People whom you are persuaded to take into your Bosoms: But from such Bosom-Friends, *Good Lord deliver us.*[71]

Another such pamphlet of the same year is hardly less explicit when it incorporates among its arguments against the Jews "an Instance on Record with regard to a *Jew at Venice* [which] seems to shew, that nothing less than our Flesh, as well as our Money, will satisfy their unchristian Appetites."⁷² The supposed distinction between Christian charity and Jewish cutthroat dealing does not seem to have been missed by the theatrical managers, for *The Merchant of Venice* was frequently chosen for benefit performances put on to relieve Christian indigence.⁷³ The same distinction was sufficiently ingrained to be effectively parodied more than two decades later in Richard Sheridan's play, *The School for Scandal* (1777), in which Charles Surface's willingness to sell to him the gallery of family portraits prompts the Jew broker, Mr. Premium (actually his uncle, Sir Oliver, in disguise), to utter by way of imprecation, "what the plague h ive you no Bowels for your own kindred?—Odds Life—do you take me for Shylock in the Play, that you would raise Money of me, on your own Flesh and Blood?"⁷⁴ Through the double-edged rhetoric of dramatic irony, Sheridan at one and the same time humorously echoes Shylock's actions and mocks the mercenary instincts shared by both Christian and Jew.

Outside the theater, however, Shylock's name is used with abandon as a synonym for an evil and disreputable Jew. The *London Evening-Post*, a newspaper dedicated in its anti-Jewish sentiment at the time of the Naturalization Bill, frequently invokes the cipher figure as a butt for its humor. In a mock advertisement, anticipating the enfranchisement of the Jews, one "Gamaliel Rubens Shylock" puts himself forward as a candidate for the "Vacancy in the Great Sanhedrin" occasioned "by the Death of your late worthy Representative, Judas Fonseca, Esq."⁷⁵ Another issue contains an inconsequential piece entitled "The Prophecies of Shylock" and yet another, a verse conversation, "Shylock and Zimri," on the benefits of naturalization. The fears of a Jewish conspiracy to buy up and overwhelm the country, often made explicit at such times of public attention, are reflected in the following report:

A few Days since a Gentleman travelling on the Uxbridge Road, overtook a Farmer, who look'd very disconsolate; on which he ask'd him the Matter? When the Farmer replied; *Lord, Sir, I have no Sleep for these three Nights, the Thoughts of the* Jews *overrunning us distracting me: For we hear, in the Country, that the* Jews *will Circumcise all their Tenants;* and my Landlord having ruin'd himself by *Cards* and *Dice,* is about selling my Farm, and several others in the Neighbourhood, and we hear to a *Jew.* For last Week two strange-looking Men (one they called *Shylock*) came to look at mine: *They had long Snouts and white turn'd up Eyes, sunk into their Heads, and black Beards, like my Boar;* and I have heard, *the Swine were turned into Jews.* They talk'd *a strange Linguo.*⁷⁶

The transformation of Shylock from the proud Jew who refuses pork as unclean meat ("the habitation which your prophet the Nazarite conjured the devil into": I.iii.29–30) to a swinish figure with a long snout and a black beard, speaking an incomprehensible language, ironically reflects the passage from stage figure to cipher that accompanied Macklin's rehabilitation of Shakespeare's play. In eighteenth-century popular culture, Shylock was both a murderous moneylender in league with the Devil and an epitome of a Jew.

Whether as a liberal reaction to extreme forms of intolerance and prejudice or simply a greater acceptance by the host population of a traditionally oppressed minority, it is noticeable that by the end of the eighteenth century a growing awareness of the repugnant nature of the traditional stereotyping of the Jews has begun to develop. In an unusual essay, "An Apology for the Character and Conduct of Shylock," published in 1796, within a few years of Macklin's final performance in the part, Richard Hole is among the first to advance a more humane interpretation of Shakespeare's Jew. Hole contends that an impartial perception of Shylock is only realizable if "we should divest ourselves of that prejudice we have contracted against him on account of his being a JEW—a prejudice equally unjust and illiberal."[77] When a more equitable view is adopted, Shylock emerges as a far less vindictive figure than he has become in the popular regard:

> Those who condemn him for his stern unforgiving disposition, do not consider that he had suffered the most intolerable injuries from Anthonio—that he had been publicly insulted, been spurned and spit upon by him, been deprived by his means "of his well-won thrift," and been robbed of his daughter and property by one of his associates. Who can reflect on this, and not make allowance for his meditating so severe a retaliation! (557)

Instead of having been regarded as the object of our commiseration, Shylock has "never appeared on the English stage but as an object of abhorrence" (571), with the result that no account is ever taken of the behavior of his oppressors:

> So engrossed are our minds with the detestation of him, that no one who peruses, or sees the "Merchant of Venice" represented, ever conceives an unfavourable opinion of the undutiful Jessica, or the prodigal Lorenzo.—And why? because the person whom he robs of his wealth, and of his daughter, is a JEW. (565)

By offering a more sympathetic interpretation of Shylock, the essay also exemplifies the beginnings of a significant attitudinal change toward the

Jews. For Hole, the inveterate malice directed against the Jews is largely anthropological, affording "a striking instance . . . of the lax state of morality, and the dominion of religious prejudices in the darker ages!" (572). Implicitly, he appears to be saying that such bigotry should have no place in a more enlightened era. Although John Nichols the literary anecdotist thought that Hole intended merely an ironic vindication of the character of Shylock, the tenor of his essay has usually been accepted at face value.[78]

We have already seen that in a periodical essay of 1785 Richard Cumberland had defended his fictitious Jewish correspondent, Abraham Abrahams, against the anti-Jewish scurrilities of the mob. Nine years later, in his play *The Jew*, Cumberland attempted to give focus to the same theme by creating in Sheva, its eponymous hero, a benevolent usurer, evidently intended as a dramatic counterpart to Shylock. The noble object of the play, as recognized by one of its contemporary reviewers, was "to conquer the illiberal prejudices of mankind and level the repulsive and uncharitable distinctions of sect and of country."[79] Although of no outstanding literary merit, *The Jew* is nevertheless an important landmark as perhaps the first English play that quite consciously sets out to vindicate the Jews from a dramatic prejudice that can be traced back in an unbroken line through half a millennium to the Miracle plays of the Middle Ages. In the preface to an early nineteenth-century text of Cumberland's play, the editor alludes to *The Merchant of Venice*, striking a similar chord to that of Richard Hole in exculpating the role of Shylock and offering further an energetic defense of his creator:

> The popular prejudice against the Jew was hardly mitigated in Shakespeare's time. That mighty master, however, cannot be said to have joined in the vulgar cry, when he drew the amazing character of Shylock; for the Jew (the story of the pound of flesh is not Shakespeare's) is circumvented and defrauded by a quibble. He is more than triumphant in all his arguments; and the practice of Christians is blown to atoms when he brings against it his tremendous artillery of withering sarcasm and unanswerable fact. Every provocation that unjustifiable and unmanly insult could offer—anathemas against the faith of his forefathers—abuse of his nation and name—indecent contumely and violence against his person—public reprobation of his practices in trade—everything that could irritate and madden, was inflicted upon him, by cool heads and cold hearts; and all—because he was a Jew![80]

Of all Shakespeare's plays, *The Merchant of Venice* is arguably the one with a critical history most closely bound to its theatrical history. Although other actors had continued to present Shylock as a malevolent villain after the tradition established by Macklin, it was inevitable that in a climate of greater tolerance toward the Jews a more humane stage interpretation should emerge. That interpretation was reserved for the hitherto unknown actor Edmund Kean (later rumored to be the illegitimate child of a Jewish father), who, at Drury Lane in 1814, introduced to great acclaim a Shylock who for the first time could be deemed recognizably human rather than monstrous. Instead of impersonating the spirit of hatred of Jew for Christian, Kean's Shylock was a man stung into anger by the bitter wrongs perpetrated against him and his tribe. His was a far more intellectualized Shylock whose sufferance could actually be felt by the audience. If dogmatic in asserting his right, he could be seen to epitomize the (so-called) Jewish law of "an eye for an eye," rather than the demonic venom of a relentless assassin. Kean's Shylock was far more in tune with a more liberal age, even though his interpretation fell well short of the "sympathetic" Shylock of Henry Irving later in the century. It is perhaps significant to note that when Kean essayed a similar revival of the role of Barabas in *The Jew of Malta*, the attempt was singularly ineffective, perhaps because Marlowe's play lends itself far less readily to the interpretation of an actor wishing to stress human credibility.[81]

Yet one more pertinent manifestation of the repudiation of the endemic stereotyping of the Jews is evinced in the works of the Anglo-Irish novelist Maria Edgeworth. In several of her earlier novels and tales, she introduced unsavory Jew-figures drawn mainly from traditional literary sources. The apogee of these is the character of Mr. Mordicai, in *The Absentee* (1812), a monstrously unscrupulous Jew, who in a bizarre deathbed scene threatens a son with the arrest of his dying father if the latter's debts are not settled on the spot. The Jew's demand, "—the bond or the body, before I quit this house," is too powerful an echo to leave any doubt of his literary ancestry.[82] After Edgeworth received "an extremely well-written letter . . . from America, from a Jewish lady, complaining of the illiberality with which the Jewish nation had been treated in some of . . . [her] works,"[83] she sought to make amends in her next novel, *Harrington* (1817). As a young man during the 1760s, the hero of the novel, William Harrington Harrington, thrills at the opportunity of meeting "the most celebrated Jew in all England, in all Christendom, in the whole civilized world" and of seeing a few days later this same "Jew" playing Shylock:

> The play went on—Shylock appeared—I forgot every thing but him.—
> Such a countenance!—Such an expression of latent malice and re-

venge, of every thing detestable in human nature! Whether speaking or silent, the Jew fixed and kept possession of my attention. It was an incomparable piece of acting: much as my expectations had been raised, it far surpassed any thing I had conceived—I forgot it was Macklin, I thought only of Shylock. In my enthusiasm I stood up, I pressed forward, I leaned far over towards the stage, that I might not lose a word, a look, a gesture. (40, 59)

Harrington's enjoyment is most suddenly assuaged by the recognition of the upsetting effect of the performance upon a fine young Jewess (shortly to be disclosed as the heroine of the novel) who has sat down close by in the same box:

> Now, my pleasure in the play was over. I could no longer enjoy Macklin's incomparable acting; I was so apprehensive of the pain which it must give to the young Jewess. At every stroke, characteristic of the skilful actor, or of the master poet, I felt a strange mixture of admiration and regret. I almost wished that Shakespeare had not written, or Macklin had not acted the part so powerfully: my imagination formed such a strong conception of the pain the Jewess was feeling, and my inverted sympathy, if I may so call it, so overpowered my direct and natural feelings, that at every fresh development of the Jew's villainy I shrunk as though I had myself been a Jew. (60)

Edgeworth's concern to give due emphasis to the larger adverse effect of Macklin's Shylock is a good indication of a new empathy toward the Jews and of a consciousness of shame at their mistreatment in the previous age. Her novel is an act of exorcism, an attempt (albeit, in literary terms, not a very convincing one) to erase the bogeyman of "the traditionary representations and vulgar notions of a malicious, revengeful, ominous looking Shylock as ever whetted his knife."[84] After the early years of the nineteenth century, the cipher figure of Shylock perseveres as rarely more than a figure of speech.

When we turn again finally to the *Oxford English Dictionary*, we find that the allusive employment of the word *Shylock* to represent in a more general sense "an extortionate usurer" seems firmly entrenched in English usage even to the present day, although mercifully perhaps not always linked by reflex to its ethnic source. Curiously, the earliest nineteenth-century example quoted by *OED* appears to reinvigorate the stereotype in all its medieval viciousness. It is drawn from the *Journal of a West India Proprietor* (1815), by Matthew Gregory Lewis, the author of sensationalist Gothic fiction and drama, and from such a pen the brief quotation seems unerringly melodramatic and gruesome: "It had such a kind of Shylocky taste of raw flesh about it." Has this West Indian

Shylock been inducted into the hideous rites of cannibalism? What macabre tale has the gnomic whimsy of a drudging lexicographer left half concealed? Can Shylock have undergone yet one further terrible metamorphosis? Beyond the dictionary, we need the context of Lewis's *Journal* to avoid suspense, for Lewis is describing his first taste of a watermelon:

> I never met with a worse article in my life; the pulp is of a faint greenish yellow, stained here and there with spots of moist red, so that it looks exactly as if the servant in slicing it had cut his finger, and suffered it to bleed over the fruit. Then the seeds, being of a dark purple, present the happiest imitation of drops of clotted gore; and altogether (prejudiced as I was by its appearance), when I had put a single bit into my mouth, it had such a kind of Shylocky taste of raw flesh about it (not that I recollect having ever eaten a bit of raw flesh itself), that I sent away my plate, and was perfectly satisfied as to the merits of the fruit.[85]

Macklin's vicious Jew could hardly have enjoyed a more unexpected evisceration!

CHAPTER 8

THE JEW BILL

THE CONTROVERSY that accompanied the passage and repeal within the same year (1753) of the Jewish Naturalization Act, popularly known as the Jew Bill, provides a kind of historical epicenter to our study. At no other time during the whole period under scrutiny in this book did the social, political, and economic position of the Jews in England excite so much unbridled passion and arouse so much raw publicity. Well over eighty pamphlets, at least a score of satirical prints, an uncounted tally of popular songs and ballads, column after spiteful column in newspapers and periodicals in opposition or defense attest to the extraordinary clamor and controversy brought about by the widespread expectation of an imminent Jewish naturalization. So many malodorous presumptions concerning the Jews that for so long had lurked in the English popular imagination unexpectedly emerge to receive explicit airing in the turbulent conflict aroused by the bill. Even after we take necessary account of the inevitable distorting effect caused by rhetorical amplification at a time of heated altercation, no other moment in the history of the Jews in eighteenth-century England gives us as complete an opportunity to gauge the prevailing temperature of contemporary anti-Semitic prejudice. In the full nastiness of the popular reaction triggered by the Naturalization Act, we may witness the last full-blown embodiment of those attitudes to the Jews that we have earlier been able to trace to the late Middle Ages and to the period of their expulsion.

Yet in terms of its overall significance to the state of affairs in Hanoverian England, the dispute over the Jew Bill, for all the utter hubbub that it begat for a good half of 1753, has come to be viewed as an episode of scarcely more than lilliputian magnitude, ignored for the most part, or at best fleetingly treated by later historians. It is regarded, in the words of a comparatively recent interpreter, as "simply a curious interlude in English politics—arousing tremendous passions at the time, but with no lasting effects whatever."[1] Even the author of the only full-length study of the bill, Thomas W. Perry, to whose work we shall shortly turn, acknowledges its "essential insignificance" as "a minor and momentary flare-up whose importance must not be exaggerated."[2] Historically valid as such statements are in recording the negligible influence of the bill in the political context of its time, they nevertheless singularly omit to take account of its repercussive consequences upon populist English attitudes to contemporary Jews. By raising to the arena of public debate so many ignoble prejudices that had for so long largely subsisted just below the surface, the bill had the twin effect of frustrating until the next century any further realistic attempt at Jewish emancipation but also of kindling nascent liberal response to the general injustices of their situation and treatment.

As such, given the monstrous public outcry that it was to provoke, the scope of the bill, which received its first reading in the House of Lords on April 3, 1753, was surprisingly narrow. Its very modest objective was to offer foreign-born Jews, who could prove a minimum of three years' residence in Great Britain or Ireland, the opportunity by private petition to Parliament to be naturalized without having to be received into the Anglican sacrament.[3] Since the fulfillment of such a procedure was both complicated and expensive, the bill was intended as a privilege that might be enjoyed almost exclusively by the few elite Sephardi merchants and brokers who had the capacity to petition in this way. A propulsive assumption behind the bill was that, given the global network of their trading connections, the naturalization of these wealthy Jews would prove of untold economic benefit to the state. As an auxiliary safeguard to avoid the remotest possibility of abuse, a clause was inserted into the bill by its promoters—a coterie of liberal Whigs—stipulating that any Jews so naturalized would be disabled from purchasing or inheriting an advowson or right of ecclesiastical patronage. The uncontentious passage within a few days of the bill through its three readings in the House of Lords and its similar reception at its first reading in the House of Commons give no hint of the massive popular ire that was about to be unleashed against its proponents and also, of course, against the whole tribe of those whom it had vainly sought to assist.

That the ruling Whigs under Henry Pelham found themselves totally unprepared and taken aback by the public furor precipitated by the Naturalization Act is indicative of their gross misjudgment in believing that its objectives would be regarded as wholly uncontentious. Parliamentary opposition to the bill emerged only during its second and third readings in the Commons and even then (for it was passed by a handsome majority and received the royal assent on June 7) it would have been next to impossible to predict the ferociousness of the clamor that would be raised up and down the country in the coming months. Initial opposition to the bill appears to have been instigated by an ultrapatriotic Tory remnant in the Commons, in conjunction with a caucus of London merchants and traders who feared that the naturalization of the Jews could threaten or compromise their own commercial position. In challenging the long-held Whig assumption that ease of immigration and naturalization were actively to be encouraged, these opponents of the bill hollowly vocalized an underlying Tory principle of support for the more orthodox values of High Church Anglicanism and ferociously expanded this to an insular distrust of all that was alien. More by callous opportunism than by venal design, they succeeded in fomenting the traditional xenophobia of the mob and targeting it against the Jews as a means of deriding the Whig administration prior to an impending general election.[4] In the popular frenzy that ensued, what was intended as a limited measure to aid a small number of the more affluent was propagated, albeit fallaciously, as a bill providing for the general naturalization of all foreign Jews wishing to enter the country.

Because it had been the conspicuous intention of the parliamentary opponents of the bill to lambast the government by clutching for any straw that might ignite a political fire, Thomas Perry concludes his *Public Opinion, Propaganda, and Politics in Eighteenth-Century England* by arguing that

> the controversy of 1753 . . . at bottom . . . was not, as it first appears, a singular and isolated outburst of anti-Semitic passion . . . , but rather a renewal—albeit a somewhat artificial one, aimed at an approaching election—of a long-standing dispute over immigration and naturalization policy. (178)

For Perry, the

> astonishing absence of any physical violence against individual Jews or their property is the best evidence for the argument that the passions stirred up by the clamor were largely directed, and were by the fomenters intended to be directed, against the Court politicians rather than against the Jews.[5]

The anti-Jewish aspect of the clamor, he explains, should not therefore be interpreted as an explosion of anti-Semitic bigotry but may rather be understood as a topical opportunity by which opponents of the bill could "demonstrate their zeal not against Jews, but against naturalizations" (178–79). Ultimately, he contends, "the 'anti-Jewish' clamor of 1753 was meant, even at its ugliest, to prepare the ground not for a pogrom, but for a general election" (75).

In the light of our own study, Perry's assessment, for all its valid emphasis upon the immediate political and propagandist elements that lay behind parliamentary opposition to the bill, seems sadly deficient in appreciating how fully the force of popular prejudice could as late as the mid-eighteenth century continue to give sustenance to the negative image of the Jew that we have followed unremittingly from the Middle Ages. It is ultimately little more than a playing with words to suggest that the evocation of this image as an illiberal weapon of election propaganda *should not* be confused with anti-Semitism. The absence of physical violence against actual Jews in England (so few in number as they were in 1753) does not alter the fact that endemic attitudes persisted in casting them in the popular imagination as infernal bogeymen shamelessly conspiring to undermine the Christian church and simultaneously plotting to rob the native Englishman of his inherited birthright. The facility with which they were so shamelessly exploited simply discloses how entrenched these attitudes remained. As Jacob Katz writes by way of timely response to Perry's thesis,

> the easy success of the propaganda and the nature of the arguments used during the campaign are telling testimonies to the image of the Jew prevailing in the public mind. It was the image of the popular Christian tradition, combining the theological tenets of the Jews' guilt in rejecting the Christian message and an aversion to the foreign tradesman whose greed and cunning remain unchecked.[6]

If antipathy to the Naturalization Act did not spill over into actual bloodshed, the mob frenzy that it aroused provides as close an approximation as we are likely to find in eighteenth-century England to the kind of popular hysteria that in pre-expulsion days may have sparked a pogrom. The fury with which the passing of the act was assailed, writes the nineteenth-century church historian John Overton, shrewdly glancing back to medieval times, "would really lead us to believe that the feeling towards the Jews was not much changed since the days of Front de Boeuf and Isaac of York."[7]

Indeed, following the bill's enactment, chronic fears were murmured among its supporters of the imminence of vicious assault upon members of the Jewish community and of gross incursions upon their property. "Such an abominable spirit" is brewing against them, writes Thomas Herring, archbishop of Canterbury, at the height of the turmoil, "that I expect in a little time they will be massacred." In a similar idiom, Lord Temple, an unyielding champion of the bill, speaking in the Upper House at the time of its repeal, spells out the anxiety shared by several of its supporters who had "trembled lest fires should be rekindled in

Smithfield to burn Jews."[8] But, perhaps because of an inability or un-willingness among its adversaries to control the situation centrally, op-position to the bill never translated itself into this kind of coordinated violence. Instead, through the summer and autumn months of 1753, public life became almost totally dominated by the rampant temper of what another of the bill's advocates, Lord Chesterfield, disdainfully calls "that narrow mob-spirit of *intoleration* in religious, and inhospitality in civil matters."[9] A function of this chapter will be to probe the rhetoric of "intoleration" at the time of the Jew Bill insofar as it may illumine our understanding of the processes of stereotyping. Specifically, I wish to examine the representation of the Jew as an implied or stated threat to the status quo in religious and civil matters, and, most particularly, the depiction of the so-called rich Jew and his assumed connection with stock-jobbing and with global trade and dealing.

The sense of an almost ineradicable difference between Jew and Chris-tian, as perceived through English eyes at the time of the Jew Bill, is initially revealed in the surviving texts of opposition speeches during the parliamentary debates on the question of naturalization.[10] One of the more commonly repeated hierarchic assumptions by proponents of the bill in response to the unexpected outcry that it provoked was that the hue and cry that it had ignited was largely confined to the mob. In the space of a few months, observes Horace Walpole, "the whole nation found itself inflamed with a Christian zeal . . . [though] this holy spirit seized none but the populace and the very lowest of the clergy."[11] Yet, despite an honorable defense of the principles of the bill by the higher clergy in the House of Lords, it is significant that many of the more tell-ing aspersions leveled against contemporary Jews in pamphlets, ser-mons, and street cries were first intonated upon the lips of opposition gentlemen in the Commons. The perception of the unconverted Jew in his traditional role as the extrinsic Other permeates their rhetoric and is later merely elaborated upon in the more expressly demotic forum of popular literature. Although deeply rooted in popular culture, anti-Semitic prejudice in mid-eighteenth-century England is rarely, if ever, bound merely to the language and sentiment of the mob.

A typical point of view of the scattering of mainly Tory country gentlemen and knights of the shire who first voiced their opposition to the bill is exemplified by Sir Edmund Isham, the M.P. for Northamp-tonshire, whose speech to the Commons during its second reading (May 7) distinguishes between Jews and other would-be immigrants:

Let us consider, Sir, that the Jews are not like French refugees, or German Protestants: these in a generation or two become so incorporated with us, that there is no distinguishing them from the rest of the people: their children, or grandchildren, are no longer French or German, or of the French or German nation, but become truly English, and deem themselves to be of the English nation. But the unconverted Jews can never be incorporated with us: they must for ever remain Jews, and will always deem themselves to be of the Hebrew not the English nation.[12]

For Sir Edmund, the fact that the Jews appear unassimilable, that unlike Protestant denizens or other foreigners they have proved incapable of coalescing with the host group, makes their presence in England so particularly unwelcome. Familiarity with Jewish history (which inevitably means their biblical history) will serve only to endorse his argument, for, he adds,

though the Israelites were 430 years in Egypt, yet they never incorporated with that people, but kept themselves always a distinct people; and though they were but one family when they first went into that country, and for most of the time were kept in continual bondage, and numbers of their male children at last destroyed, yet when they were led out of it by Moses, they amounted to about 600,000 fighting men, besides women, children, and servants. (1380)

The Bible is randomly used in such discourse as an infallible prognosticator of the demographic and behavioral patterns of contemporary Jews whose true incapacity (we may argue) is in their inability to release themselves from being grossly stereotyped by the exploitation of a common knowledge of their pentateuchal past. The familiar charge of "swamping" by multitudes of Jews becomes in 1753 a keynote of the uproar against their naturalization. In his speech to the Commons, Isham warns of the dangers of "opening this sluice for letting the torrent in upon us" and of "the numbers that will flock hither in consequence of this Bill" (1380–81). The smear that by rank conspiracy the Jews are on the point of forever supplanting English life and culture is amply echoed elsewhere. A conversation overheard in a London coffeehouse and recorded semihumorously in a polemical pamphlet voices well the wider anxiety sweeping the country through the summer of 1753 that "there may be a Design to make us all *Jews*, and to have us circumcised."[13] In a similarly overheard conversation, a gentleman sheltering from the rain near the Royal Exchange reports a Jew saying, "I hope to live now to see the day not to meet a Christian in this place or an Englishman in the kingdom."[14]

The threat of the Jew as Other as perceived in pamphlet attacks on the bill is as a perpetual menace to the very fabric of Church and State. "Naturalizing the *Jews*, who are Infidels and *Antichrists*," writes a typical scribbler, "will soon let in all Infidelity bare-fac'd; and open a Door to even the Great Antichrist."[15] As the Jews, demands another, do not seem "in the least disposed to incorporate with us by becoming *Christians*, why should we be *lavish* of our *birth-right*; and *appear abroad* . . . as endeavouring to incorporate ourselves with them . . . ?"[16] "When I reflect upon the *well-known Restlessness* of this People to make themselves a *King*, and lord it over others," remarks an anonymous pamphleteer, "I dread to think what the Consequence may be, of having such Persons near us."[17] The sense of their Otherness is pointedly represented by Jonas Hanway, who stipulates that the Jews "are not entitled to naturalization, for two plain reasons; the first is, because they are *Jews*; the next is, because they *are not christians*."[18] In all these examples, the assumption writ large of inalienable differences separating them casts the presence of the Jews as a perpetual reminder of the supposed fragility of the status quo in a Christian state and of the pressing need that this should be preserved. The pathological fears expressed in the rhetoric generated by the Jew Bill seem to oppugn the general claim put forward by several modern historians that the age may be interpreted as one of increasing political and cultural stability.[19] The xenophobia or, more particularly, Jew hatred excited by the bill supports a rather different view of the era that sees it as one that is deeply uncertain of the resilience of its institutions and subversively ill at ease with itself. As has recently been remarked by scholars questioning the received historiography of the period, "few contemporaries were as convinced as later historians that theirs was an age of stability."[20] The rhetoric provoked by the Jew Bill radically undermines too complacent an assumption of stability.

A paramount objective at the heart of the more fanatical opposition to the Jew Bill was the desire to defend the Anglican Church against the putative threat of a headlong encroachment by Judaism. The climate generated by those antagonistic to the bill made it seem, according to one contemporary, "as if *Christianity* itself was at Stake, and ready to be swallow'd up in the Gulph of *Judaism*, and that the whole Nation was in Danger of being over-run with Infidels and Blasphemers." The old rallying cry of "the Church in danger," which earlier in the century had been used to stir electoral passions, was tellingly revamped in 1753 into such catchphrases as "Christianity and Old England for ever," "No long beards nor whiskers" and "No Jews; Christianity and the constitution."[21] The most frequently repeated of these phrases, the notorious distich "No Jews! No wooden shoes!" blends contemporary prejudice against the Jews with periodic fears of a French invasion and a consequent reinstatement of Catholicism.[22]

A fanciful reflection of public anxiety over the perils awaiting the English Church is conspicuous, too, in the renewal of the rumor, first encountered in the mid-seventeenth century, that the Jews were intent upon converting St. Paul's Cathedral into the principal temple for the pursuance of their religious practice. In the anonymous print, *A Prospect of the New Jerusalem*, a throng of bearded Jews upon an eminence overlooking Wren's St. Paul's, with the city of London spread beneath, contemplate rapturously the many steepled metropolis that will become their new seat of worship after the passing of the Naturalization Bill. The caption quotes Numbers 32:5, "let this land be given unto thy servants for a possession," and collectively attributes the triumph of Christ's natural enemies, the Jews, to a cabal of the Church of Rome in outlandish conjunction with the Devil, infidels, heretics, and Turks. Accompanying the Jews, in the foreground to the print, is a grotesque figure of the Devil, with a bag of money marked £500,000 in one hand, and gesticulating with the other hand in the direction of two brothers on a distant hill, the parliamentary authors of the bill, Henry Pelham and the Duke of Newcastle, who were rumored to have been bribed into action by the Jews. Hardly visible in the foreground on the left is the cowering figure of Britannia, her lance and shield fallen beneath her, symbolizing the final extirpation of old England by her foes.[23] The promised land of the Jews, it was feared, could be attained only at the expense of the indigenous English. The disquietude first sounded within Parliament that "they may [soon] have synagogues for the propagation of Judaism in every corner of the country" becomes amplified up and down the land into a clarion call to "fellow Britons, christians and protestants" to rouse yourselves for "it is not *Hannibal* at your gates, but the *Jews*, that are coming for the keys of your church doors."[24]

The effectiveness of the strange hodgepodge of arguments, both temporal and spiritual, utilized by opponents of the bill is contingent upon a dogmatic insistence of the truth of the proposition that the Jews are by their nature both at permanent enmity with and constantly endeavoring to corrupt the values of Christians and Christianity. We have already seen how belief in this underwrites the representation of their religious ceremony in anti-Semitic discourse. This is no less the case in the popular expression of theological arguments against their naturalization, in which they are reiteratively portrayed as "the most professed enemies to Christianity, . . . the greatest revilers of Christ himself,"

A Prospect of the New Jerusalem. Engraving, 1753. (Courtesy of the Jewish Historical Society of England.)

"great scoffers at *Christianity*," and "open and avowed Opposers of those Principles of Christianity upon which our Constitution is founded."[25] To naturalize the Jews, it is argued, would be to obstruct God's decree that they should be dispersed. "He scattered them over the Earth as Fugitives and Vagrants," comments a typical naysayer to the bill, "and yet we gather them together as if they were free-born *Englishmen*: They are the Outcasts of Heaven, yet we incorporate them."[26] By permitting the bill to become law, contests the incorrigible Sir Edmund Isham in his address to the House, "we are giving the lie to all the prophecies in the New Testament, and endeavouring, as far as we can, to invalidate one of the strongest proofs of the Christian religion."[27] In pitting Judaism against Christianity, these opponents to the bill grossly magnify the sense of difference between the two religions, while also repeating the familiar twofold paralogism that the legendary obstinacy of the Jews blinds them from identifying the true Messiah, yet their cursed state persists unabated until they do.

As a consequence, the Jews are seen as "the last People under the Copes of Heaven . . . worthy of such an extraordinary Privilege" as naturalization.[28] In particular, it is claimed, the evidence of history (usually drawn from the grossly anti-Semitic accounts of the thirteenth-century Benedictine monk Matthew Paris, or the seventeenth-century Puritan controversialist William Prynne) suggests that their presence in England should be viewed as highly deleterious to the welfare of the indigenous population. "Every aera which was in this country favourable for the Jews," insists one of the more vociferous parliamentary opponents of the bill, "was an unfortunate aera for the nation."[29] Their alleged rapaciousness in former times is cited as indicative of their future conduct should the bill succeed. Not only will they buy up all the land and replace Christianity with Judaism but, in the baseness of their infidelity, they will conspire to topple the house of Hanover itself and supplant it with an Hebraic dynasty. Less than a decade after the Jacobite revolt of 1745, the loyal support that had been given to monarchy and government by wealthy Jewish merchants and brokers (an obligation not forgotten by the legislative promoters of the bill) was rudely concealed in anti-Judaic diatribe by reckless allegations of treachery. As those "ravenous Wolves, the devouring, blaspheming Jews . . . acquire more Wealth and Strength, more Influence, Interest and Power, from their Naturalization," expostulates Christianus, a pseudonymous correspondent in the rabidly Tory *London Evening Post*, "Will they not snatch the first favourable Opportunity that offers, throwing off their Allegiance to the King, and set up a King of their own?"[30]

If precedent for this commonly voiced claim could not be found in British history, it was always possible to concoct whimsical parallels by reference to the Bible. After all, the whole question of patrimony and of deceit by the Jews had been well rehearsed, among other places, in the story of Jacob and Esau (Genesis 25 and 27). The bill, it was argued by one of its Tory parliamentary opponents, William Northey, must be looked upon as an attempt by alien Jews to rob Englishmen of their birthright as Christians. But, he adds tellingly, where Esau may have been prepared to sell "his birthright to his brother Jacob for a mess of pottage, when he was faint and at the point of dying for hunger . . . we are going to give it away for nothing, and when we are under no necessity."[31] A similar but less expected parallel is forged in such discourse by reference to the Book of Esther, in which the Jew Mordecai supplants Haman, who had vowed to extirpate his people, as the favorite and chief minister of King Ahasuerus. The revenge meted out by the Jews under Mordecai, Queen Esther's uncle, against Haman and his supporters, whereby "they put to death in two days 76,000 of those they were pleased to call their enemies, without either judge or jury" is evoked as a timely reminder of the resentment and cruelty with which they may treat others when put in a position of power. Their ambition, it is alleged by parabolic allusion to the same story, is "to put their foot upon the necks of the people who have always been and always will be their declared enemies." The consequence of naturalizing the Jews will be the inevitable subservience of the English, selling not only their birthright but themselves into perpetual bondage.[32]

Significantly, the caption to the print, The Circumcised Gentiles, or a Journey to Jerusalem (1753), quotes a verse from the Book of Esther (8:17), "And in every Province, and in every City whithersoever the Kings Commandment and his decree came, the JEWS had Joy and gladness, a feast and a good day: and many of the People of the land became JEWS; for the fear of the JEWS fell upon them." The engraving prophetically reveals the consequence of the naturalization of the Jews. A shabbily dressed Ashkenazic Jew with prominent nose and grizzled beard is shown mounted on an ass, the title of the print perhaps implying an ironic travesty of Christ's entry into Jerusalem. Here, however, the Jew is accompanied upon the ass by a Church of England bishop (possibly one of those prelates derided as an apostate for supporting the bill),[33] who rides side-saddled behind him. He has his eyes turned heavenwards, holds a "TALMUD" under his left arm, and proclaims in apology for fallen Christendom, "We have err'd and stray'd from thy ways like lost Sheep." The Jew gestures disrespectfully at him and says, "Me am Naturalize and have Converted mine Broder dat is behind." He holds before him a box labeled "ISRAEL'S Court Plaister for Green Wounds." The significance of this is made apparent by a third figure on foot before them and leading the ass with a long rope, who declares, "I dont know how it fares with your Brother behind but this I am sure of that if Circumscision agrees as ill with him as it does with me he wont keep his SEAT long." He carries a moneybag marked "100,000" in allusion to the bribery by which the Jews were alleged to have bought votes in favor of naturalization. Behind him, the simple ass, symbolizing perhaps the lot of the common people under the yoke of the Jews, brays its innocence from such corrupt dealing by announcing, "I have the honour to represent my Country Gratis, which is more than my Leader can say." Two papers severally marked "General Election" and "JEWS . . . 96 CHRISTIANS 55" foretell the triumph of a Jewish theocracy. The familiar outline of the dome of St. Paul's and the rejected New Testament lying open in the dust are further cogent reminders of this. The print provides a visual exposition of prophetic fears that the Jews are hatching outrageous schemes to remold the fabric of English life so as to make it conformable with their own ceremonial practice.[34]

In the humor of the times, frequent recourse is made to prophecy and prognostication as a means of lampooning some of the more extravagant fears that had been blown about against the Jews. By clever parody of reports from the official *London Gazette,* the squibbing "News for One Hundred Years Hence," first published in the *Craftsman* but widely reprinted, includes news items supposedly culled from the "Hebrew Journal" of 1853 by which era it was assumed that, as a consequence of the Jews' naturalization, the country would have fallen under the complete domination of the Jews. Indeed, we discover by reading through items hot from the press of February 14, 1853, that Great Britain is now renamed Judaea Nova; Parliament has been replaced by a Sanhedrin which but yesterday night threw out "the Bill for naturalizing Christians . . . by a very great Majority"; on Monday last, it is reported, "a Dispensation passed the Great Seal to enable Abraham Levy to hold a Living in the Synagogue of Paul's"; a week earlier, we learn, the outlawed smuggler George Briton was cast into Newgate after having been "taken on the Coast of Sussex in the very Fact of running Pork into this Kingdom, in Defiance of the . . . Penal Laws"; among the malefactors "crucified at Tyburn, pursuant to their Sentence" on Wednesday last were several "unhappily educated in the Errors of the Christian Religion, . . . [who] chose to lay down their Lives rather than be curtail'd of the Honour of their Ancestors by the Act of Circumcision"; an order, sent recently

The Circumcised Gentiles, or a Journey to Jerusalem. Engraving, 1753.
(Courtesy of the British Museum, Department of Prints and Drawings.)

from the Lord Chamberlain's Office, forbids the theaters "under the severest Penalties, to exhibit a certain scandalous Piece, highly injurious to our present happy Establishment, entitled, *The Merchant of Venice*"; and so on.[35] Elsewhere, such pieces as "The Prophecies of Shylock" foretelling God's revelation to the Jews that the land they "are now to possess is fruitful and pleasant, and its Inhabitants . . . ripe for Destruction" and a bizarre parody of the Book of Genesis that enjoins them to seize the daughters of Englishmen for wives and their land for dowries exemplify the imaginative use of prophecy to underscore supposed dangers once lurking in the wings but now heralded by the Naturalization Act.[36] The uncomfortable humor of these pieces bears witness to larger apprehensions by which, as Roy Wolper laconically observes, "the laughter, sure as it was, was less than sure."[37]

At its grossest level, anti-Semitism at the time of the Jew Bill manifests itself by reactivation of the familiar diabolized stereotype in all its medieval odiousness. In the more extreme rhetoric employed by adversaries of the bill, the Jews are branded as perpetual crucifiers, as robbers, traitors, and murderers, who in fulfillment of rabbinical injunction make it their bounden duty to reenact their dastardly deeds of ritual infanticide.[38] They are stigmatized as children of the Devil, fetid and infectious, bringing with them leprosy and venereal disease with which to smite the men and women among whom they settle.[39] In their supposed greed, they are portrayed as grasping moneylenders and venal stock-jobbers sucking dry the assets of the state and plundering the public at large in singleminded pursuit of financial gain. The image of the Jews as bloodthirsty usurers casts its detestable shadow over discourse on their contemporary status as merchants and traders. To this we must now turn our attention in a separate section.

The Jews' return to England from the second half of the seventeenth century coincided with the rapid post-Restoration development of the city of London as the center of what Peter Dickson has aptly dubbed "the Financial Revolution in England." According to Dickson, particularly during the first half of the eighteenth century, the "fear of dislocation of the social order by the rise of new economic interests, and dislike of commercial and financial manipulation of all kinds" were often reinforced by an intense anti-Jewish prejudice. Because a number of the more prominent financiers were indeed Jews but as much because of their age-old association in popular lore with usury, coin-clipping, and other such base pecuniary dealing, it was convenient to label all brokers and jobbers as Jews. The term *stock-jobbing*, used freely but largely pejoratively to denote the speculative transaction of stocks, bills of exchange, and public funds, became widely associated with Jewish dealing.[40] The locational focus of much of the jobbing, 'Change Alley, also became a functional metonym by which to refer to financial trafficking by the Jews. The name implicitly links the brokers on the Royal Exchange with their supposed biblical forebears, the money-changers whose tables were overthrown by Christ (Matt. 21:12).

In fact, by a regulation of 1697 that would not be rescinded until 1830, the number of Jewish brokers officially allowed to perform their business on the Royal Exchange was limited to twelve out of a discrete total of at least one hundred. Although no such formal curb was applied to stock-jobbing, the expense of obtaining a license naturally restricted the number of Jews capable of practicing in this way.[41] Nevertheless, at the time of the Jew Bill, it was frequently asserted that the introduction of broking and jobbing following the "glorious" Revolution of 1688 had been instrumental in deluging the country with Jews. "We had no great inundation of them," opines Nicholas Fazakerley, "until the pernicious trade of stockjobbing was set up soon after the revolution, when Jews, and all other foreigners, were invited by act of parliament to practise that trade of usury upon the state, which by Edward the 1st's law they had been forbid to practise upon the subject."[42] If not seen necessarily as the sole trade pursued by the Jews, their avocation in stock-jobbing and bond dealing is viewed as the cornerstone of their renewed presence in England. The peculiar resonance of this belief can only be fully understood when we recognize that, through this avocation, a mental association is forged that inextricably links the stock-jobbing Jew of the eighteenth century with his putative ancestor, the bloodthirsty usurer of an earlier age. When we recall the imaginative omnipresence of the most famous of such usurers both on stage after 1741 and, by extension, as a cipher figure, it is not difficult to comprehend why the association should have been so devastating in determining English attitudes to the Jews and their financial dealings. The echoes of Shylock's "Let him look to his bond" (III.i.51) extend far beyond the theater.

By far the majority of those Jews actively engaged in broking and jobbing came from the "older" Sephardi community. As we have seen, the very specific aim of the bill of 1753 appears to have been to encourage similar wealthy Jews engaged in finance and trade to settle in England, thereby placing their capital to the larger economic advantage of the country. The arguments put forward in favor of the bill assume that England's growth as a trading nation is dependent upon attracting foreign investment to which the Sephardi Jews as seasoned merchants and financiers mysteriously hold the key. For the advocates of the bill, the country stood only to benefit from the increase in trade brought about by an influx of rich Jews from all parts of the world. Their presence, it was argued, would stimulate the economy, reduce public debt, and furnish the nation with a body of men capable of providing finance for beneficial purposes. "Their genius," it was stereotypically accepted by both supporters and opponents of the bill, "is peculiarly turned to commerce."[43] If there existed a radical difference of perspective that polarized the whole ill-tempered controversy, it was as to whether the Jews would turn their commercial skills and supposed fabulous wealth to the larger common good or simply use these selfishly to pursue their own ends. Wranglers on either side of the debate each grossly magnified the scope of the commercial and financial sway of the Jews, rarely pausing to acknowledge (or incapable of seeing) that their actual economic power was really quite narrow and limited.[44]

In the minds of the bill's opponents, the Jews were engaged in an elaborate conspiracy to snatch economic control of the nation by displacing the honest English artisan from his trade and supplanting the landed gentleman through stripping him of his inherited assets. An anecdotal story proffered as "real matter of fact" shortly after the Naturalization Act had received the royal assent is illustrative of these wider fears:

> About three weeks since I had occasion to take a boat at *Whitehall* stairs, in order to go a little way down the river. We no sooner put off from the shore, than I perceived the waterman to be a very sensible fellow, and particularly knowing in politics. I therefore gave him an opportunity of discovering his sentiments on the bill in question, and he discussed it with great strength of lungs, and vehemence of observation, concluding, "D—mn the circumcised dogs; now they are naturalized, I'll engage we shall have them all turn watermen, and they will have all the business of the river to themselves, only from sunset on *Friday*, to sun-set on *Saturday*."[45]

The story conveys well the larger apprehension, unhappily shared (according to the anecdotist) by people of all ranks and condition, that the Jews would undercut English trade in order to make it their own. The opinion of the waterman—an eighteenth-century equivalent to a chat with a taxi-driver—reflects the fictionalized threat of encroachment by the Jews, while also registering their Otherness in terms of known distinctions in their ceremonial practice (namely circumcision and sabbath).

The assumption of difference in such discourse is nowhere made more apparent than by reference to the most familiar of their religious laws, the prohibition upon pork. In terms of a threat to trade, the intrusion of large numbers of Jews, it is jocularly argued, will threaten the livelihood of English butchers by a reduction in demand for such everyday fare as brawn, hams, bacon, and black-puddings.[46] The few Christians who may still remain in the country 100 years hence are invited by another humorist to join their present besieged brethren in chanting "The Roast Pork of Old England" to the tune of the popular ballad, "The Roast Beef of Old England." Instead of beef, the burlesque song exalts roast pork as "the *Englishman's* food . . . [that] ennobled our veins and enriched our blood" and forewarns of the necessity of repelling the "foes to the pork of old *England*" before they circumcise us all and make as short work of our property.[47] Elsewhere, in distant echo of the continental *Judensau*, Jews are represented astride pigs in several contemporary prints. In one, the bearded figure of a Jew exclaims "I am Natur'lized," while, beneath him, the pig that he rides calls out "Buy Buy my Pork," ironically mimicking the familiar street cries associated with Jewish pedlars and itinerant traders.[48] The print concurs with fears expressed in the parliamentary debate on the bill that the naturalization of wealthy Jews will inevitably lead to the mass entry of poor Jews. When the rich Jews have "become possessed of land estates," William Northey had dourly warned, "great numbers of poor Jews must necessarily settle . . . ; for we know, that they can make use of none but Jew butchers, bakers, poulterers, and the like trades, which of course must make them soon become very numerous in this country."[49] The discourse on the trading capacity of the Jews inevitably links the condition of both rich and poor in exaggerated fears that the Naturalization Act will unlock the gates with a consequent potential that "every *Vagabond Jew* may purchase all the Liberties and Immunities of free-born *Englishmen.*"[50]

If the native English tradesman or artisan is implicitly held up by opponents of the bill to exemplify the beleaguered values of decent hard work, the Jews by contrast, whether we speak of rich or poor, are generally represented as dronish and parasitic. Their avocation, it is argued, is not strictly in trade in the true sense of the word, since they are rarely found to engage in productive labor: "None of the Jews, even of the poorest sort," charges one of their loudest parliamentary opponents, "are ever bred to be manufacturers or mechanics, or indeed to any laborious employment." Instead, he avers, "some . . . of the richer sort may engage in foreign commerce, but the poorer deal only as brokers, pedlars, or hawkers, as we may now see from daily experience."[51] As "monied men" and "griping usurers," it is reiterated in the *London Evening-Post* and

The Jew Naturilized. Engraving, 1753. (Courtesy of Mr. Alfred Rubens, London.)

elsewhere, the rich Jews fatten themselves on the iniquities of stock-jobbing and lotteries, whereas their poorer brethren, rather than turning to the land as a means of gaining an honest living, get their bread by peddling and by cheating.[52] In parallel with this, it is further asserted that their religious observance and particularly the keeping of their dietary laws (*kashrut*) reinforce their maintenance as a separate people and prevent them from ever becoming genuinely useful citizens. "The constitution of their religion," it is claimed, "cutting them off, in some measure, from commerce with the rest of mankind, they certainly become so much less serviceable to a community."[53] The dietary "superstitions" of the Jews are put forward as a critical factor against their social integration and ultimate mercantile utility.

The random shipping together of "rich" and "poor" Jews in anti-Judaic discourse suggests how easy it was for the bill's opponents to spread the rumor that its enactment would lead to a sudden deluge of both sorts that would threaten to submerge the very existence of the state. It could be conveniently forgotten that the legislation itself had been intended to benefit only those substantial (and almost exclusively Sephardic) Jews of foreign birth whose financial and mercantile skills might have been employed to the nation's economic advantage. Although in the England of 1753 there were perhaps barely more than 100 Sephardim of substance actively involved in business and finance, their putative influence remained always far greater than their numbers suggest.[54]

As we have observed, at least in their outward appearance endenizened Sephardim, unlike their more traditional Ashkenazic coreligionists, tended to adopt the fashions and mannerisms of the English upper classes with whom they endeavored to mix. Their rather precarious social assimilation is reflected in their willingness to intermarry with Christian families and in their brittle disdain of marriage by their own to Jews of Ashkenazic background. By purchasing for themselves great estates in the country while also maintaining high profiles in the city, the wealthier Sephardic financiers, few in number as they certainly were, unwittingly helped to cultivate in the popular mind an image of a Jewish plutocracy hell-bent on laying hold of and usurping the patrimony of the English upper classes. The parliamentary opponents of the bill speak in no uncertain terms of "the vast estates they [the Jews] have acquired in this kingdom" and of fears that "the ruin, and even annihilation of the present landed interest of England" will inevitably ensue.[55] Elsewhere, a distinctly antimercantilist element enters into the more hostile rhetoric with which the Jews are described. "I think there are just grounds to apprehend," cautions one writer, "that we should *suffer* more by the exchange of the English country-gentleman, for the foreign *Jew;* than we should *gain* by the acquisition of those riches, by means of which, estates might pass from the hands of *Christians* to those of *Jews*."[56]

It bodes ill, argues another with due sanctimony, if we prefer to gain their wealth in favor of winning their souls. "Is the *Advancement of Trade*," he adds,

> a sufficient Reason for receiving this People into our Bowels? Take Care that by so doing we, instead of advancing our Trade, don't take a Mouse into our Pocket, a Serpent into our Bosom, and Fire into our Factories. As Trade now stands with us, our Merchants are obliged to

use all their Abilities to guard against the Craft and undermining Artifices of the *Jews:* What then may be expected from them, when admitted to the same Privileges and Protection of your Majesty's natural born Subjects?[57]

The supposition here that the honest Englishman can barely match the wiles and subterfuges of the Jewish dealer and that naturalization will remove his last line of defense is, of course, merely inflammatory. But the sonority of the reference conveys an impression of the Jews and their reputed sharp practice at trade that the writer readily assumes is shared by his contemporaries. In particular, the equivocal reputation enjoyed by Samson Gideon, the greatest of mid-eighteenth-century loan contractors, will have helped to sustain as accepted fact the topical allusion to "the Craft and undermining Artifices of the *Jews.*" In the public perception, many of the worst stereotypical prejudices concerning the financial dealings of the Jews seem to have been epitomized by Gideon.

Gideon's contemporary notoriety as a financier stems from the unorthodox methods by which he had negotiated vast loans in order to reduce the national debt at the time of the War of the Austrian Succession (1742–48) and during the Jacobite rising of 1745. Many of the methods that he used were, strictly speaking, illegal, and to many good Christians he came to symbolize the corrupting influence of "monied" Jews upon the trusted values of English society.[58] The use he made of his gains to purchase magnificent houses and estates for himself and his family at Belvedere in Kent, Spalding in Lincolnshire, and elsewhere was seen as indicative of the larger transfer of landed interests from the hereditary gentry to the Jews. Notwithstanding, Gideon's fiscal maneuverings are credited with having more than once saved the government of the day from financial collapse, and by the late 1740s his worth was sufficiently recognized for him to have become one of Henry Pelham's foremost advisers on economic matters. During the crisis over the Jew Bill, it was widely rumored that it was he who had bribed Pelham to push through the detested measure.

At the beginning of Thomas Fitzpatrick's dramatic skit, *The Temple of Laverna* (1753), in which Gideon appears in loose disguise as the mighty Caiphas "the very *Atlas* of the State," a fellow Jewish broker explains his temporary absence from the dealing floor by remarking,

he has been all this Morning closetted with the GREAT MAN [Pelham]; there is a grand Council held this Day upon Affairs of the greatest Importance to our Nation—we shall soon be upon a Footing with the best of them—but mum for that.—*Caiphas* brings all this about— they dare not refuse him any Thing.[59]

In the sketch, Caiphas's power in affairs of state is demonstrated more by hearsay than directly by his actions. At the Temple of Laverna (representing Jonathan's coffeehouse in 'Change Alley where Gideon transacted many of his deals), the other brokers cringe before him in total servitude, incapable of taking decisions without him. Their tractability, it is maintained, is shared by government ministers who "are never able to carry any Point . . . in the Money-way, but when he co-operates with them" and by the Christian clergy who are reliant upon his patronage in the purchase of their benefices. He is cynically described within the playlet as "the Support of our [English] Constitution in Church and State" and "the Axis upon which the Wheel turns." While himself eschewing the honors that he claims have been offered to him, Caiphas is shown as prophetically ambitious for the future preferment of his son ("him you possibly may see a Duke").[60] His "seeming Apostacy"—for Gideon had married a non-Jewish wife and all his children were baptized—is excused by one of his fellow brokers as an appropriate façade in order to allow him to wield a wider influence within the Christian world. In actuality, the broker contends, he remains "as true an *Israelite*, as ever dwelt in *Jerusalem*." The skit accentuates the belief in an insidious conspiracy by wealthy Jews to wrest power for themselves by bribery and by equivalent misuse of their money.

A very similar iconographical statement appears in the print, *The Grand Conference or the Jew Predominant* (1753). Here, Gideon is shown at the head of a table at which also sit Henry Pelham, his brother the Duke of Newcastle, an unnamed bishop, and Lord Chancellor Hardwicke, who had been instrumental in constructing the terms of the Naturalization Bill. Gideon is offering the brothers a bag of money, containing £200,000 that has been collected as a bribe by the Jews of England to expedite the migration of those of their brethren who have been tarrying impatiently in the West Indies and on the European continent. Pelham is attended on either side of him, respectively, by a good and an evil genius, the former urging caution and the other successfully prompting him to "Take the Cash my Fri[e]nd at all Events." He is egged on to accept the bribe by his brother ("It comes seasonably to me at this Juncture Circumsion or any thing"), while the dismayed bishop holds up his hands at the sorry turn that the conference has taken as a consequence of Gideon's sordid mercenary inducements. The verse caption to the design passes final judgment on the fraudulence of the proceedings:

'Tis such, that pass your L[i]b[ert]y away—
Borrow by Br[i]b[er]y, and by V[ic]e they pay,

The Grand Conference or the Jew Predominant. Engraving, 1753.
(Courtesy of the Jewish Historical Society of England.)

As JUDAS did for pelf betray our Lord,
Grant Heav'n that they may meet their just Reward![61]

The predominance of the perfidious Jew at the Grand Conference, it is inferred, will lead to the moral ruin and financial enslavement of England.

Despite being himself London-born and a Sephardi, Gideon is represented in the print speaking with an accent that is more commonly associated with the peculiar English of the foreign-born Ashkenazi pedlar. As he points to the moneybag, he declares, "Dare Gentlemens, and my very good Friends Dis be de Puss collected by our Tribe for de great Favour." Perry sees the assignment to Gideon in this and other prints of "Yiddish-German distortions" as a clever propaganda trick whereby opponents of the bill were "able to create the perfect propaganda stereotype" that combined "the wealth and power of the Sephardim with the foreignness and low social status of the Ashkenazim."[62] While the effect will have been exactly as Perry describes, to create at the same time both fear and hate, it is also likely that he attributes far more sophistication to the propagandists, who were probably as incapable as the English public at large in being able to discriminate closely between Jews of different lineal origins. The threat posed by the bill created in the popular mind a synthetic or hybridized stereotype of the incursive foreign Jew drawn from an incongruous combination of sources.

It is ironic that, despite the strong assimilationist tendencies that he shared with other well-to-do Sephardim who consciously chose as their model the lifestyle and manners of the English gentry, Samson Gideon emerges in the political propaganda of the day, complete with heavy accent and faulty grammar, as the putative leader of a feared invasion of alien Jews. No less ironic is the fact that, rather than leading such efforts, Gideon openly opposed the attempts of his fellow Sephardim to procure by act of Parliament the naturalization of foreign-born Jews, even petulantly resigning his synagogue membership in protest against his name being put forward as an advocate of the bill. Nevertheless, as the most prominent Jew of his day, it is his statue that is set to replace that of Queen Anne outside St. Paul's Cathedral in the print, *A Scene of Scenes for the Year 1853* and his name that is put forward as a candidate for the office of Messiah to those of his coreligionists who will now flock to England to feed off its riches.[63] In his idolization of money, he is inescapably seen as the chief of the Jews. From a tradition that can be traced back certainly through Isaac of Norwich and medieval usury and perhaps also to the biblical King Solomon, Samson Gideon helped to sustain an image of the Jew as a manipulating plutocrat whose financial sway and international dealing give him a jugular grip upon the political pulse of the state. Arguably, it is the haphazard mutations of that image rather than those associated with the "poor" Jew that prevailed through the nineteenth century and into more recent anti-Semitic discourse.

The extraordinary uproar and unrest during the summer and autumn months of 1753 showed no signs of abating until Pelham and his Whig friends backtracked by repealing the Naturalization Act as the first mea-

A Scene of Scenes for the Year 1853. Engraving, 1753. (Courtesy of the
Library of Congress, Washington, D.C.)

sure following the king's opening of the new session of Parliament on
November 15. With a general election impending, prudence dictated the
necessity of such an ignominious volte-face. Had "it been agreeable to
the people," wrote Tobias Smollett a few years later, the act "might have
increased the wealth, and extended the commerce, of Great Britain," but

> What rendered this unpopular measure the more impolitic, was the
> unseasonable juncture at which it was carried into execution; that is,
> at the eve of a general election for a new parliament; when a minister
> ought carefully to avoid every step which may give umbrage to the
> body of the people.[64]

If the kind of draconian remedy to the crisis cynically floated by Lord
Hardwicke of hanging two or three dozen of the agitators as a means of
quelling the mob was unacceptable, this was as much out of the uncom-

fortable realization that the act had offended potential voters as from any sympathetic response to popular feelings. As Thomas Secker, the bishop of Oxford, wrote to Hardwicke, "the Bill for permitting Jews to be naturalized hath not only raised very great Clamours amongst the ignorant and disaffected, but hath offended great numbers of better understandings and dispositions, and is likely to have an unhappy influence on the Elections of next year."[65]

However lame, the arguments that were put forward for the repeal of the act by those who a few months earlier had been its firmest advocates were a rational response to a changed situation. Among reasons justifying repeal were that to let the clamor run riot "might be the cause of the death of many of his majesty's subjects" and that, given the unsettled state of affairs, no Jew living quietly and securely abroad would in his right mind "chuse to live in a country where he is likely to be the butt of popular malice and resentment."[66] A further telling point was made that, had the act been given a different title, the clamor it caused would never have arisen:

> If instead of calling it an act for permitting the Jews to be naturalized, it had been entitled an act to prevent the profanation of the holy sacrament of the Lord's Supper, . . . no objection would have been made to it, but on the contrary every man would have applauded our zeal for the honour of the religion we profess.[67]

The agitative connotations associated in the eighteenth century with the word *Jew* could hardly have been more succinctly illustrated.

The bill repealing the Naturalization Act rushed its way within days through Lords and Commons and shortly after received the royal assent. If the machinery of British government can be cranked up at a time of national crisis, it is no less responsive at a time of panic. The unseemly dispatch with which the repeal thundered its way into the obscurity of the statute book reflects a larger paranoia that had infected the supporters as much as the opponents of the Jew Bill. "Yesterday the Parliament met," wrote Lord Chesterfield on the instant, "and the Duke of Newcastle, frightened out of his wits at the groundless and senseless clamors against the Jew Bill . . . moved for the repeal of it. . . . This flagrant instance of timidity in the administration, gives their enemies matter for ridicule and triumph."[68] The shabby dismissal of the original legislation as inconsequential and trivial by both Newcastle and Pelham during the repeal debate belies the earnestness with which the previous spring they had trumpeted it as being so greatly to the national advantage. Their humiliation was matched only by the expedient haste with which they recognized the electoral necessity of climbing down. The repeal was immediately effective in removing from the opposition one of their most persuasive rallying cries. The diatribes against the Jews which had dominated Tory newspapers such as the London Evening-Post (dismissed by a supporter of the Naturalization Act as "that Augean Stable of Filth and Calumny") and Jackson's Oxford Journal disappeared almost overnight.[69] In the general election the following May, the Whigs would win most handsomely.

The triumph of the Jew Bill's opponents, short-lived as it might have been in terms of the course of English politics, was viewed in 1753 as a victory for the democratic will of the people. As news of the repeal spread across the country, bonfires were lit and church bells were rung all day long in celebration of England's deliverance. As a valediction to the clamor, the Tory newspapers welcomed the repeal for having delivered the nation "from all apprehensions of seeing British Christians tilling and toiling for Jewish landlords." It was also seen as showing "the respect of the Legislature for the Publick Voice."[70] The taunting cry of the repealers, "Vox Populi est Vox Dei," echoed through the Commons where it was interpreted by one Tory M.P. to spell out that "the people of this kingdom . . . are . . . as good judges of their own interest or honour as the majority of either House of Parliament can pretend to be."[71]

In the print Vox Populi, Vox Dei, or the Jew Act Repealed.—Dec' A.D. 1753, many of the ingredients that fueled the controversy are emblematically depicted. A mob of Jews and Deists led by a messianic Samson Gideon and Lord Bolingbroke (the advocate of natural religion) are seen heading toward the promised land, but have been miraculously halted before Calvary, upon which stands a Cross fiercely guarded by two archangels and protected by the divine "Eye of Providence." A hand from heaven oscillates a balance in which the Gospels and Magna Carta in one scale outweigh bags of money supporting a paper marked "Iews Act of Pa[rlia]m[en]t" in the other. On the ground, the bearded figure of a Jew, his head encircled by a fanged serpent, lies prostrate, leaning on bags of gold and clutching the "Iews Act Repealed." He exclaims, "It was Ill timed, all our Ambitions hopes are fleed." Behind him, a rueful devil, also leaning on the gold, shares his vexation. The "icons" of Judaism, familiarly represented in eighteenth-century illustrated Bibles, are scattered untidily across the adjacent field and include "The Ark over set," the "Levitical Law," a "Circumcision knife" with broken blade and the "Ephod" or vestments of the high priest. To the left, a mitered bishop who has sold his soul for money is being soundly rebuked for his support of the Jew Bill in the Lords, while behind him, Sir William Calvert, the

Vox Populi, Vox Dei, or the Jew Act Repealed. Engraving, 1753. (Courtesy of the British Museum, Department of Prints and Drawings.)

Member of Parliament for the City of London, who voted for the bill in the Commons, mutters, "The Devil's in the Swine and the Swine in me." In the distance, the spires of the city with St. Paul's in the center proclaim that London has been preserved by the hand of God from ruination by the Jews.[72] In the absurdity of their famous victory, God's voice had revealed itself through the voice of the people. The threatened inundation had been staunched. In town and country across the land, John Bull and his fellow Englishmen could sleep sweetly, exulting in the knowledge that their first encounter with a Jew had been miraculously averted till at least the advent of a later day.

CHAPTER 9

TOWARD EMANCIPATION

THE DISCREET MUTATIONS in English attitudes toward the Jews from the Naturalization Act of 1753 to 1830, when Robert Grant introduced into the House of Commons his ill-fated bill to abolish the civil disabilities affecting British-born Jews, must now attract our closer attention. At first glance, the failure of the new bill, which was soundly defeated at its second reading, suggests that it would be erroneous to assume any significant attitudinal shift between the two dates. Yet, even a rudimentary comparison should reveal to us important differences of purpose in the Disabilities Bill of 1830 over the Jew Bill more than three-quarters of a century earlier. Where the bill of 1753 was restricted in scope to offering a few wealthy foreign-born individuals the opportunity to be naturalized by private petition to Parliament, the legislation proposed in 1830 was intended to give equal rights under the law to all native-born Jews. Where in 1753 the proponents of Jewish naturalization had pitched their arguments almost exclusively upon the expected economic benefits to the state, their counterparts of 1830 were primarily concerned with the wider and more humane question of how to achieve the political and civil emancipation of a disadvantaged minority living in a Christian country. Although the battle to remove those civil and political disabilities to which British-born Jews were subject proved to be far more protracted than Robert Grant could have contemplated, the failed bill of 1830 is usually taken to represent the beginning of a campaign that was to lead piecemeal over the next fifty years to their full emancipation.[1] Unlike in 1753, when the Disabilities Bill was introduced into Parliament, the British public at large appears to have been far more acquiescent in accepting the validity of debating the case of the Jews, although its thrashing by the Commons may perhaps have served to take a good deal of the steam out of the issue. In 1830, there was no repetition on the same scale of the pamphlet war and popular clamor of 1753, and (as we shall see) the dissonant voice of William Cobbett, the most influential opponent of Jewish emancipation, sounds increasingly idiosyncratic and anachronistic.

If there were minor upsurges of popular anti-Semitic feeling between 1753 and 1830, these were usually prompted not by political considerations but by the involvement of certain Jews in gang robbery and street crime. The most infamous such incident was the Chelsea murder case of 1771 in which a gang of eight or nine malefactors, all of them Jews, was found guilty of breaking into the house of the widow Hutchins in King's Road, and fatally wounding one John Slow, a laboring man, whom they had rudely stirred from his sleep. The notoriety of the deed and the punishment by hanging at Tyburn of four of the gang led to an eruption of anti-Jewish passions reminiscent of that of eighteen years before. Although no more brutal than similar crimes frequently committed by vicious street gangs and housebreakers of the period, the Chelsea murder was singled out as indicative of a larger guilt that implicated the Jews as a whole. On the street, they were physically assaulted and verbally abused. The cry of "Go to Chelsea" was for a time a popular taunt with which to revile them. Exaggerated claims were laid that nine-tenths of all burglaries, if not actually perpetrated by them, were instigated by wealthy Jews, who could live like gentlemen by acting as receivers of stolen goods. In their houses, it was alleged, pots were kept constantly alight for the immediate melting of illicit silver.[2] A mezzotint of 1777, *Jews receiving Stolen Goods*, shows an opulently dressed Jew sitting before a table in a darkened room and haggling with a couple of ruffians over the value of the loot they have brought in. Behind him, a painted oriental screen masking a bare wall and, by his side, a crouching silver poodle, its color and the droop of its ears matching those of his expensive wig, correspond ironically with the veneer of genteel respectability that he assumes. A villainous Ashkenazi Jew at the end of the table and another sly-looking accomplice leaning across the back of his chair unctuously offer support to their patron as he counts up the last night's spoils. The print upholds the widely held belief that rich and poor Jews illicitly conspire to sustain one another at the expense of the indigenous English.[3] As a close corollary, Jewish criminality evinces in the popular imagination a sense of the fallen state of those who had once been God's chosen people. If their supposed "criminality" as a people could be traced back to their betrayal of Christ and to their ancestral avocation in money-changing and usury, then it was but fair game to assume that the felonious instincts inherited by their present-day descendants were merely second nature to them. Such equations, of course, consistently omit acknowledgment that the English criminal underworld was far

Jews receiving Stolen Goods. Mezzotint, 1777. (Courtesy of Mr. Alfred Rubens, London.)

from being exclusively the province of the Jews. Although Jews' involvement in crime was undoubtedly on the increase during the latter part of the eighteenth century, the number of cases in which Jewish criminals were implicated remained throughout the period but a small fraction of the whole.

Commenting at the time upon the popular effect of the Jew Bill of 1753, Horace Walpole remarks that the whole sorry affair served to show "how much the age, enlightened as it is called, was still enslaved to the grossest and most vulgar prejudices."[4] Writing to his Berlin correspondent almost thirty years later, the German traveler to England Carl Philipp Moritz, having witnessed the dismissive treatment by his fellow passengers of a Jew who would have boarded their carriage at Kensington, considers this "antipathy and prejudice against the Jews . . . to be far more common here, than it is even with us, who certainly are not partial to them."[5] Yet, for all the supporting evidence of a strong groundswell of anti-Semitic prejudice engulfing more enlightened attitudes, there persists throughout the same period a gradual adjustment toward a greater spirit of toleration. Jacob Katz has helped us to realize that this should be interpreted as a western European rather than merely an English phenomenon. Writes Katz, during the eighteenth century,

> There occurred a transformation of European society brought about by the influence of rationalism and the effects of economic, social and political revolution. This in turn, had a bearing on the Jewish position, too, turning the Jews from barely tolerated individuals and communities into fully fledged citizens, a transformation usually designated by the term "emancipation."[6]

In defining this transformation, Katz cautions us to recognize that it would be naive to hypothesize that the change should be viewed simply as the triumph of rationalism over traditional prejudice. Rather, he suggests that the logical arguments put forward in favor of the absorption of the Jews into the political and social fabric of those western European countries in which they had settled often flew in the face of traditional anti-Semitic discrimination. When the delegates to the French National Assembly voted in 1791 to grant equal citizenship to the Jewish subjects of the country, they did so as a matter of consistency to what they saw as the larger aims of the Revolution. In ultimately rejecting the more radical (although, for some, no less logical) alternative of expelling the Jews altogether from France, the delegates saw themselves as acceding to the revolutionary principles of egalitarianism and the regeneration of mankind. By acknowledging the Jews as equals, they optimistically believed that they were also at a stroke expunging inherited inequities that they associated with the dead thinking of the *ancien régime.* The metamorphosis in attitudes, states Katz, should not therefore be construed as representing any kind of sudden inner change to the Jews themselves but must be seen as the effect of social and political changes in the countries in which they lived. Those changes, he adds, while occurring more or less simultaneously in the countries of western Europe, were subtly different within each country, depending on the social and historical background as well as on the indigenous memory of the Jewish-gentile past of each.[7]

The roots of political and civil toleration toward the Jews in England can be traced back at least to John Locke in the late seventeenth century. Locke's championing of the religious and civil rights of the Jews in several remarks in his *Letter Concerning Toleration* (1689) are peripheral to the main thrust of his argument in favor of toleration between different denominations of the Church, yet they provide an important marker to which modern writers on the subject of Jewish emancipation have turned with almost too great an alacrity.[8] Katz is once again right to remind us that Locke's conception of religious toleration for non-Christian minorities was to have no immediate social impact whatsoever and that, even as late as 1753, the advocates of Jewish naturalization "never advanced an argument of toleration that disregarded religious considerations in civil matters."[9] As we have seen, the substance of the case put forward by the promoters of the bill of 1753 had been founded on the claimed economic utility of the legislation and on the assumption that, once naturalized, the Jews would be much more ready to convert. The adverse image that prevailed in the popular imagination of the Jews as deicidal cutthroats and cunning usurers, the natural enemies of all true Christians, made any academic notion of their political emancipation empirically unachievable in 1753. The attitudinal shifts between the middle years of the eighteenth century and the new century in which their emancipation became vocabularized within the political agenda increasingly challenged the validity of many of the age-old negative suppositions.

As is perhaps to be expected, the "reasons" for the often subtle changes that take place in popular attitudes from one era to the next do not conveniently fall into any consistent or logical pattern. They are often contradictory and will sometimes appear partial or inadequate in satisfactorily explaining their presumed effect. In addition, no single explanation in itself is quite sufficient as a means of accounting for mutations in popular attitudes, nor should it be assumed that the kindling of new values automatically presupposes the demise of older ones. If the new age saw itself as more "liberal," it is worth bearing in mind that this may merely be the self-perception of certain enlightened individuals at the time rather than necessarily that their progressive ideals filtered through to exert a positive influence upon a far broader spectrum of English society. What is certain, however, is that many of the old assumptions that cast the Jews as fiendish assassins and infernal bogeymen came to be viewed toward the end of our period with an increasing skepticism coupled with what appears to be an unfeigned remorse at their vile treatment in former times.

The repudiation of the existence of innate "peculiarities" that distinguish them from the rest of humanity and a recognition that those characteristics that are deemed to belong to them are more probably the long-term consequence of their social treatment and upbringing are already evident early in the eighteenth century in John Toland's spirited defense of the Jews. "As for the *Jews*," writes Toland, "'tis evident, that since their dispersion, they have no common or peculiar inclination distinguishing 'em from others; but visibly partake of the Nature of those nations among which they live, and where they were bred." They are, he adds shortly after, "both in their origine and progress, not otherwise to be regarded, than under the common circumstances of human nature."[10] While in many respects before his time, Toland's emphasis on the essential oneness of mankind and on the social influence of (what we now might call) nurture as opposed to nature concurs with the spirit of rationalism and the denial of innate characteristics that had been propounded so influentially for the age that followed him by Locke, particularly in the *Essay Concerning Human Understanding* (1690).

What is also evident is that such ideas accord well with the egalitarian impulses of the revolutionary era all of three-quarters of a century after Toland's pamphlet defense. If the Jews are indeed innately no different from the rest of humanity, it was to be argued, then the main cause of their suffering and of their continuing separation as a people must be in the abominable treatment meted out against them by their Christian hosts in those countries to which they have been admitted. Samuel Taylor Coleridge's impassioned piece in *The Courier* (1816) captures well the mood of outrage shared by many of his generation:

> We have ever thought that the treatment which the Jews have received has been a disgrace to all countries and to all nations. The fate of never having a home—of being a people without a people's country—of being dispersed over every part of the world, is hard enough—But to have superadded the fate of being treated as criminals and outcasts—

of having the punishment of guilt without the commission of guilt—
of having their very names pass into a synonym for all that is bad and
tricking, and false and foul—to be the mock and scorn of the rabble—
to have the "very dogs bark at them" [Richard III, I.i.23] as they pass,
is a degree of suffering to which no race were ever exposed from the
creation of the world—And this has been their lot for ages. If they have
been hard and griping in their dealings, may it not have been occasioned by the treatment they have received? To treat men as if they
were incapable of virtue is to make them so.[11]

Written shortly after learning that the Senators of Lübeck had ordered
the expulsion of the Jews from their city, Coleridge's brief essay freely
expresses a wider social indignation. The "uniqueness" of the Jews, according to his account, is as much a consequence of the cruel usage that
they continue to receive in Christian countries as from their being the
descendants of the people of the Bible. If God may have ordained that
they are to remain wanderers and outcasts, he argues, that does not assume a divine sanction for others to persecute them. Indeed, if it is an
ultimate ambition among Christians to convert the Jews, then to abuse
and brutalize them is surely the incorrect way to achieve this. Coleridge's conclusion that the measure of an enlightened age is in its showing greater justice in its treatment of the Jews corresponds closely with
philo-Semitic thinking as articulated in contemporary conversionist
tracts. The arguments postulated with gathering authority during the
latter part of the eighteenth century by conversionists and by those who
believed in the necessity of radical social reform converge in condemning the ill treatment of the Jews as inappropriate or morally wrong in
the modern era. The essence of the conversionist case relies upon the
fideistic assumption that proselytizing the Jews is but the first step in
fulfilling God's larger millenarian plan, whereas the egalitarian prerog-
atives of the reformer are based far more on rationalist premises of social
justice. The paradoxical constant that allows a linkage to be established
between millenarian and rationalist arguments is in the shared belief in
humanity's duty to ameliorate the lot of the Jews.

Philo-Semitic millenarianism in England can be traced back to at
least the sixteenth and seventeenth centuries. As is well known, it
played an important part in bringing about the readmission of the Jews
during the interregnum. The claimed rediscovery by Richard Brothers
and other late eighteenth-century millenarians of a remnant of the ten
lost tribes of Israel among the English helped to invigorate an imagined
sense of identity between native Englishman and Jew that was already
deep-rooted in popular religious belief. The visionary equation of Jeru-

salem and Albion, most immediately recollected today as elemental to the inspiration and creative thought of William Blake, was another way of heralding the essential oneness of mankind. Blake's address to the Jews in Plate 27 of *Jerusalem* (1804–20) proclaims as "True, that Jerusalem was & is the Emanation of the Giant Albion" and that Christian and Jew "are united . . . in One Religion, the Religion of Jesus, the most Ancient, the Eternal & the Everlasting Gospel."[12] While the meaning of the imaginative synthesis of Jerusalem and Albion in such discourse may have been to symbolize the ultimate reconciliation of Christian and Jew, the accommodation is achieved in terms that are characteristically one-sided. English millenarianism rarely, if ever, pauses to consider the Jews as Jews. Its palliation of traditional anti-Semitic attitudes seems often more a fortuitous byproduct than ideologically central to its program.[13]

The rapid spread and popular appeal during the latter part of our period of missionary and exegetical work by evangelicals and millenarians may be interpreted as a spontaneous response to the general abatement in religious zeal of the age. The increasing secularization of English society meant that the Church had to work that much harder to insure that its voice was heard. A widening of Christian education to embrace all levels of society became a primary goal of the Church. By setting a curriculum in charity schools based almost exclusively on religious texts, missionary bodies such as the Society for Promoting Christian Knowledge, founded in 1699, achieved varying success in bringing the Bible from the pulpit to the classroom. But, the high level of illiteracy, estimated at about half the population in the middle years of the eighteenth century, suggests that oral instruction by sermon and narration remained still the far more common way of disseminating knowledge of the Bible and, as an unfortunate byproduct, of instilling embryonic ideas about the accursed state of the Jews.

Moreover, the limited availability of printed texts in many households where there were readers will almost certainly have been a factor that vicariously determined elementary attitudes to the Jews. The testimony of sundry autobiographers confirms that, apart from the family Bible, the most commonly available reading material at home to them in the late eighteenth century were chapbooks and broadside ballads. "The precious, dog-eared pages were read and reread," writes a recent commentator, "until imperceptibly they merged back into the communal and oral tradition whence they had originally come."[14] Typically, these works rendered into print (adorned with crude pictorial woodcuts) religious and folkloric stories that had been retold in popular oral culture through time immemorial. The radical author Thomas Holcroft, born in 1745 the son of a shoemaker, divulges that he learned to read when his father set him the task of reciting "eleven chapters a day in the Old Testament," yet "an inestimable treasure," "too precious to be ever forgotten," was the gift by a good-natured apprentice in his father's shop of two chapbooks that "were soon as familiar to me as my catechism."[15] According to John Clare the poet, his father, though but barely literate, would boast over a horn of ale of his ability to sing or recite over a hundred ballads, "could read a little in a bible or testament and was very fond of the supersti[ti]ous tales that are hawked about a sheet for a penny." Although it was well grounded in the Bible, Clare feared that the method employed by many village schools of learning passages by rote made reading from it seem to many a young boy an "irksome inconvenience." With far greater alacrity, he himself turned to ballads and sixpenny chapbooks which, "thro the indefatigable savings of a penny and halfpenny" here and there, he would buy "as oppertunity offered when hawkers offerd them for sale at the door." He urged that his own "stock of learning was gleaned from the Sixpenny Romances . . . for I firmly believed every page I read and considerd I possesd in these the chief learning and literature of the country." Such tales, he remarked, "have memorys as common as Prayer books and Psalters with the peasantry." Among ballads that he knew (and may have possessed in broadsheet or chapbook form) was "The Wandering Jew," which he considered to declare "More of our saviour the[n] (the bible learns)."[16]

Holcroft's and Clare's attitudes to contemporary Jews are left unrecorded in their respective autobiographical writings, but their revelations of the childhood influence of chapbooks, ballads, and oral literature in rural England attest to the strength of a demotic tradition in which it was not uncommon to depict the Jews as crucifiers, Judases, murderers of innocent Christian children, and eternal wanderers. The weakening hold of this largely oral tradition brought about (it has been claimed) by the great migration of the English populace from the country to the city at the beginning of the Industrial Revolution may help to account for the accompanying attenuation of ancient superstitions concerning the Jews during the latter part of the eighteenth century and the early years of the nineteenth century.[17]

Inevitably, any attempt to reconstruct how the telling and retelling of biblical tales in rural England during the eighteenth century colored popular attitudes toward contemporary Jews must rely upon the chance survival of such intelligence in written and printed texts. Perhaps the most revealing account—would that we had more of the same—is that given by Carl Philipp Moritz, who describes the conversation of a group of country farmers traveling with him on a coach near Dunstable in 1782:

> One of them brought the history of Samson on the carpet, which the clergyman of his parish, he said, had lately explained, I dare say, very satisfactorily; though this honest farmer still had a great many doubts about the great gate which Samson carried away, and about the foxes with the fire-brands between their tails. In other respects, however, the man seemed not to be either uninformed or sceptical.
>
> They now proceeded to relate to each other various stories chiefly out of the Bible; not merely as important facts, but as interesting narratives, which they would have told and listened to with equal satisfaction, had they met them anywhere else. One of them had heard these stories from his minister in the church, not being able to read them himself.
>
> The one that sat next to him now began to talk about the Jews of the Old Testament, and assured us that the present race were all descended from those old ones. "Aye, and they are all damned to all eternity!"—said his companion, as coolly and as confidently as if at that moment he had seen them burning in the bottomless pit.[18]

The earnestness with which the farmers struggle to accept at face value the literal truth of a biblical narrative that stretches their credulity runs counter to the facility with which they are prepared to accept as irrefutable fact that the Jews are eternally damned. The retelling to them by the rural clergy of familiar scriptural tales triggers in the minds of the farmers an appalling nexus that implicates both biblical and modern Jews. The memoir is a good illustration of the deep-seated vein of anti-Judaic prejudice that obdurately persisted at the almost intangible line of demarcation between oral and written culture.

At the beginning of Maria Edgeworth's novel, *Harrington* (1817), a similar connection is forged in the impressionable imagination of the eponymous hero by a maid-servant who frightens her young charge with "stories of Jews who had been known to steal poor children for the purpose of killing, crucifying, and sacrificing them at their secret feasts and midnight abominations." During the early years of his life, deeply affected by her shocking nursery tales, he is haunted by recurring nightmares of faces "grinning, glaring, receding, advancing, all turning at last into the same face of the Jew with the long beard and terrible eyes." Whenever he hears the cry of the Jewish old-clothes man passing along the street, he breaks out in a cold sweat, which his mother (unaware of the pernicious influence of the maid) crassly puts down to an "exquisite sensibility of the nervous system." With the pedagogical hindsight of maturity, Harrington looks back at these early episodes of his life by reflecting on the difference between "the present improved state of education" and that which pertained in his infancy when it was dangerously common to entrust the care of young children to the bigotry of ignorant nurse-maids. Edgeworth attributes endemic anti-Semitism in the third quarter of the eighteenth century (the period of Harrington's childhood) to the credulity of the infant imagination and to the profusion of tales based on "old story books, where the Jews are as sure to be wicked as the bad fairies, or bad genii, or allegorical personifications of the devils, and the vices in the old emblems, mysteries, moralities, &c." The common representation of the Jew in more recent works of fiction as "a mean, avaricious, unprincipled, treacherous character," she suggests, merely gives authority to "the erroneous association of ideas" that has been imbibed in earliest childhood from oral folklore and superstition. Far from being innate or latent within the English character, Edgeworth sees prejudice against the Jews as the consequence of injurious educational influences and therefore ultimately remediable. Her book is written in the avowed and optimistic belief that, once awakened to the problem, future authors will be that much more circumspect in their representation of the Jews. Educational advances bringing a greater responsiveness are, for Edgeworth, the key to that improvement.[19]

In the complex and uneasy process by which during the eighteenth century English society was transformed to the new mercantilism of a predominantly urban-based culture, the place of the Jews may only occasionally have attracted wider attention. Yet, because those Jews who settled in England after the readmission migrated mainly to the metropolis and to the larger towns, it was not difficult to associate them with the progress of trade. Their traditional involvement in the spheres of commerce and finance gave explicit validity to such an association. Joseph Addison's frequently quoted *éloge* of the trading habits of the Jews is an early eighteenth-century example of an increasing acceptance of their place in the fabric of the new mercantilism:

> They are, indeed, so disseminated through all the trading Parts of the World, that they are become the Instruments by which the most distant Nations converse with one another, and by which Mankind are knit together in a general Correspondence. They are like the Pegs and Nails in a great Building, which, though they are but little valued in themselves, are absolutely necessary to keep the whole Frame together.[20]

Increasingly, during the longer eighteenth century, the Jew came to be regarded by his Christian neighbor more as an object of commercial interest than as a theological pariah. The economic arguments put up in 1753 by the supporters of the Jew Bill are one manifestation of a gradual adjustment that implicitly called into question so many traditional assumptions. The utility of the Jews, as one pamphleteer remarked, is as "a People to whom we of this Nation are greatly obliged for the Increase of our Trade, and consequently of our Wealth."[21] Although the opponents of the bill would throw against this view a farrago of pietistical nonsense attacking Jewish commerce as a form of financial idolatry, they too were obliged to give weight to economic arguments that were often distinct from the old theological ones. Yet, however tenuously, it was still feasible for them to link these arguments to traditional perceptions, for instance, by reference to the biblical story of the money-changers cast by Christ from the Temple or to the medieval role of the Jew as usurer. Brokerage and stock-jobbing are deemed merely as alternative forms of usury to which the present-day Jews, congenitally indistinguishable from their ancestors, remain inured. The economic and utilitarian grounds put forward for accepting the Jews could too easily be conjoined unfavorably with a mental image that persisted in seeing them as a fallen race fatally propelled by a singular love of gain.

Already in 1753, decent allowance was made among a few of their more enlightened defenders that the economic status of the Jews in former times was the consequence of their social condition and treatment and *not* a reflection of any kind of innate mercenary disposition. The pseudonymous Philo-Patriae, for example, strenuously contests that "Men's Geniuses, Nationally considered, are equal; where there is any Difference, it must arise either from Education or Circumstances." In the case of the Jews, he avows,

> Their Avarice, or Love of Money, may be accounted for, from the restrictive Laws in many Places, which confined them to Traffick and Gain, the necessary Consequence of which has been, that enriching themselves became their chief View in worldly Affairs; but . . . , where in free Countries they have had different Educations and Views, we find them capable of thinking like other Men.

For Philo-Patriae, the "common Notion . . . that the *Jews* are cleverer Traders, and better skilled than others in the Art of Commerce" is open to question as a general proposition because it fails to take account of the particular circumstances that may have made them so. The barbarism and superstition brought about by the ascendancy of the Catholic

Church after the fall of the Roman Empire, he alleges, "not only exerted their Tyranny against the *Jews*, but even against all Learning." By reducing the Jews to the pursuit of banking or usury that had been ruled taboo to the community of Christians, the Church unavoidably made them into pariah figures. In a more egalitarian age that is prepared to grant them the same general liberties enjoyed by others, he argues, the Jews will soon appear little different from the rest of humanity. Their utility as traders is subsumed within a broader plea that commerce will only truly flourish in a state that has fully liberalized its values.[22]

More than three-quarters of a century later, the advocates of emancipation were far more concerned with these larger humane questions than with debating the economic utility of the Jews. What had been merely peripheral in the bitter atmosphere of the Jew Bill became focal. If their propensity as commercial traders remained an issue that attracted comment by their defenders, it was usually by way of historical explanation for their present condition. William Hazlitt's discerning essay on the "Emancipation of the Jews," for instance, contains a suggestive paragraph in which he accounts for their present avocation in trade as the outcome of their ignoble handling in Christian countries through the ages:

> The Jews barter and sell commodities, instead of raising or manufacturing them. But this is the necessary traditional consequence of their former persecution and pillage by all nations. They could not set up a trade when they were hunted every moment from place to place, and while they could count nothing their own but what they could carry with them. They could not devote themselves to the pursuit of agriculture, when they were not allowed to possess a foot of land. You tear up by the roots and trample on them like noxious weeds, and then make an outcry that they do not take root in the soil like wholesome plants. You drive them like a pest from city to city, from kingdom to kingdom, and then call them vagabonds and aliens.

The social alienation of the Jews, according to Hazlitt, becomes explicable only in the light of their longer term treatment by their hosts. Although recognizing their class difference, he implicitly links the status of rich and poor Jews, moneyed brokers and vagabond pedlars, by maintaining that the present condition of each has been largely determined by the refusal of others to allow them to put down roots in any one country and by their consequent dependence for their livelihood on portable property. "If they are vicious," he writes, "it is we who have made them so. Shut out any class of people from the path to fair fame, and you reduce them to grovel in the pursuit of riches and the means to live." The blame for the present condition of the Jews lies squarely in the behavior of their hosts. Hazlitt's ardent plea is for a fairer and more humane treatment of the Jews in a supposedly more enlightened age.[23]

If sometimes ulterior to the more pressing humanitarian arguments, popular discourse showing forbearance to the Jews in the early nineteenth century often pays at least lip service to their commercial or other utility within the wider social fabric of the nation. The pedlar and the old-clothes dealer, so often reviled in the past, are seen as fulfilling tasks, however menial, that are both integral and necessary to society. In many ways, some of these discourses are more revealing of the otherwise intangible mutations in contemporary attitudes to the Jews than the high-minded and ideologically based clarion calls to emancipate them from their abject status as a disadvantaged minority. They impart an unvarnished willingness to engage with them as Jews rather than to conceptualize their situation within an abstract dialogue concerning the natural rights of man. Often too, they depict Jews in "mixed" colors that thrust together both good and bad stereotypical traits.

In the series entitled "Philosophy of the Streets of London" included in William Pinnock's *Guide to Knowledge* (1832), the utility of Moses Aaron, the Jewish old-clothes dealer, is perceived in his ability to extract wealth from what appears to everyone else as no more than rags and rubbish. As a scavenger of other people's detritus, he is rather unflatteringly equated both in his "dusky" complexion and his behavior with a rapacious species of bird:

> The Jew is in truth the raven of the city, just as his dusky brother is the raven of the wilds; and both the wilds and the city are all the better for the raven. He of the wilds eats up carrion and offal which otherwise would taint the air, and render it unwholesome for more cleanly creatures. So also the Jew collects the refuse and offal of the wardrobe of the house, which, if retained, would keep the place in a litter, be unsightly to look at, and useful to nobody.

If his unprepossessing aspect—"his dark eyes, his long beak and his croaking sound"—makes Moses Aaron seem mean and uncouth, that should not (argues Pinnock) detract from the strict probity with which "his word once passed is irrefragable as the Laws of the Medes and Persians." His integrity needs no external blandishment. Far from being condoned, the exclusion of "his race from the general citizenship of the world for nearly two thousand years, and the cruel persecution . . . which that race has been made to suffer for a great part of the time" is deemed here to be "the most disgraceful spot on Christian history." Rather than rebuking this Jew as a miserly Christ-killer in the traditional manner, we are urged to admire him for the tenacity with which he pursues his trade and for his unassuming generosity to others. Yet, diminishing the onus of his theological guilt is curiously insufficient to absolve him from what is perceived to be his natural vocation:

> Driving bargains is his whole trade; and in justice we ought to judge of the man who lives by that, on the same principles as we would judge of the man who earns his living in any other way. "A hard-working man" is about the best, and deservedly the best character we can give a mechanical labourer; and as bargaining is the Jew's work, why should not a "hard-bargaining Jew" be the very perfection of his character.[24]

The stereotype that emerges of this corvine philosopher of the streets reconstitutes traditional perceptions by emphasizing his mastery of the hard bargain to the exclusion of other more overtly theological traits. The justification of his menial role points firmly to the acceptance of the Jew as a constituent of the commercial life of London. If he is far from being acknowledged yet as a social equal, his economic utility is no longer in doubt.

The qualified acceptance of this "new" role for the Jew as distinct from his once-ubiquitous position as a pariah figure in popular fantasy can also be marked by his progressive involvement in a variety of different quarters of English life. Exposure to actual Jews in everyday situations impelled subtle attitudinal shifts that brought into question the veracity of many of the old preconceptions. As well as the more familiar association during the eighteenth century of the "rich" with brokerage and the "poor" with peddling and street trading, individual Jews became professionally engaged and sometimes well known in such leisure activities as the theater, in music and singing, and in boxing.[25] Their high profile in the latter, as a direct consequence of the pugilistic feats of the celebrated Daniel Mendoza (1763–1836), dubbed "The Star of Israel," provides one of the most pointed illustrations of the way in which accepted prejudices against the Jews could be at least implicitly challenged. Mendoza's epic contests against Richard Humphries and his introduction into boxing of more "scientific" skills over brute force served as a focus for reappraisal of at least one widely held prejudice. Earlier in the century, it had been common to judge the seemingly instinctive tendency to nonaggression among the Jews as indicative that they were without doubt a people "distinguish'd for Pusillanimity and Cowardice."[26] They were considered in the popular perception as "among the most peaceable in *England*" and, in their apparent lack of interest in warfare, "the least of any people . . . addicted to a military life."[27] At the time of the Jew Bill of 1753, their opponents could imply that their almost proverbial aversion to physical altercation of any kind meant that they could never be trusted to fight for king and country and were therefore to be deemed totally unworthy of naturalization. "I know not upon what authority it is said," writes Jonas Hanway, casting about for good reasons to abrogate the proposed legislation, "but I have been told, that a *Jew* will not fight in defence of a *Christian* country."[28] Even if it is true that they themselves "are not a warlike people as the Saxons were," maintains one of their more outspoken parliamentary antagonists, that is no guarantee that they may not use their great command of money to "prevail with one half of the natives to assist them in subduing the other."[29] Their reputed cowardice is converted into allegations of wholesale treachery. For Charles Johnstone, writing almost three decades later, their pusillanimity has become congenitally linked to their predacious love of money. "Spit in a *Jew*'s face," declares the malicious hero of one of his episodic novels, "give him a box on the ear with one hand, so you give him but a farthing at the same time with the other, he will pocket the affront and thank you."[30] The exposure of Jewish cowardice is determined here by the dubious commission of a cruel and lurid sadistical game.

After Mendoza's rise in the late 1780s, such charges soon became far less tenable. To castigate with cowardice a man so obviously capable of striking back smacked too much of tempting fortune. As Francis Place informs us,

> the art of boxing as a science . . . soon spread among the young Jews, and they became generally expert at it. The consequence was in a very few years seen and felt too. It was no longer safe to insult a Jew unless he was an old man and alone. . . . But even if the Jews were unable to defend themselves, the few who would [now] be disposed to insult them merely because they are Jews, would be in danger of chastisement from the passers-by and of punishment from the police.[31]

The sporting prowess of Daniel Mendoza and Jewish boxers of a similar mold did much to assuage traditional antipathies. The self-respect that many poorer Jews were able to find by virtue of no longer being afraid to defend themselves and the heroic status accorded to Mendoza served as a clear challenge to the traditional allegation of Jewish cowardice. In the judgment of a writer who was to describe their situation more than a generation later, toward the beginning of the Victorian age, the Jews are worthy of praise as "a remarkably peaceable people" with no longer any hint of their presumed innate cowardice:

> They are very rarely to be found engaged in any of the personal outrages that are so common in the metropolis. And even in the very few in-

stances in which the name of a Jew is to be found mixed up in any scuffle or affray that takes place, it will almost always be found that he is not the aggressor. A Jew is a singularly quiet, inoffensive member of society.[32]

Although they were still unemancipated in 1842 when this was written, it is not entirely accidental perhaps that their social acceptance here is linked to their supposed placidity as a people. If by negative connotation "peaceable" might have been employed elsewhere as little more than an ironic euphemism for "cowardly," the more positive reading tips the balance in favor of seeing the Jews as a people who are responsible, forbearant, and (most critically) socially harmless.

Far less well known is that Jews were in fact actively involved in military service both in the army and navy from the middle years of the eighteenth century and particularly during the Napoleonic wars. According to Cecil Roth, when on one occasion George III reviewed a regiment of soldiers drawn from the London East End, the king "was struck by the number of zoophoric names (such as Lyon, Wolf, Hart and so on) borne by those in its ranks."[33] At the height of the threat of a French invasion in 1803, many Jews considered it a patriotic duty to enlist. In a humorous engraving of that year, entitled *The Loyal Jew—and French Soldier or Beard against Whiskers!!*, a bearded Ashkenazi stands bayonet to bayonet against a French infantryman who has challenged him to surrender, exclaiming in broken English: "Vut Shurender Jean Bools property—never while I am a Shew.—I'll let you know Mounsheer, dat I fight for King Sheorge, and de Shynagogue!!"[34] When, as late as 1810, George Crabbe wrote, "Nor war nor wisdom yields our Jews delight. / They will not study, and they dare not fight,"[35] he was obdurately refusing to lay to rest a prejudice that had far less currency than it might have had only fifty years before. In weighing contradictory claims, we can see that the old belief by which the Jews were branded as natural cowards proves itself to be no less malleable and as much open to question as any other traditional prejudice against them. That it remained something of a recurrent charge in later periods may perhaps be explained by recalling the strength of the allied tradition by which they were commonly depicted as eternal wanderers with no land of their own to defend.

The difficulty of excising ancient prejudices from the face of popular belief even in an age that saw itself as one that valued toleration and enfranchisement over bigotry and inequity may be persuasively illustrated by reviewing the attitude to the Jews pursued by the journalist William Cobbett (1763–1835). Cobbett was indisputably the most influential radical populist of his day, and his strong support for Catholic

The Loyal Jew—and French Soldier or Beard against Whiskers!! Engraving, 1803. (Courtesy of the Jewish Historical Society of England.)

emancipation (achieved by act of Parliament in 1829) and for the Reform Bill of 1832 are signal examples of the progressive thinking that permeates his journalism in the *Political Register,* which he founded and published weekly from 1802 until his death. In particular, his thought is molded both by a profound concern to uphold the social integrity of rural England in an age of dispersion and by a compassionate desire to defend the English laboring man from the fatal encroachment of economic and industrial change. Cobbett attributes this change and the consequent devastation of rural values to the intrusion of financial speculators and nonproductive middlemen. A typical list of such people (one of many in Cobbett's writings) includes "exchange and insurance-brokers, loan and lottery contractors, agents and usurers, in short . . . all the Jew-like race of money-changers." Another similar array comprises "the *Forgers*, . . . the *Jews*, and . . . the *Tax-gatherers*."[36] Despite his acute sensitivity in recording the momentous changes to English society wrought by enclosure of the land and by the Industrial Revolution, Cobbett's primitive comprehension of the complexities of finance led him to lay the blame for the "new" capitalism that he so intensely despised on what he saw as the parasitism of credit men and money-brokers. The association of these paper-money men with the Jews runs as a noxious thread through his voluminous popular journalism.

For Cobbett, the Jews and their agents are England's natural enemies who are constantly colluding to destroy the continuity of the life of the small farmer and honest laborer. Their presence is both symptomatic and causative of national downfall. "The Jews," he writes, "have never been found numerous and opulent in any country which was not fast going to decay." "Every nation," he avers, "that has fostered the Jews has become miserable in proportion to their numbers and influence." "In our country, the history of them is quite sufficient to convince any man of the ruinous consequences of permitting even their existence to any considerable extent." His wider xenophobia and dislike of certain kinds of change find reiterative focus in his deep-seated aversion to the Jews. Their expulsion from these islands along with that of the "Italians and Negroes and Germans and other foreigners" becomes for him the only panacea to pauperism and national misery. Economically, he sees them as capable of holding the nation to ransom by their swindles and extortions. In the city, they have established a lethal grip on the financial health of the state by exacerbating the government's reliance upon public debt. In the country, they have forged a similar stranglehold by utilizing their pedlars and "Rag-men" as so "many '*bankers*,' as they are called. . . . So that there is not a village, however small, into which some or other of these deceivers does not poke his nose, either directly or indirectly." The presumption of a conspiracy against the state involving both "rich" and "poor" Jews, already well rehearsed by earlier writers, is also explicit in Cobbett's thinking.[37]

The economic ubiquity of the Jews, as he perceives it, and their shameless substitution of paper money for gold convey frightening intimations of national ruin. The consequence of allowing them too great a share of the public interest, he contends, will be the imminent thraldom of so many unborn generations of the English people. Fear of such enslavement causes him to pitch his resentment into the zealotry of a personal crusade "to prevent the labouring man's child in the cradle from having more than half its labour mortgaged to Jews and jobbers." Cobbett imagines the Jews as a people who will never work themselves but through their degenerate peculation insouciantly exploit the labor of others. He sees them as poised to take over the state by reducing the English populace to the lowest level of miserable subsistence. In the afflatus of his phantasmic vision of a future national bondage, he imagines that "the children's children of Englishmen . . . [will] toil like slaves and live on crusts that fall from the table of . . . pampered Israelites, or Israelitish Christians." His peremptory response to the liberal pleas of those contemporary voices arguing so strenuously for greater toleration is that a very large section of the London press has been bought and "is absolutely in the pay of the Jews . . . , the tool of the Jews for pecuniary reward."[38] The rhetorical effect of his invective allows him simultaneously to reassert his own steadfast independence from such base dealing and to insist on the veracity of even his most hyperbolic claims. The pugnaciousness of his argument acts as a partial camouflage for the naiveté of many of his more unsupportable opinions concerning the economic hegemony of the Jews. Its "logic" only makes sense when matched with more overtly theological perceptions of the Jews which, as he grew older, Cobbett exploited with increasing vigor.

In common with some earlier writers, Cobbett links the economic and theological strands of his discourse by claiming that money rather than deity is the true object of Jewish worship. The assumption is given sporadic airing when enunciating his attitude to the Jews in the *Political Register* but receives its most comprehensive and damning treatment in a sermon that he published at his own expense in 1830 under the title *Good Friday; or, The Murder of Jesus Christ by the Jews*. In this rabid piece of anti-Semitism, designed to frustrate the promoters of the first Disabilities Bill, Cobbett melds traditional theological perceptions of their deicidal culpability with the conviction that the Jews are to be blamed no less for bringing about the economic ills that have beset those countries that have deigned to give them succor:

> With regard to the TEMPORAL GOOD of a nation, what can be more pernicious than to give countenance and encouragement to a race, whose god is *gain*; who live solely by money-changing; who never labour in making, or causing to come, any thing useful to man; who are usurers by profession, and extortioners by habit and almost by instinct; who, to use the words of the prophet, carry on "usury and increase, and greedily gain of their neighbours by extortion"? This pro-

pensity they appear to have in their very nature: it seems to be inborn with them to be continually drawing to themselves the goods of all around them. In all the states, where they have been encouraged, they have first assisted to rob and enslave the people, and, in the end, to destroy the government.[39]

Unlike his more liberal contemporaries, Cobbett remains uncompromising in his verdict that the Jews are innately greedy and will pursue their mercenary instincts even to the annihilation of the state. He enunciates the calamitous events of the French Revolution as a perfect exemplum of their subversive influence. They were, he asserts wildly, "the agents in bringing about that state of misery, which finally produced the lamentable catastrophe. They every where are on the side of oppression, assisting tyranny in its fiscal extortions" (16–17).

The crudity of Cobbett's thinking on the Jews of his own day is apparent from the frequency with which he utilizes traditional theological perceptions as a springboard to berate them. They are, he claims with bewildering velocity, "the descendants of the *murderers of Christ*; . . . they continue to boast of the exploit, and one of their greatest parental cares is to teach their children to blaspheme his name, and that too, in the most horrible manner." Their biblical ancestors who perpetrated "the bloody deed" against Christ may have ceased to exist but, writes Cobbett, "the earth be still polluted by their descendants in mind and heart as well as in their natural bodies; and . . . these still persevere in the utterance of their blasphemous calumnies." Their worship does not deserve the dignity of being pronounced a religion, but should rather be termed as "the '*Jewish depravity*;' . . . for our forefathers knew too well the meaning of words, to call the blasphemy of these creatures '*religion.*'" As a people "whose very name indicates that they would, if they could, crucify him again," they are to be considered as "worse than dogs," meant by God to be instinctively shunned by humanity as God has taught other animals to shun the serpent and the crocodile. Moreover, propriety should dictate shutting them off from the rest of humanity, since they flout their unbelief so ostentatiously by their "blackguard appearance of a Sunday, when they put on their nasty old clothes for the express purpose of insulting Christians." Admit into the country, Cobbett beseeches, even the Catholic Church and the Spanish Inquisition than give room to these professed infidels who, "in their blasphemous assemblies called synagogues, call Jesus Christ an impostor, and treat his faith and doctrine with the utmost contempt!"[40]

Whipping through this venomous panoply of traditional smears and accusations from the pen of one of the most widely read writers of his age may leave us with the impression that little had changed in popular attitudes to the Jews among the English since the long period of their expulsion. Perhaps William Cobbett gives a tad more emphasis to economic over theological arguments but the Jew that emerges from his diatribe appears as unwelcomely familiar as that conceived by William Prynne in the seventeenth century or by William Romaine in the middle of the eighteenth. Yet there are significant differences. As a journalist who throughout his long career showed an ear finely attuned to fluctuations in popular opinion but still remained obsessively anti-Semitic, we may assume without strain that Cobbett would have lost no opportunity to stigmatize wherever and whenever he could. "I certainly am," he declares with unseemly pride, "an enemy of all Jews."[41] However, while quite happy to echo and impute a belief in the vernacular libel that the Jews were (and are still) engaged in deeds of ritual murder, he invariably seems to fall just short of spelling out the charge in so many words. In *Good Friday*, among the most truculent of his innumerable attacks, he comes particularly close when he challenges the assimilationist tendencies of certain Jews:

> A mourning coat or cloak may cover a body containing a soul as far from being a *Christian,* as those of the *Jews* themselves, even while they are in the performance of their blasphemous rites, repeating in effigy (as on certain days is said to be their custom) the bloody deed for which their race has been condemned to wander throughout the earth.[42]

The hearsay charge that Cobbett attributes in parenthesis to popular belief rather than proven fact arraigns Jewish ritual with iconically reenacting the crucifixion. If not quite indicting the Jews of his own day as ruthless assassins compulsively disposed to turn against their Christian neighbors, he imputes hardly less. They are, he says, "exactly like those *spies,* whom tyrants employ when they suspect that their power is in danger, and who, in the words of the Psalmist, 'lie in wait to shed innocent blood'" (19).

Elsewhere, in an essay in the *Political Register,* coincident to *Good Friday* in also being occasioned by the Disabilities Bill, Cobbett embroiders his childhood recollection of the infamous Chelsea murder of 1771 to give the deed all the dubious aura of a ritual slaying: "A servant man was murdered by these bloody Jews, in a manner so barbarous, and attended with such circumstances of mutilation, and of studied *insult to human nature,* as to rouse the indignation of all England from one end of the country to the other."[43] Endelman, who provides an ample summary of the Chelsea murder, legitimately suggests that certain details concerning the Jews as perpetrators that appear nowhere else are most likely to have been the product of Cobbett's fertile imagination. Among these, he surmises that the allusion to the mutilation of the servant's body may have been intended to imply that his attackers castrated him.[44] However, it seems far more plausible here that Cobbett is once again endeavoring to create a mental image by which his reader will associate this particular killing with the larger imputation that the Jews engage compulsively in deeds of ritual murder. That he stops just short of directly stating this shows his tacit recognition that the libel no longer has the same currency as certainly had been the case less than a century earlier. In the sundry defamations against the Jews sprinkled through Cobbett's enormous literary output, we can detect heavily coded simulacra of so many longstanding popular beliefs that had entered eighteenth-century English culture virtually intact but proved themselves more and more incredible as their veracity was laid open to dispassionate scrutiny.

Unlike in 1753, when many voices were raised in universal clamor against the Naturalization Act, Cobbett turns out to be almost unique among popular writers in execrating the Jews so publicly at the time of the first Disabilities Bill.[45] The rejection of the bill at its second reading on May 17, 1830, may certainly have owed a great deal to a sustained tradition of hostility toward the Jews in England but that hostility failed to translate itself into extra-parliamentary agitation of the kind that had characterized events nearly eighty years before. Although he expressly abominates and denounces "modern 'liberality'" for hugging to its "bosom the devil himself" by opening its arms indiscriminately to the Jews, Cobbett desists from advocating any further action than rhetorical assault and the rebuttal of demands for their emancipation: "Do I call upon you to destroy them, or to hunt them from the land like beasts of prey? By no means: the principles of Christianity, the principles of Him against whose name they utter their blasphemies, are their sure protection."[46] Throughout, Cobbett seems instinctively to sense how far he can decently push his aspersions without appearing completely illiberal, yet one senses that only his acute register of public opinion prevents him from endeavoring to recreate an even more negative image of the Jews.

In his extravagant account of the Chelsea murder which occurred when he was eight, he almost casually recalls how the roots of his own prejudice are inescapably grounded in his memory of childhood: "For many years after that affair, we never used to see a Jew, in the country, without driving him away, with a cry of '*Chelsea*' at his heels. I have pelted them many a time with snow-balls, or rotten apples, or clods of dirt; and I thought I was doing my duty."[47] Cobbett's candid revelation here suggests the complexity of the process by which Christian anti-Semitism can often be traced to irrational apprehensions and fears concerning the Jews that have been capriciously implanted from earliest infancy. The illogical association of the Jews of his own day with those accused of murdering Christ and their further implication in a host of latter-day deeds that perversely simulate the original crime of their forefathers leave no room for viewing them as anything other than vicious in their own right. By combining such traditional perceptions with the argument, increasingly voiced by their antagonists from the time of their readmission, that the Jews are responsible for the imminent financial and moral collapse of the state and its institutions, Cobbett seems to stand at the crossroads between medieval theological and modern economic anti-Semitism. If the old stereotype of the Jew as the cohort of the Devil no longer excited quite the same literal fears that had been voiced by the anti-Judaic writers of late medieval and Renaissance England, the example of William Cobbett shows us that, however anachronistically, it could still provoke disturbing resonances in the popular imagination of the early nineteenth century.

Those resonances are still powerfully apparent at the *terminus ad quem* to our study in Charles Dickens's unsavory creation of the Jew Fagin in *The Adventures of Oliver Twist* (1837–39). In certain respects, the portrayal of Fagin presents a more characteristic picture of the endurance of endemic anti-Semitic attitudes than we have witnessed in Cobbett's vicious and malicious propaganda. Where Cobbett flagrantly expends his energy in his endeavors to revile the Jews, Dickens (if we may believe the consensus of his critics) had no such conspicuous intention. "That Dickens could create Fagin," writes Harry Stone, "is a reflection of his indifference to the implications of his portrait. . . . [His] attitude towards the Jews was negligent at best, and he probably gave little thought to Fagin's anti-Semitic ramifications."[48] Yet, whether inadvertently anti-Semitic or otherwise, the extraordinary imaginative impact of Fagin depends in large measure upon a tacit acknowledgment by both author and reader of a shared response to the character's "Jewishness." At best unconsciously, Dickens's imagination delves into the annals of an inveterate anti-Semitism. We can see in Fagin, however watered down, many aspects of the complex negative stereotype of the Jew that, despite the persuasive liberalism of the age, persisted as a feature of English popular culture through the early years of the nineteenth century.

Critical commentary has tended to argue that Fagin is at best a Jew in no more than name. His "main claim to Jewishness," contends Stone, "is the fact that Dickens constantly labels him 'the Jew'" (234). "Thoughtful readers," states Montagu Modder, "will see that, although Fagin belongs to the Jewish people, he retains no distinctive peculiarities of his religion. . . . As a Jew he lacks actuality."[49] Both critics cite Dickens's much later disclaimer to a Jewish correspondent in which he explains that, as a "fence" or receiver of stolen goods, Fagin was only made a Jew "because it unfortunately was true of the time to which the story refers, that that class of criminal almost invariably *was* a Jew."[50] Both also point out that at one of our final glimpses of Fagin, as he awaits in prison his impending fate by hanging, he shoos away with curses a group of "venerable men of his own persuasion [who] had come to pray beside him."[51] Stone comments that it "seems strange that Dickens could believe these touches would offset the implications of the remainder of his portrait" while Modder uses it as support for his contention that Fagin "is just as much an outcast Jew, as Bill Sykes is an outcast Christian."[52] The significant point that these discussions fail to amplify is that, while it remains manifestly clear that his behavior and actions in no way reflect the actualities of Judaism, Fagin's "Jewishness" emanates far more visibly from Dickens's imaginative reinvigoration of attributes of the endemic anti-Semitic stereotype that for so long had haunted the Christian consciousness.

Physiognomically, he endows Fagin with a "villainous-looking and repulsive face . . . obscured by a quantity of matted red hair," the color originally associated with Judas and commonly worn through the centuries by the Jew in drama.[53] His exaggerated nose (more evident in George Cruikshank's illustrations to the novel than in Dickens's own account) is almost certainly a borrowing from the stage. In a wonderful moment of pure theater, upon meeting Noah Claypole (alias Morris Bolter), Fagin teasingly sinks "his voice to a confidential whisper" to bamboozle the simple countryman with the warning that "one need be sharp in this town." He accompanies this by striking "the side of his nose with his right forefinger,—a gesture which Noah attempted to imitate, though not with complete success, in consequence of his own nose not being large enough for the purpose" (289). Cruikshank's illustration, *The Jew & Morris Bolter begin to understand each other*, captures perfectly the comic incongruity of this brief misalliance of sharpness and simplicity. In his dress, Dickens associates Fagin with contemporary Jewish old-clothes men, his typical apparel being "a greasy flannel gown" (50) or "an old torn coverlet" (317). On his first morning in Fagin's foul back

George Cruikshank, *The Jew & Morris Bolter begin to understand each other.* Engraving, 1839. (Courtesy of the Brotherton Library, University of Leeds.)

room or den, Oliver considers that "the old gentleman must be a decided miser to live in such a dirty place, with so many watches" (53). Some while later, after being rescued by Mr. Brownlow, Oliver's own "old clothes" or "sad rags" are sold to a Jew (84), suggesting that Dickens may be appealing to the common perception that reflexively links old-clothes dealing with the shadowy network of Jewish larceny.

Dickens's stereotypical association of Fagin with a class of criminal perceived by him as almost invariably Jewish is based on a circumstantial awareness of the reputed nefarious practices of this kind of Jew.[54] However, the connection in the popular imagination of Jews with crime probably owes as much to theological traditions that stress their greater cosmic guilt. It is significant that, at an elemental level, Dickens endows Fagin with many vestigial characteristics of the traditional diabolized Jew-figure. References to Fagin frequently turn upon invidious comparison with the Devil: plunged into deep thought as he plots with Bill Sikes the robbery at Chertsey, his grimace becomes "an expression of villany perfectly demoniacal" (123); later, when Fagin lays his "withered old claw" on Sikes's shoulder, the housebreaker (no cherub himself) claims to be reminded "of being nabbed by the devil" (302); Sikes apprises the Jew by way of bizarre compliment in the same episode that Fagin's deceased father is in all probability roasting in hell where the Devil will be "singeing his grizzled red beard by this time, unless you came straight from the old un without any father at all betwixt you."[55] The epithet "merry old gentleman," which Dickens frequently uses to label Fagin, remains even today a fairly standard euphemism with which to describe the Devil.[56]

In common with many earlier representations of the diabolized Jew-figure, Fagin is depicted throughout the novel in terms that render him less than human, both brutish and repulsive: a "lynx-eyed Jew" (266), "a black-hearted wolf" (304), a "thundering old cur" (319), and so on. Seating Fagin uncomfortably in "his old lair" shortly before Nancy's murder, of which he is at the very least an accessory before the fact, the novelist comprehensively bestializes his features: "His right hand was raised to his lips, and as . . . he bit his long black nails, he disclosed among his toothless gums a few such fangs as should have been a dog's or rat's" (317). In the selfsame scene, the tormented conscience that traditionally belongs to the Wandering Jew wishing to atone for his crime against humanity finds a secularized adjunct in Fagin's physiognomic cast: "the Jew sat watching . . . , with face so distorted and pale, and eyes so red and bloodshot, that he looked less like a man, than like some hideous phantom: moist from the grave, and worried by an evil spirit."

The chimerical aspect of this figure is also apparent in Dickens's evocation of Fagin's "shrivelled body" slinking from its den:

> The mud lay thick upon the stones: and a black mist hung over the streets; the rain fell sluggishly down: and everything felt cold and clammy to the touch. It seemed just the night when it befitted such a being as the Jew, to be abroad. As he glided stealthily along, creeping beneath the shelter of the walls and doorways, the hideous old man seemed like some loathsome reptile, engendered in the slime and darkness through which he moved: crawling forth, by night, in search of some rich offal for a meal. (120–21)

In the lurid half-light of a vile metamorphosis, the Jew becomes no longer human but a predacious nocturnal creature that has recovered its primordial element. Dickens denotes the untold Otherness of the Jew by magnifying grotesque and reptilian traits that link him to traditional representations of the Devil.

Although sometimes diluted, the influence upon Dickens's imagination in *Oliver Twist* of popular beliefs concerning the Jews manifests itself even more remarkably in a number of crucial details. The old fabrication (an unfailing source of endless "low" humor) that their apparent abhorrence conceals a secret appetite for the flesh of the pig is given a new twist by Dickens when Fagin is first revealed to Oliver (and the reader) in his inner sanctum or "den" employing his toasting-fork to turn the saveloys or (pork?) sausages that he is busily frying over his fire (50; also 75). As we have seen, Fagin is a receiver who lives not upon his own "work" but, as was alleged of the Jews, upon the misdeeds of those whom he controls. As such, he is represented (if we may borrow Sikes's words) as a "white-livered thief" (93) and a "false-hearted wagabond" (260), a coward and a double-crosser who will blithely betray even those closest in trust to him when his own survival appears at stake. In order to perpetrate his despicable crimes, it is imputed at least twice (78, 305) that Fagin would resort without remorse even to poisoning, yet one more wicked deed with which the Jews had been traditionally tarnished. By making Fagin orchestrate Oliver's kidnapping (82), Dickens also revives the hideous specter of the Jew as one who willfully abducts young Christian boys for the purpose of enmeshing them in crime and then, once they have become dispensable, expediting their death as a means of reaping personal benefit. In the first scene that he is left alone with Fagin, as Oliver begins to awake from his slumber, he catches sight of the miserly old Jew gloating over an array of intricate jewels, gold watches, and magnificent trinkets that he extracts from a secret casket. "What a fine thing capital punishment is!" murmurs Fagin to himself, unaware that

Oliver is no longer asleep and is listening, "Dead men never repent; dead men never bring awkward stories to light. Ah, it's a fine thing for the trade! Five of 'em strung up in a row; and none left to play booty, or turn white-livered!" (52). At that instant, Fagin's glance falls on the waking boy, their eyes meet albeit momentarily, and in a spasm of fury the Jew seizes hold of a bread knife and waves it quivering over the hapless Oliver. The gesture, though one utilized repeatedly elsewhere by Dickens in different forms to represent (as Harry Stone puts it) "murderous adult aggression against defenseless childhood," achieves an additional intensity of purpose here as it evokes the frightening specter of the perfidious Jew preparing to enact yet again his allotted crime of ritual murder.[57] Interpreted through the eyes of an innocent but extremely distraught young boy, Fagin's action demythologizes the reader's very worst inner fears concerning the Jews. The innuendo of the blood libel is unmistakable.

According to M. J. Landa, despite Dickens never intending a harmful portrayal of the Jews, the immediate effect of Fagin (whom he dubs as "second in command to Shylock" in the gradation of English images of the Jew) may well have been to hold back their struggle for emancipation at a particularly crucial moment. He points out that in London restrictions on Jewish traders were rescinded in 1831, "a Jew was called to the Bar in 1833, the first Jewish sheriff was elected in 1835, and the following year saw the first Jewish alderman." But, he claims, with the appearance of Fagin in 1837 at a critical time in Anglo-Jewish relations, endemic attitudes noticeably hardened and it was not until 1858 that a practicing Jew was finally admitted to Parliament.[58] No doubt, Landa grossly simplifies the complex processes that led to full emancipation and similarly exaggerates the influence of Fagin in determining cultural attitudes, but he is right in recognizing that Dickens's Jew magnetized many latent prejudices that may otherwise have remained dormant. That the author later acknowledged that he had unthinkingly compromised the good standing of the Jews is apparent from his efforts many years after to emend the text of *Oliver Twist*; where he had previously referred to his villain as "the Jew," Dickens fairly consistently altered this to read "Fagin" or simply "he."[59] His attempt to counterbalance Fagin through the virtuous Jew, Riah, in *Our Mutual Friend* (1864), however unconvincing as a character portrayal, is further evidence of Dickens's humane concern to undo an earlier wrong. It is Riah who provides us with a final apologia for the predicament of the Jews living in a predominantly gentile society:

It is not, in Christian countries, with the Jews as with other peoples. Men say, "This is a bad Greek, but there are good Greeks. This is a bad

Turk, but there are good Turks." Not so with the Jews. Men find the bad among us easily enough—among what peoples are the bad not easily found?—but they take the worst of us as samples of the best; they take the lowest of us as presentations of the highest; and they say "All Jews are alike."[60]

The blurring of distinctions here by which in the common perception the bad Jew has become the denominator through whom his people as a whole are to be judged attests to Dickens's implicit recognition of the sinister forces that he had casually unleashed when he created Fagin. The author's humanitarianism, for all its generosity and great-heartedness, cannot ultimately annul or eradicate the specter of the vile Jew. The fine tradition of liberalism that had emerged with the Enlightenment but also the legacy of Shylock and of Fagin constitute the divided inheritance that will promiscuously help to formulate the attitudes to the Jews of the emergent Victorian age.

EPILOGUE

EMANATING from the intertextual discourse with which this book has been concerned, several fundamental questions remain unresolved or invite closer attention than has so far been possible. In particular, I wish to give some thought to three practical issues that unfold intrinsically from this discussion. The first is to consider the extent to which the treatment of the Jew may differ from the representation of other religious, ethnic, or national groups in eighteenth-century English discourse. Several writers within the period, and also some more recently, have endeavored comparison. A further discussion will help to construct an axis upon which the paradigmatic status of the Jew as Other can once more be reviewed. Arising from this, a second consideration turns upon the claim that the rhetoric of anti-Semitic discourse during the eighteenth century was largely innocent and that, nowadays, in an age that is far more sensitive to intolerance we may too easily employ our own liberal suspicions in a manner that is crudely unhistorical. The uncouthness of partisan debate and the unrefined quality of eighteenth-century humor, runs this argument, should not be mistaken for anti-Semitism. Last we need to reexamine the belief that the progressive liberalization of English attitudes toward the Jews, particularly within the latter part of the period, may have helped to attenuate (though not eradicate) endemic prejudices. The nub of this final question returns us to the theoretical analysis of the mutative quality of ethnic stereotypes and to a broader conundrum in present-day social psychology that posits "education" as an optimistic counter to traditional forms of prejudice. With each one of these issues, the main source of my discussion will be in terms of their representation in the eighteenth century rather than necessarily attempting, except perhaps incidentally, to contribute to debate on the nature of prejudice in the modern world.

In dramaturgical and fictional analysis, it has not been unusual to compare the representation of the Jew with that of other (more overtly) national types. "As a born minor character," writes Edgar Rosenberg,

> the Jew often appears as merely one more stock figure in a series of fringe types, along with a flat-footed Irishman, or a French fop, or a

whoring nobleman, or a niggardly Scotsman, and so on. In that case he enjoys no privileged handicaps: his foolishness is treated on crudely the same level as the foolishness of the others. Certainly he is not much better than any of the rest, but not distinctively worse either.[1]

Yet, even if "merely one more stock figure," the literary depiction of the Jew, intentionally or otherwise, is likely to arouse complex emotions in an audience or reader that are distinct from those evoked by the portrayal of, say, an Irishman or a Scot or a Frenchman. In the latter case, the depiction may depend upon the well-tried employment of certain formulaic characteristics such as flat-footedness, parsimony, or foppishness. They are characteristics that by convention have become attached to popular representations of specific national types but they are also ones that it would not be difficult to encounter elsewhere, particularly in the everyday world of the host group. By contrast, the stereotype of the Jew frequently defies close affinity with any other. In the case of the most common characteristic attached to the Jew, namely usury or money-lending, the association inexorably awakens a dormant nexus of negative perceptions that provokes an uncomfortable mental link with the pariah figure of old. Because the equivalent vocation as practiced by the host group has achieved since the eighteenth century some respectability under the different guise of banking, it is conveniently forgotten in most cases that the lending of money at interest is far from being the exclusive preserve of the Jew. A judicious change of nomenclature creates a telling change of perception. Sociolinguistic demarcation makes irresistible the "unique" villainy of the Jew as perceived by the host group.

The survival of the Jews from biblical times as a separate people, often interpreted in the parlance of philo-Semitism as living witness to Christianity of God's larger millennial plan, is employed in anti-Semitic discourse as confirmation of their total unassimilability. A propagandist such as William Romaine at the time of the Jew Bill insists that "our State can have no natural-born Subjects but Christians" and amusingly scorns the idea of "a natural-born *Jew Christian Foreign Englishman,* [which] is such a Medley of Contradictions, that all the Rabbies in the World will never be able to reconcile them."[2] Similarly, William Cobbett, writing in the early nineteenth century, determines that unlike those of other nations the Jews are not only incapable but also unwilling to assimilate with their hosts:

If a German, a Frenchman, a Spaniard, or a man of any other country settle amongst us, he soon coalesces and becomes amalgamated with the rest of us, and at any rate his progeny is sure to be English. But a

Jew is of no nation, and his children are Jews, never uniting and coalescing with any other race, but making it their religion and their
study to remain distinct and separate from all.[3]

The alterity or Otherness of the Jews, according to this view, is entirely
of their own making. Their unity, argues Cobbett voicing a commonly
held conviction, is only among themselves. "They are united together
though spread in all countries," he writes, "a mass widely extending
amongst other materials, but gravitating uniformly and alone to its own
centre."[4] The myth expressed here of a Jewish conspiracy extending
across national boundaries but centripetally deployed to its own selfish
advantage bolsters the belief that it is impossible to absorb them within
the fabric of the state. Distinct from other foreigners, the bounds that
separate Jews and native Englishmen remain perpetual. They are, claims
the poet George Crabbe, a people "whose common Ties are gone, / Who,
mix'd with every Race, are lost in none."[5] The Jews exemplify in English
discourse the ultimate paradigm of the eternal Other.

If, at least in terms of assimilation, *national* identity becomes in anti-
Semitic colloquy an insurmountable distinguishing factor between Jew
and other foreigner assaying "Englishness," it could perhaps be argued
that a more valid parallel might be drawn between the treatment of the
Jews and of other non-Protestant *religious* groups. In particular, the situation of the Catholics, whose political disabilities were finally removed
by act of Parliament of 1829, might be thought to share certain similarities with that of the Jews. Indeed, reaction to the first Roman Catholic
Relief Act (1778), resulting in the Gordon Riots of 1780, was of a scale
far more widespread and bloody than the clamor occasioned by the Jew
Bill of 1753. Official figures at the time, almost certainly a gross under-
estimate, put the number of fatalities at 285, although most of the deaths
were as a consequence of furious confrontation between an agitated mob
and the troops sent to quell them. Few if any of those who died were
Catholics. The stream of pamphlets against the encroachment of Catholicism that poured from the press during these violent years contained, among other things, allegations of Jesuitical plots to blow up the
banks of the River Thames for the purpose of inundating the city of London and indiscriminate rumors of a clandestine conspiracy to assassinate
King George III.[6] A closer comparison of popular rhetoric generated by
the Jewish Naturalization and the Catholic Relief acts would be of un-
doubted merit for what it might reveal about patterns of stereotyping of
religious minorities in eighteenth-century England. In the absence of
such a study, it should be mentioned that (except later when Jewish disabilities reentered the parliamentary agenda) explicit analogy between

the situation of Catholics and Jews is rare in eighteenth-century discourse. Reference to Catholicism in the context of the Jews is usually confined to berating the monks for their invention prior to the Reformation of malicious rumors concerning nefarious Judaic practices but is sometimes employed more deliberately as an antipapal stick. Fundamentally, however, similarities between the predicament of Jew and Catholic in eighteenth-century England are probably superficial. The English Catholics comprised a far more substantial minority than the Jews; physiognomically and in the manner of their dress, they were indistinguishable from the Protestant majority with whom they could trace a shared lineality; and in general they were far more integrated into the social fabric, many of their members being drawn from the nobility and the gentry.[7] Foreign Catholics would, of course, tend to be regarded as French, Spanish, Italian, and so on.[8]

A more overtly ethnic-based, or "exo-cultural," similitude might likewise be detected in terms of the representation of Jews and blacks in eighteenth-century English discourse. The demographic insignificance of each as a fraction of the country's total population is belied (although more so in the case of the Jews) by the frequency of allusion to them. Accusations (some of which retain a lamentably familiar ring in xenophobic depictions of minorities even to our own age) of "swamping," foul living, sexual excess, and olfactory indecency are all too frequently aimed at each, but only rarely (at least in anti-Judaic texts) through direct comparison between the two groups.[9] Except obliquely by reference to a Jew's "blackness" or "dusky" complexion, contemporary analogy between the situation of these two groups remains largely incidental. A surprising exception to this occurs, however, in the House of Lords debate that accompanied the repeal of the Jewish Naturalization Act in November 1753. In the speech of John Russell, fourth Duke of Bedford, a prominent Whig (rather than Tory) opponent of the original bill, we can catch echoes of received wisdom in his contention that two rules of prudence should dictate in cases of naturalization:

> first, not to naturalize at once, or in a short time, such a number of foreigners as may, by uniting together, become any thing near to an equal match for the natives: and secondly, never to naturalize such foreigners whose latest progeny must always continue a people separate and distinct from the people that naturalized them.

The first of these rules, he argues, should be uncontentious, but the second deserves some illustration. The conjectural example he provides is to invite us to imagine that for strengthening our sugar colonies, and for peopling them with subjects instead of slaves, a scheme were proposed for naturalizing all the blacks born in any of them without any other condition whatsoever: I will say, that our adopting such a scheme would be ridiculous, because their progeny would always continue to be a distinct people; but if the conditions were added that no such blacks should be naturalized unless they declared themselves Christians, and that no such black man should be naturalized unless he married a white woman, nor any black woman unless she married a white man, the ridicule of the scheme would be very much softened, because their progeny would in time unite and coalesce with the rest of the people: it might a little alter the complexion of the people of these islands; but they would all become the same people, and would look upon themselves in no other light than as subjects of Great Britain.[10]

The function of the illustration is as part of his argument to try to preclude the Jews from the rights of citizenship on the grounds that of all the peoples of the world they are the least able to assimilate with any other nation. Their separation from the rest of humanity, according to Bedford, means that the only terms upon which they would agree to "naturalize" would be by endeavoring to convert others to Judaism. The preposterousness of the argument is in accord with widely held fears of the Jews' yearning to proselytize the English. What is unusual here because so contrary to the dynamics of modern-day prejudice is the presumption (floated perhaps only half seriously) that, on the strict condition that they convert and intermarry, there need be no barrier to the assimilation of the blacks. Their difference is treated not as a matter of external pigmentation but of inner faith. In that they may change; the Jews, whose Otherness is irreversible, will not.

Despite the emphasis on an enduring difference that emerges again and again in eighteenth-century popular discourse concerning the Jews, it would be remiss to assume that their treatment in England was any harsher than in other European countries. On the contrary, we should remember that during the whole period under discussion, despite sporadic attacks upon individuals, there were no actual pogroms against the Jews, nor were they forced (as in many other states) to remove themselves to a benighted existence in the ghetto. Even if still lacking the formal recognition that would eventually arrive through full emancipation, they enjoyed without interruption a civil and religious freedom that was almost unique. Their comparative liberty in the open exercise of their faith and in the pursuit of trade led an early nineteenth-century commentator, Robert Southey, to contend, albeit sardonically, that England had become "the heaven of the Jews."[11] Hardly himself the advocate of the Jews, it is Southey's opinion that the muted opposition and the sheer apathy of the English toward them have been the contributory factors in allowing them willy-nilly to establish residence in London and elsewhere in the country. Whereas in a previous generation, he maintains (citing a famous but probably apocryphal tale), King John had condemned a Jew to have a tooth drawn every day till he consented to lend him money, the present-day English by contrast have become blithely indifferent to those who even fifty years before would have been openly condemned as the professed enemies of Christianity. As a consequence, the deep-rooted vein of anti-Judaic sentiment that had existed in former times has been reduced to little more than empty gesture. Were a fresh attempt made to naturalize them, he claims, it would now meet with little open antagonism.[12]

Southey's account of contemporary English attitudes to the Jews implicitly questions whether anti-Semitic abuse, so facilely employed in eighteenth-century popular culture, still retains its ancient pungency or should be seen as merely residual, a quaint palimpsest or rhetorical throwback to an earlier age in which such diatribe may have once been invested with the ardor of conviction. The problem is compounded when it is recalled that xenophobic terminology is deeply ingrained in the English language and culture and far from confined to being directed against any one particular group. At least one modern historiographer, Thomas W. Perry, whose work on the Jew Bill has earlier concerned us, has employed this latter point to claim that it is too easy to misunderstand the deplorably low level of eighteenth-century partisan debate by simply exaggerating its "specifically anti-Semitic bitterness." Anglo-Jewish historians, he contends, "knowing little about the tone of eighteenth-century political controversy, but being familiar with the language of anti-Semitic bigotry in all ages, naturally tend" to misinterpret the rhetoric of the age. Too easily, they misread what is rarely more than the boisterous language of party politics for persecution or (as he calls it) "rabid anti-Jewish hysteria."[13] Perry's argument may be persuasive in suggesting a gap between the rhetoric and the application of anti-Semitism during the eighteenth century—no pogrom ensued as a consequence of the clamor over the Jew Bill—but it plays down the extent to which the emotive connotations associated with the word "Jew" are a reflection of deeper endemic attitudes.[14] Unquestionably, prejudice against the Jews in eighteenth-century England is not on the same brutal level as in some other countries in which they were far more openly and systematically persecuted. Nor does it appear to have had the strength or substance that we might associate with English attitudes of an earlier age. However, the slipperiness of endeavoring to define anti-Semitism (as Perry does) merely by insisting on a *qualitative* distinction between prejudice and persecution is nowhere better exposed than in the subtly reductive analysis of Thomas Babington Macaulay speaking as a newly elected Member of Parliament in defense of the Jews during the passage of the first Disabilities Bill of 1830. The distinction, as Macaulay presents it, becomes little more than metaphysical:

> Any person may build a theory upon phrases: with some, perhaps, burning would be persecution, while the screwing of thumbs would not be persecution; others may call the screwing of thumbs persecution, and deny the justice of that expression when used to whipping. But according to my impression, the infliction of any penalties on account of religious opinions, and on account of religious opinions alone, is generally understood as coming within the meaning of the term, for all the purposes of political argument. It is as much persecution in principle as an *auto da fé*, the only difference is in degree. Defining persecution, then, as I do, I cannot conceive any argument to be adduced in favour of the mildest degree of this injustice, which, logically speaking, though not morally, indeed, might not be used with equal force in favour of the most cruel inflictions from similar motives.[15]

If we borrow or adopt for our purposes this robust definition offered by Macaulay before the House of Commons as the centerpiece of a remarkable maiden speech, its distinction of physical persecution from "persecution in principle" (or prejudice) is primarily one of degree or scale. Clearly, the definition relies upon a liberal disposition that considers a refusal to release an oppressed minority from its political disabilities as a form of persecution no less real than physical assault. In this sense, it recognizes persecution and prejudice as points on a mental scale on which there is crucially only a moral (and not a logical) distinction between different levels of intolerance.

Applied more widely, Macaulay's definition provides an excellent antidote to those who refuse or are unable to discern anti-Semitism unless accompanied by physical violence or distinguished by a hatred that has been precisely targeted. Rhetorical assaults on the Jews in eighteenth-century discourse are but rarely directed at individuals (except when seen as examples of the tribe) but that does not in any way mitigate their potency as invective nor absolve those who employ them from anti-Semitism. At best, it might be possible to contend that much of this anti-Semitism may have been unconscious, although this seems more cogent as an argument in favor of admitting its deep-rooted and endemic hold on the eighteenth-century English mind. Evidence of this "unconscious" anti-Semitism is not too hard to unearth. For instance, a favored method employed and publicly advocated by a leading educationalist, the Quaker Joseph Lancaster (1778–1838), to punish misconduct at his school was to make the culprit parade from class to class decorated in the garb of a pedlar while the other boys followed behind imitating in a taunting fashion the dismal tones of Jewish street hawkers. He was convinced that the cause of rude behavior toward Jews was "more on account of the manner in which they cry 'old clothes,' than because they are Jews" and, consequently, saw no harm in ridiculing them as a means of subduing delinquency at school. Neither he nor Sydney Smith who wrote vigorously in his defense could comprehend (despite it being spelled out to Lancaster by the redoubtable Mrs. Trimmer) that, however unconsciously, such mockery could also inculcate in the boys a dislike of Jews.[16]

The extent to which anti-Semitic attitudes remained part and parcel of the cultural vocabulary of the era may be represented here by reference to the scolding reaction of an anonymous theatrical reviewer commenting in 1802 on the behavior of some Jews in the audience who had obstreperously interrupted the performance of Thomas Dibdin's play, *Family Quarrels*, that contained an offensive song about the licentious antics of some Jewish harlots. If it can be deemed acceptable, begins the reviewer, to amuse an audience with the depiction of a frivolous Frenchman, an effeminate Italian, an irascible Welshman, or a sycophantic Scot, why may not an actor also humorously assume the disguise of a Jew to sing about "Miss Moses, Miss Levi, and Miss Abram" without raising "a barbarous howl" from "a parcel of *old cloathsmen* and *pedlars*"? Ever since (he sanctimoniously progresses) the theater complimented them by introducing in Richard Cumberland's Sheva the figure of a good Jew,

> like the viper in the fable . . . [the Jews] turn and sting the hand that has fostered them. . . . They now grow arrogant and presuming, appearing to claim as a right what we have liberally conceded to them as an indulgence; and after we have made a public renunciation, through the medium of the drama, of the prejudices which have been imputed to us respecting the Jews, they take the most obvious method of *reviving* those prejudices (if such they were), and of convincing us that our concessions have been impolitic, and our eulogium unwarranted. Let them be cautious how they proceed. It is dangerous to trifle with the English nation. For these people, who already enjoy, perhaps,

more privileges than are consistent with the Christian religion, and who, in this country, are, and ever have been, more favoured than in any other on the face of the globe, it is more particularly unsafe and unwise to render themselves obnoxious to the public.[17]

The admonition provides us with a timely reminder of the one-way nature of English discourse concerning the Jews, from whom it counsels silence rather than protest as a fitter strategy for acceptance in a (so-called) liberal society. The implication here is that, innocent humor or otherwise, the Jews will have to put up with the slurs and jibes against them should they wish to retain the present status quo and live at peace with their hosts. In England at least, that has always proved the uneasy compromise, the insecure *modus vivendi*, of a marginal group adjusting to the mores of the dominant culture. The imagined threat posed by the Jew as Other, so often inflated by the host group into an imminent menace to its very existence, translates itself into intimations of reprisal against his coreligionists should they presume to overstep. "It is not easy to fix a bound to the just resentment of the British public," warns the same reviewer. "After the horrible murder at Chelsea, several years ago, by a confederacy of Jews, none of their race durst, for a long time, venture beyond the *purlieus* of Houndsditch, without experiencing, in some degree, the effects of popular fury."[18] It is perhaps not entirely surprising that only a few Jews were sufficiently unafraid and prepared to show open enthusiasm in support of the endeavors of those liberal Englishmen like Macaulay and Robert Grant who strove a few years later to attain their political emancipation.[19]

No one doubts that toward the latter part of our period we may witness the gradual emergence of increasingly liberal and progressive attitudes toward the Jews. No less than that of other disadvantaged groups, their predicament becomes grist to the mill of reform in an age of emancipation and radical social change. In part, we would be correct in reading this as inchmeal evidence of the loosening hold upon the collective imagination of medieval beliefs concerning the Jews that had been passed down more or less intact in popular culture from generation to generation. The renewed and peaceful presence of the Jews in England following Cromwell's toleration combined with the pervasive effect of the rational Enlightenment and of liberal attitudes severely strained the credibility of ancient tradition that had painted them as compulsive mutilators of children and inimical desecrators of the Cross. Even at the height of the controversy over the Naturalization Bill, while warning of the perpetual danger that he believes they pose, the pseudonymous Archaicus, one of the most virulent of their opponents, has to concede, albeit grudgingly, that "the *modern Jews* have lost much of *the old Jewish Venom,* and are become much more *candid, humane,* and *civil,* than their *Ancestors.*"[20] A similar point from a very different perspective is made by Philo-Patriae, one of their staunchest defenders in 1753, who argues that in previous times "the restrictive Laws in many Places . . . confined them to Traffick and Gain, . . . but . . . , where in free Countries they have had different Educations and Views, we find them capable of thinking like other Men." "I ever was of Opinion," he maintains a few pages later, "that Men's Geniuses, Nationally considered, are equal; where there is any Difference, it must arise either from Education or Circumstances."[21] By humanizing the Jews and stressing the impact of cultural factors, Philo-Patriae implicitly questions the validity of linking them as aliens with the Devil and the assumption of their unregenerate Otherness. By recognizing a significant alteration to their situation through their exposure to "different Educations and Views" in a free society, he seems to be wielding a double-edged sword that is also intended to challenge the persistence among the English of illiberal ideas about the present state of the Jews.

Increasingly after 1753, writers of a liberal bias tend to acknowledge that the far greatest responsibility for the predicament of the Jews lies in their vile treatment through the ages in Christian countries. "These usages" against them, claims the miscellaneous writer William Hone in the early nineteenth century, "were instituted and justified by a dreadful perversion of scripture, when rite and ceremony triumphed over truth and mercy. Humanity was dead, for superstition Molochized the heart." One should not assume, he insists, that the persecution of the Jews belongs only to a remote era. Recalling the pandemonium brought about by the Jew Bill, Hone ruefully reminds his readers to recall "that three quarters of a century have not elapsed since hatred to the Jews was a national feeling." The ignominious repeal of the Act of Naturalization, he feels, became a license for treating them no less shoddily than before:

> From that hour to the present, the Jews have been subjected to their old pains, penalties, disqualifications, and privations. The enlightenment of this age has dispelled much of the darkness of the last. Yet the errors of public opinion then respecting the Jews, remain to be rectified now by the solemn expression of a better public opinion. Formerly, if one of the "ancient people" had said in the imploring language of the slave, "Am I not a *man,* and a brother?" he might have been answered, "No, you are not a *man,* but a *Jew.*" It is not the business of the Jews to petition for justice, but it is the duty of Christians to be just.[22]

In unpacking this suggestive passage, we should recognize that it is written in the conviction that urgent legislative action is necessary if the state of the Jews is to be finally ameliorated. Yet, it is far less optimistic than many other accounts in assessing the effect of the radical values of the Enlightenment upon Christian perceptions of the Jews, which it appears to be saying have continued to ignore their plight. Hone seems to be positing a view that implies the existence of a mental blindspot in public opinion that prevents those humane principles that have gained acceptance elsewhere from being applied as sedulously in Christian attitudes to the Jews. A similar view is acknowledged on a more personal level by his contemporary, Charles Lamb, who speaks of his own inbred antipathy toward the Jews:

> I confess that I have not the nerves to enter their synagogues. Old prejudices cling about me. I cannot shake off the story of Hugh of Lincoln. Centuries of injury, contempt, and hate, on the one side,—of cloaked revenge, dissimulation, and hate, on the other, between our and their fathers, must, and ought, to affect the blood of the children. I cannot believe it can run clear and kindly yet; or that a few fine words, such as candour, liberality, the light of a nineteenth century, can close up the breaches of so deadly a disunion. A Hebrew is nowhere congenial to me.

In describing his mental constitution as "a bundle of prejudices—made up of likings and dislikings—the veriest thrall to sympathies, apathies, antipathies," Lamb contends that it is in the nature of each of us to respond less favorably to those who appear least like ourselves. Recognition of difference prompts only "an unhealthy excess" of national or ethnic bias. The centuries of mutual mistrust between Englishman and Jew cannot therefore be eradicated simply by invoking the progressive spirit of the age.[23]

The wider significance of this more pessimistic assessment of the supposed assuaging effect of liberal values upon endemic anti-Semitism is to act as a counter to the relatively upbeat analysis of many Anglo-Jewish historians and literary critics who have traditionally tended to quote the noble discourses of Macaulay and others as "proof" of a positive sea change in English attitudes during the latter part of our period and beyond. The employment of hand-picked quotations from liberal writers as empirical evidence in support of an optimistic interpretation has been subjected to ferocious inquisition by Edgar Rosenberg in his study of Jewish stereotypes in English fiction. Rosenberg argues that the desire to come up with positive conclusions has led to a tendency to slant the evidence by proffering carefully chosen philo-Semitic utterances "as potent antidotes to the disreputable characters in Dickens" and others. Endeavoring by such means to dip the scales to achieve the desired effect, he maintains, proves to be a fruitless effort, since in reality it cannot hope to "dislodge [the spirit of] Fagin by one inch." He cites Gotthold Ephraim Lessing's dictum in *Nathan der Weise* (1779) that "we have not freed ourselves from superstition by detecting it" as an apt reminder of the futility of believing that the rational pronouncements of sane men can in any real sense eliminate the dangerous potency of a universally accepted myth. Too easily, he claims, we fall into the trap of assuming that by their appeal to reason, enlightened thinkers could somehow argue the myth out of existence. For Rosenberg, the rational defense of the Jews and the outcry against their continued persecution by high-minded writers in the late eighteenth and early nineteenth centuries had ultimately little or no effect in denting embedded prejudice.[24]

While Rosenberg correctly cautions us against the danger of assuming that the philanthropic expression of benign values will substitute for less worthy ones, his discussion upholds far too rigid a separation between literary stereotypes, which he sees as fairly static and durable, and the currents of political and social history that are much more flexible. He categorically disavows that a stereotype may mutate through time to reflect the evolutions and gradations of social change. For him, the medieval stereotype of the Jew as usurer or mutilator remains ineradicably fixed in the popular consciousness and no amount of special pleading can shift that repulsive image. There is little sense in his study that liberal values may mollify or that changes in social attitudes may modify the hideous stereotype of old. From his fundamentally pessimistic perspective, no attenuation is possible because the literary stereotype is almost completely insulated from social reality. Rosenberg's stereotype of the Jew appears more as an enduring archaeological fossil than as a complex figure that may be decoded to reveal changing categories of difference.

Perhaps no adequate compromise can be achieved between the tendency to make naively optimistic statements about evolving English attitudes to the Jews and the more negative viewpoint expressed by Rosenberg. However, a pragmatic response to these extremes of wishful thinking and downright pessimism depends upon a reiteration of the belief that such polarities are not unusual, even characteristic, in the intricate analysis of stereotyping. Without the other, each of these poles renders only a partial reading of a much more complex whole that can only make sense if we are prepared to accept its inherent diversities and contradictions. It remains beyond question that, despite the efforts of liberal thinkers and dewy-eyed philanthropists, many of the old adverse assumptions concerning the Jews continued to infect the consciousness of Victorian England. Yet it is equally true to suggest that an increased awareness of their past persecution contributed to a developing cognizance of the moral iniquity of a failure to try at a minimum to uproot and expose the excesses of latent prejudice. Without the progressive stance of those who struggled so boldly on behalf of the Jews, the door to their eventual emancipation would have remained firmly closed. The desire of the reformers to repair accumulated wrongs both acknowledges the persistence of the problem and hints at the possibility of change. Rosenberg's view that stereotypes are insensitive to social vibrations and therefore fundamentally static insufficiently appreciates the long-term influence and percolating effect of more liberal attitudes toward the Jews.

However, although the progressive secularization of English society during the eighteenth century helped to modify and attenuate many malicious beliefs concerning the Jews, it did not eradicate but merely altered the nature of anti-Semitism for the age that followed. The gradual displacement of traditional perceptions did not automatically create an environment in which less hostile attitudes could readily emerge. In fact, the adjustment from the more overtly theological anti-Semitism inherited from the Middle Ages is often accompanied by a shifting emphasis on the economic and social condition of the Jews. By way of example, we may examine the passage of the unsavory notion that as a consequence of their trespass against Christ the Jews emitted a diabolic foul odor (*foetor judaicus*) which could be purged only by the balm of baptism. In the seventeenth century, their supposed smell is typically construed by the historiographer James Howell as a mark of their division from the rest of humanity: they are, he says, "the most contemptible people, and have a kind of fulsome scent, no better than a stink, that distinguisheth them from others."[25] Despite efforts to rebut this outlandish fallacy, it still retained sufficient currency to be recalled by anti-Semitic writers at the time of the Jew Bill. The very name of the Jews, avows Archaicus, has been "declar'd . . . to *stink* in a Figure [i.e., figuratively], as their Persons are even said to do, literally."[26] The more vicious deduction of another contemporary wrangler is that their malodorousness extends from their persons to their demeanor and to their dwelling places. They are, he claims, "in general so indolent, slothful, and nasty that they stink as they go, as well as their Habitations." The charge, he alleges, may indeed be verified by taking a walk incognito "from *Leadenhall-Street* . . . into *Duke's-Place, Bever's-Marks,* . . . and so thro' to *Houndsditch*" (the squalid sections of London populated mainly by destitute Ashkenazim), whereby "any Person will allow [that] they are the nastiest People by Nature under Heaven."[27] From our point of view, the particular interest of this short account lies in the facility with which the writer can translate a longstanding theologically based superstition into a caustic social criticism of contemporary Jews. Their supposed olfactory indecency, traditionally linked to their cosmic crime against humanity, becomes a measure by which they may be further condemned for their present tainted condition. By subtle mutation, an age-old stereotypical trait revamps itself before a new circumstance. Later writers show little or no awareness of the mythical *foetor judaicus*, although many make it their business to record the stench in the streets surrounding Rag Fair where Jewish old-clothes men would barter their wares.[28] Even Samuel Taylor Coleridge, whose copious reading among the byways and relics of literature may have made him aware of ancient belief, makes no mention of the *foetor judaicus* in a crafted anecdote recorded in his *Table Talk:*

> Once I sat in a coach opposite a Jew—a symbol of old clothes' bags—
> an Isaiah of Holywell Street. He would close the window; I opened it.
> He closed it again; upon which, in a very solemn tone, I said to him,
> "Son of Abraham! thou smellest; son of Isaac! thou art offensive; son
> of Jacob! thou stinkest foully. See the man in the moon! he is holding
> his nose at thee at that distance; dost thou think that I, sitting here,
> can endure it any longer?" My Jew was astounded, opened the window
> forthwith himself, and said, "he was sorry he did not know before I
> was so great a gentleman."[29]

Most writers on the subject persist in reproaching the Jews more broadly for their foul living, sometimes associating this with the duskiness of their complexion and sometimes too with their reputation for lasciviousness. The author of *Kidd's London Directory* (c. 1835), for instance, by way of demonstration of the "outcast" character of the Jews, remarks in elementary timbre that "their skin [is] so impregnated with filth as to defy the power of fuller's soap."[30] Even more generally, an avowed anti-Judaic writer like William Cobbett can refer at random to their "blackguard appearance" and their "*filth*," conscious that he is striking a resonance that will be familiar to the majority of his readers.[31] The evoked stereotype relies most tangibly on socioeconomic perceptions, yet is reinforced all the more by its strong theological undertones.[32] For all the efforts of the liberal intelligentsia toward the end of our period, the anatomy of the Jew in anti-Semitic discourse still reeks quite pungently with the odor of the Devil. This is even acknowledged by a fair-minded reviewer of Cobbett's *Good Friday* sermon, writing in 1830, who points out how easy it remains to arraign the Jews with accusations that they

> are . . . "filthy;"—they wear a wrong coat, or they stink. All the persecuted stink. One of the first receipts for having a man persecuted, is to impugn the credit of his corporal presence. But what does it all come to, but that there is a certain caste of believers among the Christians, who wish the Jews were at the devil?[33]

The "certain caste of believers" may no longer have been able to express their more abhorrent opinions without the expectation of being challenged but it is evident that at the end of our period many of their prejudices still commanded a considerable sway in the popular imagination.

In our own day, Julia Kristeva has spoken of the need to make peace with our own inner demons rather than blaming the outsider for all our problems. The foreigner as Other, she writes, "lives within us: he is the hidden face of our identity, the space that wrecks our abode, the time in which understanding and affinity founder. By recognizing him within ourselves, we are spared detesting him in himself."[34] For the Englishman of 1830, the compunction to acknowledge a refracted image of his own biases and shortcomings in the scapegoat of the Other and then to forgive remained little more than primitive. Too easily, as a contemporary traveler shrewdly observes,

> Whether you dine, or pray, or converse, or correspond with a pure and conscientious Jew, some peculiarity forces upon your notice, that he is not one of the people; and in these, more than in the peculiarities of their religious creed, rests the execution of the curse, which still keeps the descendants of Israel a distinct and despised people among the Gentile nations.[35]

Although the better part of two centuries had elapsed since their readmission, a cloud of fundamental ignorance concerning the true nature of their customs, habits, and beliefs still shrouded the average Englishman's perception of the Jews.

NOTES

Unless otherwise stated, reference to the Bible in English is to the Authorized Version.

Abbreviations

DNB   *Dictionary of National Biography,* ed. Leslie Stephen and Sidney Lee. 63 vols. 1885–1900.

George Cat.   F. G. Stephens and M. Dorothy George, *Catalogue of Political and Personal Satires Preserved in the Department of Prints and Drawings in the British Museum.* 11 vols. (in 12). 1870–1954.

OED   *Oxford English Dictionary,* 2d ed. 20 vols. 1989.

Rubens   Alfred Rubens, *A Jewish Iconography,* rev. ed. 1981.

STC   A. W. Pollard and G. R. Redgrave. *A Short-Title Catalogue of Books Printed in England, Scotland, and Ireland and of English Books Printed Abroad, 1475–1640.* 2d ed. 3 vols. 1976–91.

Wing   Donald Wing, *Short-Title Catalogue of Books Printed in England, Scotland, Ireland, Wales, and British America and of English Books Printed in Other Countries, 1641–1700.* 2d ed. 3 vols. New York, 1972–88.

Introduction

1. Daniel Defoe, *The Fortunate Mistress or Roxana* (1929), 142, 164, 172, 197.

2. Fanny Burney, *Cecilia or Memoirs of an Heiress,* ed. Judy Simons, 2 vols. (1986), 1:183 (bk. 3, chap. 1); Charles Johnstone, *Chrysal or the Adventures of a Guinea* (1760–65), ed. E. A. Baker [1907], 224 (vol. 2, chap. 18).

3. *The Correspondence of Alexander Pope,* ed. George Sherburn, 5 vols. (Oxford, 1956), 2:50 (letter to Robert Digby, July 20, 1720); Edmund Burke, *A Letter from Mr. Burke to a Member of the National Assembly,* 3d ed. (1791), 17; "Unparalleled Wickedness," *Cobbett's Political Register* 44 (December 21, 1822): 741.

4. M. J. Landa, *The Jew in Drama* (1926), 12.

5. See H. S. O. Henriques, *The Jews and the English Law* (Oxford, 1908), 186. Cecil Roth, *A History of the Jews in England* (Oxford, 1941), claims that as "late as 1818 it was [still] possible to maintain in the courts Lord Coke's doctrine" respecting the legal status of the Jews (247).

6. Song 7, "Praise for the Gospel," in Isaac Watts, *Divine Songs Attempted in Easy Language for the Use of Children* (1715), facsimile edition, ed. J. H. P. Pafford (Oxford, 1971), 9.

7. John Breuhowse [pseud.], *The Highland Spectator: Or, Observations on the Inhabitants of Various Denominations in London and Westminster* (1744), 94.

8. Quoted in William Jones of Nayland, *Memoirs of the Life, Studies, and Writings of the Right Reverend George Horne, D.D. Late Bishop of Norwich* (1795), 332.

9. Howard D. Weinbrot, *Britannia's Issue: The Rise of British Literature from Dryden to Ossian* (Cambridge, 1993), 403–74, has recently shown the vitality of interest during the eighteenth century in the Israelites as antecedents to the English. Although his study brings out well what he calls "the flowering of Britain's Hebraic seed" (405), Weinbrot does not always distinguish with sufficient rigor between representations of the Jews of the Bible and attitudes to their "living" counterparts in the eighteenth century. He is right, however, to stress that "much British hostility to . . . [contemporary] Jews . . . was part of the ongoing movement towards national affirmation" (448).

10. See, for instance, John Ashton, *Social England under the Regency*, 2 vols. (1890), 1:25; J. Rumney, "Anglo-Jewry as Seen through Foreign Eyes (1730–1830)," *Transactions of the Jewish Historical Society of England* 13 (1936): 331–32.

11. I am most grateful to Judith Samuel, at present researching the history of the Jews of Bristol, for reporting to me that her reading of three local papers, the *Bristol Gazette, Bristol Mirror,* and *Felix Farley's Bristol Journal,* dated the beginning of January to the middle of February 1811, revealed no reference to the incident. However, the White Hart at Bristol is listed as a coaching inn in Kearsley's *Traveller's Entertaining Guide through Great Britain* (1803), 424, and Cary's *Traveller's Companion* (1822), 168. Mrs. Samuel informs me that it was situated in Broad Street.

12. *The Temple of Mirth; or Fete of Comus and Bacchus* (c. 1800), 150–51. The same anecdote, entitled "Popular Justice," appears in *The Lively Jester* [1800?], 62.

13. [Charles Johnstone], *The History of John Juniper, Esq., alias Juniper Jack*, 3 vols. (1781), 3:280. *OED* gives no discrete reference under "out-jew" but it defines the verb "to jew" (earliest quotation, 1824) as "to cheat or overreach, in the way attributed to Jewish traders or usurers." It quotes "1833 L. Dow *Dealings of God* (1849) 189 If they [*sc.* the Jews] will *Jew* people, they cannot flourish among Yankees, who are said to 'outjew' them in trading." Cf. the phrase "to out-Herod Herod."

14. Peter Burke, *Popular Culture in Early Modern Europe* (1978), 58 and *passim*. Two further studies that have helped to mold my thinking on concepts of popular culture are Morag Shiach, *Discourse on Popular Culture: Class, Gender and History in Cultural Analysis, 1730 to the Present* (1989), and Steven L. Kaplan, ed., *Understanding Popular Culture: Europe from the Middle Ages to the Nineteenth Century* (Berlin, 1984).

15. Burke, *Popular Culture in Early Modern Europe*, 167–68.

16. The term is preferred, but with little sense of close definition, by Thomas Perry in his study of the Jew Bill, *Public Opinion, Propaganda, and Politics in Eighteenth-Century England* (Cambridge, Mass., 1962). See also Shiach, *Discourse on Popular Culture*, 30.

17. Samuel Sandmel, *Anti-Semitism in the New Testament* (Philadelphia, 1978), xx.

18. On this, see, for instance, Geoffrey Alderman's review of Gavin Langmuir's *Towards a Definition of Antisemitism* (1990) in *Jewish Journal of Sociology* 33, no. 2 (December 1991): 117.

Chapter 1. Stereotypes

1. Archaicus [pseud.], *Admonitions from Scripture and History, from Religion and Common Prudence, Relating to the Jews* (1753), 18.

2. A Christian [pseud.], *The Case of the Jews Considered* (1753), 14.

3. See Joshua Trachtenberg, *The Devil and the Jews: The Medieval Conception of the Jew and its Relation to Modern Antisemitism*, 2d ed. (Philadelphia, 1983), 182–83.

4. On this, see Robert A. Stewart, Graham E. Powell, and S. Jane Chetwynd, *Person Perception and Stereotyping* (1979), 4–5.

5. Walter Lippmann, *Public Opinion*, 15th ed. (New York, 1956).

6. It is not included for purposes of definition by M. H. Abrams, *A Glossary of Literary Terms*, 4th ed. (New York, 1981), nor by Roger Fowler, *A Dictionary of Modern Critical Terms*, rev. ed. (1987).

7. Lippman, *Public Opinion*, 120.

8. On this, see Gordon W. Allport, *The Nature of Prejudice* (Boston, 1954), 189, 192.

9. Sander L. Gilman, *Jewish Self-Hatred* (Baltimore, 1986), 4.

10. A Country Gentleman [pseud.], *Reflections upon Naturalization, Corporations and Companies; Supported by the Authorities of both Ancient and Modern Writers* (1753), 80.

11. Konstantyn Jelenski, *Kultura* (Paris, 1968); quoted by Sander Gilman, *Difference and Pathology: Stereotypes of Sexuality, Race and Madness* (Ithaca, N.Y., 1985), 29.

12. Britannia [pseud.], *An Appeal to the Throne against the Naturalization of the Jewish Nation* (1753), 12–13.

13. Lippman, *Public Opinion*, 96.

14. Arthur G. Miller, "Historical and Contemporary Perspectives on Ste-

reotyping," in Miller, ed., *In the Eye of the Beholder: Contemporary Issues in Stereotyping* (New York, 1982), 27.

15. Allport, *The Nature of Prejudice*, 247–53; see also S. Freud, *Moses and Monotheism* (New York, 1939), in *The Origins of Religion*, Pelican Freud Library 13 (1985).

16. Miller, "Historical and Contemporary Perspectives on Stereotyping," 19.

17. J. O. Bartley, *Teague, Shenkin, and Sawney* (Cork, Ireland, 1954), 1.

18. Edgar Rosenberg, *From Shylock to Svengali: Jewish Stereotypes in English Fiction* (Stanford, Calif., 1960), 10.

19. Michael Echeruo, *The Conditioned Imagination from Shakespeare to Conrad: Studies in the Exo-cultural Stereotype* (1978), 13–14.

20. Edward Said, *Orientalism* (1978), 6.

21. *Orientalism* is not concerned with the cultural stereotyping of the Jews, although Said does occasionally confess that there are similarities between the predicament of Muslim and Jew. At its most primitive, particularly in the nineteenth century, Middle Eastern Arabs and Jews are perceived by Western writers as indistinguishably oriental, the singular difference being that "Arabs are [sometimes viewed as] simply Jews on horseback" (102). At its most arguable, the distinction becomes polemicized by Said into an overt political vehicle that discriminates between Jew and Arab by maintaining that Zionism is "a strange, secret sharer of Western anti-Semitism." For all the cleverness of his discussion and his recognition of the hegemonies maintained by ethnic stereotyping, Said remains curiously blind to the fact that his argument merely counters myth with myth. If *Orientalism* is concerned with the cultural analysis of "anti-Semitism . . . in its Islamic branch" (27–28), he shows little appetite to widen his inquiry to include the much more deep-rooted history and demonology of anti-Semitism in its Jewish branch. The incompleteness of perspective is evident in Said's perverse failure to emphasize that Islamic anti-Judaism, though less well documented than Christian anti-Semitism, long pre-dates the advent of political Zionism; on this, see, for instance, Dennis Prager and Joseph Telushkin, *Why the Jews?* (New York, 1985), 110–26. To argue that, as a result of the Zionist movement, "one Semite [i.e., the Jew] went the way of Orientalism, the other, the Arab, was forced to go the way of the Oriental" (307) is to ignore the long history of the subordination and degradation of Jews in Arab lands. Caught up in the perspective of Western orientalism, the logic of Said's argument breaks down when he uses the same rhetorical strategies, that he has castigated elsewhere, as a means to denounce Zionism, and, by inference, the Jews.

22. See, particularly, Gilman, *Difference and Pathology*, 16–21.

23. Gilman, *Jewish Self-Hatred*, 4–5.

24. Sander L. Gilman, *Seeing the Insane* (New York, 1985), xi.

25. Gilman, *Difference and Pathology*, 21.

26. Ibid., 18.

27. Ibid.

28. Ibid., 27.

29. As will be apparent in chapter 9, I could not resist leaping seven small years beyond 1830 in order to involve Dickens and Fagin.

30. Archaicus [pseud.], *Admonitions from Scripture and History*, 28–29.

31. Lippman, *Public Opinion*, 126.

32. Robert Wuthnow, "Anti-Semitism and Stereotyping," in Miller, ed., *In the Eye of the Beholder*, 169.

33. Douglas Bethlehem, *A Social Psychology of Prejudice* (1985), 133.

34. S. M. Lipset and W. Scheider, *Anti-Semitism and Israel: A Report on American Public Opinion*, unpublished manuscript (Stanford University, Department of Sociology, 1979); quoted by Wuthnow, "Anti-Semitism and Stereotyping," 169.

35. Traditionally, stereotypes were thought by social psychologists to be "particularly rigid and resistant to change." More recent research has shown that, on the contrary, they "are capable of being systematically adjusted in accordance with the prevailing circumstances" (Stewart et al., *Person Perception and Stereotyping*, 2, 7–8).

36. Miller, "Historical and Contemporary Perspectives on Stereotyping," 14.

37. Wuthnow, "Anti-Semitism and Stereotyping," 171.

38. D. Katz and K. W. Braly, "Racial Stereotypes of 100 College Students," *Journal of Abnormal and Social Psychology* 28 (1933): 280–90.

39. Miller, "Historical and Contemporary Perspectives on Stereotyping," 12–13.

40. Allport, *The Nature of Prejudice*, 202.

41. See Miller, "Historical and Contemporary Perspectives on Stereotyping," 14, 25.

42. However, it is pretty evident that many of the more avowedly anti-Semitic pieces published in 1753 were the work of opposition Tory hacks, who saw the Jew Bill as an opportunity to whip up frenzy against the unbroken hegemony of the Whig party that had been in power since 1714. On this, see Perry, *Public Opinion, Propaganda, and Politics in Eighteenth-Century England*, 31–43.

43. Rosenberg, *From Shylock to Svengali*, 17.

44. Joseph Priestley, *Letters to the Jews*, 2d ed. (Birmingham, 1787), 3.

45. *Causes and Consequences of the French Emperor's Conduct Towards the Jews* (1807), 105.

46. Bernard Glassman, *Anti-Semitic Stereotypes without Jews* (Detroit, 1975), 187.

47. Todd Endelman, *The Jews of Georgian England, 1714–1830: Tradition and Change in a Liberal Society* (Philadelphia, 1979), 94–96.

Chapter 2. Jews and Devils

1. Exchequer of Receipt, Jews' Roll, no. 87, Hilary Term, 17 Hen. III, Public Record Office, London.

2. Luke Owen Pike, *History of Crime in England*, 2 vols. (1873–76), 1:190.

3. Bohun Lynch, *A History of Caricature* (1926), 20–21.

4. V. D. Lipman, *The Jews of Medieval Norwich* (1967), 105.

5. Cecil Roth, "Portraits and Caricatures of Medieval English Jews," *Essays and Portraits in Anglo-Jewish History* (Philadelphia, 1962), 22–23.

6. Michael Adler, *Jews of Medieval England* (1931), 20n.

7. Roth, "Portraits and Caricatures of Medieval English Jews," 23. See also Ruth Mellinkoff, "Cain and the Jews," *Journal of Jewish Art* 6 (1979): 16–38.

8. See Trachtenberg, *The Devil and the Jews*, 46–47. M. D. Anderson, *A Saint at Stake: The Strange Death of William of Norwich 1144* (1964), proposes that the drawing represents "Isaac . . . in Hell . . . shown in the centre as the King of Demons, crowned and with a triple face. . . . The triple face, originally applied to pagan gods, became an ambiguous element in medieval iconography, being applied both to the Holy Trinity and to the Infernal Rulers. The drawing suggests another possible interpretation of a fifteenth-century misericord in Cartmel Priory (Lancs.) which represents a triple-faced King with markedly Semitic features" (55).

9. Roth, "Portraits and Caricatures of Medieval English Jews," suggests that Avegaye and Mokke are possibly husband and wife (23). Adler, *Jews of Medieval England*, considers the two to be Isaac's "local agents" (20).

10. Alfred Rubens, *A History of Jewish Costume* (New York, 1973), identifies Isaac's crown as that of the king: "It has three fleur-de-lys on it like the crown on the first Great Seal of Henry III" (94). He considers that Isaac wears the crown "possibly to indicate that he is the king's property." Guido Schoenberger, *The Drawings of Mathis Gothart Nithart called Gruenewald* (New York, 1948), no. 35, reproduces Gruenewald's *The Three Heads* (c. 1520–25) and avers that "in the *Bible Moralisée*, and its derivations from the 13th to the 15th century, Satan usually appears three-headed with a radiant crown . . . having the special significance of Antichrist" (44). Cf. Bodleian MS 2706, *Bible Moralisée*, French thirteenth century, fol. 198.

11. Trachtenberg, *The Devil and the Jews*, 216.

12. See H. Michelson, *The Jew in Early English Literature* (Amsterdam, 1926), 41.

13. William Langland, *The Vision of Piers Plowman*, ed. A. C. Schmidt (1978), 222–23 (B text, passus XVIII, ll. 94, 101–7) (lurdaynes = villains; cheve = prosper).

14. See Michelson, *The Jew in Early English Literature*, 46–48, 51–52; Jacob Lopes Cardozo, *The Contemporary Jew in the Elizabethan Drama* (Paris, 1925), 254–66. Geoffrey Bullough, *Narrative and Dramatic Sources*

of Shakespeare (1957), 1:452–54, 486–90, records a variant or analogue to the story in Anthony Munday's *Zelauto or The Fountaine of Fame* (1580), in which the "extorting Usurer" is a Christian rather than a Jew and the bond stipulates the loss (not of a pound of flesh but) of the right eyes of his two intended victims.

15. Glassman, *Anti-Semitic Stereotypes without Jews*, 19.

16. Hyam Maccoby, *Judas Iscariot and the Myth of Jewish Evil* (1992), 107–8. Despite the popular association, Cardozo, *The Contemporary Jew in the Elizabethan Drama*, cautions us that red "is in no sense typical of Jewish physique" (60). Interestingly, a common belief that retained some currency until a much later age was that a likely outcome of copulation during a woman's menses was the birth of a red-haired child: see Paul-Gabriel Boucé, "Some Sexual Beliefs and Myths in Eighteenth-Century Britain," *Sexuality in Eighteenth-Century Britain* (1982), 36. Professor Boucé writes to me (privately) that he believes that Judas's red hair was part of this "diffuse, but pervasive myth." The irony of deeming red hair a characteristic of the Jews in general becomes apparent when it is recalled that pentateuchal law is adamant in its insistence that connubial lovemaking is unclean in the period of menstruation when the "issue in . . . [a woman's] flesh be blood" (Lev. 15:19).

17. But see Ruth Mellinkoff, "Judas's Red Hair and the Jews," *Journal of Jewish Art* 9 (1982): 31–46, who concludes that it is "both possible and even probable that Judas and Shylock wore red wigs on the stage, but to date I have not found firm evidence" (45). However, Landa, *The Jew in Drama* (1926), insists that the change of Shylock's hair from red to black and curly can be traced to Charles Macklin's performance in 1741 (12).

18. Thomas Kyd, *The Spanish Tragedy*, ed. J. R. Mulryne (1970), 135. The reference occurs in an additional passage (first printed in 1602) and considered to be by another writer. Cf. William Shakespeare, *As You Like It*, III.iv.6, and John Marston and others, *The Insatiate Countess* (1613), II.ii.36, ed. George Melchiori (Manchester, 1984), 98.

19. John Dryden, *Amboyna* (Wing D2232), I.i.

20. "A Dialogue or Communication between Satan and our Conscience" (c. 1550), *The Writings of John Bradford, M.A.*, ed. Aubrey Townsend, 2 vols. (Cambridge, 1848–53), 1:211.

21. Vaughan, *Silex Scintillans* ("Rules and Lessons," l. 45), *The Works of Henry Vaughan*, ed. L. C. Martin (Oxford, 1957), 437; cf. George Herbert, "Self-condemnation," ll. 17–18, in *The Works of George Herbert*, ed. F. E. Hutchinson (Oxford, 1978), 170–71.

22. For an early fifteenth-century pictorial representation of this, see Henry John Cheales, "On the Wall-Paintings in All Saints' Church, Friskney, Lincolnshire," *Archaeologia* 53, pt. 2 (1893): 427–32. Cf. the Croxton *Play of the Sacrament* (c. 1460s) in which the Jews prick the stolen Host with four holes in the shape of a cross before stabbing the center with a fifth wound that causes it to bleed; see Gail McMurray Gibson, *The Theater of*

Devotion: East Anglian Drama and Society in the Late Middle Ages (Chicago, 1989), 36. A variant of the theme lies in the accusation that the Jews indulged in the desecration of Christ's image or picture; see, for instance, Thomas Beard, *The Theatre of Gods Iudgements*, 2d ed. (1612 [STC 1660]), 46–47.

23. See, for instance, the Chester play of "The Sacrifice of Isaac," *English Miracle Plays Moralities and Interludes*, ed. Alfred W. Pollard, 7th ed. (Oxford, 1923), 21–30. A very different interpretation of Abraham emerges from medieval biblical exegesis (and indeed remains present even today in the Catholic mass), where he is saluted as "our Father in Faith." I am grateful to Prof. Jack Watt for alerting me to this.

24. The suggestion is made by Cardozo, *The Contemporary Jew in the Elizabethan Drama*, 22.

25. Montagu Frank Modder, *The Jew in the Literature of England* (Philadelphia, 1939), 12–13.

26. W.H. [William Hughes], *Anglo-Judaeus, or the History of the Jews whilst here in England* (1656 [Wing H3321]), 46, 48.

27. William Prynne, *A Short Demurrer to the Jewes Long Discontinued Remitter into England* (1656 [Wing P4078]), 27.

28. *Pamphlets Relating to the Jews in England during the Seventeenth and Eighteenth Centuries*, ed. P. Radin (San Francisco, 1939), 21–22 (*To His Highnesse the Lord Protector of the Commonwealth. The Humble Addresses of Menasseh ben Israel* [1655?]).

29. For the equation of Antichrist and Jew, see Christopher Hill, *Antichrist in Seventeenth-Century England* (1971), 175–76, 178–81; Trachtenberg, *The Devil and the Jews*, 32–43.

30. P. Fairlambe, *The Recantation of a Brownist* (1606); quoted by David S. Katz, *Philo-Semitism and the Readmission of the Jews to England, 1603–1655* (Oxford, 1982), 163. On the conjunction of Jews with dogs, cf. R. Po-Chia Hsia, *The Myth of Ritual Murder: Jews and Magic in Reformation Germany* (New Haven, 1988), 26, 28.

31. *A Brief Compendium of the Vain Hopes of the Jews Messias*, 11 (Wing B764). Katz, *Philo-Semitism and the Readmission of the Jews to England*, describes Bargishai, who also went under the name of Paul Isaiah, as "a professional convert from Judaism" (223). See also Wilfred S. Samuel, "The Strayings of Paul Isaiah in England (1651–1656)," *Transactions of the Jewish Historical Society of England* 16 (1952): 77–87.

32. Thomas Calvert, *The Blessed Jew of Marocco or a Blackmoor Made White* (York, 1649 [Wing C321]); quoted by Glassman, *Anti-Semitic Stereotypes without Jews*, 93–94.

33. The dog (cf. Cerberus) and the goat are both associated with the Devil (see Trachtenberg, *The Devil and the Jews*, 46–47, 84); the cock is linked with Peter's denial of Christ (Matt. 26:34, 27:74) and the prickthorn with the crucifixion (the crown of thorns).

34. Latimer, *Remains*, ii, p. 42 (quoted in Michelson, *The Jew in Early English Literature*, 138).

35. Francis Bacon, *The Essays or Counsels Civil and Moral of Francis Lord Verulam*, ed. Henry Lewis, Collins' English Classics (n.d.), 237. Lewis notes that "in the Middle Ages it was customary to enforce by law certain styles of dress upon the different ranks and professions of society, and it was not uncommon to compel Jews to wear head-dresses of yellow."

36. *Pamphlets Relating to the Jews in England*, ed. Radin, 20–21. Cf. John Blaxton, *The English Usurer, or Usury Condemned* (London, 1634 [STC 3129]), 50, who remarks that a Christian usurer "is worse than a *Iew*, for one *Iew* will not take vsury of another: but the Vsurer will take vsury of his Christian brethren."

37. *Pamphlets Relating to the Jews in England*, ed. Radin, 22.

38. See A. Cohen, *An Anglo-Jewish Scrapbook, 1640–1840* (1943), 215, and D'Blossiers Tovey, *Anglia Judaica* (Oxford, 1738), 259–60.

39. See Tovey, *Anglia Judaica*, 267.

40. See ibid., 106; Katz, *Philo-Semitism and the Readmission of the Jews to England*, 4, 17; Trachtenberg, *The Devil and the Jews*, 48; Browne, *Pseudodoxia Epidemica*, bk. 4, chap. 10, ed. Robin Robbins, 2 vols. (Oxford, 1981), 1:324–29.

41. See Michelson, *The Jew in Early English Literature*, 107.

42. Venetia Newall, "The Jew as Witch Figure," in Newall, ed., *The Witch Figure* (1973), 114. Hyam Maccoby, *The Sacred Executioner* (1982), links the bizarre fantasy that Jewish men menstruated with their supposed need to feed on Christian blood as a means to replenish the loss of their own (154).

43. Allen Edwardes [pseud.], *Erotica Judaica* (New York, 1967), 197. Edwardes also remarks that the ecclesiastical mind regarded intercourse with a Jew as equivalent to bestiality (172), for which biblical prescription states that "if a Man lyeth with a Beaste, he shall be put to Death; and ye shall kill the Beaste also" (Lev. 20:15). See also Salo Wittmayer Baron, *A Social and Religious History of the Jews*, 2d ed., 18 vols. (New York, 1952–83), 11:77–87, on "Mixed Mating."

44. Newall, "The Jew as Witch Figure," 98.

45. Prynne, *A Short Demurrer to the Jewes Long Discontinued Remitter into England*, 1. The epithet "off-scowring" is biblical (Lam. 3:45, 1 Cor. 4:13) but came to be applied to the Jews in general, e.g., "Like the *Jews* to the *Gentiles*, all others are the Offscowrings of the World"; George Savile, *Political Thoughts and Reflections*, written c. 1680, in *The Works of George Savile Marquis of Halifax*, ed. Mark N. Brown, 3 vols. (Oxford, 1989), 2:235.

46. E.I., *The Land of Promise, and the Covenant Thereof* (London, 1641 [Wing E11]), 37. Matt. 12:34 speaks of the "generation of vipers" and the phrase is repeated at 23:33: "Ye serpents, ye generation of vipers, how can you escape the damnation of hell?"

47. *The Devilish Conspiracy, Hellish Treason, Heathenish Condemnation, and Damnable Murder, Committed, and Executed by the Iewes, against the Anointed of the Lord, Christ the King* (Wing W902), 21. Though published anonymously, the preacher of the sermon was John Warner, bishop of Rochester (1581–1666); see *DNB*.

48. The development of English philo-Semitism has been admirably documented by Katz, *Philo-Semitism and the Readmission of the Jews to England.*

49. See Harold Fisch, *The Dual Image: A Study of the Figure of the Jew in English Literature* (1959), 11.

50. John Foxe, *A Sermon Preached at the Christening of a Certaine Iew at London,* translated out of Latine into English by Iames Bell (1578 [STC 11248]), sigs. Eiii$^{r/v}$ and Eiv^v.

51. *The Case of the Jevves stated: or the Jews Synagogue Opened* (London, 1656 [Wing C1094]), 1. For a further discussion of the significance of this account, see chapter 6.

52. See, for instance, Joseph Copley, *The Case of the Jews is Altered, and their Synagogue Shut to all Evil-Walkers, or a Vindication of the Jewes* (1656 [Wing C6084]).

53. See Trachtenberg, *The Devil and the Jews,* 102.

54. Christopher Marlowe, *The Jew of Malta,* ed. N. W. Bawcutt (1978), II.iii.; cf. Thomas Nashe, *The Unfortunate Traveller* (1594), in *The Works of Thomas Nashe,* ed. Ronald B. McKerrow, 5 vols. (Oxford, 1966), 2:311: "If I [Zadoch the Jew] must be banisht, . . . I will poyson their springs & conduit heades, whence they receiue al their water round about the citie [Rome]."

55. *Popish Plots and Treasons, from the beginning of the reign of Queen Elizabeth. Illustrated with Emblems and explain'd in Verse,* quoted by Sidney Lee, "Elizabethan England and the Jews," *Transactions of the New Shakespeare Society* (1887–92): 162.

56. George Carleton, *A Thankful Remembrance of God's Mercie* (1624 [STC 4640]), 164.

57. Lee, "Elizabethan England and the Jews," 160. Among others, Trachtenberg, *The Devil and the Jews,* 93, points out that the renown of the Jews in medicine often had a consequent effect of linking them with sorcery and the black arts.

58. A.R. [Alexander Ross], *A View of the Jewish Religion* (1656 [Wing R1983]), sig. *2^r.

59. Thomas Cartwright, *Helpes for Discovery of the Truth in Point of Toleration* (1648 [Wing C700]), 2.

Chapter 3. Following Readmission

1. On this, see Glassman, *Anti-Semitic Stereotypes without Jews,* 106–33. Cecil Roth, *Magna Bibliotheca Anglo-Judaica,* new ed. (1937), 206–9,

277–78, lists more than fifteen pamphlets concerning the Jews published between 1655 and 1657.

2. W.H., *Anglo-Judaeus*, 31. On Hughes, see also David S. Katz, "English Redemption and Jewish Readmission in 1656," *Journal of Jewish Studies* 34 (1983): 80–81.

3. W.H., *Anglo-Judaeus*, 46.

4. Katz, *Philo-Semitism and the Readmission of the Jews to England*, 41.

5. Prynne, *A Short Demurrer to the Jewes Long Discontinued Remitter into England*, 58. In the same pamphlet, Prynne also calls the Jews deceivers and Antichrists, but, as Hill, *Antichrist in Seventeenth-Century England*, points out, "this was an incidental argument among many others . . . against their readmission" (180). Hill further remarks that, despite Prynne, Protestants tended to reject "the medieval theory [still] retained by sixteenth- and seventeenth-century catholic theologians—that Antichrist had not yet come and that when he did come he would be a Jew" (175). However, the equation in English popular culture of Antichrist and the Jews persists well into the eighteenth century.

6. For a selection, see Cohen, *An Anglo-Jewish Scrapbook*, 154–55, 198–201.

7. *Coryat's Crudities*, 3 vols. (1776) 1:298–99 (first published 1611).

8. *The Wandering-Jew, Telling Fortunes to English-men* (STC 11512), 13.

9. See Trachtenberg, *The Devil and the Jews*, 71. Cf. Acts 13:1–12 for a biblical representation of a Jew as sorcerer.

10. Alfred Rubens, *A Jewish Iconography*, rev. ed. (1981), 262; also Champfleury, *Histoire de l'Imagerie Populaire* (Paris, 1869). Roger of Wendover's account in his *Flores Historiarum*, written at St. Albans around 1228, is reprinted in English translation by George K. Anderson, *The Legend of the Wandering Jew* (Providence, 1965), 18–19.

11. Baron, *A Social and Religious History of the Jews*, points out that "England was the first country to follow the lead of the Lateran Council" of 1215 and order its Jews to wear a badge as a distinguishing mark (11:98).

12. On the Jew badge, see Cohen, *An Anglo-Jewish Scrapbook*, 249–53.

13. It is always possible that the woodcut may have been copied from a hitherto untraced continental print. There is no allusion to Egremont's Jew badge in *The Wandering-Jew Telling Fortunes to English-men*. Curiously, too, in the pamphlet the Jew is depicted wearing "buskins on his legges" (13), although in the cut he is barefooted as was typical to most folktales (Baron, *A Social and Religious History of the Jews*, 11:181).

14. *The Wandering-Jew*, 40, 58.

15. See Lucien Wolf, "The Jewry of the Restoration: 1660–1644," *Transactions of the Jewish Historical Society of England* 5 (1902–5): 5; Glassman, *Anti-Semitic Stereotypes without Jews*, 135.

16. "London," in *The Jewish Encyclopedia*, new ed. (New York, 1927), 8:158.

17. Tovey, *Anglia Judaica*, 302.
18. *The Other Side of the Question* (1753), iv, footnote.
19. Endelman, *The Jews of Georgian England*, 172.
20. Patrick Colquhoun, *A Treatise on the Police of the Metropolis*, 5th ed. (1797), 159.
21. See Endelman, *The Jews of Georgian England*, 172, 341.
22. Thomas Violet, *A Petition against the Jewes* (1661 [Wing V584]), 2.
23. *Seasonable Remarks on the Act Lately Pass'd in Favour of the Jews* (1753), 12.
24. *A Letter from a Gentleman to his Friend Concerning the Naturalization of the Jews* (1753), 4, 12–13.
25. John Tutchin, *England's Happiness Consider'd* (1705), 22.
26. Mohamed Caraffa, the Grand Turk [pseud.], *The Exclusion of the English; An Invitation to Foreigners* (1748), 18–19.
27. Archaicus [pseud.], *Admonitions from Scripture and History*, 27.
28. *The Other Side of the Question*, 33.
29. See Glassman, *Anti-Semitic Stereotypes without Jews*, 134; H. R. S. Van der Veen, *Jewish Characters in Eighteenth-Century English Fiction and Drama* (Groningen, 1935), 83–84. Unless otherwise noted, all references to Van der Veen are to this edition.
30. [Jonas Hanway], *A Review of the Proposed Naturalization of the Jews* (1753), 85; letter of "Christianus," *London Evening Post*, July 12–14, 1753; Archaicus [pseud.], *Admonitions from Scripture and History*, 20, 27; *A Modest Apology for the Citizens and Merchants of London, Who Petitioned the House of Commons against Naturalizing the Jews* (1753), 8, 12; J.E., Gent, *Some Considerations on the Naturalization of the Jews* (1753), 13; *London Evening Post*, July 14, 1753.
31. The earliest *OED* example dates from 1606. See also R. W. Dent, *Proverbial Language in English Drama Exclusive of Shakespeare, 1495–1616* (Berkeley, 1984), 445, and Geoffrey Hughes, *Swearing: A Social History of Foul Language, Oaths and Profanity in English* (Oxford, 1991), 130–31.
32. W.H. [William Hughes], *Anglo-Judaeus*, 47.
33. [Hanway], *A Review of the Proposed Naturalization of the Jews*, 85.
34. See Perry, *Public Opinion, Propaganda, and Politics in Eighteenth-Century England*, 8–9.
35. Letter of Dr. Joshua van Oven to Patrick Colquhoun, London, March 24, 1801, printed in *Anglo-Jewish Letters*, ed. Cecil Roth (1938), 211. Endelman, *The Jews of Georgian England*, 116, cites another example from the second quarter of the nineteenth century: "The very word, according to the Rev. Charles B. Taylor, Rector of St. Peter's, Chester, was 'associated with what is vulgar and degraded and contemptible. . . . The Jewish name is commonly coupled with a reproach, with the idea of low cunning and sordid avarice'"; Henry John Marks, *Narrative of H. J. Marks*, intro. Charles B. Taylor (1838), v.
36. Cobbett MSS., c. 1833; quoted by Lewis Melville, *The Life and Let-

ters of William Cobbett in England and America, 2 vols. (1913), 1:21. On Cobbett and the Jews, see John W. Osborne, "William Cobbett's Anti-Semitism," *The Historian* 47, no. 1 (1984): 86–92, and chapter 9 of this book.

Derogatory compounds such as "Jew-bail," "Jew-boy," and "Jew-craft" (all listed by *OED*) also make their first appearance in eighteenth-century usage. An antedating of the earliest *OED* listing (1785) of "Jew-bail" (meaning insufficient or worthless bail) occurs in the anonymous pamphlet, *The Merchant's Complaint to the Lawyers at the Devil. Shewing the Hardships, Inconveniences, and Injustice, To which Every Honest Man of Property is Exposed, from Jew Bail, Sham Pleas, Demurrers, Writs of Error, and Injunction Bills* (1771), which comprises a sustained attack on the practice. Without employing the term itself, Charles Johnstone, *The Pilgrim: Or, A Picture of Life*, 2 vols. [1775], 2:229–43, purveys a savagely anti-Semitic delineation of the iniquity. It is rendered graphically in Isaac Cruikshank's *The Last Day of Term* (1786) (Rubens, no. 868), and in two prints by Thomas Rowlandson, *A Lady in Limbo or Jew Bail Rejected* (1785; reissued 1802) (Rubens, no. 907), and *Kitty Careless in Quod or Waiting for Jew Bail* (c. 1800) (George Cat., no. 11802; Rubens, no. 902).

37. Quoted by *OED*, "Jew," 2. A similar expression is used by W.H. [William Hughes], *Anglo-Judaeus*: "Better we cannot express more cut-throat dealing then [sic] thus, *None but a Jew would have done so*" (47); also cf. Thomas Nashe, *Christs Teares over Iervsalem* (1593), in *The Works of Thomas Nashe*, ed. McKerrow: "the Prouerbe which we vse to a cruell dealer, saying, Goe thy waies, thou art a Iewe" (2:159).

38. Van der Veen, *Jewish Characters in Eighteenth-Century English Fiction and Drama*, 26–28, 53–54.

39. Maria Edgeworth, *Castle Rackrent* (1800), ed. George Watson (Oxford, 1969), 36. Van der Veen, *Jewish Characters in Eighteenth-Century English Fiction and Drama*, gives further examples of this common phrase as used earlier in the eighteenth century by Jonathan Swift and Samuel Foote (29, 150). Cf. George Farquhar, *Love and Business* (1701), in *The Works of George Farquhar*, ed. Shirley Strum Kenny, 2 vols. (Oxford, 1988), 2:320: "People, like the *Jews*, that are tolerated in all Governments for the Interest of the Publick, while their main Drift is to enrich themselves; and who by their Gettings and Cunning have brought their Riches and Practice into a Proverb."

40. *An Apology for the Naturalization of the Jews* (1753), 2.

41. [John Toland], *Reasons for Naturalizing the Jews in Great Britain and Ireland, on the same Foot with all other Nations* (1714), 19.

42. *The Commonplace Book of the Rev. Robert Kirk of Aberfoyle*, in Donald Maclean and Norman G. Brett-James, "London in 1689–90," *Transactions of the London and Middlesex Archeological Society* 7, pt. 1 (1935): 151.

43. *Anglo-Jewish Letters*, ed. Roth, 64.

44. *The Diary of Samuel Pepys*, ed. Robert Latham and William Mat-

thews, 11 vols. (1970–83), 4:335. Cohen, *An Anglo-Jewish Scrapbook*, notes that "Pepys was unaware that his visit was on the Festival of the Rejoicing of the Law [Simchat Torah] when decorum was relaxed" (276).

45. Henry Newcome, *Autobiography*, ed. R. Parkinson (Chetham Society), 2 vols. (1852), 2:262; quoted in Cohen, *An Anglo-Jewish Scrapbook*, 276.

46. See Endelman, *The Jews of Georgian England*, 106, 172. According to the *OED*, the earliest employment in English of the terms *Sephardi* and *Ashkenazi* considerably post-dates the eighteenth century.

47. *Reasons Offered to the Consideration of Parliament, for Preventing the Growth of Judaism* (c. 1738), 8–9.

48. *The Ceremonies of the Present Jews* (1728), vi.

49. *Seasonable Remarks on the Act Lately Pass'd in Favour of the Jews*, 13.

50. *London Evening-Post*, July 19–21, 1753.

51. In Leviticus 19:27, the Jews are given a prohibition not "to round the corners of your heads, neither shalt thou mar the corners of thy beard."

52. *A Narrative of the Remarkable Affair between Mr. Simonds, the Polish Jew Merchant and Mr. James Ashley, Merchant of Bread-Street* (1752), 18.

53. [Thomas Bridges, of Hull], *The Adventures of a Bank-Note*, 4 vols. (1770–71), 4:165.

54. The best of the eighteenth-century commentators on the plates, the German Georg Christoph Lichtenberg, describes him as "a Portuguese Jew"; see *Commentaries on Hogarth's Engravings*, trans. Innes and Gustav Herdan (1966), 16. M. J. Landa tentatively identifies him as Philip Mendez da Costa, a Jewish rake, who brought a widely publicized breach of promise action against his wealthy cousin, Kitty Villareal; see "Kitty Villareal, the Da Costas and Samson Gideon," *Transactions of the Jewish Historical Society of England* 13 (1936): 289–90. Ronald Paulson, *Hogarth: His Life, Art, and Times*, 2 vols. (New Haven, 1971), guesses that the Jew may have been Samson Gideon, "the greatest Jewish merchant in London during the first half of the century, [who] was born in 1699 and would have been the right age for the Harlot's keeper in the 1730s" (1:534 n. 47).

55. See Van der Veen, *Jewish Characters in Eighteenth-Century English Fiction and Drama*, 109, and 109–22, 142–43, for a full account of Hogarth's influence.

56. According to Fisch, *The Dual Image* (1971), the immoral aspect of Isaac, the bad Jew in Smollett's *Roderick Random* (1748), also "owed something to the portrayal of the Jew as a whoremonger in Hogarth's series of paintings *The Harlot's Progress*. . . . The quality of licentiousness is henceforward added as a spring for the broth of literary anti-semitism" (45).

57. Eliza Haywood, *The History of Miss Betsy Thoughtless*, ed. Dale Spender (1986), 197. David Dabydeen, *Hogarth, Walpole and Commercial Britain* (1987), notes fictional parallels, slightly pre-dating *A Harlot's Prog-*

ress, in which the "deceiving of dandified Jewish merchants . . . by whores
. . . is to be found" (86). He cites *The Life and Intrigues of the Late Celebrated Mrs Mary Parrimore, the Tall Milliner of Change-Alley* (1729) and
The Ramble or, A View of Several Amorous and Diverting Intrigues (c.
1730). A more immediate echo occurs in Fielding's burlesque play, *The
Covent-Garden Tragedy* (1732), performed only weeks after the publication
of *A Harlot's Progress*. In wooing Kissinda, Lovegirlo remarks (scene IX.28–
32):

> I'll take thee into Keeping, take thee Rooms
> So large, so furnish'd, in so fine a Street,
> The Mistress of a *Jew* shall envy thee,
> By *Jove*, I'll force the sooty Tribe to own,
> A Christian keeps a Whore as well as they.

Burlesque Plays of the Eighteenth Century, ed. Simon Trussler (Oxford,
1969), 193.
  58. *Jackson's Oxford Journal*, August 11, 1753, reprinted from the
London Evening Post, August 4–7, 1753; as quoted by Paulson, *Hogarth*,
2:198–99.
  59. Rubens, *A Jewish Iconography*, lists approximately 170 such prints
(nos. 1066–1235). The only one that predates Hogarth is J. Boydell's *A View
of Stocks Market* (1753), in which the pedlar figure is too indistinct to be of
significance.

Chapter 4. Wandering Jew, Vagabond Jews

  1. The belief that at least one of Christ's followers would not taste death
until the second coming is supported by his response to Peter at John 21:20–
23, concerning "the disciple whom Jesus loved" (St. John) who, "if I will . . .
[shall] tarry till I come."
  2. Anderson, *The Legend of the Wandering Jew*, 94–95.
  3. Bishop Thomas Percy, *Reliques of Ancient English Poetry* (1765),
2:291–96.
  4. See Anderson, *The Legend of the Wandering Jew*, 61.
  5. Ibid., 117.
  6. *The Wandering Jew, Or the Shoemaker of Jerusalem* (n.d.), 2–3, 4,
7–8.
  7. On this, see R. Edelmann, "Ahasuerus, the Wandering Jew: Origin and
Background," in Galit Hasan-Rokem and Alan Dundes, eds., *The Wandering
Jew: Essays in the Interpretation of a Christian Legend* (Bloomington, Ind.,
1986), 1–10.
  8. See Anderson, *The Legend of the Wandering Jew*, 76, 104, 105, 107.
(The italics in the quoted passages are mine.)
  9. Rosenberg, *From Shylock to Svengali*, 188–89, 196.
  10. On the westward migration of "beggar Jews" (*Betteljuden*) in the sev-

enteenth and eighteenth centuries, see Moses A. Shulvass, *From East to West: The Westward Migration of Jews from Eastern Europe during the Seventeenth and Eighteenth Centuries* (Detroit, 1971).

11. *Seasonable Remarks on the Act Lately Pass'd in Favour of the Jews*, 14.

12. George Cat., no. 7423 (January 5, 1788); *Transactions of the Jewish Historical Society* 7 (1915): 267.

13. J.E., Gent, *Some Considerations on the Naturalization of the Jews*, 17.

14. Archaicus [pseud.], *Admonitions from Scripture and History*, 16, 27.

15. *Look Before You Leap, or, the Fate of the Jews* (c. 1795), 5–6.

16. The Reverend John Brown of Haddington, *A Dictionary of the Holy Bible* (1813), projects the common denotation of "vagabond," which he explains as "one who has no settled abode," but adds that the word "ordinarily signifies one who is also naughty and wicked" (692).

17. Henry Francis Offley, *Richard Brothers, Neither a Madman nor an Impostor* (1795), xvi–xvii.

18. A By-Stander [pseud.], *A True State of the Case Concerning the Good or Evil which the Bill for the NATURALIZATION of the JEWS May Bring upon Great-Britain* (1753), 5–6.

19. Archaicus [pseud.], *Admonitions from Scripture and History*, 14.

20. *An Historical and Law-Treatise Against Jews and Judaism* (1732), 20.

21. John Tutchin, *England's Happiness Consider'd, in Some Expedients* (1705), 22.

22. [William Romaine], *An Answer to a Pamphlet, entitled, Considerations on the Bill to Permit Persons Professing the Jewish Religion to be Naturalized*, 3d ed. (1753), 18.

23. [Edward Weston], *ΔΙΑΣΠΟΡΑ. Some Reflections Relating to The Naturalization of Jews* (1754), 50–51. The copy of this book in the Solomons Collection of the Jewish Theological Seminary, New York, has a manuscript note identifying the author.

24. Priestley, *Letters to the Jews*, Part II, 41, 40.

25. Archaicus [pseud.], *The Rejection and Restoration of the Jews, According to Scripture, Declar'd* (1753), 17.

26. Britannia [pseud.], *An Appeal to the Throne against the Naturalization of the Jewish Nation* (1753), 15–16.

27. On this, see Katz, *Philo-Semitism and the Readmission of the Jews*, passim; Endelman, *The Jews of Georgian England*, 50–59.

28. Thomas Pocock, "The Life of Menasseh Ben-Israel," in *Of the Term of Life*, translated from the Latin of Menasseh (1709), xviii–xix.

29. Britannia [pseud.], *An Appeal to the Throne against the Naturalization of the Jewish Nation*, 16.

30. *A Letter from a Gentleman to his Friend Concerning the Naturalization of the Jews*, 5.

31. *A Modest Apology*, 8.

32. J.E., Gent, *Some Considerations on the Naturalization of the Jews*, 15.

33. [Hanway], *A Review of the Proposed Naturalization of the Jews*, 42. The same statement appears in *A Letter from a Gentleman to his Friend Concerning the Naturalization of the Jews*, 11.

34. [Jacob Bryant], *A Treatise upon the Authenticity of the Scriptures, and the Truth of the Christian Religion*, 2d ed. (Cambridge, 1793), 41.

35. *An Historical and Law-Treatise against Jews and Judaism*, 18.

36. Lewis Stephens, *The Excellencies of the Kindness of Onesiphorus to St. Paul, when He Was a Prisoner in Rome: Exemplified in a Discourse Preach'd before the Inhabitants of the Parish of St. Patrock in Exeter, on Sunday the 6th of July, 1735: Occasioned by their Delivering Joseph Otto-lenghe, a Poor Convert Jew, out of South-gate Prison, into which He Was Cast by a Jew, after his Conversion to Christianity*. Published at the Request of the Parishioners of St. Patrock's, For the Benefit of the Said Poor Convert Jew (Exeter, [1735]), 14.

37. The print was published by S. Alken, Soho, September 30, 1785 (Rubens, no. 1070).

38. Robert Southey, *Letters from England* (1807), ed. Jack Simmons (1951), 396–97.

39. Colquhoun, *A Treatise on the Police of the Metropolis*, 159.

40. On this, see Endelman, *The Jews of Georgian England*, 192–226, 297–300, who shows that Jewish criminal activity became an increasingly acute social problem in the late eighteenth century; Harold Pollins, *Economic History of the Jews in England* (East Brunswick, N.J., 1982), 65, who cites examples from earlier in the century.

41. *The London Chronicle: or, Universal Evening Post* 7, no. 477, January 15–17, 1760.

42. Ibid., no. 480, January 22–24, 1760; cf. *The Gentleman's Magazine* 30 (1760): 43. Recently Bernard Susser, *The Jews of Southwest England* (Exeter, 1993), has added some important details to the case. He identifies "Mr. Sherenbeare" as one Mr. Sherrenbeck, a Plymouth Jew, to whom Jackson offered the articles that he had stolen from Little Isaac. He also records that the site where the deed was perpetrated "is still known as Murder Hill, and the woods were renamed Jew's Woods."

43. For examples, see Cecil Roth, "The Jew Peddler—An Eighteenth-Century Rural Character," in *Essays and Portraits in Anglo-Jewish History*, 134–35; Endelman, *The Jews of Georgian England*, 114.

44. Quoted from the Francis Place manuscripts (British Library), as transcribed by J. Rumney, "Anglo-Jewry as Seen through Foreign Eyes (1730–1830)," *Transactions of the Jewish Historical Society of England* 13 (1936): 331.

45. Southey, *Letters from England*, 393, 398.

46. J.E., Gent, *Some Considerations on the Naturalization of the Jews*, 9.

47. "Jews," *Cobbett's Political Register* 81 (20 July 1833): 145.

48. *Reasons Offered to the Consideration of Parliament, for Preventing the Growth of Judaism*, 8.

49. Johnstone, *Chrysal or the Adventures of a Guinea*, 224.

50. *Esther's Suit to King Ahasuerus: In Behalf of the Jews* (1753), 4–5.

51. Henry Fielding, *The History of Tom Jones A Foundling*, ed. Martin C. Battestin, 2 vols. (Oxford, 1974), 2:632 (bk. 12, chap. 4).

52. The incident, though probably fictitious, was reported in the *Pennsylvania Gazette* of March 13, 1753; see Jacob R. Marcus, *The Colonial American Jew, 1492–1776*, 3 vols. (Detroit, 1970), 2:553.

53. See chapter 5.

54. The two anecdotes appeared in *The Encyclopedia of Wit* [1804], 109, 432–33, and are quoted in full by Endelman, *The Jews of Georgian England*, 98.

55. *A Peep into the Synagogue, or a Letter to the Jews* (n.d. [1790s?]), 23, 26–27.

56. Samuel Taylor Coleridge, *Table Talk*, August 14, 1833, in *The Table Talk and Omniana*, ed. T. Ashe (1923), 244–45. The street market at Holywell Street, off the Strand, London, demolished c. 1900, was for many years a hub of the trade in old clothes and rags, largely operated by poor Jews.

57. Lord Byron, *The Complete Poetical Works*, ed. Jerome J. McGann, 7 vols. (Oxford, 1980–93), 3:268, "Magdalen" (1814), ll. 19–20.

58. *A Peep into the Synagogue*, 22.

59. According to Otto Jespersen, no specific "Anglo-Jewish dialect or mode of speech" had developed in Elizabethan England, and there is no "single trait in Shylock's language that can be called distinctly Jewish"; *Growth and Structure of the English Language* (Leipzig, 1919), 218. A visitor to the Sephardi synagogue at Creechurch Lane 1690, some thirty-five years after the readmission, says of the Jews there that they had "bad English, some Latin, but all of them Hebrew" (*The Commonplace Book of the Rev. Robert Kirk of Aberfoyle*, 151). In an introduction to a reprint of Van der Veen, *Jewish Characters in Eighteenth Century English Fiction and Drama* (New York, 1972), 16, Edgar Rosenberg maintains that the earliest example of "Jewish stage-gibberish" is to be found in Knipe's *City Ramble* (1715). However, the common use of such "gibberish" and its attribution to Ashkenazi Jews is much more apparent from mid-century.

60. Unidentified print, possibly by Woodward; collection of the Jewish Theological Seminary, New York. The irony of a German Jew bargaining at a knockdown price to sell off the king of England (albeit himself a Hanoverian!) is not easily missed.

61. Published by Hodgson & Co. Newgate St. January 1824; collection of the Jewish Theological Seminary, New York. The alternative title to the print may conceivably echo Hazlitt's delineation of the pedlar in Hogarth's *Canvassing for Votes* (1757) as "a very Jew in grain"; see *The Round Table* (1817), *The Complete Works of William Hazlitt*, ed. P. P. Howe, 21 vols. (1930–34), 4:30. William Cobbett, *Cobbett's Political Register* 46 (1823), has

a passing reference to "the old pun, *Jews in grain*" (330). Cf. *The Universal Songster, or, Museum of Mirth*, 3 vols. (1825–26), 1:262–63, which includes "The Jew in Grain; or, the Doctrine of an Israelite," a song similarly describing a Jew's dexterity as a cheat.

62. Maria Edgeworth, *Harrington* (1817), chap. 2, in *Tales and Novels*, 10 vols. (1857), 9:13.

63. "Treatment of the Jews," in *The Courier*, June 18, 1816, *Essays on His Times in The Morning Post and The Courier*, ed. David V. Erdman, 3 vols. (Princeton, 1978), 3:144–45. The attribution of this piece to Coleridge is conjectural.

64. Jon Bee [John Badcock], *A Living Picture of London for 1828* (1828), 111.

65. See *OED*, which cites examples from 1705 to 1842 and also quotes a corresponding verb (*to smouch*), meaning to acquire dishonestly or pilfer. The noun survived in colonial usage in South Africa during the nineteenth century, where it denoted an itinerant (often Jewish) pedlar or old-clothes man and is thought to have been introduced by tradesmen of the Dutch East Indies Company. In Dutch, the derogatory word *smous* meant a Jew or usurer. The origin of the word may be a corruption of the Jewish proper name, Moses. See Rev. Charles Petman, *Africanderisms* (1913), 453; Jean Branford, *A Dictionary of South African English*, 3d ed. (Capetown, 1987), 330; and cf. the related German word *mauscheln*, originally meaning "to extort usurious interest *in the manner of a Jew*" as discussed by Gilman, *Jewish Self-Hatred*, 139 and *passim*.

66. See Van der Veen, *Jewish Characters in Eighteenth-Century English Fiction and Drama*, 215–17.

67. Thomas Collier, *A Brief Answer to Some of the Objections and Demurs Made against the Coming and Inhabiting of the Jews in This Commonwealth* (1656 [Wing C5269]), 8.

68. *A Letter from a Gentleman to his Friend Concerning the Naturalization of the Jews*, 12.

69. *A Modest Apology*, 14, vii. On the historical background to the belief that the Jews curse Jesus, see Trachtenberg, *The Devil and the Jews*, 181–83.

70. *A Declaration of the Conversion of Mr. Aron de Almanza, a Spanish Merchant, with his Two Children and Nephew, from Judaism to the Protestant Religion* (1703), 6. The word *Elganafa* may be related to the Yiddish term *ganef* (or *gonef*), meaning a thief or crook that has been traced in English usage from c. 1835; see Kellow Chesney, *The Victorian Underworld* (1970), 128n, and Leo Rosten, *The Joys of Yiddish* (1971), 140–42.

71. Henry Mayhew, *London Labour and the London Poor*, 4 vols., facsimile reprint (New York, 1967), 2:117. I am tempted to believe that Shakespeare may be alluding to this superstition in *The Merchant of Venice* when Shylock complains of his treatment by Antonio: "You call me misbeliever, cut-throat dog, / And spet upon my Jewish gaberdine" (I.iii.106–7). See also

[John Toland], *Reasons for Naturalizing the Jews in Great Britain and Ireland*, 19, quoted in chap. 3, p. 49; Trachtenberg, *The Devil and the Jews*, 51; Endelman, *The Jews of Georgian England*, 93.

72. See, for instance, Eino Railo, *The Haunted Castle* (New York, 1964), 197–201; Rosenberg, *From Shylock to Svengali*, 206–19; Anderson, *The Legend of the Wandering Jew*, 177–80.

73. Matthew Gregory Lewis, *The Monk* (1795), ed. Howard Anderson (Oxford, 1973), 168.

74. Anderson, *The Legend of the Wandering Jew*, 179.

75. See Railo, *The Haunted Castle*, 198; Rosenberg, *From Shylock to Svengali*, 214–15.

76. Rosenberg, *From Shylock to Svengali*, 210.

77. Anderson, *The Legend of the Wandering Jew*, 179.

78. Trachtenberg, *The Devil and the Jew*, 70–71, 232, n. 35.

79. *OED* quotes Gabriel Harvey, "A souerain Rule, as deare as a Iewes eye" (*Pierce's Superogation or A New Prayse of the Olde Asse*, 1593) and Shakespeare, "There will come a Christian by, / Will be worth a Iewes eye" (*The Merchant of Venice*, II.v.43).

80. Robert Burton, *The Anatomy of Melancholy*, ed. Holbrook Jackson, 2 vols. (1964), 1:211. The phrase is picked up at the time of the Jew Bill by a writer in the *Gazeteer*, May 30, 1753, who describes a dream in which he imagines "a good company of goggle-eyed creatures, with long whiskers"; see *A Collection of the Best Pieces in Prose and Verse, Against the Naturalization of the JEWS* (1753), 14.

81. Isaiah Shachar, *Studies in the Emergence and Dissemination of the Modern Jewish Stereotype in Western Europe*, Ph.D. diss., University of London, 1967, writes: "The perception of the Jew by his looks emerged only in the late seventeenth century and not before. It is essentially a modern, not a medieval notion" (325).

82. See chap. 3, p. 50.

83. William Hurd, *A New Universal History of the Religious Rites, Ceremonies, and Customs of the Whole World* (n.d., c. 1788), 22. Cf. John Breuhowse [pseud.], *The Highland Spectator*, 94: "Though they [the Jews] are blended and mixed with the Inhabitants of all the Nations of the Earth, they are so effectually distinguished from all other People, that they are always known at the first Glance . . . the very Preservation of that People is certainly intended by Divine Providence for making the Judgments of God the more visible to Man."

84. *Seasonable Remarks on the Act Lately Pass'd in Favour of the Jews*, 26.

85. *A Modest Apology*, 8–9.

86. See John Livingston Lowes, *The Road to Xanadu*, (1927; Princeton, 1986), 230–31; Anderson, *The Legend of the Wandering Jew*, passim.

87. [James Grant], *Travels in Town*, 2 vols. (1839), 2:320.

88. John Fisher Murray, *The World of London*, 1st ser., 2 vols. (1843), 1:249, 252 (originally published in *Blackwood's Magazine*).

89. William Rae Wilson, *Travels in the Holy Land, Egypt, etc.*, 4th ed., 2 vols. (1847), 2:338 (quoted by Cohen, *An Anglo-Jewish Scrapbook*, 332). Wilson's account of his travels was first published in 1823.

90. On "oriental" versions of the Wandering Jew, see Anderson, *The Legend of the Wandering Jew*, 119, 188–89.

91. This view is well argued by Hyam Maccoby, "The Wandering Jew as Sacred Executioner," in Hasan-Rokem and Dundes, eds., *The Wandering Jew*, 236–60.

92. *Journals of Dorothy Wordsworth*, ed. Mary Moorman (Oxford, 1971), 42 (October 3, 1800). That Jewish pedlars visited the Lake District at this time is apparent from a reference in Mayhew, *London Labour and the London Poor*, 122. An elderly street seller, interviewed by Henry Mayhew, remembered that in his youth he "had travelled all over England, selling quills, sealing-wax, pencils, sponges, braces, cheap or superior jewellery, thermometers and pictures. He had sold barometers in the mountainous parts of Cumberland, sometimes walking for hours without seeing man or woman."

93. Coleridge, *Table Talk*, 101–2.

94. Lowes, *The Road to Xanadu*, 15, 227.

95. Coleridge, "Treatment of the Jews," 145.

96. For details, see Anderson, *The Legend of the Wandering Jew*, 183–87; M. Roxana Klapper, *The German Literary Influence on Shelley* (Salzburg, 1975), 58–106; *The Poems of Shelley*, vol. 1, ed. Geoffrey Matthews and Kelvin Everest (1989), 38–41. Cf. De Quincey's self-identification with the figure of the Wandering Jew in *Confessions of an English Opium-Eater* (1822) and elsewhere, discussed by John Barrell, *The Infection of Thomas de Quincey* (New Haven, 1991), 29–32.

Chapter 5. Conversion

1. Roth, *Magna Bibliotheca Anglo-Judaica*, 275–95, lists 127 conversionist tracts published between 1578 and 1839, although he cautions that the welter of conversionist propaganda, following the establishment at the turn of the nineteenth century of the London Society for Promoting Christianity among the Jews, inevitably leaves his bibliography incomplete.

2. For a modern version of this ongoing view, see Murdo A. Macleod, "The Witness of the Church to the Jewish People," in David W. Torrance, ed., *The Witness of the Jews to God* (Edinburgh, 1982), 71–80.

3. A popular example of the "folk conversion" of a Jew is the poetic tale of "The Monk and Jew," in *The New Winter Evening's Companion, of Fun, Mirth, and Frolic, Containing a Great Variety of Merry Tales, and Diverting Entertainments, for the Winter Evening Fireside* (Kilmarnock, 1822), 20–21. When Mordecai "upon whose face / The synagogue you plain might trace"

falls through the ice into a stream, a passing monk refuses to help him to safety till he turns Christian and acknowledges "our papal father . . . / Heav'ns vicar." Once the despairing Jew complies, the monk responds:

Your peace, my friend is made on high:
Full absolution here I give:
Saint Peter will your soul receive
Wash'd clean from sin, and duly shriven,
New converts always go to heaven;
No hour for death so fit as this:
Thus, thus, I launch you into bliss!
His convert launch'd beneath the ice.

Significantly, the duped conversion is made by a Catholic priest. Rubens, *A Jewish Iconography*, 101, reproduces (no. 957) an illustration to a version of "The Monk and Jew" published in 1820. I have traced its source to *Poems, Consisting of Tales, Fables, Epigrams &c. &c.* (1770), humorously ascribed on its title page to "Nobody" but identifiable as the work of the actor James Robertson (1714–95) of York. Robertson's *Poems* went through several editions.

4. Philo-Patriae [pseud.], *Considerations on the Bill to Permit Persons Professing the Jewish Religion to be Naturalized by Parliament* (1753), 7.

5. [The Querist], *Some Queries, Relative to the Jews* (1753), Letter 3 (signed "Norvicensis"), 27. The correspondence included with this pamphlet is based on a series of letters sent to the printer of the *Norwich Mercury*.

6. Richard Kidder, *A Demonstration of the Messias. In which the Truth of the Christian Religion is Defended, especially against the Jews*, 2 vols. (1684, 1699), 2:80.

7. Stephens, *The Excellencies of the Kindness of Onesiphorus to St. Paul*, 20–21.

8. Priestley, *Letters to the Jews*, 6.

9. Abraham Cowley, *Poems* (1656), sig. B2^v (Wing C6682).

10. [Johanna Cartenright and Ebenezer Cartwright], *The Petition of the Jewes for the Repealing of the Act of Parliament for their Banishment out of England* (1649 [Wing C695]), 2. The authors, widowed mother and son, both Baptists, were English nationals resident in Amsterdam; see Katz, *Philo-Semitism and the Readmission of the Jews to England*, 177.

11. On this, see Katz, *Philo-Semitism and the Readmission of the Jews to England*, 89–126; Christopher Hill, "Till the Conversion of the Jews," in Richard H. Popkin, ed., *Millenarianism and Messianism in English Literature and Thought, 1650–1800* (Leiden, 1988), 12–36.

12. Isa. 11:10–12; cf. Rom. 15:12.

13. [The Querist], *Some Queries, Relative to the Jews*, 27–28.

14. Philo-Patriae [pseud.], *Considerations*, 8. Edgar R. Samuel, "The Jews in English Foreign Trade—A Consideration of the 'Philo Patriae' Pamphlets of 1753," in John M. Shaftesley, ed., *Remember the Days: Essays on Anglo-Jewish History Presented to Cecil Roth* (1966), 123–43, has argued that the

author of this and a further similarly signed pamphlet was in fact a Jew, one Joseph Salvador. The attribution remains insecure. As Todd Endelman, *The Jews of Georgian England*, points out: "The conversionist sentiments of Philo-Patriae hardly seem compatible with someone who chose to remain a Jew and obtain his privileges through legislative relief, rather than through baptism" (327n). Mel Scult, *Millennial Expectations and Jewish Liberties* (Leiden, 1978), calls Philo-Patriae "the chief spokesman for the administration" (64).

15. *The Writings of Mr. Richard Brothers, God's Anointed King* (1798), 100.

16. Thomas Taylor, *An Additional Testimony Given to Vindicate the Truth of the Prophecies of Richard Brothers* (1795), 4.

17. *The Writings of Mr. Richard Brothers*, 87. The twelve rays of light upon the ensign allude to the twelve tribes of Israel.

18. George Cat., no. 8627; Rubens, no. 206.

19. David Levi, *Letters to Nathaniel Brassey Halhed, M.P., in Answer to his Testimony of the Authenticity of the Prophecies of Richard Brothers, And his Pretended Mission to Recall the Jews* [1795], 46–47.

20. Ibid., 39; see also Offley, *Richard Brothers, Neither a Madman nor an Impostor*, xvii–xix, who raises the comparison of Brothers with Moses. There are excellent modern accounts of Brothers and his mission in Ronald Matthews, *English Messiahs* (1936), and Clarke Garrett, *Respectable Folly* (Baltimore, 1975).

21. [Romaine], *An Answer to a Pamphlet*, 24, 28, 29.

22. Kidder, *A Demonstration of the Messias*, 2:88.

23. [Gilbert Burnet], *The Conversion & Persecutions of Eve Cohan, Now Called Elizabeth Verboon, A Person of Quality of the Jewish Religion* (1680 [Wing B5772]), 4.

24. *The Principal Motives and Circumstances that Induced Moses Marcus to Leave the Jewish, and Embrace the Christian Faith* (1724), xxi.

25. On this, see Henriques, *The Jews and the English Law*, 6–8.

26. Burnet, *The Conversion & Persecutions of Eve Cohan*, 24.

27. See Thomas Barnardston, *Reports of Cases Determined in the Court of King's Bench* (1744) in *The English Reports* 94 (1909), 406, 425 [5 GEO. II. 1732]; *The Gentleman's Magazine* 2 (1732): 773; H. R. Plomer, G. H. Bushnell, and E. R. McC.Dix, *A Dictionary of the Printers and Booksellers at Work in England Scotland and Ireland from 1726 to 1775* (Oxford, 1932), 186; Henriques, *The Jews and the English Law*, 9–10; Roth, *A History of the Jews in England* (1949), 203.

28. *Remarks on the Reverend Mr. Tucker's Letter on Naturalizations* (1753), 28.

29. *A Declaration of the Conversion of Mr. Aron de Almanza*, 7.

30. Stephens, *The Excellencies of the Kindness of Onesiphorus to St. Paul*, 14.

31. Georgette de Montenay, *A Book of Armes, or Remembrances* (Frank-

furt, 1619), 222, quoted by Huston Diehl, *An Index of Icons in English Emblem Books, 1500–1700* (Norman, Okla., 1986), 135.

32. [Hanway], *A Review of the Proposed Naturalization of the Jews*, 41.

33. *Remarks on the Reverend Mr. Tucker's Letter on Naturalizations*, 26–27. The echoes are of 2 Cor. 6:14–15: "Be ye not unequally yoked together with unbelievers. . . . And what concord hath Christ with Belial? or what part hath he that believeth with an infidel?"

34. Archaicus [pseud.], *The Rejection and Restoration of the Jews*, 32–33. The biblical quotations in this passage are inaccurately cited: "Mat. iii. 37" does not exist and the second passage comes from Acts 7:52.

35. Stephens, *The Excellencies of the Kindness of Onesiphorus to St. Paul*, 29.

36. [Grant], *Travels in Town*, 2:322.

37. In a groundbreaking article, Everett V. Stonequist argued that "marginality" may be viewed as a predicament for all Jews living in a predominantly gentile society; "The Marginal Character of the Jews," in Isaque Graeber and Steuart Britt, eds., *Jews in a Gentile World* (New York, 1942), 296–310. However, his definition of marginality may appropriately be applied to the convert from Judaism:

The marginal man is the individual who lives in, or has ties of kinship with, two or more interacting societies between which there exists sufficient incompatibility to render his own adjustment to them difficult or impossible. He does not quite "belong" or feel at home in either group. This feeling of homelessness or of estrangement does not arise in the same way or for the same reasons in all individuals, nor is it identical in all situations. For many it is a matter of incomplete cultural assimilation in one or both societies, for others it arises less because of lack of cultural assimilation than from failure to gain social acceptance, and in some cases it originates less because of obvious external barriers than because of persistent inhibitions and loyalties. (297)

38. Richard Brinsley Sheridan, *The Duenna*, I.iii; *The Dramatic Works of Richard Brinsley Sheridan*, ed. Cecil Price, 2 vols. (Oxford, 1973), 1:237.

39. Kidder, *A Demonstration of the Messias*, 2:91–92.

40. See Endelman, *The Jews of Georgian England*, 255–56. The son, Sampson Gideon, made a baronet in 1759, eventually married the elder daughter of Sir John Eardley Wilmot in 1766 (not, as Endelman implies, during his father's life) and was created Baron Eardley of Spalding in 1789.

41. Walpole to Richard Bentley, July 9, 1754, in *Horace Walpole's Correspondence*, ed. Wilmarth Lewis (1973), 35:178–79. This anecdote is repeated many years after by John Francis, *Chronicles and Characters of the Stock Exchange* (1849), who remarks that it "was related with great unction at the period" (90).

42. [Isaac D'Israeli], *The Genius of Judaism* (1833), 143.

43. "Imperfect Sympathies," *The Essays of Elia*, in *The Works of Charles Lamb*, ed. William Macdonald, 12 vols. (1903), 1:121.

44. Joseph Samuel C. F. Frey, *Judah and Israel*, 4th ed. (New York, 1841), 5.

45. George L. Berlin, "Joseph S.C.F. Frey, the Jews, and Early Nineteenth-Century Millenarianism," *Journal of the Early Republic* 1 (1981): 27–49, provides a good summary of Frey's exposition of many of these charges.

46. Frey, *Judah and Israel*, 5–6. The descriptive subtitle of a popular early nineteenth-century chapbook concerning the conversion of one, Moses the Jew, may be read as a bare summary of what had become by Frey's time an almost determinate pattern: "an account of his deliverance from the bloody hands of his father, . . . who employed three ruffians to murder him, his narrow escape . . . , his embracing the Christian Religion, and his baptism . . . " (*The Substance of Three Sermons Preached at Edinburgh, the 8th, 9th, and 10th Days of July 1787, by Moses the Jew, who was Lately Converted to the Christian Religion* [Nottingham?], 1812, p. 1). I have been unable to verify whether the pamphlet is fact or fiction, although the lineaments of the narrative are suspiciously familiar.

47. For a full exposition of the subject, see Gilman, *Jewish Self-Hatred*. B. Z. Sobel, *Hebrew Christianity: The Thirteenth Tribe* (New York, 1974), 98–109, also includes some interesting remarks.

48. Frey, *Judah and Israel*, 58. According to Felix Goldmann, article on "Converts," *The Universal Jewish Encyclopedia*, 10 vols. (New York, 1939–43), "The custom of mourning for a converted Jew as though he were dead, although occurring in sporadic cases, has no basis whatsoever in Jewish religious law" (3:344).

49. For details, see Scult, *Millennial Expectations and Jewish Liberties*, 90–123; Berlin, "Joseph S.C.F. Frey, the Jews, and Early Nineteenth-Century Millenarianism"; Lee M. Friedman, *The American Society for Meliorating the Condition of the Jews and Joseph S.C.F. Frey its Missionary* (Boston, 1925).

50. M. Sailman, *The Mystery Unfolded; or, an Exposition of the Extraordinary Means Employed to Obtain Converts by the Agents of the London Society, for Promoting Christianity amongst the Jews* [1817], 7.

51. Scult, *Millennial Expectations and Jewish Liberties*, 97; Roth, *A History of the Jews in England*, 242. Much of this cost will have been incurred in missionary activities, the running of a school for young Jewish converts, the publication of pamphlets and the New Testament in Hebrew and the salaries of its staff.

52. P. P. Pasquin, *Jewish Conversion: A Christianical Farce* (1814), 4–5; quoted by Endelman, *The Jews of Georgian England*, 74.

53. See chap. 2, p. 34.

54. Violet, *A Petition against the Jewes*, 2.

55. *Anglo-Jewish Letters*, ed. Roth, 64.

56. [Charles Leslie], *A Short and Easie Method with the Jews*, 4th ed. (1715), iv. The work was first published in 1699 as the second part of *A Short and Easie Method with the Deists*.

57. *Remarks on the Reverend Mr. Tucker's Letter on Naturalizations*, 13–14.

58. See chap. 3, pp. 45–47, and chap. 8, pp. 192, 202.

59. Philo-Patriae [pseud.], *Considerations,* 13, 16.

60. Edward Goldney, Senr., *A Friendly Epistle to the Jews* (1760), 10. See also James Picciotto, *Sketches of Anglo-Jewish History,* rev. and ed. Israel Finestein (1956), 136.

61. See Endelman, *The Jews of Georgian England,* 145–46, 268–69, 283. A far more venal explanation sometimes emerges in anti-Semitic diatribe. For instance, William Romaine, *An Answer to a Pamphlet,* alleges that as "Money is [the] Idol. . . . they most ardently worship . . . [,] they do not try to convert others, because they can get nothing by it. Make it a more lucrative Job than plundering the Public, and there will not be one *Jew* left in *Change-alley.* They will go through Sea and Land to make Proselytes, if they can but make a Fortune by it" (29).

62. Sarah Fielding, *The Adventures of David Simple,* ed. Malcolm Kelsall (1969), 32–34, 43.

63. See Percy Colson, *The Strange History of Lord George Gordon* (1937). The sections of this book on Gordon's conversion were largely written by Cecil Roth and reprinted in an abridged version by him in *Essays and Portraits in Anglo-Jewish History,* 183–210.

64. The print was published by T. Harmar on February 11, 1788; see George Cat., no. 7424; Rubens, no. 1514; Israel Solomons, "Lord George Gordon's Conversion to Judaism," *Transactions of the Jewish Historical Society of England* 7 (1915): 222–71; Franziska Forster-Hahn, *Johann Heinrich Ramberg als Karikaturist und Satiriker,* in *Hannoversche Geschichtsblätter,* Neue Folge Band 17 (Hannover, 1963), 180 (no. 14).

65. See, for instance, *Moses Gorden or the Wandering Jew,* chap. 4, p. 63.

66. [Dent], *The Birmingham Moses,* December 12, 1787; George Cat., no. 7209; Rubens, no. 1511.

67. *The Christian Turned Jew. Being the Most Remarkable Life and Adventures of Lord G.G.,* quoted by Colson, *The Strange History of Lord George Gordon,* 225. On the supposed effect of pork on Jews, see chapter 6.

68. Edmund Burke, *Reflections on the Revolution in France* (*The Writings and Speeches of Edmund Burke,* vol. 8, ed. L. G. Mitchell [Oxford, 1989], 135).

69. The calumny that the Jews were intent on importing the libertarian values of the Revolution is fairly common after the declaration of war between France and England in 1793. En route to Bath in March 1793, Thomas Telford, Scottish architect, records witnessing the gross behavior "at a Paltry Alehouse, . . . of [some] drunken Blackguards bellowing *Church & King*— with most tremendous vociferation, while to thicken the Plot there happened at that very moment to arrive a poor ragged German Jew, whom the whole of the discerning loyalists immediately accused of being a *frenchman* come to take away their *liberties*" (letter to Andrew Little, March 10, 1793, Gibbs-Little transcripts, Iron Gorge Museum Trust, Salop). I am grateful to Dr. Terry Friedman for bringing Telford's letter to my attention. I have been unable to establish definitively whether the linkage in the popular percep-

tion between Frenchmen and Jews was already a factor when Burke was writing in 1790, although indiscriminate allegations of Jewish treachery were familiar enough. See also Endelman, *The Jews of Georgian England*, 275–76.

70. According to the Roman historian, Tacitus (A.D. 55–117), *The Histories*, trans. W. Hamilton Fyfe, 2 vols. (Oxford, 1912), 2:207, "Though immoderate in sexual indulgence, they [the Jews] refrain from all intercourse with foreign women: among themselves anything is allowed" (bk. 5, sec. 5). The second-century church father Justin Martyr alleges that "the Jewish teachers permitted four and even five wives, and that they lusted after beautiful women" (Dialogue with the Jew Tryphon, sec. 114, quoted in *The Jewish Encyclopedia*, 7:396). Interestingly, Gavin I. Langmuir, *History, Religion, and Antisemitism* (Berkeley, 1990), 31, informs us that "the attack on Jewish sexual morality, so frequent in Christian rhetoric as a corollary of Christian asceticism, is almost totally absent in pagan works."

71. Tutchin, *England's Happiness Consider'd*, 25.

72. *Reasons Offered to the Consideration of Parliament, for Preventing the Growth of Judaism*, 14–15.

73. *The Rape of the Lock*, Canto II, ll. 7–8, in *The Poems of Alexander Pope*, ed. John Butt (1963), 223.

74. Antony Easthope, *Poetry as Discourse* (1983), 115, comments: "Here the (tendentious) joke is produced by play between whether the antecedent of 'Which' is 'breast' or 'cross.' In the apparent meaning, men are persuaded to kiss her cross and in the real meaning they kiss her breast."

75. *A Letter from a Gentleman to his Friend Concerning the Naturalization of the Jews*, 12.

76. [Bridges], *The Adventures of a Bank-Note*, 4:133.

77. *London Evening-Post*, October 18–20, 1753 (no. 4047).

78. Rubens, no. 846. The theme of the print harks back to Plate 2 of *A Harlot's Progress* (1732), discussed in chapter 3, and is also recalled in such engravings as the anonymous *Beau Mordecai Inspir'd* (1773) (Rubens, no. 842, George Cat., no. 4525) and Thomas Rowlandson's *Introduction or Moses with a Good Bargain* (1806) (Rubens, no. 919).

79. Mezzotint, published by F. Adams, 1772; Rubens, nos. 839 and 840, the latter a reduced sized mezzotint with the alternative title, *The Enamour'd Israelite*.

Jews (often in unholy alliance with Turks) were also commonly credited with having imported into England the practice of sodomy. On this, see Rictor Norton, *Mother Clap's Molly House: The Gay Subculture in England, 1700–1830* (1992), 123.

80. Josiah Tucker, *A Letter to a Friend Concerning Naturalization*, 2d ed. (1753), 16.

81. Philo-Patriae [pseud.], *Further Considerations on the Act to Permit Persons Professing the Jewish Religion, to be Naturalized by Parliament* (1753), 6.

Chapter 6. Ceremonies

1. Timothy Scribble [Ashley Cowper], *The Norfolk Poetical Miscellany,* 2 vols. (1744), 2:382–84. Onesimus is named after the Phrygian slave on whose behalf St. Paul wrote his Epistle to Philemon. The notion that rabbis regularly performed the circumcision operation is a common error: see n. 69 below.

2. Archaicus [pseud.], *Admonitions from Scripture and History,* 20. Alexander Cruden, *Unabridged Concordance to the Old and New Testaments and the Apocrypha* (1769; rpt., Grand Rapids, Mich., 1969), 115, remarks that, in biblical times, the dog was by "the law . . . declared unclean, and was very much despised among the *Jews:* the most offensive expression they could use, was to compare a man to a dead dog."

3. *An Historical and Law-Treatise Against Jews and Judaism,* 20, quoted in chap. 4, p. 66; cf. *London Evening Post,* July 12–14, 1753 (letter from Christianus, Cambridge, July 10), quoted in chap. 8, p. 196. According to Cruden, *Unabridged Concordance to the Old and New Testaments and the Apocrypha,* "The Scripture takes notice of these remarkable things of the *wolf:* that it lives upon rapine: that it is violent, cruel, and bloody: that it is voracious and greedy: that it goes abroad by night to seek its prey: that it is the great enemy of flocks of sheep: . . . that the persecutors of the church, and false pastors, are also ravening *wolves*" (562).

4. Archaicus [pseud.], *The Rejection and Restoration of the Jews,* 36. Cruden, *Unabridged Concordance to the Old and New Testaments and the Apocrypha* remarks on the "serpentine disposition, being a subtil, crafty, and dangerous enemy to mankind," akin to the Devil (433).

5. Tutchin, *England's Happiness Consider'd,* 23.

6. *An Historical and Law-Treatise against Jews and Judaism,* 20.

7. J.E., Gent, *Some Considerations on the Naturalization of the Jews,* 13; cf. *The Other Side of the Question,* 33, quoted in chap. 3, p. 47. Cruden, *Unabridged Concordance to the Old and New Testaments and the Apocrypha,* describes the locust as "a certain vile insect. Their nature is to be many together, therefore vast multitudes are resembled by them, *Nah. 3.15.* In *Arabia,* and other countries that are infested by them, they come in vast numbers upon their corn when ripe, and what they do not eat they infect with their touch and the moisture coming from them; and afterwards dying in great numbers, they poison the air, and cause a pestilence" (284).

8. [Toland], *Reasons for Naturalizing the Jews in Great Britain and Ireland,* 23.

9. Colin Haydon, *Anti Catholicism in Eighteenth-Century England, c. 1714–80: A Political and Social Study* (Manchester, 1993). Dr. Haydon's volume appeared after this book had gone to press and I am conscious that I have been unable to give it the prominence it deserves.

10. Among works that endeavored to describe contemporary Jewish ritual and ceremony, the following may be cited: Lancelot Addison, *The Pres-*

ent *State of the Jews* (1675 [Wing C526]); Isaac Abendana, *Discourses of the Ecclesiastical and Civil Polity of the Jews* [1706; second ed. 1709]; *Ceremonies of the Present Jews* (1728); Bernard Picart (engraver), *Ceremonies and Religious Customs of the Various Nations of the Known World* (1733–37), 1:27–242; Abraham Mears, *The Book of Religion, Ceremonies and Prayers; of the Jews* (1738); John Allen, *Modern Judaism: Or, A Brief Account of the Opinions, Traditions, Rites, and Ceremonies, of the Jews in Modern Times* (1816).

11. Ben Jonson, *Every Man in His Humour*, I.ii.67, in *The Complete Plays of Ben Jonson*, ed. G. A. Wilkes, 4 vols. (Oxford, 1981–82), 1:189.

12. Marlowe, *The Jew of Malta*, ed. Bawcutt, II.iii.7.

13. Thomas Fuller, M.D., *Gnomologia: Adages and Proverbs; Wise Sentences and Witty Sayings, Ancient and Modern, Foreign and British*, no. 3106, quoted in *The Oxford Dictionary of English Proverbs*, 3d ed. (Oxford, 1980), 405, which draws attention to Shylock's negative response to Bassanio's invitation, *The Merchant of Venice*, I.iii.28, "[Bassanio] If it please you to dine with us.—[Shylock] Yes, to smell pork. . . . I will buy with you, sell with you . . . ; but I will not eat with you, drink with you, nor pray with you."

14. Cruden, *Unabridged Concordance to the Old and New Testaments and the Apocrypha*, 485.

15. *The Merchant of Venice*, III.v.32–33; cf. III.v.21–23.

16. Richard Steele, *The Spectator*, no. 14, March 16, 1711, ed. Donald F. Bond, 5 vols. (Oxford, 1965), 1:63.

17. Thomas Gray to Horace Walpole, Cambridge, March 17, 1771, in *Horace Walpole's Correspondence*, ed. Lewis (1948), 14:188.

18. Laurence Sterne, *The Life and Opinions of Tristram Shandy, Gent.*, bk. 9, chap. 4, ed. Ian Campbell Ross (Oxford, 1983), 490; cf. Johnstone, *Chrysal or the Adventures of a Guinea*, 319 (vol. 2, chap. 52): "I saw them roast some poor Smouches [Jews] at Lisbon because they would not eat pork."

19. Johnstone, *Chrysal or the Adventures of a Guinea*, 223 (vol. 2, ch. 17). Southey, *Letters from England*, vouches so many years later in 1807 that the English "pork-butchers are commonly Jews" (397).

20. James Boswell, *Life of Johnson* (Oxford, 1965), 1291 (June 10, 1784).

21. Isaiah Shachar, *The Judensau: A Medieval Anti-Jewish Motif and Its History*, Warburg Institute Surveys (1974), 5:2.

22. L. Alexander, *Memoirs of the Life and Commercial Connections, Public and Private, of the Late Benj. Goldsmid., Esq., of Roehampton* (1808), laments that in Germany, "all that had been done there for them [the Jews], was abolishing in many places an infamous toll, which placed the Jews upon a level with quadruped animals" (35). Paul van Hemert, *State of the Jews in the Beginning of the Nineteenth Century*, trans. from the Dutch by Lewis Jackson (1825), remarks that toward the end of the eighteenth century they "began, though very slowly, to abolish the Jew-tax, and the hateful words of *'Jews and pigs pay toll here,'* which were seen upon the turnpikes on some

roads in Germany" (7). See also *The Collected Writings of Thomas de Quincey*, 14 vols., ed. David Masson (Edinburgh, 1889–90), 10:384, 12:275.

23. George Cat., no. 12146; Rubens, no. 940; Shachar, *The Judensau*, 63 and pl. 60. A reversed version of the print is entitled *Mrs. Smouch Longing for Piggy* (Rubens, no. 941), a copy of which may be found in the collection of the Firestone Library, Princeton University. The imputation that Jews willingly engage in acts of sodomy with animals is an occasional motif in eighteenth-century English popular discourse: see, for instance, *An Essay Towards the Character of the Late Chimpanzee* (1739), in which a debauched "*Jew* Gentleman was so enamour'd of her [the ape] that he made Proposals of Marriage, and was determin'd to have her at all Events" (20–21). In the song, "Isaac Mo; or, the Jew and the Pig," in *The Universal Songster, or, Museum of Mirth*, 3 vols. (1825–26), when the pig is satisfied, having "done his play," the Jew invites him to come home and live with him, but is shortly after tried and "hang'd as dead as bacon" for stealing the porker (1:19).

24. Rubens, no. 947.

25. See Henry Wilson and James Caulfield, *The Book of Wonderful Characters* [1869], xii; also Ricky Jay, *Learned Pigs and Fireproof Women* (1986), 35. The motif closely parallels an equally incredible belief that the notorious *foetor judaicus* (Jewish odor) would straightaway transform into the sweetest fragrance as a consequence of conversion; see chap. 2, p. 35.

26. Engraved and published by Henry Roberts near Hand Alley facing Great Turnstile in Holborn, London, April 23, 1764, price sixpence. Rubens, no. 866, records a later version, dated 1785.

27. A particularly nasty scatological version of the forced feeding of a Jew is represented in the print *Moses & Abram's Bad Bargain* (1786), in which "the Famous Lord Croker" compels a Jewish old-clothes man to defecate over the garments that he is about to buy and then makes his "Brother" eat up all the excrement. (A copy of the print with verses set to music is in the Solomons Collection at the Jewish Theological Seminary.) For a variant of the same anecdote but with "Lord Grandby" for Croker, see *Garrick's Jests* [1785?], 29–30. I have been unable to verify the story, although its source may be by analogy with the forcing of a Jew to swallow pork sausages. Cf. 2 Kings 18:27, Isa. 36:12. In Germany, it was for many years popularly believed (by Luther, among others) that devils fed on human excrement and a well-known episode in the adventures of Til Eulenspiegel describes how a peasant tricks some Jews into purchasing his feces as a rare medicament; see Hsia, *The Myth of Ritual Murder*, 213–14.

28. Thomas Telford to Andrew Little, March 10, 1793 (Gibbs-Little transcripts, Ironbridge Gorge Museum Trust, Salop; letter brought to light by Dr. Terry Friedman).

29. *Annual Register for 1769* (1770), 93, cited by Endelman, *The Jews of Georgian England*, 114.

30. Endelman, *The Jews of Georgian England*, 114–15.

31. See Colson, *The Strange History of Lord George Gordon*, 225.

32. *The Gentleman's Magazine* 46 (1776): 189, cited by Endelman, *The Jews of Georgian England*, 114.

33. Walter Scott, *Ivanhoe* (Oxford, 1912), 78. A similar jest is depicted in Richard Newton's caricature, *Tricks upon Travellers* (1795), in which a butcher conceals a young sucking-pig in a Jew pedlar's box much to the latter's consternation; see George Cat., no. 8746, Rubens, no. 1083.

34. *Mordecai's Beard*, the manuscript of which is in the Larpent Collection, Huntington Library, San Marino, California, is discussed by Van der Veen, *Jewish Characters in Eighteenth-Century English Fiction and Drama*, 215–18. Van der Veen also cites *A Specimen of Jewish Courtship* (1787), a one-act playlet, in which Shadrach and Leah scruple over the consumption of roast pork but conclude that "every Jew will eat de Christian's meat if he can do it slyly" (213–14).

35. [Bridges], *The Adventures of a Bank-Note*, 3:196–97.

36. *Remaines of Gentilisme and Judaisme* (c. 1686), in John Aubrey, *Three Prose Works*, ed. John Buchanan-Smith (Fontwell, Sussex, 1972), 134. At the start of the nineteenth century, William Hone, *The Every-Day Book* (Tegg's edition), 2 vols. (n.d.), confirms that the custom was "still maintained in some parts of England" (2:220).

37. [George Colman and Bonnel Thornton], *Connoisseur*, no. 13, April 25, 1754, in *The British Essayists*, 30 vols. (1827), 18:53–54. Perry, *Public Opinion, Propaganda, and Politics in Eighteenth-Century England*, considers that the "account was not mere whimsical invention" and adds that "this sort of concrete symbolism . . . [only] went out about the middle of the next century—probably because of the increase in literacy" (120).

38. [Colman and Thornton,] *Connoisseur*, no. 2, February 7, 1754 (*The British Essayists*, 8).

39. William Blake, "The Everlasting Gospel," c. 1818, in *Complete Writings*, ed. Geoffrey Keynes (1966), 757. Cf. Henry Fielding, "*Juvenal's* Sixth Satire Modernized in Burlesque Verse," ll. 244–45: "Sure with less Sin a *Jew* might dine, / If hungry, on a Herd of Swine," in *Miscellanies*, vol. 1 (originally published 1753), ed. Henry Knight Miller (Oxford, 1972), 103.

40. [William King], *The Dreamer* (1754), 141. A surprisingly common variant of this supposed fraternity of pig and Jew manifests itself in the tale of a Jew living abroad who, in order to preserve the remains of his dead brother for burial in England, has his carcass cut up and pickled before shipping it home in a barrel marked "pork." During the long voyage, the hungry sailors are forced to prise open the barrel and consume its contents. The tale recurs during the early nineteenth century in broadside ballads, e.g., "The Barrel of Pork," in John Ashton, *Modern Street Ballads* (1888), 170–72, and in a print, *Pickled Pork*, signed "Giles Grinagain," that survives in at least two separate states (copy dated 1802 at the Jewish Theological Seminary, New York; Rubens, no. 913, dated 1804). According to G. Legman, *Rationale of the Dirty Joke: An Analysis of Sexual Humor*, 2d ser. (New York, 1975),

555, the tale may be traced to the *Facetiae* (no. 131) of the Italian Humanist, Poggio Bracciolini, c. 1451.

41. Isaac Israel ("formerly a Jew, but now a Christian"), *Christ Jesus the True Messiah* (1682 [Wing I1057]), 24.

42. See George Cat., no. 9562, Rubens, no. 1273, who conjecturally identifies him as Jacob Franco (1762–1817), a member of one of the most prominent late eighteenth-century Sephardi Anglo-Jewish families.

It is interesting to note that the far more common use, particularly during the 1790s, by Gillray and others of a pig motif is as an instant recollection of Burke's infamous reference to the common people as "a swinish multitude" in *Reflections on the Revolution in France*, 130. On this, see E. P. Thompson, *The Making of the English Working Class* (1963), 90. The possibilities implicit in the association of "a swinish multitude" and the Jews do not appear to have been exploited. The two motifs remain largely separate.

43. *Matthew Henry's Commentary on the Whole Bible*, ed. Leslie F. Church (1970), 33 (on Gen. 17:6–14). Cf. *New Catholic Encyclopedia* (1967), 3:880, for modern support of this thoroughly orthodox Christian view: "It is through faith in Christ, who was Himself circumcised, that the new Israel is grafted on the root of Abraham, and therefore the physical circumcision has become unnecessary (Gal. 5.6; 6.15)." The interpretation of the Church of England does not differ.

44. *Matthew Henry's Commentary on the Whole Bible*, ed. Church, 215–16, on Luke 2:21.

45. Ibid., 560, on Rom. 4:11. Strictly speaking, Henry's interpretation of circumcision as "the initiating sacrament of the Old Testament" is inaccurate since Judaism does not consider it as a sacrament that "gives the Jew his religious character as a Jew. An uncircumcised Jew is a full Jew by birth" (*The Jewish Encyclopedia*, 4:95).

46. Other commentaries are even more vehement in asserting that the continued practice of circumcision by the Jews is a "shameful and contemptible" defiance of the earnest endeavors of "all the Prophets and Apostles . . . to beat them out of their Misconstructions," in Samuel Mather, *The Figures or Types of the Old Testament*, 2d ed. (1705), 82, 177. Following Christ's death and resurrection, remarks the Reverend John Brown of Haddington, reflecting a commonly held view, the observance of circumcision "became wicked and damnable, because it imported that the true Messiah had not made satisfaction for sin, and was a practical rejection of him and his atonement" (*A Dictionary of the Holy Bible*, 167).

47. According to Freud, those who do not practice it "look on it as very strange and are a little horrified by it, but those who have adopted circumcision are proud of it. They feel exalted by it, ennobled, as it were, and look down with contempt on the others, whom they regard as unclean"; see Freud, *Moses and Monotheism*, 268. Freud sees circumcision as a kind of "key-fossil" that helps us to unlock "a portion of the primaeval past which is [otherwise] gladly forgotten" (279, 336). As a symbolic substitute for man's

dread of castration, it recalls the absolute power in primitive times of the primal father who could ordain the circumcision of his sons. For Freud, to Christian eyes the crime of the Jews is in their refusal to admit their complicity in the murder of Christ and by extension to acknowledge the new primacy accorded to the son. "Judaism," he writes, had been a religion of the father; Christianity became a religion of the son" (332). By abandoning circumcision, Christianity could put itself forward as a universal religion, embracing all mankind, rather than one that was deliberately restricted to a "chosen" few. Anti-Semitism arises as the complex emotion of those who, under a thin veneer of Christianity, displace their actual (but unconscious) contempt toward their own religion by redirecting it against the Jews. Cf. Bruno Bettelheim, *Symbolic Wounds* (1955), 128–43.

Lionel Trilling, "The Changing Myth of the Jew" (1930?), in *Speaking of Literature and Society*, ed. Diana Trilling (Oxford, 1982), 54ff., picks up an intriguing variant to an aspect of Freud's father-son theory when he remarks on the prevalence in English literature of "the Jew-and-daughter myth" in which "generally the young Jewess abhors the practices of her father." Examples that he cites include a version of the ballad "The Jew's Daughter," *The Merchant of Venice*, and Scott's *Ivanhoe* (1819). A Latin analogue is traced by Beatrice D. Brown, "Mediaeval Prototypes of Lorenzo and Jessica," *Modern Language Notes* 44 (April 1929): 227–32, and a later English version occurs in the tale, "The Professor of Toledo," *Bentley's Miscellany* (1838), 3:544–52. See also Baron, *A Social and Religious History of the Jews*, 11:83.

48. Legman, *Rationale of the Dirty Joke*, 2d ser., 528–618, gives many examples of this drawn from both ancient and modern humor. Cf. Allport, *The Nature of Prejudice*, 248.

49. *Joe Miller's Jests; or, the Wits Vade-Mecum*, 14th ed. [1750?], 89 (anecdote no. 510 in this edition; the quotation marks are my addition). The anecdote may be traced back to the *Laconics* of Thomas Brown of Shifnel (1663–1704), in *The Works of Mr. Thomas Brown*, 4 vols. (1708–11), 4:19, which went through several editions. Many years later, it is passingly alluded to by Thomas Babington Macaulay, *The History of England* (1848–55), 2 vols. (1880), 2:544n.

50. Macaulay, *The History of England*, 2:541–51, gives a fine account of the economic crisis under William III, caused by coin-clipping and blamed popularly on the Jews. The charge of coin-clipping against the Jews may be traced back at least to medieval times.

51. The ordinary of Newgate referred to in the anecdote was Sam Smith (d. 1698), elegized by Tom Brown (*The Works of Mr. Thomas Brown*, vol. 4).

52. *The Twin-Rivals*, IV.i., in *The Works of George Farquhar*, ed. Kenny, 1:550. Mr. Bill Myers, at present preparing a new edition of the play, points out to me (private correspondence) that he believes the appellation given by Farquhar to the father is insulting to Jews, citing the fact that the Moabites were descended of an incestuous union between Lot and his eldest daughter. He quotes Psalms 108:8–9, "Judah *is* my lawgiver; Moab *is* my washpot."

53. César de Saussure, *A Foreign View of England in the Reigns of George*

I and George II, translated by Mme. van Muyden (1902), 329–30. The "sponsor" was the *sandek* (or godfather) who held the child on his lap during the operation.

54. *Adventures Underground. A Letter from a Gentleman Swallowed up in the Late Earthquake to a Friend on His Travels* (1750), 18–19. The supposed victim of this fictitious attack was the celebrated "Orator" Henley (1692–1756).

55. *London Evening Post,* August 11–14, 1753; *A Collection of the Best Pieces in Prose and Verse,* 77.

56. From "The Jolly Knight's Declaration to his Constituents" in *Oxfordshire in an Uproar; or the Election Magazine* (Oxford, [1753]), 60.

57. J.E., Gent, *Some Considerations on the Naturalization of the Jews,* iii.

58. *Esther's Suit to King Ahasuerus,* 22. For other examples of the circumcision theme at the time of the Jew Bill, see Perry, *Public Opinion, Propaganda, and Politics in Eighteenth-Century England,* 98–99, 131; G. A. Cranfield, "The *London Evening-Post* and the Jew Bill of 1753," *The Historical Journal* 8 (1965): 16–30; also *The Christian's New Warning Piece: Or, a Full and True Account of the Circumcision of Sir E. T. Bart* (1753), reproduced in facsimile by Roy S. Wolper, ed., *Pieces on the "Jew Bill" (1753),* Augustan Reprint Society 217 (Los Angeles, 1983).

59. Israel Solomons, "Satirical and Political Prints on the Jews' Naturalisation Bill, 1753," *Transactions of the Jewish Historical Society of England* 6 (1912): 208; also Herbert M. Atherton, *Political Prints in the Age of Hogarth* (Oxford, 1974), 166.

60. Solomons, "Satirical and Political Prints on the Jews' Naturalisation Bill, 1753," 230–31 (although not in Rubens). I have not seen this print.

61. Ibid., 226; Rubens, no. 824. There is a copy of this print in the collection of the Library of Congress and the Print Room of the British Museum possesses the original drawing.

62. Ralph Straus, *The Unspeakable Curll* (1927), 62, considers that this last pamphlet may have been penned in 1717. All three were published anonymously.

63. *A Strange but True Relation how Edmund Curll, of Fleetstreet, Stationer, Out of an extraordinary Desire of Lucre, went into* Change Alley, *and was converted from the Christian Religion by certain Eminent Jews: And how he was circumcis'd and initiated into their Mysteries* [1717?], in *The Prose Works of Alexander Pope,* ed. Norman Ault (Oxford, 1936), 1:317–22.

64. The reference to "Papists" contains particular irony as Pope himself was a Catholic.

65. Pope is one of a minority of writers aware that the practice, almost always associated in the eighteenth-century English mind with Jewry, also pertains in Islam. In a familiar letter, written at the same period to Lady Mary Wortley Montagu, who was accompanying her husband during his embassy

to Constantinople, he mockingly accuses her of "exhorting Mr Wortley to be circumcised. But he satisfies you by demonstrating, how in that condition, he could not properly represent his Brittannick Majesty" (letter of November 10, 1716, *The Correspondence of Alexander Pope*, ed. Sherburn, 1:369). As elsewhere, if somewhat whimsically, circumcision is represented here as an emblem of an inalienable Otherness. Were he to undergo the rite, Pope sniggers, Mr. Wortley would appear "incomplete" as British ambassador. The same letter is also revealing of Pope's self-absorbed dread of circumcision (and of his own sexual inadequacies) in the prurient humor with which he chats to Lady Mary. "I shall look upon you no longer as a Christian," he writes, "when you pass from that charitable Court [Vienna] to the Land of Jealousy [Turkey], where the unhappy Women converse with none but Eunuchs, and where the very Cucumbers are brought to them Cutt" (368).

66. *Seasonable Remarks on the Act Lately Pass'd in Favour of the Jews*, 27–28.

67. *The Reply of the Jews to the Letters Addressed to them by Doctor Joseph Priestley* (Oxford 1787), 29.

68. Ibid., 33. A short notice in *The Gentleman's Magazine* 57, pt. 2 (1787), praises the tenor of the pamphlet and conveys a sense of how controversial Priestley's ministry to the Jews was considered: "This smart retort on the Doctor, by some waggish Oxonian, in the guise of a Jew, is the best and shrewdest detection of his sophisms, contradictions, and inconsistencies, that has yet appeared" (620).

69. *A Peep into the Synagogue*, 32–33. Traditionally, the rite is performed not by a priest as stated here, but by a "mohel" (circumciser), a layman specially trained for the task. Cecil Roth assumes that the author of the tract "was obviously an Ashkenazi" Jew; "An Early Voice for Synagogue Reform in England," *Essays and Portraits in Anglo-Jewish History* (Philadelphia, 1962), 211–18. If Roth is right, the error here appears as an odd aberration.

70. Milton, *Samson Agonistes* (1671), ll. 975, 1100; cf. "the *circumcised* cast off clothes-man," in *The Life and Adventures of a Cat* (1760), ed. Victor Link (Braunschweig, 1973), 34. *The Ramble*, 45; cf. John Spencer, *A Discourse Concerning Prodigies* (1663), "the circumcised Nation," cited in *OED*. Nashe, *The Unfortunate Traveller* (1594), in *The Works of Thomas Nashe*, ed. McKerrow, 2:307; William Tindale, translation of the New Testament (1534), cited in *OED* (cf. "your old son of circumcision," in *The Jew Decoyed; or The Progress of a Harlot* [1735], cited by Van der Veen, *Jewish Characters in Eighteenth-Century English Fiction and Drama*, 117); *London Evening-Post*, July 28–31, 1753 (fictitious letter from Timothy Freeman, written in a country dialect).

71. *Horace Walpole's Correspondence*, ed. Lewis (1973), 35:179 (letter to Richard Bentley, July 9, 1754).

72. Menasseh Ben Israel, *Of the Term of Life*, translated from the Latin by Thomas Pocock (1709), 74–75.

73. On this, see, for instance, Nigel Davies, *Human Sacrifice* (1981), 67–68; Venetia Newall, *An Egg at Easter* (1971), 217; Freud, *Moses and Monotheism*, 217, 328, 332.

74. Legman, *Rationale of the Dirty Joke*, 1st ser. (1969), 784. A different slant is taken by M. C. N. Salbstein, *The Emancipation of the Jews in Britain: The Question of the Admission of the Jews to Parliament, 1828–1860* (East Brunswick, N.J., 1982), 17–18. In reviewing the hostility of Jews and Christians toward the end of the Middle Ages, he writes:

Fears of contamination . . . were mutual. The eucharistic-sacramental association of wine was responsible for the Jewish ban on its trade and consumption at all times of the year, whilst the explanation for the further thirteenth-century English prohibition of the nursing of Jewish children for the three days after Easter lay, paradoxically, in the fear entertained by Jewish parents that Christian nurses might smuggle into their households the leavened bread forbidden during Passover—which festival usually fell concurrently with Easter—and so by incorporation infuse the children with the Body and Blood of Christ.

75. See *The Oxford Book of Ballads*, ed. Arthur Quiller-Couch (Oxford, 1910), 353–55, and Thomas Percy, *Reliques of Ancient English Poetry*, 3 vols. (1765), 1:32.

76. *The Case of the Jevves Stated*, 1; cf. *Matthew Paris's English History*, translated from the Latin by J. A. Giles, 3 vols. (1852–54), 1:277.

77. See Trachtenberg, *The Devil and the Jews*, who points out that the use of a species of dark red gum, popularly known as dragon's blood, to relieve an infant's pain after circumcision may have caused the more gullible to be persuaded into mistaking it for Christian blood (149–51). Legman, *Rationale of the Dirty Joke*, 2d ser., 536–38, suggests further that circumcision is "the hidden parallel or justification" for the blood accusation because of a traditional practice among Jewish *mohelim* (ritual circumcisers) of cleansing the wound by sucking the blood from the penis of the infant and spitting it out.

78. *Seasonable Remarks on the Act Lately Pass'd in Favour of the Jews*, 19–20.

79. Ibid., 28.

80. Among examples are *Moses Chusing His Cook* (Ramberg, 1788) (Rubens, no. 1514), briefly discussed in chap. 5, *Jews at a Luncheon or a Peep into Dukes Place* (Rowlandson, 1794) (Rubens, no. 888, George Cat., no. 8536), *Pork* (c. 1812) (Rubens, no. 942), *Jewish Disabilities—First Remove* (1847) (Rubens, no. 1029).

81. Edgeworth, *Harrington*, in *Tales and Novels*, 9:2–3.

82. James Leigh Hunt, *The Autobiography*, ed. Roger Ingpen, 2 vols. (1903), 1:112; cf. Iona Opie and Peter Opie, *The Lore and Language of Schoolchildren* (1959), 346; Southey, *Letters from England* (also quoted in chap. 4, p. 73).

83. *Remarks on the Reverend Mr. Tucker's Letter on Naturalizations*, 31.

84. Tobias Smollett, *The Adventures of Peregrine Pickle*, ed. James L. Clifford (1964), 284.

85. "The Jews," *Cobbett's Political Register* 65 (January 5, 1828): 23.

86. "To the People of Kensington, Chelsea and Fulham," *Cobbett's Political Register* 48 (October 25, 1823): 216.

87. Tutchin, *England's Happiness Consider'd*, 24.

88. [Romaine], *An Answer to a Pamphlet*, 11, 16.

89. *Reasons Offered to the Consideration of Parliament for Preventing the Growth of Judaism*, preface.

90. Britannia [pseud.], *An Appeal to the Throne against the Naturalization of the Jewish Nation*, 16–17.

91. Its early twentieth-century editor, E. A. Baker (Johnstone, *Chrysal or the Adventures of a Guinea*, vii), notes that the work went through at least twenty editions.

92. Copley, *The Case of the Jews is Altered*, 2. Copley clinically takes apart the superstition deriving from Matthew Paris that Jewish ceremony involved ritual circumcision followed by infanticide. "'tis a likely matter," he writes, "that the Jews should first circumcise a Child to make him a Jew, and then murder him" (1).

93. Percy, *Reliques of Ancient English Poetry*, 1:32.

94. [Toland], *Reasons for Naturalizing the Jews in Great Britain and Ireland*, 27.

95. "Emancipation of the Jews," in *The Complete Works of William Hazlitt*, ed. Howe (1930–34), 19:324.

96. A popular representation of the theme appears in an illustrated version, *The Miraculous Host Tortured by the Jew* (1822), published by William Hone. According to Alfred Rubens, *Portrait of Anglo-Jewry, 1656–1836* (1959), Hone published the narrative in order to "expose some of the absurd nonsense circulated about the Jews" (34). It seems improbable that it was always read with this idea in mind.

97. See the print, *One of the Benefits of the Jewish Emancipation* (1847) (Rubens, no. 1028).

98. "To the Freeholders of the County of Kent," *Cobbett's Political Register* 42 (June 22, 1822): 738–39. Elsewhere, Cobbett castigates the Jews for what he describes as "the performance of their blasphemous rites, repeating in effigy (as on certain days is said to be their custom) the bloody deed for which their race has been condemned to wander throughout the earth"; *Good Friday; or, The Murder of Jesus Christ by the Jews* (1830), 9–10. For all the virulence of his anti-Semitism, it is instructive that Cobbett, unlike some of his eighteenth-century confrères, is constrained from asserting the charge of ritual infanticide. For a fuller discussion, see chap. 9, pp. 231–38.

Chapter 7. "Ev'ry child hates Shylock"

1. *Horace Walpole's Correspondence*, ed. Lewis (1961), 30:141 (letter of October 11, 1757); see also 21:39n.

2. I employ the term *cipher* both in its figurative sense, "a person who fills a place, but is of no importance or worth, a nonentity, a 'mere nothing'"

(*OED*, definition 2) and also, semeiologically, as a "disguised manner of writing . . . intelligible only to those possessing the key" (*OED*, definition 5).

3. Edward D. Coleman, *The Jew in English Drama: An Annotated Bibliography* (New York, 1943), vii.

4. On this, see, for instance, M. J. Landa, *The Shylock Myth* (1942), 30.

5. *The Works of Charles and Mary Lamb*, ed. E. V. Lucas, 6 vols. (1903–12), 1:42.

6. "Shakespeare: The Young Dramatist," in *The Age of Shakespeare*, The Pelican Guide to English Literature, ed. Boris Ford (1962), 2:185.

7. *Saturday Review*, November 8, 1879; *The Theatre*, December 1879 (all quoted from Lelyveld, *Shylock on the Stage*, 1961, 89, 83).

8. Lelyveld, *Shylock on the Stage*, 91.

9. See the New Variorum edition of *The Merchant of Venice*, ed. H. H. Furness, 8th ed. (Philadelphia, 1888), 396, 399 (hereafter *Merchant of Venice*, ed. Furness). The full version of Lee's article, "The Original Shylock," may be found in *The Gentleman's Magazine* (February 1880), 185–200.

10. *The Merchant of Venice*, Arden edition, ed. J. R. Brown (1967), xxiii–iv.

11. See Wilbur Sanders, *The Dramatist and the Received Idea* (Cambridge, 1968), 38–60.

12. See Christopher Marlowe, *The Jew of Malta*, ed. T. W. Craik (1979), xvi; also T. W. Craik, *The Tudor Interlude* (Leicester, 1958), 51. I am indebted to N. W. Bawcutt's introduction and notes to the Revels edition of the play (1978) for many details in this paragraph. Quotations are from Bawcutt's text of the play.

13. Quoted in *Merchant of Venice*, ed. Furness, 461–63.

14. *The Merchant of Venice* was published eight times during the seventeenth century. Quartos appeared in 1600, 1619, 1637 and 1652 (the latter a reissue of the previous edition). All four folios (1623, 1632, 1663, and 1685) contain the play. See Arden edition, ed. Brown, xx.

15. From title page of 1701 first edition.

16. George Granville, *The Jew of Venice* (1701), "Prologue."

17. Ibid., act I, p. 8. Bassanio's "portly" physique accords with descriptions of Betterton, who, superlative actor as he was, "labour'd under an ill Figure, being clumsily made, having a great Head, a short thick Neck, stoop'd Shoulders, and had fat short Arms, which he rarely lifted higher than his Stomach"; Anthony Aston; quoted in *A Biographical Dictionary of Actors, Actresses, Musicians, Dancers, Managers & Other Stage Personnel in London, 1660–1800*, ed. Philip H. Highfill Jr., Kalman A. Burnim and Edward Langhans (Carbondale, Ill., 1972), 2:92.

18. See Lelyveld, *Shylock on the Stage*, 15.

19. See the New Cambridge edition of *The Merchant of Venice*, ed. M. M. Mahood (Cambridge, 1987), 43.

20. Nicholas Rowe, *Some Account of the Life,&c., of Mr. William Shakespear* (1709), xix (quoted in *Merchant of Venice*, ed. Furness, 421).

21. Quoted in John Downes, *Roscius Anglicanus*, ed. the Reverend Montague Summers, [1929], 275 (editor's note); Colley Cibber, *An Apology for His Life* (1938), 252.

22. Downes, *Roscius Anglicanus*, 52.

23. The best account of the characterization of Shylock in *The Jew of Venice* is by J. Harold Wilson, "Granville's 'Stock-Jobbing Jew,'" *Philological Quarterly* 13 (1934): 1–15. Mahood, in the New Cambridge edition of *The Merchant of Venice*, claims that "the extra lines that Granville provided suggest that the Jew was played less as a 'low comedy' part than as a sort of Fagin" (43), but she offers no further evidence to support this view. The argument by William S. E. Coleman, "Post Restoration Shylocks prior to Macklin," *Theatre Survey* 8 (1967): 17–36, that "the case for a comic Shylock prior to Macklin is virtually unprovable" (28) appears to contradict all the evidence. Coleman contends that, in Granville's adaptation, the role of Shylock is "proportionately larger" (20), but pays no attention to the actual enlargement of the part of Bassanio.

24. [William Cooke], *Memoirs of Charles Macklin Comedian* (1804), 90.

25. For details, see Lelyveld, *Shylock on the Stage*, 19. Van der Veen, *Jewish Characters in Eighteenth-Century English Fiction and Drama*, tells us that between 1701 and 1741 *The Jew of Venice* "was performed about forty times" (95).

26. Charles Gildon, *Remarks on the Plays of Shakespeare*, Rowe's edition (1710), 7:321 (quoted in *Merchant of Venice*, ed. Furness, 421).

27. Rowe, *Some Account of the Life, &c, of Mr. William Shakespeare*, xix (quoted in *Merchant of Venice*, ed. Furness, 421).

28. F. T. Wood, "*The Merchant of Venice* in the Eighteenth Century," *English Studies* 15 (1933), remarks that, curiously, as Macklin "had never been conspicuous in Shakespearean roles . . . Granville's Shylock would have suited him admirably. He had played Peachum in *The Beggar's Opera*, Lord Foppington in Colley Cibber's *The Careless Husband*, Trappanti in the same author's *She Would and She Would Not*, and Marplot in Mrs. Centlivre's *The Busy Body*" (212).

29. On this point, see particularly John Russell Brown, "The Realization of Shylock," in John Russell Brown and Bernard Harris, eds., *Early Shakespeare*, Stratford-upon-Avon Studies 3 (1961), 187–88.

30. [Cooke], *Memoirs of Charles Macklin Comedian*, 91.

31. [Colman and Thornton], *Connoisseur*, no. 1, January 31, 1754, in *The British Essayists* (1827), 18:1.

32. Quoted by William W. Appleton, *Charles Macklin: An Actor's Life* (Cambridge, Mass., 1961), 46. Macklin's commonplace book is now in the Folger Library, Washington D.C.

33. [Cooke], *Memoirs of Charles Macklin Comedian*, 94–95.

34. Edgeworth, *Harrington*, in *Tales and Novels*, 9:40.

35. Georg Christoph Lichtenberg, *Vermischte Schriften* (Göttingen, 1867), 3:266 (quoted in translation in *Merchant of Venice*, ed. Furness, 374). As

Furness notes, the performance that Lichtenberg saw took place shortly after Macklin had won a much publicized lawsuit and this in part accounts for the initial applause of the audience.

36. James Thomas Kirkman, *Memoirs of the Life of Charles Macklin, Esq.*, 2 vols. (1799), 1:259.

37. [Cooke], *Memoirs of Charles Macklin Comedian*, 93.

38. Lichtenberg (quoted in *Merchant of Venice*, ed. Furness), 374–75. Johan Zoffany's painting, part of the Hughes-Stanton collection in 1955, shows Shylock's hands clasped in a manner reminiscent of Lichtenberg's description; see R. Mander and J. Mitchenson, *The Artist and the Theatre* (1955), 58–60.

39. The engraving was executed by T. Cooke and based on a drawing by Ramberg now in the British Museum (see the list of portraits of Macklin in *A Biographical Dictionary*, ed. Highfill et al., 10:27 [no. 26]).

40. Reported in *The Morning Post and Daily Advertiser*, November 9, 1781; quoted by Appleton, *Charles Macklin*, 52. The action of whetting the knife is depicted in an anonymous engraving of *Mᵣ Macklin in the Character of Shylock*, published by Wenman as a frontispiece to an edition of the play of 1777.

41. John Doran, *Their Majesties' Servants* (New York, 1865), 2:187 (quoted by Lelyveld, *Shylock on the Stage*, 31).

42. [Cooke], *Memoirs of Charles Macklin Comedian*, 93.

43. James Boaden, *Memoirs of the Life of John Philip Kemble* (1825), 1:440 (quoted by Lelyveld, *Shylock on the Stage*, 31).

44. Kirkman, *Memoirs of the Life of Charles Macklin*, 264.

45. Quoted in *A Biographical Dictionary*, ed. Highfill et al., 10:10; *The Pin Basket. To the Children of Thespis* (1796), quoted in *A Biographical Dictionary*, ed. Highfill et al., 10:23–24. Nearly fifty years earlier, some verses in the *Dublin Journal* (September 30–October 3, 1749) have a similar resonance:

When in the frantic Jew we see him rage,
We then no longer view him on a Stage . . .
When from his Eyes the Jewish Vengeance darts
Ev'n Nature at her own Performance starts!

Quoted by Esther K. Sheldon, *Thomas Sheridan of Smock-Alley* (Princeton, 1967), 134.

46. Mrs. Inchbald, ed., *The British Theatre*, 25 vols. (1808), 2:3; quoted in *A Biographical Dictionary*, ed. Highfill et al., 10:10.

47. William Hazlitt, *Characters of Shakespeare's Plays* (1817), 276 (quoted in *Merchant of Venice*, ed. Furness, 379–80).

48. Appleton, *Charles Macklin*, 178ff., gives a fairly full account of the background to these disturbances. For more details of Macklin's performance as Macbeth, see Denis Donoghue, "Macklin's Shylock and Macbeth," *Studies* 43 (1954): 421–30.

49. Published in the *Macaroni Magazine* (December 1, 1773), 2:41. The print is described in the George Cat., no. 5203.

50. [Cooke], *Memoirs of Charles Macklin Comedian*, 95; see also p. 418.

51. Kirkman, *Memoirs of the Life of Charles Macklin*, 1:191–92, 202. Mary Nash, *The Provoked Wife: The Life and Times of Susannah Cibber* (1977), 81–84, provides a detailed account of this unfortunate event.

52. Appleton, *Charles Macklin*, 33.

53. There is a copy of this print in the Harvard Theater Collection. It is reproduced in *A Biographical Dictionary*, ed. Highfill et al. (1982), 7:43. Dr. Derek Nuttall, the author of *A History of Printing in Chester from 1688 to 1965* (Chester, 1969), writes to me in a private letter that he considers that "the inclusion of the word 'Chester' is pertinent to the letter and is not to be read as an imprint." He adds that "there was no printer, in or near Chester, at the middle of the eighteenth century who had an intaglio press; and . . . the quality of the work is far superior to that which might be expected of a provincial engraver (even of a century later), and is of the style one would expect from a London artist."

54. Munday, *Zelauto or The Fountaine of Fame*. In this case, the price of the loan includes the *right* eye of each of his intended victims. See Bullough, *Narrative and Dramatic Sources of Shakespeare* (1957), 1:452.

55. Appleton, *Charles Macklin*, 3–6, has established his date of birth as 1699 but earlier biographers seem to have relied more on guesswork. Cooke (*Memoirs of Charles Macklin Comedian*) informs us that the actor himself "was often inaccurate . . . in very essential parts of his own history . . . [by] the neglect of a little arithmetical knowledge" (318).

56. Lelyveld, *Shylock on the Stage*, 22.

57. Stead Collection, New York Public Library; quoted by Lelyveld, *Shylock on the Stage*, 36–37.

58. [Cooke], *Memoirs of Charles Macklin Comedian*, 316–17.

59. Lelyveld, *Shylock on the Stage*, 24.

60. One other play with which Macklin's name was constantly linked was his own *Love à la Mode*, a farce first performed in 1759. In it, Macklin played the part of Sir Archy MacSarcasm, an avaricious Scottish knight, and occasionally in the same performance he played that of Beau Mordecai, a foppish Jew. The play was most popular when performed as an afterpiece to *The Merchant of Venice*. The name Beau Mordecai is identical to that given to the Jew in Theophilus Cibber's pantomime entertainment, *The Harlot's Progress*, a part which Macklin himself took at Drury Lane in 1738. See Lelyveld, *Shylock on the Stage*, 32–33; Van der Veen, *Jewish Characters in Eighteenth-Century English Fiction and Drama*, 134–43.

61. Kirkman, *Memoirs of the Life of Charles Macklin*, 1:261.

62. *Moral Essays*, Ep. 1 (1734), l. 114 (*The Poems of Alexander Pope*, ed. Butt, 553).

63. An equivalent eighteenth-century clarification of the epithet "Shy-

302 / Notes to Pages 178–183

lock" appears in Scribble [Cowper], *The Norfolk Poetical Miscellany*, 2: 245n: "A known Appellation for any *Scrivener*, or sharping, usurious *Money-lender.*"

64. William Shakespeare, *The Merchant of Venice* (Dublin, 1805), 32 (quoted by Michelson, *The Jew in Early English Literature*, 153).

65. Richard Cumberland, *The Observer* (1785), no. 38, in *The British Essayists* (1823) 32:252–53.

66. For examples, see Endelman, *The Jews of Georgian England*, 114–15.

67. Cumberland, *The Observer*, 254, 255.

68. Van der Veen, *Jewish Characters in Eighteenth-Century English Fiction and Drama*, 65–74, 219–40, details Cumberland's championing of the Jews.

69. *Diary of Richard Cross* (September 8, 1753), Folger Shakespeare Library; quoted by Harry William Pedicord, *The Theatrical Public in the Time of Garrick* (New York, 1954), 42–43.

70. [Arthur Murphy], *Gray's-Inn Journal*, 2 vols. (1756), 1:300. For a discussion of Murphy's attitude to the Jews, see Bonnie Ferrero, "Samuel Johnson and Arthur Murphy: Curious Intersections and Deliberate Divergence," *MLN* 28, no. 3 (1991): 18–24.

71. J.E., Gent., *Some Considerations on the Naturalization of the Jews*, 17–21. The author identifies himself as "bred and born in, and brought up to the Church of *England*, as by Law establish'd, or as we commonly call a *Protestant.*" His insistence that he has not penned "a Line by Way of Malice or Prejudice against the *Jews*" (24) suggests that the intention of the pamphlet may have been satirical. If so, the irony is grossly misplaced.

72. *Seasonable Remarks on the Act Lately Pass'd in Favour of the Jews*, 28.

73. Lelyveld, *Shylock on the Stage*, 22 and note. Lelyveld quotes "one of Garrick's Drury Lane receipt book lists," now in the Folger Library, that records "the profits of 2/10 for a *Merchant of Venice* evening, 'For a young Gentlewoman in distress thro' ye Bankruptcy of her Guardian,'" but he does not supply a date for this performance.

74. *The School for Scandal*, III.iii (*The Dramatic Works of Richard Brinsley Sheridan*, ed. Price, 1:403).

75. *London Evening-Post*, July 12–14, 1753. The same piece appeared in several other journals; see Wolper, ed., *Pieces on the "Jew Bill" (1753)*, viii, xi.

76. *London Evening-Post*, August 11–14 and 28, September 13–15, 1753.

77. T.O. [Richard Hole], "An Apology for the Character and Conduct of Shylock," Essay 26 in *Essays by a Society of Gentlemen, at Exeter* (Exeter, 1796), 553.

78. See John Nichols, F.S.A., *Literary Anecdotes of the Eighteenth Century*, 9 vols. (1812–15), 8:93; *The Merchant of Venice*, ed. Brown (Arden edition), xxxiv.

79. *The Universal Magazine* (May 1794), as quoted by Van der Veen, *Jewish Characters in Eighteenth-Century English Fiction and Drama*, 230.

80. Richard Cumberland, *The Jew* "With Remarks, Biographical and Critical, by D.—G" [c. 1824], 5–6.

81. This paragraph is largely indebted to Lelyveld, *Shylock on the Stage*, 39–60, who gives a full account of Edmund Kean and his era.

82. Maria Edgeworth, *The Absentee*, chap. 4, Everyman edition, ed. Brander Matthews (n.d.), 134; also quoted by Van der Veen, *Jewish Characters in Eighteenth-Century English Fiction and Drama*, 77.

83. Edgeworth, *Tales and Novels*, 9:iii (preface to the reader by Richard Lovell Edgeworth, the author's father). The "Jewish lady" who wrote to Miss Edgeworth from America in August 1815 was Rachel Mordecai. Her letter and subsequent correspondence are collected in *The Education of the Heart: The Correspondence of Rachel Mordecai Lazarus and Maria Edgeworth*, ed. Edgar E. Macdonald (Chapel Hill, N.C., 1977).

84. Edgeworth, *Tales and Novels*, 9:10. At the end of the novel, Edgeworth appears to balk at the notion of a Christian marrying a Jew. The dénouement reveals that the heroine, Miss Montenero, is actually the daughter of a Christian mother. Sir Walter Scott's comments, in a letter to Joanna Baillie, dated from Drumlanrigg Castle, July 24, 1817, are instructive:

I think Miss Edgeworths last work delightful though Jews will always be to me Jews. One does not naturally or easily combine with their habits and pursuits any great liberality of principle although certainly it may and I believe does exist in many individual instances. They are money-makers and money brokers by profession and it is a trade which narrows the mind. I own I breathed more freely when I found Miss Montenero was not an actual Jewess.

The Letters of Sir Walter Scott, ed. H. J. C. Grierson, 12 vols. (1932–37), 4:478. See also Michael Ragussis, "Representation, Conversion, and Literary Form: *Harrington* and the Novel of Jewish Identity," *Critical Inquiry* 16, no. 1 (1989): 113–43.

85. M. G. Lewis, *Journal of a West India Proprietor, 1815–17*, ed. Mona Wilson (1929), 52.

Chapter 8. The Jew Bill

1. Cranfield, "The *London Evening-Post* and the Jew Bill of 1753," 30.

2. Perry, *Public Opinion, Propaganda, and Politics in Eighteenth-Century England*, 45, 180.

3. The legal position of native-born English Jews in 1753 did not differ substantially from those born abroad. Among disabilities shared in common with native-born Catholics and some Dissenters, they were disbarred from standing for Parliament and from voting; they could hold neither municipal office nor appointment under the Crown; they were denied the freedom of

the city of London, so effectively preventing them from practicing any retail trade within the city boundaries; and they were also refused admission to the universities.

In addition, foreign-born Jews (estimated as perhaps half the total of 1753) as *aliens* were incapacitated from holding land or real property in the kingdom; obliged to pay as high as double subsidy on imported tonnage and poundage; excluded from ownership of British vessels; and prohibited from acting as factors or merchants in the lucrative trade with the colonies. Some of these encumberments could be got around by utilizing the names of native-born Jews but such arrangements were uneasy. The alien duty on imports was abolished in 1784. See Perry, *Public Opinion, Propaganda, and Politics in Eighteenth-Century England*, 13–14; Henriques, *The Jews and the English Law*.

4. Perry, *Public Opinion, Propaganda, and Politics in Eighteenth-Century England*, 44, 70, and *passim*.

5. Perry, *Public Opinion, Propaganda, and Politics in Eighteenth-Century England*, 75. However, *The London Magazine* 22 (1753): 578, 613–14, reports the horrific murder near Abergavenny in Wales of the pedlar, Jonas Levi, by one William Price. After Levi had been strangled with a belt, his skull had been battered to pieces and his box of wares plundered. Endelman, *The Jews of Georgian England*, is surely right to suggest that the viciousness of the attack at a time of heightened agitation against the Jews "may not be mere coincidence" (114). Levi's death may have been the only fatality consequent upon the passing of the Jew Bill. *Harrop's Manchester Mercury*, no. 96 (January 8, 1754), gives us a short inventory of items taken from the pedlar's box by recording that Price's arrest

was occasioned chiefly by his audaciously carrying in his Pockets several Watches, and wearing at his Knees and in his Shoes genteel Silver Buckles, Ornaments unsuitable to him; and, in some measure, to his great Generosity towards his Female Acquaintance . . . in bestowing on them Gold Rings, Stone Girdle-Buckles, Snuff-Boxes, &c. in too liberal a Manner.

He was found guilty of Levi's murder on March 21, 1754, executed the following day and his body delivered to the surgeons; *The London Magazine* 23 (1754): 139–40.

6. Jacob Katz, "The Term 'Jewish Emancipation': Its Origin and Historical Impact," in *Emancipation and Assimilation* (Farnborough, Hants., 1972), 29–30. See also Endelman, *The Jews of Georgian England*, 60n.

7. Charles J. Abbey and John H. Overton, *The English Church in the Eighteenth Century*, 2 vols. (1878), 2:396. Front-de-Boeuf and Isaac of York are characters in Scott's *Ivanhoe* (1819) set in the Middle Ages.

8. *Maty's Review* (1782), i.241, quoted by Charles J. Abbey, *The English Church and Its Bishops, 1700–1800*, 2 vols. (1887), 2:39; Horace Walpole, *Memoirs of King George II*, ed. John Brooke, 3 vols. (New Haven, 1985), 1:240 (second reading, November 20, 1753).

9. *The Letters of Philip Dormer Stanhope 4th Earl of Chesterfield*, ed. Bonamy Dobrée, 6 vols. (1932), 5:2063.

10. Several of the most significant speeches were reprinted during 1753 in *The London Magazine* 22. These were reproduced with additions from other sources in Cobbett's *Parliamentary History of England*, vols. 14 and 15, printed by T. C. Hansard (1813), from which I quote in this chapter.

11. Walpole, *Memoirs of King George II*, 1:238. Cf. Cobbett, *Parliamentary History of England:* "The question was debated perhaps, with more heat without doors, than it was within" (14:1367–68); "the clamour that has been so artfully raised, and so industriously propagated without doors, against this act of legislature" (15:93); "The clamour was . . . chiefly among the vulgar and ignorant, and among them . . . it was in some places, and upon some occasions, like to become riotous" (15:145).

12. Cobbett, *Parliamentary History of England*, 14:1380.

13. *A Letter to the Publick on the Act for Naturalizing the Jews* [1753], 7–8. The pamphlet was written in favor of the Bill.

14. *Jackson's Oxford Journal*, no. 12 (1753): 3, as quoted by R. J. Robson, *The Oxfordshire Election of 1754* (Oxford, 1949), 89.

15. Archaicus [pseud.], *Admonitions from Scripture and History*, 27.

16. *A Letter from a Gentleman to his Friend Concerning the Naturalization of the Jews*, 8.

17. *Remarks on the Reverend Mr. Tucker's Letter on Naturalizations*, 13.

18. [Hanway], *A Review of the Proposed Naturalization of the Jews*, 33.

19. See, for instance, J. H. Plumb, *The Growth of Political Stability in England, 1675–1725* (1967); W. A. Speck, *Stability and Strife: England, 1714–1760* (1977).

20. Jeremy Black and Jeremy Gregory, eds., *Culture, Politics, and Society in Britain, 1660–1800* (Manchester, 1991), 9.

21. *The Jews Advocate* (1753), 54; Speck, *Stability and Strife*, 91; Gerald Berkeley Hertz, *British Imperialism in the Eighteenth Century* (1908), 77.

22. It is so explained in the *Oxford Dictionary of English Proverbs*, 568. Other authorities suggest, however, that the reference to wooden shoes alludes to the footwear worn by Huguenot refugees from France (see, for instance, Hertz, *British Imperialism in the Eighteenth Century*, 67). The first part of the cry is quoted on a placard beneath an effigy of a Jew carried by the mob in the background to the second plate of William Hogarth's *Election* series (1754). In Southwark, a similar Jew effigy was set alight by the mob; see Nicholas Rogers, *Whigs and Cities* (Oxford, 1989), 383.

23. Rubens, no. 821; George Cat., no. 3204; Solomons, "Satirical and Political Prints on the Jews' Naturalisation Bill, 1753," 217–18; Atherton, *Political Prints in the Age of Hogarth*, 163, 167. At least three other Jew Bill prints incorporate the image of St. Paul's, namely, *A Scene of Scenes for the Year 1853*, discussed in chapter 6, *Vox Populi, Vox Dei*, or the *Jew Act Repealed* (Rubens, no. 825, George Cat., no. 3202), and *The Circumcised Gentiles, or a Journey to Jerusalem*, described later in this chapter. Cf. [Mur-

phy], *Gray's-Inn Journal*, 1:276: "TRUE INTELLIGENCE. . . . We hear that a Scheme is on foot among the *Jews* to purchase St. *Paul*'s Church in order to hold a Synagogue there; but this wants Confirmation" (no. 43, August 11, 1753).

24. Cobbett, *Parliamentary History of England*, 14:1372 (speech of William Northey, Tory M.P. for the borough of Calne, Wiltshire); *A Collection of the Best Pieces in Prose and Verse*, 12.

25. Cobbett, *Parliamentary History of England*, 14:1388 (speech of Sir John Barnard); *A Letter from a Gentleman to his Friend Concerning the Naturalization of the Jews*, 12; [Romaine], *An Answer to a Pamphlet*, 31.

26. *A Modest Apology*, 7. Cf. *The Life and Adventures of a Cat*, ed. Link: "These loyal subjects [the Jews] are the very people, to whom we were on the point of linking ourselves, by a voluntary act of naturalization, as if we had entertained a presumptuous design of frustrating all prophecies, and making null the predictions of their dispersion, and of these people being a scattered people over the face of the whole earth" (49).

For a discussion of the wider perception of the Jews as a dispersed people, see chapter 4.

27. Cobbett, *Parliamentary History of England*, 14:1381.

28. J.E., Gent, *Some Considerations on the Naturalization of the Jews*, 11.

29. Cobbett, *Parliamentary History of England*, 14:1405 (speech of Nicholas Fazakerley). Fazakerley's grossly simplified historical overview castigates William the Conqueror and Oliver Cromwell for allowing in the Jews, while Edward I is acclaimed—"the only king we ever had, before his present majesty, that perfectly understood, and steadily pursued the true interest of England" (1404)—for having kicked them out.

30. *London Evening Post*, July 12–14, 1753 (letter of Christianus, Cambridge, July 10). Similar apprehensions were expressed in the House of Lords by the Duke of Bedford at the time of the repeal of the Act; see Cobbett, *Parliamentary History of England*, 15:105–6.

31. Cobbett, *Parliamentary History of England*, 14:1366.

32. Ibid., 14:1403, 1408 (speech of Nicholas Fazakerley), and 15:140–41 (speech of Thomas Prowse in the Commons debate to repeal the Naturalization Act). Curiously, in the pamphlet *Esther's Suit to King Ahasuerus*, the same biblical story was employed as a vehicle for defending the Jews.

33. Abbey and Overton, *The English Church in the Eighteenth Century*, 398:

The silence of the Bishops caused bitter invectives to be uttered against them. . . . The Bishop of Norwich, who was not only silent, but actually voted for the bill, was the object of special vituperation. "Soon after holding a confirmation, he was called upon by the mob to administer the rite of circumcision, and a paper was affixed to the church doors, stating that the next day, being Saturday, his lordship would confirm the Jews, and the day following the Christians."

34. Rubens, no. 822; George Cat., no. 3205; Solomons, "Satirical and Political Prints on the Jews' Naturalisation Bill, 1753," no. 5. Atherton, *Political Prints in the Age of Hogarth*, 165–66, also provides a useful account of this print.

35. Taken from "News for One Hundred Years Hence," *Jackson's Oxford Journal*, July 21, 1753, reproduced in facsimile in Wolper, ed., *Pieces on the "Jew Bill" (1753)*, which includes bibliographical notes on the frequency with which the piece was reprinted. Perry, *Public Opinion, Propaganda, and Politics in Eighteenth-Century England*, 101–2, notes that in printing this piece the *London Magazine* "appended an interesting partial disclaimer, commenting that such lampoons were 'far from agreeable to the true spirit of Christianity.' Yet the magazine did, after all, reprint it—as did the *London Evening Post* and *Jackson's Oxford Journal*." Arthur Murphy's sequel, "More News for One Hundred Years Hence," *Gray's-Inn Journal*, no. 51 (October 6, 1753), also reproduced by Wolper, is far less pungent. The print, *A Scene of Scenes for the Year 1853* (discussed in chapter 6), is based on a similar idea.

36. "The Prophecies of Shylock" appeared in the broadside, *The Jews Triumph, and England's Fears, Set Forth*, 1753 (George Cat., no. 3206; Solomons, "Satirical and Political Prints on the Jews' Naturalisation Bill, 1753," no. 6), which contains woodcut copies of the prints, *A Prospect of the New Jerusalem* and *The Circumcised Gentiles*, already discussed in this chapter. Solomons, "Satirical and Political Prints on the Jews' Naturalisation Bill, 1753," 219–20, reproduces the text of "The Prophecies of Shylock" from which I quote. It was also printed in the *London Evening-Post*, August 28, 1753, as was the parodic "thirty-fourth Chapter of GEN—," October 18–20, 1753. The belief that naturalized Jews would debauch Christian women is merely a revamping of a common enough charge.

37. Wolper, ed., *Pieces on the "Jew Bill" (1753)*, ix.

38. See, for instance, *Remarks on the Reverend Mr. Tucker's Letter on Naturalizations*, 31; Archaicus [pseud.], *The Rejection and Restoration of the Jews*, 32–33, and *Admonitions from Scripture and History*, 24.

39. See, for instance, *A Modest Apology*, 12; [Romaine], *An Answer to a Pamphlet*, 11; J.E., Gent, *Some Considerations on the Naturalization of the Jews*, 13; Ben Saddi the Jeweller [pseud.], *A Fragment of the Chronicles of Zimri the Refiner* (Edinburgh, 1753), 8–9.

40. P. G. M. Dickson, *The Financial Revolution in England: A Study in the Development of Public Credit, 1688–1756* (1967), 32–35. A partially dated letter of James Howell from London, 3 Jan. —, to Mr. R. Lewis at Amsterdam, probably written shortly after the Restoration, suggests that already then the unpleasant association forged between Jews and dealing was all too well understood: "touching *Judaism*, some corners of our City smell as rank of it as yours doth there"; James Howell, *Epistolae Ho-Elianae*, ed. Joseph Jacobs, 2 vols. (1892), 2:617. For a further definition of stock-jobbing, see also chapter 7.

41. Henriques, *The Jews and the English Law*, 200–201; Roth, *A History of the Jews in England*, 194–95; Endelman, *The Jews of Georgian England*, 21–22. Pollins, *Economic History of the Jews in England*, points out that there was "no clear distinction . . . between the brokers, who acted for principals, and the jobbers who bought and sold stock on their own account. The names were used interchangeably and it was not uncommon to combine broking and jobbing with other activities" (56). He adds that an act of 1708 removed the upper limit of a hundred brokers although the number of Jews remained limited to twelve.

42. Cobbett, *Parliamentary History of England*, 14:1405.

43. *A Letter from a Gentleman to his Friend Concerning the Naturalization of the Jews*, 13.

44. Pollins, *Economic History of the Jews in England*, 53–60, quantifies Jewish involvement in British overseas trade as between 1 and 2 percent of the total. Given their noticeable absence from domestic banking, he views the range of their financial activities as somewhat restricted. It may only be deemed large relative to the small size of the community.

45. *The Craftsman*, July 7, 1753, reprinted in *A Collection of the Best Pieces in Prose and Verse, Against the Naturalization of the JEWS*, 53–54.

46. *Seasonable Remarks on the Act Lately Pass'd in Favour of the Jews*, 19–20.

47. *A Collection of the Best Pieces in Prose and Verse, Against the Naturalization of the JEWS*, 76–77; also *London Evening-Post*, July 28, 1753, quoted by Cranfield, "The *London Evening-Post* and the Jew Bill of 1753," 23, and Perry, *Public Opinion, Propaganda, and Politics in Eighteenth-Century England*, 198–99. Richard Leveridge's celebrated ballad, "The Roast Beef of Old England" (c. 1730), was frequently parodied during the eighteenth century: see Claude M. Simpson, *The British Broadside Ballad and Its Music* (New Brunswick, N.J., 1966), 604–6.

48. "The Jew Naturilized," Rubens, no. 827. In *Shylock's Race from the Chequer Inn to Paris* (Rubens, no. 826), the Jewish financier Samson Gideon is shown crossing the English Channel mounted on a pig with the Devil riding behind him.

49. Cobbett, *Parliamentary History of England*, 14:1371.

50. *A Modest Apology*, iv.

51. Cobbett, *Parliamentary History of England*, 14:1390–91 (speech of Sir John Barnard).

52. *London Evening-Post*, June 30, July 3, July 21, 1753 (quoted by Cranfield, "The *London Evening-Post* and the Jew Bill of 1753," 21). The phrase, "a set of monied men," appears in Cobbett, *Parliamentary History of England*, 14:1367, but, according to Dickson, *The Financial Revolution in England*, 225, it had been employed as early as the mid-1740s as a coded term of disparagement to describe Samson Gideon and other rich Jews involved in city dealing.

53. *A Letter from a Gentleman to his Friend Concerning the Naturalization of the Jews*, 4.

54. See Endelman, *The Jews of Georgian England*, 31–32, on the number of Jewish merchants in London in 1753.

55. Cobbett, *Parliamentary History of England*, 14:1389, 1426 (speeches of Sir John Barnard and the Earl of Egmont).

56. *A Letter from a Gentleman to his Friend Concerning the Naturalization of the Jews*, 12–13.

57. Britannia [pseud.], *An Appeal to the Throne against the Naturalization of the Jewish Nation*, 22–23.

58. See Lucy Sutherland, "Samson Gideon: Eighteenth-Century Jewish Financier," in *Politics and Finance in the Eighteenth Century*, ed. Aubrey Newman (1984), 388–89; Dickson, *The Financial Revolution in England*, 222–24.

59. The sketch appeared in two numbers of Arthur Murphy's *Gray's-Inn Journal* but may have been printed earlier in *The Craftsman*. It is reproduced in Wolper, ed., *Pieces on the "Jew Bill" (1753)*, who establishes its authorship (vi) and from which I quote. Endelman, *The Jews of Georgian England*, 28–29, who notes Caiphas's ancestry in the similarly named high priest of Jerusalem at the time of Jesus, also includes some useful remarks on the piece. Laverna was the Roman goddess of rogues and thieves.

60. Gideon's baptized son, Sampson, was made a baronet at the age of 13 in 1759 and much later in life became Baron Eardley (see chapter 5).

61. George Cat., no. 3203; Solomons, "Satirical and Political Prints on the Jews' Naturalisation Bill, 1753," no. 3. See also Atherton, *Political Prints in the Age of Hogarth*, 165, 167; Perry, *Public Opinion, Propaganda, and Politics in Eighteenth-Century England*, 4, who offers the alternative identity of Dr. John Hill, an opposition journalist, for the figure of Hardwicke.

62. Perry, *Public Opinion, Propaganda, and Politics in Eighteenth-Century England*, 110–11. Cf. *The Racers Unhors'd 1753* (Solomons, "Satirical and Political Prints on the Jews' Naturalisation Bill, 1753," no. 18, p. 228), in which Gideon exclaims: "Vat Sall Ik do voor myn gelt[,] myn gelt dat is all, myn gelt myn gelt."

63. Albert M. Hyamson, *The Sephardim of England* (1951), 131–32. Cf. *Connoisseur*, no. 2, February 7, 1754 (in *The British Essayists*, 18:8), which describes a painting of "the Triumph of Gideon" which "if a late project in favour of our brethren had not miscarried, should have been hung up in St. Peter's Chapel, as a memorial to our victory over the Uncircumcised."

64. Tobias Smollett, *Continuation of the Complete History of England*, 5 vols. (1760–65), 1:144–45. Smollett introduced Manasseh, a "benevolent Israelite," into his novel, *The Adventures of Ferdinand Count Fathom*, published in the same year as the Jew Bill. Despite the enthusiastic discussions of Van der Veen, *Jewish Characters in Eighteenth-Century English Fiction and Drama*, 41–48, and Tuvia Bloch, "Smollett and the Jewish Naturalization Bill of 1753," *American Notes and Queries* 6 (1968): 116–17, the publication of the novel before the bill had been debated in Parliament rules out conjecture that Smollett's characterization of Manasseh was influenced by the controversy; see Ian Campbell Ross, "Smollett and the Jew Bill of 1753,"

American Notes and Queries 16 (1977): 54–55. Manasseh is, however, perhaps the earliest noble Jew in English literature and a likely prototype of Richard Cumberland's Sheva in *The Jew* (1794). It is tempting to suggest (although with no supporting evidence) that in creating Manasseh, Smollett may have been aware that the Naturalization Bill was pending. He alludes to it again briefly in a political satire, *The History and Adventures of an Atom* (1769), ed. Robert Adams Day (Athens, Ga., 1989), 14. Elsewhere, the controversy barely impinges directly on the works of "canonical" writers.

65. Cobbett, *Parliamentary History of England,* 15:100 (speech of Lord Hardwicke in the debate in the House of Lords on the repeal of the Naturalization Act); British Library Add. MSS. 35592, f. 84, Secker to Hardwicke, June 1753 (quoted by Robson, *The Oxfordshire Election of 1754,* 93).

66. Cobbett, *Parliamentary History of England,* 15:145, 93 (speeches of Henry Pelham and the Duke of Newcastle).

67. Ibid., 110 (speech of the Earl of Granville).

68. *The Letters of Philip Dormer Stanhope 4th Earl of Chesterfield,* ed. Dobrée, 5:2059 (letter to Dayrolles, November 16, 1753).

69. Cranfield, "The *London Evening-Post* and the Jew Bill of 1753," 27–28.

70. Robson, *The Oxfordshire Election of 1754,* 96; Perry, *Public Opinion, Propaganda, and Politics in Eighteenth-Century England,* 160.

71. Cobbett, *Parliamentary History of England,* 15:133 (speech of Sir Roger Newdigate).

72. Rubens, no. 825; George Cat., no. 3202; Solomons, "Satirical and Political Prints on the Jews' Naturalisation Bill, 1753," no. 16. The two figures reprimanding the unnamed bishop for his support of the Bill may be identified as the evangelical preachers Charles Wesley and George Whitefield, perhaps intended to represent the lower clergy, many of whom had been violently opposed to it. The unexpected alliance of Deists and Jews may be accounted for in terms of the former's strenuous denial of revealed religion of the kind exemplified in the print. Atherton, *Political Prints in the Age of Hogarth,* notes that the late Lord Bolingbroke's "already declining reputation" (164) was further reduced by the publication in 1754 of an edition of his works "revealing how extensive were his Deist convictions." (On this, see also Perry, *Public Opinion, Propaganda, and Politics in Eighteenth-Century England,* 88n). As a consequence of his support of the Jew Bill, Sir William Calvert was to lose his seat in the 1754 election, coming bottom of the poll. He re-entered Parliament in 1755 as the representative for the rotten borough of Old Sarum (Perry, *Public Opinion, Propaganda, and Politics in Eighteenth-Century England,* 165–68).

Chapter 9. Toward Emancipation

1. For details, see Henriques, *The Jews and the English Law,* chaps. 8–10; Salbstein, *The Emancipation of the Jews in Britain;* Abraham Gilam, *The Emancipation of the Jews in England* (1982).

2. Endelman, *The Jews of Georgian England*, 198–203, gives a detailed account of the Chelsea murder case. A later jest-book, *The Festival of Mirth* (1800), 70, contains an anecdote that suggests that the repercussions of the case were perhaps less enduring than Endelman maintains. See also Camden Pelham [pseud.], *The Chronicles of Crime; or, the New Newgate Calendar*, 2 vols. (1886), 1:227–29; R. Leslie-Melville, *The Life and Work of Sir John Fielding* [1934], 259–68.

3. George Cat., no. 5468; Rubens, no. 844, who notes that the plate was also issued with the alternative title, *A Scene in Dukes Place*. Endelman, *The Jews of Georgian England*, 214–15, gives further examples of this theme.

4. Walpole, *Memoirs of King George II*, 1:238.

5. Carl Philipp Moritz, *Travels of Carl Philipp Moritz in England in 1782*, introduced by P. E. Matheson (1924), 103.

6. Katz, *Emancipation and Assimilation*, ix.

7. Ibid., 3–4; Jacob Katz, *Out of the Ghetto: The Social Background of Jewish Emancipation, 1770–1870* (Cambridge, Mass., 1973), 3, 167–68 and *passim*. On attitudes to the Jews in eighteenth-century France, see Arthur Hertzberg, *The French Enlightenment and the Jews* (New York, 1968).

8. See John Locke, *A Letter Concerning Toleration* (1689), ed. Mario Montuori (The Hague, 1963): "If a Jew do not believe the New Testament to be the word of God, he does not thereby alter anything in men's civil rights" (79); "neither *Pagan* nor *Mahometan*, nor *Jew*, ought to be excluded from the civil rights of the commonwealth because of his religion. The Gospel commands no such thing. . . . If we allow the *Jews* to have private houses and dwellings amongst us, why should we not allow them to have synagogues? Is their doctrine more false, their worship more abominable, or is the civil peace more endangered by their meeting in public than in their private houses?" (103).

9. Katz, *Out of the Ghetto*, 40.

10. [Toland], *Reasons for Naturalizing the Jews in Great Britain and Ireland*, 18–19, 20. Katz, *Emancipation and Assimilation*, 26–30, provides a useful discussion of some of Toland's ideas.

11. Samuel Taylor Coleridge, "Treatment of the Jews," *The Courier*, June 18, 1816, in *Essays on His Times in The Morning Post and The Courier*, 3 vols., ed. David V. Erdman (Princeton, 1978), 3:144.

12. Blake, *Complete Writings*, 649.

13. A curiously unsung exception to this may be found in the work of the lawyer, Thomas Witherby (d. 1830), whose defense of the Jews (written in the form of a Christian dialogue) boldly attempts to trace back the historical roots of anti-Semitism to what he interprets as a patristic "desire to exalt the Christian religion at the expence of the Jewish religion." The greatest heresy of the early Church, according to Witherby, was in biting the hand of the very faith that had given it its being. The poisonous vein of heresy so created was to become inflated in later ages by the pious frauds of the monks with their disgraceful allegations of ritual murder. Although greatly diluted, the influence of their trumped-up charges remains for him even in the early

nineteenth century a powerful factor in determining contemporary attitudes to the Jews. The compelling enigma at the heart of Witherby's thinking is that, by adopting the Old Testament, the Church had from its inception recognized its need for Judaism as a fundamental sustaining force, yet had consistently misdirected this into wanton persecution and eradication of the Jews themselves. His work is emphatic in spelling out what he sees as the precariousness of Christianity without Judaism. "The Jewish and the Christian religion," he maintains, "are so inseparably united, that unless the true foundation, THE JEWISH RELIGION, is preserved, the Christian church must become weak and unstable" (An Attempt to Remove Prejudices Concerning the Jewish Nation, 2 parts, 1803–4, pt. 2 [Dialogue 8], 372). To illustrate what he sees as the continued Christian need for Judaism, Witherby explains that throughout history it is only by way of the Jews or by those who have recently converted from them that God has continued to reveal himself to the world (pt. 2 [Dialogue 10], 472). By endeavoring to confound what still remains "the general opinion, the prevailing opinion" that the Jews are to be "distinguished as a knavish . . . , hard dealing, hard-hearted people," he sees himself as contributing toward a new Christian enlightenment that will be fulfilled in the return of the chosen people to the promised land and the eventual second coming of the Messiah (pt. 1 [Dialogue 1], 2, 4). The abatement of prejudice against the Jews, because so tied up with his prophetic reading of the Holy Scriptures, becomes for Witherby the key to unlocking his larger millennial expectations. It is therefore a task that he declares to be "of the GREATEST IMPORTANCE: of greater importance than any other subject, be it what it may" (pt. 1, preface, v–vi). Only by clearing away such prejudice will the full truth of the Gospels ultimately be revealed.

14. David Vincent, Literacy and Popular Culture: England, 1750–1914 (Cambridge, 1989), 198.

15. Memoirs of the Late Thomas Holcroft, Written by Himself (1852), 8, 10–11. The two books were The History of Parismus and Parismenes and The Seven Champions of Christendom.

16. John Clare's Autobiographical Writings, ed. Eric Robinson (Oxford, 1983), 2, 5–6, 56–57; George Deacon, John Clare and the Folk Tradition (1983), 30–32, 210. Clare's alternative title for "The Wandering Jew" was "The restless Jew." Cf. George Crabbe, The Parish Register (1807), pt. 1, ll. 111–14, in The Complete Poetical Works, ed. Norma Dalrymple-Champneys and Arthur Pollard, 3 vols. (Oxford, 1988), who also lists "The Wandering Jew" among the "humbler works the pedlar's pack supplied."

17. See Richard D. Altick, The English Common Reader (Chicago, 1957), 94–95. The same scholar (112–13) also cites the experience of a writer from a more conventionally literate and orthodox background than that of Clare or Holcroft. Charlotte Elizabeth Browne (1790–1846), the daughter of a Norwich clergyman, first became attuned to "the exquisite narratives of the Old Testament" from her father reading aloud to his children the stories of Abel, Noah, Moses, Gideon, and so on. They were, she says, "merely read as his-

tories, the fact being carefully impressed on our minds that God was the author, and that it would be highly criminal to doubt the truth of any word in that book." However, by her own confession, at the tender age of 7 Miss Browne "became entangled in a net of dangerous fascination" when she was permitted to read *The Merchant of Venice:* "The character of Shylock burst upon me. . . . I revelled in the terrible excitement that it gave rise to; page after page was stereotyped upon a most retentive memory, without an effort, and during a sleepless night I feasted on the pernicious sweets thus hoarded in my brain." This one "ensnaring book," she hysterically claimed, was responsible for perverting her mind by initiating a taste for works of the imagination and turning it away from its fitter preoccupation with God. Later, after having recognized the error of her ways and returning with missionary zeal to the Protestant fold, she took considerable delight in endorsing the evangelical work of those attempting the conversion of the Jews. See Charlotte Elizabeth Browne Phelan Toona, *Personal Recollections* (1841), 15, 24–25, 130–31.

18. Moritz, *Travels of Carl Philipp Moritz in England in 1782*, 216. It is unclear from the context whether "the history of Samson" alludes to a chapbook version, though I have been unable to identify such. The story of Samson is at Judges 13–16.

19. Edgeworth, *Harrington*, in *Tales and Novels*, 9:1–18 (chaps. 1–2). Edgeworth is self-reproachful in recognizing that, despite believing in her own candor and toleration, even she had been guilty of unthinkingly introducing despicable Jewish characters into her *Moral Tales* (1801) that had been intended for young readers.

20. Addison and Steele, *The Spectator*, no. 495 (September 27, 1712), 4:255.

21. *Esther's Suit to King Ahasuerus* [p. 3].

22. Philo-Patriae [pseud.], *Further Considerations*, 6, 10–11, 16, 41–42. Cf. Josiah Tucker, *A Second Letter to a Friend Concerning Naturalizations* (1753), who sees the origin of medieval anti-Semitism in the cynical exploitation of the Jews by "our Princes . . . [who] used them as *Spunges*, to suck up the Treasure of the Nation; and then, when they had a mind to *squeeze them dry*, . . . let loose the popular Odium and Fury upon them" (36).

23. *The Complete Works of William Hazlitt*, ed. Howe, 19:321. Salbstein, *The Emancipation of the Jews in Britain*, 65, notes that the essay was published posthumously in *The Tatler* of March 1831, six months after its author's death.

24. W. Pinnock, ed., *The Guide to Knowledge*, no. 13 (September 15, 1832), 103–4.

25. Alfred Rubens, "Jews and the English Stage, 1667–1850," *Transactions of the Jewish Historical Society of England* 24 (1974): 151–70, furnishes a valuable outline of Jewish involvement in the first three of these activities.

26. *Reasons Offered to the Consideration of Parliament, for Preventing*

the Growth of Judaism, 8. Similarly, more than a century earlier, James Howell condemns the Jews as "the most timorous people on earth, and so utterly incapable of Arms, for they are neither Soldiers nor Slaves: And this their Pusillanimity and Cowardice ... may be imputed to their various thraldoms, contempt and poverty, which hath cow'd and dastardiz'd their courage" (Howell, *Epistolae Ho-Elianae,* 1:314–15).

27. A Christian [pseud.], *The Case of the Jews Considered,* 30; Tobias Smollett, *Travels through France and Italy,* ed. Frank Felsenstein (Oxford, 1979), Letter XIII (January 15, 1764), 119.

28. [Hanway], *A Review of the Proposed Naturalization of the Jews,* 78.

29. Cobbett, *Parliamentary History of England,* 15:105 (speech of the Duke of Bedford).

30. [Johnstone], *The History of John Juniper,* 1:261.

31. British Library Add. MSS 27287, fol. 145–46, quoted by M. Dorothy George, *London Life in the Eighteenth Century* (1930), 132.

32. [James Grant], *Life and Shadows of London Life,* 2 vols. (1842), 2:251.

33. Cecil Roth, "The Jews in Defence of Britain," *Transactions of the Jewish Historical Society of England* 15 (1946): 14. Roth does not cite the source of his information. For a recent study of Jewish involvement in the navy during the same period, see Geoffrey L. Green, *The Royal Navy and Anglo-Jewry, 1740–1820* (1989).

34. Rubens, no. 909; reproduced by Cecil Roth, *Transactions* 15, frontispiece.

35. George Crabbe, *The Borough* (1810), IV, ll. 214–15, in Crabbe, *The Complete Poetical Works,* 1:396. In a footnote to the text, Crabbe remarks: "Some may object to this assertion; to whom I beg leave to answer, that I do not use the word *fight* in the sense of the Jew Mendoza."

36. *Cobbett's Political Register,* 6:618, Letter III to the Rt. Hon. Wm. Pitt, "On the Causes of the Decline of Great Britain" (October 27, 1804), and 40:1123, "To the Money Hoarders," no. 1 (November 10, 1821).

37. Ibid., 48:207, "To the People of Kensington, Chelsea and Fulham" (October 25, 1823); 65:23, "The Jews" (January 5, 1828); 69:731, "To Big O" (June 1, 1830); 11:431, "To the Free and Independent Electors of the City and Liberties of Westminster" (March 21, 1807); 40:1119, "To the Money Hoarders."

38. Ibid., 42:733, 739, "To the Freeholders of the County of Kent" (June 22, 1822); 65:22, "The Jews"; see also 48:214 (October 25, 1823).

39. Cobbett, *Good Friday,* 16. The quoted passage is from Ezekiel 22:12, part of the text cataloguing the sins of Jerusalem on which Cobbett bases his sermon.

40. *Cobbett's Political Register,* 65:21, "The Jews"; Cobbett, *Good Friday,* 11–12; *Cobbett's Political Register* 82, no. 8 (November 23, 1833): 480; 48:216, "To the People of Kensington, Chelsea and Fulham" (cf. 69:730, "To Big O"; Cobbett, *Good Friday,* 22); 65:23, "The Jews" 48:217, "To the People of Kensington, Chelsea and Fulham."

41. *Cobbett's Political Register,* 48:206, "To the People of Kensington, Chelsea and Fulham."

42. Cobbett, *Good Friday,* 9–10.

43. *Cobbett's Political Register,* 69:732, "To Big O."

44. Endelman, *The Jews of Georgian England,* 201.

45. On this, see Ursula Henriques, *Religious Toleration in England, 1787–1833* (1961), 191–92.

46. Cobbett, *Good Friday,* 21–23. Cobbett's sanctimonious disavowal of revenge against the Jews is scornfully derided by an anonymous reviewer in *The Westminster Review* 13 (July 1830): 188–97.

47. *Cobbett's Political Register,* 69:733, "To Big O."

48. Harry Stone, "Dickens and the Jews," *Victorian Studies* 2 (1958–59): 234–35. A similar conclusion is reached by Landa, *The Jew in Drama,* 166.

49. Modder, *The Jew in the Literature of England,* 218.

50. Letter to Mrs. Eliza Davis, July 10, 1863 (quoted by Stone, "Dickens and the Jews," 245; Modder, *The Jew in the Literature of England,* 220). The full correspondence between Mrs. Davis and the author is reproduced by Cumberland Clark, *Charles Dickens and His Jewish Characters* (1918).

51. Charles Dickens, *Oliver Twist,* ed. Kathleen Tillotson (Oxford, 1966), 361. All references in the text are to this edition.

52. Stone, "Dickens and the Jews," 235; Modder, *The Jew in the Literature of England,* 218.

53. Dickens, *Oliver Twist,* 50. In *Sketches by Boz* (1833–37), Dickens announces his detestation of "red-headed and red-whiskered Jews who forcibly haul you into their squalid houses, and thrust you into a suit of clothes, whether you will or not"; *The Works of Charles Dickens,* 40 vols. (1906–8), 1:88.

54. Landa, *The Jew in Drama,* 159–69, supposes that Fagin may be based on Ikey Solomons, a receiver of stolen goods, who was sentenced to transportation to Van Diemen's Land in 1830. Van der Veen, *Jewish Characters in Eighteenth-Century English Fiction and Drama,* 31–35, suggests that Dickens may have been influenced by Henry Fielding's references to the Jews as receivers in *An Enquiry into the Causes of the Late Increase of Robbers* (1751). In placing the scene of the violent house burglary in *Oliver Twist* at Chertsey, is it possible that Dickens's subconscious imagination recollects the more or less homonymic name of "Chelsea," so closely associated with Jewish criminality in the previous era?

55. Elsewhere, he is described by Sikes as "infernal" (76) and by Nancy as "Devil that he is, and worse than devil as he has been to me" (313).

56. Rosenberg, *From Shylock to Svengali,* 125. The "toasting-fork" (50) that Fagin wields over his fire is perhaps intended to allude distantly to the forked tail worn by the Devil in traditional iconography.

57. Harry Stone, *Dickens and the Invisible World: Fairy Tales, Fantasy, and Novel-Making* (1979), 100. It is interesting that other examples that Stone gives of this motif, in which neither the aggressor nor the child is Jewish, are of a later date than *Oliver Twist.*

58. Landa, *The Jew in Drama*, 165–66.

59. The revisions were made in the 1867 collected "Charles Dickens edition." Curiously, most of the changes to "Fagin" occur in the later chapters of the novel.

60. Charles Dickens, *Our Mutual Friend*, ed. Stephen Gill (1971), 795 (bk. 4, chap. 9).

Epilogue

1. Edgar Rosenberg, "Tabloid Jews and Fungoid Scribblers," introduction to reprint of Van der Veen, *Jewish Characters in Eighteenth-Century Fiction and Drama* (New York, 1972), 20.

2. [Romaine], *An Answer to a Pamphlet*, 42.

3. *Cobbett's Political Register*, 10:405, "Jewish Predominance" (September 6, 1806). The essay is signed "Ethnicus" but is almost certainly by Cobbett himself.

4. Ibid.

5. Crabbe, *The Borough* (1810), IV, ll. 226–27, in *The Complete Poetical Works*, 1:396.

6. M. D. R. Leys, *Catholics in England, 1559–1829: A Social History* (1961), 134–35. Haydon, *Anti-Catholicism in Eighteenth-Century England*, also gives a vivid account of the effect of the Gordon riots.

7. John Bossy, *The English Catholic Community, 1570–1850* (1975), 185, estimates the number of Catholics in England and Wales in 1770 as about 80,000 or approximately 1 percent of the total population.

8. English attitudes toward Irish Catholics are as usual far more complex. The hegemony of the Anglo-Irish minority over the Catholics must have grossly distorted such attitudes. According to Wendy Hinde, *Catholic Emancipation: A Shake to Men's Minds* (Oxford, 1992), at the time of the Act of Union of 1801, the members of the Protestant Church of Ireland (i.e., Anglo-Irish) "numbered about 800,000 scattered among more than six million Catholics" (11).

9. Many of these features and also the shared status of blacks and dogs (a bestial analogy likewise foisted on the Jews) are discussed by David Dabydeen, *Hogarth's Blacks: Images of Blacks in Eighteenth-Century English Art* (Mundelstrup, Denmark, 1985), *passim*. Cf. James Walvin, *Black and White: The Negro and English Society, 1555–1945* (1973), 159–76. Twentieth-century social psychologists have reported comparable stereotypical traits still being attributed to blacks and Jews; see, for instance, Bruno Bettelheim and Morris Janowitz, *Dynamics of Prejudice* (New York, 1950), *passim*.

10. Cobbett, *Parliamentary History of England*, 15:106.

11. Southey, *Letters from England*, 398. Southey adds caustically that "alas, they have no other heaven to expect!" His letters are written from the fictional perspective of a Spanish Catholic.

12. Ibid., 392–93.

13. Perry, *Public Opinion, Propaganda, and Politics in Eighteenth-Century England,* 194–95.

14. In a recent survey of the linguistic use since Anglo-Saxon times of oaths and profanity, Geoffrey Hughes, *Swearing,* concludes that in "the English word-field of ethnic abuse," the Jews are "most consistently seen as an out-group." It is notable, he adds, that "there are comparatively few terms of abuse between the English, the Scots and the Welsh, but far more are targeted against the obvious out-groups, namely the Jews, the Irish and the 'new Britons,' . . . particularly those that have distinctive appearance, food, language, religion and cultural traditions" (135).

15. *Hansard's Parliamentary Debates,* n.s., 23 (1830): 1313 (April 5, 1830). Cf. Macaulay's further remarks on the subject, published anonymously in *The Edinburgh Review* 52 (1831): 363–74.

16. Sydney Smith, "Trimmer and Lancaster," *Edinburgh Review* (1806), in *Selections from the Writings of the Rev. Sydney Smith,* 2 vols. (1854), 1:12. Lancaster's *Improvements in Education* (1803) was widely known, going through several editions. His pedagogical system upheld that to shame a wrongdoer in public was a more effective means of punishment than physical chastisement. Sarah Trimmer's response to Lancaster, *A Comparative View of the New Plan of Education,* was published in 1805.

17. *The Monthly Mirror* 14 (1802): 404–5 (*The Dramatic Guardian,* no. 9). Endelman, *The Jews of Georgian England,* 217–18, provides a useful summary of the disturbance.

18. *The Monthly Mirror* 14 (1802): 405. On the Chelsea murder (1771), see chapter 9. Houndsditch is an area of London that was for many years populated by and associated with Jews of the poorer sort.

19. Endelman, *The Jews of Georgian England,* 278.

20. Archaicus [pseud.], *The Rejection and Restoration of the Jews,* 36.

21. Philo-Patriae [pseud.], *Further Considerations,* 6, 41–42.

22. Hone, *The Every-Day Book,* 1:152–53 (entry for February 23).

23. Charles Lamb, "Imperfect Sympathies," *The Essays of Elia,* in *The Works of Charles Lamb,* ed. Macdonald, 1:120–21.

24. Rosenberg, *From Shylock to Svengali,* 17, 39.

25. Howell, *Epistolae Ho-Elianae,* 1:314 (June 3, 1633). Cf. John Weemse, *A Treatise of the Foure Degenerate Sonnes* (1636): "the Iewes have a loathsome and stinking smell, and . . . a stinking breath" (330); quoted by David Katz, *Philo-Semitism and the Readmission of the Jews to England, 1603–1655* (Oxford, 1982), 17.

26. Archaicus [pseud.], *Admonitions from Scripture and History,* 16.

27. J.E., Gent, *Some Considerations on the Naturalization of the Jews,* 13.

28. See Betty Naggar, "Old-Clothes Men: Eighteenth and Nineteenth Centuries," *Transactions of the Jewish Historical Society of England* 31 (1990): 172, 180–81.

29. Samuel Taylor Coleridge, *Table Talk*, July 8, 1830, in *The Table Talk and Omniana*, 102. For Holywell Street, see chap. 4, n. 56, above.

30. *Kidd's London Directory*, n.d., pt. 3, *London in All Its Dangers*, 12. Fuller's soap (or earth) is a hydrous silicate of allumina that was formerly used in cleansing cloth (*OED*).

31. *Cobbett's Political Register*, 65:23, "The Jews"; Cobbett, *Good Friday*, 4. As a sermon, the latter comments on a text from Ezekiel in which God catalogues the sins of the Jews and vows to consume their "filthiness" (22:15) by fire.

32. Significantly, an influential study of ethnic intolerance conducted shortly after World War II and based on interviews with American veterans suggests that at least for that group the slur of racial smell had been (unconsciously) transferred from Jews to blacks. Similarly, the charges that they will not work and that they are sexually immoral were more frequently leveled at blacks (Bettelheim and Janowitz, *Dynamics of Prejudice*, 32–47). The mutative character of these stereotypical traits probably owes a good deal both to socioeconomic factors and to education.

33. *Westminster Review* 13 (1830): 193.

34. Julia Kristeva, *Strangers to Ourselves*, trans. Leon S. Roudiez (New York, 1991), 1; also interview in *Talking Liberties* (Channel 4 television pamphlet), ed. Derek Jones and Rod Stoneham (1992), 16.

35. [John Russell], *A Tour in Germany, and Some of the Southern Provinces of the Austrian Empire in the Years 1820, 1821, 1822*, 2 vols. (Edinburgh, 1824), 1:47. The passage is quoted by D'Israeli, *The Genius of Judaism*, 236.

BIBLIOGRAPHY

The bibliography is divided into primary and secondary texts. Unless otherwise indicated, place of publication is London. Where appropriate, abbreviations to some standard reference works are cross-referenced.

Contemporary Newspapers and Journals

The Annual Register
Cobbett's Political Register
The Gentleman's Magazine
Harrop's Manchester Mercury
Jackson's Oxford Journal
The London Chronicle: or, Universal Evening Post
London Evening-Post
The London Magazine
The Monthly Mirror
The Times
The Westminster Review

Other Primary Texts

Abendana, Isaac. *Discourses of the Ecclesiastical and Civil Polity of the Jews.* [1706; second ed. 1709].
Addison, Joseph, and Richard Steele. *The Spectator.* Edited by Donald F. Bond. 5 vols. Oxford, 1965.
Addison, Lancelot. *The Present State of the Jews.* 1675 (Wing C526).
Adventures Underground. A Letter from a Gentleman Swallowed up in the Late Earthquake to a Friend on His Travels. 1750.
Alexander, L. *Memoirs of the Life and Commercial Connections, Public and Private, of the Late Benj. Goldsmid., Esq., of Roehampton.* 1808.
Allen, John. *Modern Judaism: Or, A Brief Account of the Opinions, Traditions, Rites, and Ceremonies, of the Jews in Modern Times.* 1816.
Anglo-Jewish Letters. Edited by Cecil Roth. 1938.
An Apology for the Naturalization of the Jews. 1753.
Archaicus [pseud.]. *Admonitions from Scripture and History, from Religion and Common Prudence, Relating to the Jews.* 1753.
———. *The Rejection and Restoration of the Jews, According to Scripture, Declar'd.* 1753.

Ashton, John. *Modern Street Ballads.* 1888.

Aubrey, John. *Three Prose Works.* Edited by John Buchanan-Smith. Fontwell, Sussex, 1972.

Bacon, Francis. *The Essays or Counsels Civil and Moral of Francis Lord
Verulam.* Edited by Henry Lewis. N.d.

Bargishai, Eleazar. *A Brief Compendium of the Vain Hopes of the Jews
Messias.* 1652 (Wing B764).

Beard, Thomas. *The Theatre of Gods Iudgements.* 2d ed. 1612 (STC 1660).

Bee, Jon [John Badcock], *A Living Picture of London for 1828.* 1828.

Ben Saddi the Jeweller [pseud.]. *A Fragment of the Chronicles of Zimri the
Refiner.* Edinburgh, 1753.

Blake, William. *Complete Writings.* Edited by Geoffrey Keynes. 1966.

Blaxton, John. *The English Usurer, or Usury Condemned.* 1634 (STC
3129).

Boswell, James. *Life of Johnson.* Oxford, 1965.

Bradford, John. *The Writings of John Bradford, M.A.* Edited by Aubrey
Townsend. 2 vols. Cambridge, 1848–53.

Breuhowse, John [pseud.]. *The Highland Spectator: Or, Observations on
the Inhabitants of Various Denominations in London and Westminster.* 1744.

[Bridges, Thomas, of Hull]. *The Adventures of a Bank-Note.* 4 vols.
1770–71.

Britannia [pseud.]. *An Appeal to the Throne against the Naturalization of
the Jewish Nation.* 1753.

[Brothers, Richard]. *The Writings of Mr. Richard Brothers, God's Anointed
King.* 1798.

Brown, John, of Haddington. *A Dictionary of the Holy Bible.* 1813 (first
published 1769).

Brown, Thomas, of Shifnel. *The Works of Mr. Thomas Brown.* 4 vols.
1708–11.

Browne, Charlotte Elizabeth. *See* Elizabeth Browne Phelan Toona

Browne, Sir Thomas. *Pseudodoxia Epidemica.* Edited by Robin Robbins. 2
vols. Oxford, 1981.

[Bryant, Jacob]. *A Treatise upon the Authenticity of the Scriptures, and
the Truth of the Christian Religion.* 2d ed. Cambridge, 1793.

Burke, Edmund. *A Letter from Mr. Burke to a Member of the National
Assembly.* 3d ed. 1791.

———. *Reflections on the Revolution in France.* Vol. 8 of *The Writings
and Speeches of Edmund Burke.* Edited by L. G. Mitchell. Oxford,
1989.

[Burnet, Gilbert]. *The Conversion & Persecutions of Eve Cohan, Now
Called Elizabeth Verboon, A Person of Quality of the Jewish Religion.* 1680 (Wing B5772).

Burney, Fanny. *Cecilia or Memoirs of an Heiress* (1782). Edited by Judy
Simons. 2 vols. 1986.

Burton, Robert. *The Anatomy of Melancholy*. Edited by Holbrook Jackson. 2 vols. 1964.

Lord Byron. *The Complete Poetical Works*. Edited by Jerome J. McGann. 7 vols. Oxford, 1980–93.

A By-Stander [pseud.]. *A True State of the Case Concerning the Good or Evil which the Bill for the NATURALIZATION of the JEWS May Bring upon Great-Britain*. 1753.

Calvert, Thomas. *The Blessed Jew of Marocco or a Blackmoor Made White*. York, 1649 (Wing C321).

Caraffa, Mohamed, the Grand Turk [pseud.]. *The Exclusion of the English; An Invitation to Foreigners*. 1748.

Carleton, George. *A Thankful Remembrance of God's Mercie*. 1624 (STC 4640).

[Cartenright, Johanna, and Ebenezer Cartwright]. *The Petition of the Jewes for the Repealing of the Act of Parliament for their Banishment out of England*. 1649 (Wing C695).

Cartwright, Thomas. *Helpes for Discovery of the Truth in Point of Toleration*. 1648 (Wing C700).

The Case of the Jevves stated: or the Jews Synagogue Opened. 1656 (Wing C1094).

Causes and Consequences of the French Emperor's Conduct Towards the Jews. 1807.

The Ceremonies of the Present Jews. 1728.

A Christian [pseud.]. *The Case of the Jews Considered*. 1753.

The Christian's New Warning Piece: Or, a Full and True Account of the Circumcision of Sir E. T. Bart. 1753.

Cibber, Colley. *An Apology for His Life*. 1740, 1938.

Clare, John. *John Clare's Autobiographical Writings*. Edited by Eric Robinson. Oxford, 1983.

Cobbett, William. *Good Friday; or, The Murder of Jesus Christ by the Jews*. 1830.

———. *Parliamentary History of England*. Vols. 14 and 15. Printed by T. C. Hansard, 1813.

Coleridge, Samuel Taylor. *Essays on His Times in The Morning Post and The Courier*. Edited by David V. Erdman. 3 vols. Princeton, 1978.

———. *The Table Talk and Omniana*. Edited by T. Ashe. 1923.

A Collection of Testimonies in Favor of Religious Liberty, in the Case of the Dissenters, Catholics, and Jews, by a Christian Politician, 1790.

A Collection of the Best Pieces in Prose and Verse, Against the Naturalization of the JEWS. 1753.

Collier, Thomas. *A Brief Answer to Some of the Objections and Demurs Made against the Coming and Inhabiting of the Jews in This Commonwealth*. 1656 (Wing C5269).

[Colman, George, and Bonnel Thornton]. *Connoisseur*. Vol. 18 of *The British Essayists*, ed. Robert Lynam and others (30 vols.). 1827.

Colquhoun, Patrick. *A Treatise on the Police of the Metropolis.* 5th ed. 1797.

[Cooke, William]. *Memoirs of Charles Macklin Comedian.* 1804.

Copley, Joseph. *The Case of the Jews is Altered, and their Synagogue Shut to all Evil-Walkers. Or, A Vindication of the Jewes.* 1656 (Wing C6084).

Coryat, Thomas. *Coryat's Crudities.* 3 vols. 1776 first published 1611).

A Country Gentleman [pseud.]. *Reflections upon Naturalization, Corporations and Companies; Supported by the Authorities of Both Ancient and Modern Writers.* 1753.

The Court Jester. [1795?].

Cowley, Abraham. *Poems.* 1656 (Wing C6682).

Cowper, Ashley. *See* Timothy Scribble.

Crabbe, George. *The Complete Poetical Works.* Edited by Norma Dalrymple-Champneys and Arthur Pollard. 3 vols. Oxford, 1988.

The Crisis, or an Alarm to Britannia's True Protestant Sons. 2 pts., 1754.

Cruden, Alexander. *Unabridged Concordance to the Old and New Testaments and the Apocrypha.* 1769. Reprint, Grand Rapids, Mich., 1969.

Cumberland, Richard. *The Jew* (1794), "With Remarks, Biographical and Critical, by D.—G" [c. 1824].

———. *The Observer* (1785). Vol. 32 of *The British Essayists,* ed. Alexander Chalmers. 1823.

A Declaration of the Conversion of Mr. Aron de Almanza, a Spanish Merchant, with his Two Children and Nephew, from Judaism to the Protestant Religion. 1703.

Defoe, Daniel. *The Fortunate Mistress or Roxana* (1724). 1929.

De Quincey, Thomas. *Collected Writings.* Edited by David Masson. 14 vols. Edinburgh, 1889–90.

Dickens, Charles. *Oliver Twist* (1837–39). Edited by Kathleen Tillotson. Oxford, 1966.

———. *Our Mutual Friend* (1864). Edited by Stephen Gill. 1971.

———. *The Works of Charles Dickens.* 40 vols. 1906–8.

[D'Israeli, Isaac]. *The Genius of Judaism.* 1833.

Downes, John. *Roscius Anglicanus* (1708). Edited by the Reverend Montague Summers. [1929].

Dryden, John. *Amboyna.* 1673 (Wing D2232).

Dury, John. *A Case of Conscience, Whether it Be Lawful to Admit Jews into a Christian Commonwealth?* 1656 (Wing D2838).

E.I. *The Land of Promise, and the Covenant Thereof.* London, 1641 (Wing E11).

An Earnest and Serious Address to the Freeholders and Electors of Great-Britain. 1753.

Edgeworth, Maria. *The Absentee* (1812). Edited by Brander Matthews. N.d.

———. *Castle Rackrent* (1800). Edited by George Watson. Oxford, 1969.

———. *Tales and Novels.* 10 vols. 1857.

The Education of the Heart: The Correspondence of Rachel Mordecai Lazarus and Maria Edgeworth. Edited by Edgar E. Macdonald. Chapel Hill, N.C., 1977.

The Encyclopedia of Wit. [1804].

English Miracle Plays Moralities and Interludes. Edited by Alfred W. Pollard. 7th ed. Oxford, 1923.

An Essay Towards the Character of the Late Chimpanzee. 1739.

Essays by a Society of Gentlemen, at Exeter. Exeter, 1796.

Esther's Suit to King Ahasuerus: In Behalf of the Jews. 1753.

The Fair Hebrew: Or, A True, but Secret History of Two Jewish Ladies, who Lately Resided in London. 1729.

Farquhar, George. *The Works of George Farquhar.* Edited by Shirley Strum Kenny. 2 vols. Oxford, 1988.

The Festival of Mirth. 1800.

Fielding, Henry. *The History of Tom Jones A Foundling* (1748). Edited by Martin C. Battestin. 2 vols. Oxford, 1974.

———. *Miscellanies,* vol. 1 (1753). Edited by Henry Knight Miller, Oxford, 1972.

Fielding, Sarah. *The Adventures of David Simple* (1744). Edited by Malcolm Kelsall. 1969.

Foxe, John. *A Sermon Preached at the Christening of a Certaine Iew at London.* Translated out of Latin into English by James Bell, 1578 (STC 11248).

Frey, Joseph Samuel C. F. *Judah and Israel.* 4th ed. New York, 1841.

Full and Final Restoration of the Jews and Israelites Evidently Set Forth to Be Nigh at Hand. 1753.

A Full Answer to a Fallacious Apology Artfully Circulated through the Kingdom, in Favour of the Naturalization of the Jews, Verified by History and Record, by a Christian. 1753.

Garrick's Jests. [1785?].

Goldney, Edward, Senr., *A Friendly Epistle to the Jews.* 1760.

[Grant, James]. *Life and Shadows of London Life.* 2 vols. 1842.

———. *Travels in Town.* 2 vols. 1839.

Granville, George. *The Jew of Venice.* 1701.

Hansard's Parliamentary Debates.

[Hanway, Jonas]. *A Review of the Proposed Naturalization of the Jews.* 1753.

Haywood, Eliza. *The History of Miss Betsy Thoughtless* (1751). Edited by Dale Spender. 1986.

Hazlitt, William. *The Completè Works of William Hazlitt.* Edited by P. P. Howe. 21 vols. 1930–34.

Hemert, Paul van. *State of the Jews in the Beginning of the Nineteenth Century.* Translated from the Dutch by Lewis Jackson. 1825.

Henry, Matthew. *Matthew Henry's Commentary on the Whole Bible.* Edited by Leslie F. Church. 1970.

Herbert, George. *The Works of George Herbert.* Edited by F. E. Hutchinson. Oxford, 1978.

An Historical and Law-Treatise Against Jews and Judaism. 1732.

Hone, William. *The Every-Day Book.* Tegg's edition. 2 vols. N.d.

Holcroft, Thomas. *Memoirs of the Late Thomas Holcroft, Written by Himself.* 1852.

[Horne, George?]. *The Reply of the Jews to the Letters Addressed to them by Doctor Joseph Priestley.* Oxford, 1787.

Howell, James. *Epistolae Ho-Elianae.* Edited by Joseph Jacobs. 2 vols. 1892.

W.H. [William Hughes]. *Anglo-Judaeus, or the History of the Jews whilst here in England.* 1656 (Wing H3321).

Hunt, James Leigh. *The Autobiography.* Edited by Roger Ingpen. 2 vols. 1903.

Hurd, William. *A New Universal History of the Religious Rites, Ceremonies, and Customs of the Whole World.* N.d., c. 1788.

Inchbald, Elizabeth, ed. *The British Theatre.* 25 vols. 1808.

Israel, Isaac. *Christ Jesus the True Messiah.* 1682 (Wing I1057).

J.E., Gent. *Some Considerations on the Naturalization of the Jews.* 1753.

The Jews Advocate. 1753.

The Jews Triumph, and England's Fears, Set Forth. 1753.

Joe Miller's Jests; or, the Wits Vade-Mecum. 14th ed. [1750?].

Jones, William, of Nayland, *Memoirs of the Life, Studies, and Writings of the Right Reverend George Horne, D.D. Late Bishop of Norwich.* 1795.

Johnstone, Charles. *Chrysal or the Adventures of a Guinea* (1760–65). Edited by E. A. Baker. [1907].

[Johnstone, Charles]. *The History of John Juniper, Esq., alias Juniper Jack.* 3 vols. 1781.

———. *The Pilgrim: Or, A Picture of Life.* 2 vols. [1775].

Jonson, Ben. *The Complete Plays of Ben Jonson.* Edited by G. A. Wilkes. 4 vols. Oxford, 1981–82.

Kidd's London Directory. N.d. (c. 1835).

Kidder, Richard. *A Demonstration of the Messias. In which the Truth of the Christian Religion is Defended, especially against the Jews.* 2 vols. 1684, 1699.

[King, William]. *The Dreamer.* 1754.

Kirk, Robert. *The Commonplace Book of the Rev. Robert Kirk of Aberfoyle.* In Donald Maclean and Norman G. Brett-James, "London in 1689–90," *Transactions of the London and Middlesex Archeological Society* 7, pt. 1 (1935).

Kirkman, James Thomas. *Memoirs of the Life of Charles Macklin, Esq.* 2 vols. 1799.

Kyd, Thomas. *The Spanish Tragedy.* Edited by J. R. Mulryne. 1970.

Lamb, Charles. *The Works of Charles Lamb.* Edited by William Macdonald. 12 vols. 1903.

Lamb, Charles, and Mary Lamb. *The Works of Charles and Mary Lamb.* Edited by E. V. Lucas. 6 vols. 1903–12.

Langland, William. *The Vision of Piers Plowman.* Edited by A. C. Schmidt. 1978.

[Leslie, Charles]. *A Short and Easie Method with the Jews.* 4th ed. 1715.

A Letter from Angel Lyon to the Right Honourable Lord George Gordon on Wearing Beards. [1789].

A Letter from a Gentleman to his Friend Concerning the Naturalization of the Jews. 1753.

A Letter to the Publick on the Act for Naturalizing the Jews. [1753].

Levi, David. *Letters to Nathaniel Brassey Halhed, M.P., in Answer to his Testimony of the Authenticity of the Prophecies of Richard Brothers, And his Pretended Mission to Recall the Jews.* [1795].

Lewis, Matthew Gregory. *Journal of a West India Proprietor, 1815–17.* Edited by Mona Wilson. 1929.

———. *The Monk* (1795). Edited by Howard Anderson. Oxford, 1973.

Lichtenberg, Georg Christoph. *Commentaries on Hogarth's Engravings.* Translated by Innes and Gustav Herdan. 1966.

The Life and Adventures of a Cat (1760). Edited by Victor Link. Braunschweig, 1973.

The Life and Intrigues of the Late Celebrated Mrs Mary Parrimore, the Tall Milliner of Change-Alley. 1729.

The Lively Jester. [1800?].

Locke, John. *A Letter Concerning Toleration* (1689). Edited by Mario Montuori. The Hague, 1963.

London Jests: or Collection of the Choicest Joques and Repartees. 1712.

Look Before You Leap, or, the Fate of the Jews. [c. 1795].

Macaulay, Thomas Babington. *The History of England.* 2 vols. 1880.

Macklin, Charles. *Four Comedies.* Edited by J. O. Bartley, 1968.

Marlowe, Christopher. *The Jew of Malta.* Edited by N. W. Bawcutt. 1978.

———. *The Jew of Malta.* Edited by T. W. Craik. 1979.

Marston, John, and others. *The Insatiate Countess.* Edited by Giorgio Melchiori. Manchester, 1984.

Mather, Samuel. *The Figures or Types of the Old Testament.* 1683. 2d ed. 1705.

Mayhew, Henry. *London Labour and the London Poor.* 4 vols. New York, 1967 (facsimile reprint).

Mears, Abraham. *The Book of Religion, Ceremonies and Prayers; of the Jews.* 1738.

The Merchant's Complaint to the Lawyers at the Devil. Shewing the Hardships, Inconveniences, and Injustice, To which Every Honest Man of Property is Exposed, from Jew Bail, Sham Pleas, Demurrers, Writs of Error, and Injunction Bills. 1771.

The Merry Medley. [1750?].

The Miraculous Host Tortured by the Jew. 1822.

A Modest Apology for the Citizens and Merchants of London, Who Peti-

tioned the House of Commons against Naturalizing the Jews. 2d ed.
1753.

Moritz, Carl Philipp. *Travels of Carl Philipp Moritz in England in 1782.*
Introduced by P. E. Matheson. 1924.

[Moses the Jew]. *The Substance of Three Sermons Preached at Edinburgh,
the 8th, 9th, and 10th Days of July 1787, by Moses the Jew, who was
Lately Converted to the Christian Religion.* [Nottingham?], 1812.

[Murphy, Arthur]. *The Gray's-Inn Journal.* 2 vols. 1756.

Murray, John Fisher. *The World of London.* 1st ser. 2 vols. 1843.

*A Narrative of the Remarkable Affair between Mr. Simonds, the Polish
Jew Merchant and Mr. James Ashley, Merchant of Bread-Street, London.* 1752.

Nashe, Thomas. *The Works of Thomas Nashe.* Edited by Ronald B.
McKerrow. 5 vols. Oxford, 1966.

*The New Winter Evening's Companion, of Fun, Mirth, and Frolic, Con-
taining a Great Variety of Merry Tales, and Diverting Entertainments, for the Winter Evening Fireside.* Kilmarnock, 1822.

Nichols, John, F.S.A., *Literary Anecdotes of the Eighteenth Century.* 9
vols. 1812–15.

Offley, Henry Francis. *Richard Brothers, Neither a Madman nor an Impostor.* 1795.

The Other Side of the Question. 1753.

The Oxford Book of Ballads. Edited by Arthur Quiller-Couch. Oxford,
1910.

Oxfordshire in an Uproar; or the Election Magazine. Oxford, [1753].

*Pamphlets Relating to the Jews in England during the Seventeenth and
Eighteenth Centuries.* Edited by P. Radin. San Francisco, 1939.

Paris, Matthew. *Matthew Paris's English History.* Translated from the
Latin by J. A. Giles. 3 vols. 1852–54.

A Peep into the Synagogue, or a Letter to the Jews. N.d. [1790s?].

Pelham, Camden [pseud.]. *The Chronicles of Crime; or, the New Newgate
Calendar.* 2 vols. 1886.

Pepys, Samuel. *The Diary of Samuel Pepys.* Edited by Robert Latham and
William Matthews. 11 vols. 1970–83.

Percy, Thomas. *Reliques of Ancient English Poetry.* 3 vols. 1765.

Philo-Patriae [pseud.]. *Considerations on the Bill to Permit Persons Professing the Jewish Religion to be Naturalized by Parliament.* 1753.

———. *Further Considerations on the Act to Permit Persons Professing
the Jewish Religion, to be Naturalized by Parliament.* 1753.

Picart, Bernard, engraver. *Ceremonies and Religious Customs of the Various Nations of the Known World.* 1733–37.

Pinnock, William, ed. *The Guide to Knowledge.* 1832.

Pocock, Thomas. "The Life of Menasseh Ben-Israel." In *Of the Term of
Life,* translated by Pocock from the Latin of Menasseh. 1709.

Pope, Alexander. *The Correspondence of Alexander Pope.* Edited by
George Sherburn. 5 vols. Oxford, 1956.

————. *The Poems of Alexander Pope.* Edited by John Butt. 1963.

————. *The Prose Works of Alexander Pope,* vol. 1. Edited by Norman Ault. Oxford, 1936.

Priestley, Joseph. *Letters to the Jews.* 2d ed. Birmingham, 1787.

The Principal Motives and Circumstances that Induced Moses Marcus to Leave the Jewish, and Embrace the Christian Faith. 1724.

Prynne, William. *A Short Demurrer to the Jewes Long Discontinued Remitter into England.* 1656 (Wing P4078).

[The Querist]. *Some Queries, Relative to the Jews.* 1753.

A.R. [Alexander Ross]. *A View of the Jewish Religion.* 1656 (Wing R1983).

The Ramble or, A View of Several Amorous and Diverting Intrigues. [c. 1730].

Reasons for Naturalizing the Jews in Great Britain and Ireland. see Toland.

Reasons Offered to the Consideration of Parliament, for Preventing the Growth of Judaism. [c. 1738].

Remarks on the Reverend Mr. Tucker's Letter on Naturalizations. 1753.

Robertson, James [Nobody, pseud.]. *Poems, Consisting of Tales, Fables, Epigrams &c. &c.* 1770.

[Romaine, William]. *An Answer to a Pamphlet, entitled, Considerations on the Bill to Permit Persons Professing the Jewish Religion to be Naturalized.* 3d ed. 1753.

[Russell, John]. *A Tour in Germany, and Some of the Southern Provinces of the Austrian Empire in the Years 1820, 1821, 1822.* 2 vols. Edinburgh, 1824.

Sailman, M. *The Mystery Unfolded; or, an Exposition of the Extraordinary Means Employed to Obtain Converts by the Agents of the London Society for Promoting Christianity amongst the Jews.* [1817].

Saussure, César de. *A Foreign View of England in the Reigns of George I and George II.* Translated by Mme. van Muyden. 1902.

Savile, George. *The Works of George Savile Marquis of Halifax.* Edited by Mark N. Brown. 3 vols. Oxford, 1989.

Scott, Walter. *Ivanhoe* (1819). Oxford, 1912.

————. *The Letters of Sir Walter Scott.* Edited by H. J. C. Grierson. 12 vols. 1932–37.

Scribble, Timothy [Ashley Cowper]. *The Norfolk Poetical Miscellany.* 2 vols. 1744.

Seasonable Remarks on the Act Lately Pass'd in Favour of the Jews. 1753.

Shakespeare, William. *The Merchant of Venice.* New Variorum edition. Edited by H. H. Furness. 8th ed. Philadelphia, 1888.

————. *The Merchant of Venice.* Arden edition. Edited by J. R. Brown. 1967.

————. *The Merchant of Venice.* New Cambridge edition. Edited by M. M. Mahood, Cambridge, 1987.

Shelley, Percy Bysshe. *The Poems of Shelley,* vol. 1. Edited by Geoffrey Matthews and Kelvin Everest. 1989.

Sheridan, Richard Brinsley. *The Dramatic Works of Richard Brinsley Sheridan.* Edited by Cecil Price. 2 vols. Oxford, 1973.

Smollett, Tobias. *The Adventures of Ferdinand Count Fathom* (1753). Edited by Paul-Gabriel Boucé. 1990.

———. *The Adventures of Peregrine Pickle* (1751). Edited by James L. Clifford. Oxford, 1964.

———. *Continuation of the Complete History of England.* 5 vols. 1760–65.

———. *The History and Adventures of an Atom* (1769). Edited by Robert Adams Day. Athens, Ga., 1989.

———. *Travels through France and Italy.* Edited by Frank Felsenstein. Oxford, 1979.

Southey, Robert. *Letters from England* (1807). Edited by Jack Simmons. 1951.

Stanhope, Philip Dormer. *The Letters of Philip Dormer Stanhope 4th Earl of Chesterfield.* Edited by Bonamy Dobrée. 6 vols. 1932.

Steele, Richard. *See* Addison, Joseph, and Richard Steele.

Stephens, Lewis. *The Excellencies of the Kindness of Onesiphorus to St. Paul, when He Was a Prisoner in Rome: Exemplified in a Discourse Preach'd before the Inhabitants of the Parish of St. Patrock in Exeter, on Sunday the 6th of July, 1735: Occasioned by their Delivering Joseph Ottolenghe, a Poor Convert Jew, out of South-gate Prison, into which He Was Cast by a Jew, after his Conversion to Christianity.* Published at the Request of the Parishioners of St. Patrock's, For the Benefit of the Said Poor Convert Jew. Exeter, [1735].

Sterne, Laurence. *The Life and Opinions of Tristram Shandy, Gent.* (1759–67). Edited by Ian Campbell Ross. Oxford, 1983.

Taylor, Thomas. *An Additional Testimony Given to Vindicate the Truth of the Prophecies of Richard Brothers.* 1795.

The Temple of Mirth; or Fete of Comus and Bacchus. [c. 1800].

Bonnel Thornton. *See* Colman, George, and Bonnel Thornton.

[Toland, John]. *Reasons for Naturalizing the Jews in Great Britain and Ireland, on the same Foot with all other Nations.* 1714.

Toona, Elizabeth Browne Phelan. *Personal Recollections.* 1841.

Tovey, D'Blossiers. *Anglia Judaica.* Oxford, 1738.

Tucker, Josiah. *A Letter to a Friend Concerning Naturalization.* 2d ed. 1753.

———. *A Second Letter to a Friend Concerning Naturalizations.* 1753.

Tutchin, John. *England's Happiness Consider'd, in Some Expedients.* 1705.

The Universal Songster, or, Museum of Mirth. 3 vols. 1825–26.

Vaughan, Henry. *The Works of Henry Vaughan.* Edited by L. C. Martin. Oxford, 1957.

Violet, Thomas. *A Petition against the Jewes.* 1661 (Wing V584).

W.H. *See* William Hughes.

Walpole, Horace. *Horace Walpole's Correspondence.* Edited by Wilmarth
Lewis. 48 vols. 1937–83.
——. *Memoirs of King George II.* Edited by John Brooke. 3 vols. New
Haven, 1985.
The Wandering Jew, Or the Shoemaker of Jerusalem. N.d.
The Wandering-Jew, Telling Fortunes to English-men. 1640 (STC 11512).
[Warner, John, Bishop of Rochester]. *The Devilish Conspiracy, Hellish
Treason, Heathenish Condemnation, and Damnable Murder, Com-
mitted, and Executed by the Iewes, against the Anointed of the Lord,
Christ the King.* 1648 (Wing W902).
Watts, Isaac. *Divine Songs Attempted in Easy Language for the Use of
Children* (1715), facsimile edition. Edited by J.H.P. Pafford. Oxford,
1971.
[Weston, Edward]. *ΔΙΑΣΠΟΡΑ. Some Reflections Upon the Question Re-
lating to The Naturalization of Jews.* 1754.
Wilson, Henry, and James Caulfield. *The Book of Wonderful Characters.*
[1869].
Witherby, Thomas. *An Attempt to Remove Prejudices Concerning the
Jewish Nation.* 2 parts, 1803–4.
Wolper, Roy S., ed. *Pieces on the "Jew Bill" (1753).* Augustan Reprint Soci-
ety, no. 217. Los Angeles, 1983.
Wordsworth, Dorothy. *Journals of Dorothy Wordsworth.* Edited by Mary
Moorman. Oxford, 1971.

Modern Journals

Jewish Journal of Sociology
Journal of Jewish Art
Transactions of the Jewish Historical Society of England

Secondary Texts

Abbey, Charles J. *The English Church and Its Bishops, 1700–1800.* 2 vols.
1887.
Abbey, Charles J., and John H. Overton. *The English Church in the Eigh-
teenth Century.* 2 vols. 1878.
Abrams, M. H. *A Glossary of Literary Terms.* 4th ed. New York, 1981.
Adler, Michael. *Jews of Medieval England.* 1931.
Allport, Gordon W. *The Nature of Prejudice.* Boston, 1954.
Almog, Shmuel, ed. *Antisemitism through the Ages.* Oxford, 1988.
Altick, Richard D. *The English Common Reader.* Chicago, 1957.
Anderson, George K. *The Legend of the Wandering Jew.* Providence, R.I.,
1965.
Anderson, M. D. *A Saint at Stake: The Strange Death of William of Nor-
wich 1144.* 1964.

Appleton, William W. *Charles Macklin: An Actor's Life.* Cambridge, Mass., 1961.

Ashton, John. *Social England under the Regency.* 2 vols. 1890.

Atherton, Herbert M. *Political Prints in the Age of Hogarth.* Oxford, 1974.

Barnardston, Thomas. *Reports of Cases Determined in the Court of King's Bench* (1744) in *The English Reports,* vol. 94. 1909.

Baron, Salo Wittmayer. *A Social and Religious History of the Jews.* 2d ed. 18 vols. New York, 1952–83.

Barrell, John. *The Infection of Thomas de Quincey.* New Haven, 1991.

Bartley, J. O. *Teague, Shenkin and Sawney.* Cork, Ireland, 1954.

Berlin, George L. "Joseph S.C.F. Frey, the Jews, and Early Nineteenth-Century Millenarianism." *Journal of the Early Republic* 1 (1981): 27–49.

Bethlehem, Douglas. *A Social Psychology of Prejudice.* 1985.

Bettelheim, Bruno. *Symbolic Wounds.* 1955.

Bettelheim, Bruno, and Morris Janowitz. *Dynamics of Prejudice.* New York, 1950.

A Biographical Dictionary of Actors, Actresses, Musicians, Dancers, Managers and Other Stage Personnel in London, 1660–1800. Edited by Philip H. Highfill Jr., Kalman A. Burnim, and Edward Langhans. 16 vols. Carbondale, Ill., 1973–93.

Black, Jeremy, and Jeremy Gregory, eds. *Culture, Politics and Society in Britain, 1660–1800.* Manchester, 1991.

Bloch, Tuvia. "Smollett and the Jewish Naturalization Bill of 1753." *American Notes and Queries* 6 (1968): 116–17.

Bossy, John. *The English Catholic Community, 1570–1850.* 1975.

Boucé, Paul-Gabriel. *Sexuality in Eighteenth-Century Britain.* 1982.

Branford, Jean. *A Dictionary of South African English.* 3d ed. Capetown, 1987.

Brown, John Russell, and Bernard Harris, eds. *Early Shakespeare.* Stratford-upon-Avon Studies 3. 1961.

Bullough, Geoffrey. *Narrative and Dramatic Sources of Shakespeare.* 7 vols. 1957–73.

Burke, Peter. *Popular Culture in Early Modern Europe.* 1978.

Burlesque Plays of the Eighteenth Century. Edited by Simon Trussler. Oxford, 1969.

Cardozo, Jacob Lopes. *The Contemporary Jew in the Elizabethan Drama.* Paris, 1925.

Catalogue of an Exhibition of Anglo-Jewish Art and History. Victoria and Albert Museum, London. 1956.

Champfleury. *Histoire de l'Imagerie Populaire.* Paris, 1869.

Cheales, Henry John. "On the Wall-Paintings in All Saints' Church, Friskney, Lincolnshire." *Archaeologia* 53, pt. 2 (1893): 427–32.

Chesney, Kellow. *The Victorian Underworld.* 1970.

Clark, Cumberland. *Charles Dickens and His Jewish Characters.* 1918.

Coffin, Tristram P. *The British Traditional Ballad in North America.* Rev. ed. Philadelphia, 1963.

Cohen, A. *An Anglo-Jewish Scrapbook, 1600–1840.* 1943.

Coleman, Edward D. *The Jew in English Drama: An Annotated Bibliography.* New York, 1943.

Coleman, William S. E. "Post Restoration Shylocks prior to Macklin." *Theatre Survey* 8 (1967): 17–36.

Colson, Percy. *The Strange History of Lord George Gordon.* 1937.

Craik, T. W. *The Tudor Interlude.* Leicester, 1958.

Cranfield, G. A. "The *London Evening-Post* and the Jew Bill of 1753." *Historical Journal* 8 (1965): 16–30.

Dabydeen, David. *Hogarth's Blacks: Images of Blacks in Eighteenth-Century English Art.* Mundelstrup, Denmark, 1985.

———. *Hogarth, Walpole, and Commercial Britain.* 1987.

Davies, Nigel. *Human Sacrifice.* 1981.

Deacon, George. *John Clare and the Folk Tradition.* 1983.

Dent, R. W. *Proverbial Language in English Drama Exclusive of Shakespeare, 1495–1616.* Berkeley, Calif., 1984.

Dickson, P. G. M. *The Financial Revolution in England: A Study in the Development of Public Credit, 1688–1756.* 1967.

Diehl, Huston. *An Index of Icons in English Emblem Books, 1500–1700.* Norman, Okla., 1986.

Donoghue, Denis. "Macklin's Shylock and Macbeth." *Studies* 43 (1954): 421–30.

Easthope, Antony. *Poetry as Discourse.* 1983.

Echeruo, Michael. *The Conditioned Imagination from Shakespeare to Conrad: Studies in the Exo-cultural Stereotype.* 1978.

Edwardes, Allen [pseud.]. *Erotica Judaica.* New York, 1967.

Encyclopaedia Judaica. 16 vols. Jerusalem, 1971–72.

Endelman, Todd. *The Jews of Georgian England, 1714–1830: Tradition and Change in a Liberal Society.* Philadelphia, 1979.

———. *Radical Assimilation in English Jewish History, 1656–1945.* Bloomington, 1990.

Ferguson, Rosalind, ed. *The Facts on File Dictionary of Proverbs.* New York, 1983.

Fisch, Harold. *The Dual Image: A Study of the Figure of the Jew in English Literature.* 1959. 2d ed. 1971.

Forster-Hahn, Franziska. *Johann Heinrich Ramberg als Karikaturist und Satiriker.* In *Hannoversche Geschichtsblätter,* Neue Folge Band 17. Hannover, 1963.

Fowler, Roger. *A Dictionary of Modern Critical Terms.* Rev. ed. 1987.

Francis, John. *Chronicles and Characters of the Stock Exchange.* 1849.

Freud, Siegmund. *Moses and Monotheism* (New York, 1939). In *The Origins of Religion.* The Pelican Freud Library 13. 1985.

Friedman, Lee M. *The American Society for Meliorating the Condition of the Jews and Joseph S.C.F. Frey its Missionary.* Boston, 1925.

Fuchs, Edward. *Die Juden in der Karikatur.* Munich, 1921.

Garrett, Clarke. *Respectable Folly.* Baltimore, 1975.

George, M. Dorothy. *London Life in the Eighteenth Century.* 1930.

Gibson, Gail McMurray. *The Theater of Devotion: East Anglian Drama and Society in the Late Middle Ages.* Chicago, 1989.

Gilam, Abraham. *The Emancipation of the Jews in England.* 1982.

Gilman, Sander L. *Difference and Pathology: Stereotypes of Sexuality, Race and Madness.* Ithaca, N.Y., 1985.

———. *Jewish Self-Hatred.* Baltimore, 1986.

———. *The Jew's Body.* New York, 1991.

———. *Seeing the Insane.* New York, 1985.

Glassman, Bernard. *Anti-Semitic Stereotypes without Jews.* Detroit, 1975.

Gonzalez, Elana. *British Political and Social Cartoons, 1655–1832.* Library of Congress checklist, 2 vols. Washington, 1968.

Graeber, Isaque, and Steuart Britt, ed. *Jews in a Gentile World.* New York, 1942.

Green, Geoffrey L. *The Royal Navy and Anglo-Jewry, 1740–1820.* 1989.

Gross, John. *Shylock: Four Hundred Years in the Life of a Legend.* 1992.

Halimi, Suzy. "Le Jew Bill de 1753." *Annales du C.E.S.E.R.E.* (Université Paris XIII), no. 3 (1980): 3–19.

Hasan-Rokem, Galit, and Alan Dundes, eds. *The Wandering Jew: Essays in the Interpretation of a Christian Legend.* Bloomington, Ind., 1986.

Haydon, Colin. *Anti-Catholicism in Eighteenth-Century England, c. 1714–80: A Political and Social Study.* Manchester, 1993.

Henriques, H. S. O. *The Jews and the English Law.* Oxford, 1908.

Henriques, Ursula. *Religious Toleration in England, 1787–1833.* 1961.

Hertz, Gerald Berkeley. *British Imperialism in the Eighteenth Century.* 1908.

Hertzberg, Arthur. *The French Enlightenment and the Jews.* New York, 1968.

Hill, Christopher. *Antichrist in Seventeenth-Century England.* 1971.

Hinde, Wendy. *Catholic Emancipation: A Shake to Men's Minds.* Oxford, 1992.

Hsia, R. Po-Chia. *The Myth of Ritual Murder: Jews and Magic in Reformation Germany.* New Haven, 1988.

Hughes, Geoffrey. *Swearing: A Social History of Foul Language, Oaths and Profanity in English.* Oxford, 1991.

Hyamson, Albert M. *A History of the Jews in England.* 1908.

———. *The Sephardim of England.* 1951.

Jay, Ricky. *Learned Pigs and Fireproof Women.* 1986.

Jespersen, Otto. *Growth and Structure of the English Language.* Leipzig, 1919.

The Jewish Encyclopedia. New edition. 12 vols. New York, 1925.

Kaplan, Steven L., ed. *Understanding Popular Culture: Europe from the Middle Ages to the Nineteenth Century.* Berlin, 1984.

Katz, D., and K. W. Braly. "Racial Stereotypes of 100 College Students." *Journal of Abnormal and Social Psychology* 28 (1933): 280–90.

Katz, David S. *Philo-Semitism and the Readmission of the Jews to England, 1603–1655.* Oxford, 1982.

Katz, Jacob. *Emancipation and Assimilation.* Farnborough, Hants., 1972.

———. *Out of the Ghetto: The Social Background of Jewish Emancipation, 1770–1870.* Cambridge, Mass., 1973.

Klapper, M. Roxana. *The German Literary Influence on Shelley.* Salzburg, 1975.

Koestler, Arthur. *Insight and Outlook.* New York, 1949.

Kristeva, Julia. *Strangers to Ourselves.* Translated by Leon S. Roudiez. New York, 1991.

Landa, M. J. *The Jew in Drama.* 1926.

———. *The Shylock Myth.* 1942.

Langmuir, Gavin I. *History, Religion, and Antisemitism.* Berkeley, 1990.

Legman, G. *Rationale of the Dirty Joke: An Analysis of Sexual Humor.* 2 vols. New York, 1st ser., 1969, 2d ser., 1975.

Lelyveld, Toby. *Shylock on the Stage.* 1961.

Leslie-Melville, R. *The Life and Work of Sir John Fielding.* [1934].

Leys, M. D. R. *Catholics in England, 1559–1829: A Social History.* 1961.

Lipman, V. D. *The Jews of Medieval Norwich.* 1967.

Lippman, Walter. *Public Opinion* (1922). 15th ed. New York, 1956.

Lowes, John Livingston. *The Road to Xanadu.* 1927. Princeton 1986.

Lustig, Irma. "Boswell and the Descendants of Venerable Abraham." *Studies in English Literature* (Rice University) 14, no. 3 (1974): 435–48.

Lynch, Bohun. *A History of Caricature.* 1926.

Maccoby, Hyam. *Judas Iscariot and the Myth of Jewish Evil.* 1992.

———. *The Sacred Executioner.* 1982.

Mander, R., and J. Mitchenson. *The Artist and the Theatre.* 1955.

Marcus, Jacob R. *The Colonial American Jew, 1492–1776.* 3 vols. Detroit, 1970.

Matthews, Ronald. *English Messiahs.* 1936.

Mellinkoff, Ruth. "Cain and the Jews." *Journal of Jewish Art* 6 (1979): 16–38.

———. "Judas's Red Hair and the Jews." *Journal of Jewish Art* 9 (1982): 31–42.

Melville, Lewis. *The Life and Letters of William Cobbett in England and America.* 2 vols. 1913.

Michelson, H. *The Jew in Early English Literature.* Amsterdam, 1926.

Miller, Arthur G., ed. *In the Eye of the Beholder: Contemporary Issues in Stereotyping.* New York, 1982.

Modder, Montagu Frank. *The Jew in the Literature of England.* Philadelphia, 1939.

Nash, Mary. *The Provoked Wife: The Life and Times of Susannah Cibber.*
1977.
Newall, Venetia. *An Egg at Easter.* 1971.
————, ed. *The Witch Figure.* 1973.
New Catholic Encyclopedia. 15 vols. New York, 1967.
Norton, Rictor. *Mother Clap's Molly House: The Gay Subculture in
England, 1700–1830.* 1992.
Opie, Iona, and Peter Opie. *The Lore and Language of Schoolchildren.*
1959.
Osborne, John W. "William Cobbett's Anti-Semitism." *The Historian* 47,
no. 1 (1984): 86–92.
The Oxford Dictionary of English Proverbs. 3d ed. Oxford, 1980.
Oxford English Dictionary. 2d ed. 20 vols. Oxford, 1989 (*OED*).
Paulson, Ronald. *Hogarth: His Life, Art, and Times.* 2 vols. New Haven,
1971.
Pedicord, Harry William. *The Theatrical Public in the Time of Garrick.*
New York, 1954.
Perry, Thomas W. *Public Opinion, Propaganda, and Politics in
Eighteenth-Century England.* Cambridge, Mass., 1962.
Peskin, Allan. "England's Jewish Naturalization Bill of 1753." *Historia
Judaica* 19, pt. 1 (1957): 3–32.
Petman, Charles. *Africanderisms.* 1913.
Picciotto, James. *Sketches of Anglo-Jewish History.* Rev. and ed. Israel
Finestein, 1956.
Pike, Luke Owen. *History of Crime in England.* 2 vols. 1873–76.
Plomer, H. R., G. H. Bushnell, and E. R. McC.Dix. *A Dictionary of the
Printers and Booksellers at Work in England Scotland and Ireland
from 1726 to 1775.* Oxford, 1932.
Plumb, J. H. *The Growth of Political Stability in England, 1675–1725.*
1967.
Pollard, A. W., and G. R. Redgrave. *A Short-Title Catalogue of Books
Printed in England, Scotland, and Ireland and of English Books
Printed Abroad 1475–1640.* 2d ed. 3 vols. 1976–91 (STC).
Pollins, Harold. *Economic History of the Jews in England.* East Bruns-
wick, N.J., 1982.
Popkin, Richard H., ed. *Millenarianism and Messianism in English Litera-
ture and Thought, 1650–1800.* Leiden, 1988.
Prager, Dennis, and Joseph Telushkin,. *Why the Jews?* New York, 1985.
Ragussis, Michael. "Representation, Conversion, and Literary Form: *Har-
rington* and the Novel of Jewish Identity." *Critical Inquiry* 16, no. 1
(1989): 113–43.
Railo, Eino. *The Haunted Castle.* New York, 1964.
Rappaport, Ernest A. *Anti-Judaism: A Psychohistory.* Chicago, 1975.
Robson, R. J. *The Oxfordshire Election of 1754.* Oxford, 1949.

Rogers, Nicholas. *Whigs and Cities*. Oxford, 1989.
Rosenberg, Edgar. *From Shylock to Svengali: Jewish Stereotypes in English Fiction*. Stanford, Calif., 1960.
Ross, Ian Campbell. "Smollett and the Jew Bill of 1753." *American Notes and Queries* 16 (1977): 54–55.
Rosten, Leo. *The Joys of Yiddish*. 1971.
Roth, Cecil. *Essays and Portraits in Anglo-Jewish History*. Philadelphia, 1962.
———. *A History of the Jews in England*. Oxford, 1941, 1949.
———. *Magna Bibliotheca Anglo-Judaica*. New edition, 1937.
———. *The Ritual Murder Libel and the Jews*. 1935.
Rubens, Alfred. *A History of Jewish Costume*. New York, 1973.
———. *A Jewish Iconography*. Rev. ed. 1981 (Rubens).
———. *Portrait of Anglo-Jewry, 1656–1836*. 1959.
Rubin, Abba. *Images in Transition: The English Jew in English Literature 1660–1830*. Westport, 1984.
Rumney, J. "Anglo-Jewry as Seen through Foreign Eyes (1730–1830)." *Transactions of the Jewish Historical Society of England* 13 (1936): 323–40.
Said, Edward. *Orientalism*. 1978.
Salbstein, M. C. N. *The Emancipation of the Jews in Britain: The Question of the Admission of the Jews to Parliament, 1828–1860*. East Brunswick, N.J., 1982.
Samuel, Wilfred S. "The Strayings of Paul Isaiah in England (1651–1656)." *Transactions of the Jewish Historical Society of England* 16 (1952): 77–87.
Sanders, Wilbur. *The Dramatist and the Received Idea*. Cambridge, 1968.
Sandmel, Samuel. *Anti-Semitism in the New Testament*. Philadelphia, 1978.
Schoenberger, Guido. *The Drawings of Mathis Gothart Nithart called Gruenewald*. New York, 1948.
Scult, Mel. *Millennial Expectations and Jewish Liberties*. Leiden, 1978.
Seiden, Morton. *The Paradox of Hate, A Study in Ritual Murder*. South Brunswick, N.J., 1967.
Shachar, Isaiah. *The Judensau: A Medieval Anti-Jewish Motif and Its History*. Warburg Institute Surveys 5. 1974.
———. "Studies in the Emergence and Dissemination of the Modern Jewish Stereotype in Western Europe." Ph.D. diss., University of London, 1967.
Shaftesley, John M., ed. *Remember the Days: Essays on Anglo-Jewish History Presented to Cecil Roth*. 1966.
Sheldon, Esther K. *Thomas Sheridan of Smock-Alley*. Princeton, 1967.
Shiach, Morag. *Discourse on Popular Culture: Class, Gender and History in Cultural Analysis, 1730 to the Present*. 1989.

Shulvass, Moses A. *From East to West: The Westward Migration of Jews from Eastern Europe during the Seventeenth and Eighteenth Centuries.* Detroit, 1971.

Smith, Sydney. *Selections from the Writings of the Rev. Sydney Smith.* 2 vols. 1854.

Simpson, Claude M. *The British Broadside Ballad and Its Music.* New Brunswick, N.J., 1966.

Sobel, B. Z. *Hebrew Christianity: The Thirteenth Tribe.* New York, 1974.

Spater, George. *William Cobbett: The Poor Man's Friend.* 2 vols. Cambridge, 1982.

Speck, W. A. *Stability and Strife: England, 1714–1760.* 1977.

Stephens, F. G., and M. Dorothy George. *Catalogue of Political and Personal Satires Preserved in the Department of Prints and Drawings in the British Museum.* 11 vols. [in 12], 1870–1954 (George Cat.).

Stewart, Robert A., Graham E. Powell, and S. Jane Chetwynd. *Person Perception and Stereotyping.* 1979.

Stone, Harry. *Dickens and the Invisible World: Fairy Tales, Fantasy, and Novel-Making.* 1979.

———. "Dickens and the Jews." *Victorian Studies* 2 (1958–59): 223–53.

Straus, Ralph. *The Unspeakable Curll.* 1927.

Susser, Bernard. *The Jews of Southwest England.* Exeter, 1993.

Sutherland, Lucy. *Politics and Finance in the Eighteenth Century.* Edited by Aubrey Newman. 1984.

Talking Liberties (Channel 4 Television pamphlet). Edited by Derek Jones and Rod Stoneham. 1992.

Thompson, E. P. *The Making of the English Working Class.* 1963.

Thompson, Stith. *Motif-Index of Folk-Literature.* 6 vols. Bloomington, Ind., 1958.

Torrance, David W., ed. *The Witness of the Jews to God.* Edinburgh, 1982.

Trachtenberg, Joshua. *The Devil and the Jews: The Medieval Conception of the Jew and Its Relation to Modern Antisemitism.* 2d ed. Philadelphia, 1983.

Trilling, Lionel. *Speaking of Literature and Society.* Edited by Diana Trilling. Oxford, 1982.

The Universal Jewish Encyclopedia. 10 vols. New York, 1939–43.

Van der Veen, H.R.S. *Jewish Characters in Eighteenth-Century English Fiction and Drama.* Groningen, 1935. Reprinted with an introduction by Edgar Rosenberg, New York, 1972.

Vincent, David. *Literacy and Popular Culture: England, 1750–1914.* Cambridge, 1989.

Walvin, James. *Black and White: The Negro and English Society, 1555–1945.* 1973.

Weinbrot, Howard D. *Britannia's Issue: The Rise of British Literature from Dryden to Ossian.* Cambridge, 1993.

Williams, Bill. *The Making of Manchester Jewry, 1740–1875.* Manchester, 1976.

Williamson, Clark M., and Ronald J. Allen. *Interpreting Difficult Texts: Anti-Judaism and Christian Preaching.* 1989.

Wilson, J. Harold. "Granville's 'Stock-Jobbing Jew.'" *Philological Quarterly* 13 (1934): 1–15.

Wing, Donald. *Short-Title Catalogue of Books Printed in England, Scotland, Ireland, Wales, and British America and of English Books Printed in Other Countries, 1641–1700.* 2d ed. 3 vols. New York, 1972–88 (Wing).

Wolfthal, Diane. "The Wandering Jew: Some Medieval and Renaissance Depictions." In *Tribute to Lotte Brand Philip Art Historian and Detective,* ed. William W. Clark, Colin Eisler, William S. Heckscher and Barbara G. Lane, 217–27. New York, 1985.

Wolper, Roy S. "Pork as Polemic in the Jew Bill Controversy of 1753." *Transactions of the Samuel Johnson Society of the Northwest* 11 (1980): 131–43.

Wood, F. T. "*The Merchant of Venice* in the Eighteenth Century." *English Studies* 15 (1933): 209–18.

Zafran, Eric Myles. *The Iconography of Antisemitism: A Study of the Representation of the Jews in the Visual Arts of Europe, 1400–1600.* Ph.D. diss., New York University, 1973.

INDEX

Fictional characters have been omitted from the Index, with the exception of Shylock and Fagin, who lay claim to a distinct existence outside and beyond the works from which they originated.